Armenian Pontus

The UCLA conference series, "Historic Armenian Cities and Provinces," has been organized to convey the historical, political, cultural, religious, and economic legacy of a people rooted on the Armenian Plateau for more than three millennia.

Other Publications by Richard G. Hovannisian

Armenia on the Road to Independence, 1918
The Republic of Armenia (4 volumes)
The Armenian People from Ancient to Modern Times (2 volumes)
The Armenian Genocide in Perspective
The Armenian Genocide: History, Politics, Ethics
Remembrance and Denial: The Case of the Armenian Genocide
The Armenian Image in History and Literature
Enlightenment and Diaspora: The Armenian and Jewish Cases
Islam's Understanding of Itself
Ethics in Islam
Poetry and Mysticism in Islam: The Heritage of Rumi
"The Thousand and One Nights" in Arabic Literature and Society
The Persian Presence in Islam
Religion and Culture in Medieval Islam
*Looking Backward, Moving Forward: Confronting
  the Armenian Genocide*
Armenian Van/Vaspurakan
Armenian Baghesh/Bitlis and Taron/Mush
Armenian Tsopk/Kharpert
Armenian Karin/Erzerum
Armenian Sebastia/Sivas and Lesser Armenia
Armenian Tigranakert/Diarbekir and Edessa/Urfa
Armenian Cilicia
The Armenian Genocide: Cultural and Ethical Legacies

UCLA ARMENIAN HISTORY AND CULTURE SERIES
Historic Armenian Cities and Provinces, 8

Armenian Pontus

The Trebizond-Black Sea Communities

Edited by

Richard G. Hovannisian

MAZDA PUBLISHERS, Inc. ◆ Costa Mesa, California ◆ 2009

Mazda Publishers, Inc.
Academic publishers since 1980
P.O. Box 2603
Costa Mesa, California 92628 U.S.A.
www.mazdapub.com
A. K. Jabbari, Publisher

Library of Congress Cataloging-in-Publication Data

Armenian Pontus : The Trebizond-Black Sea Communities / edited by
Richard G. Hovannisian.
p. cm. — (Historic Armenian cities and provinces ; no. 8)
Includes bibliographical references and index.

ISBN 13: 978-1-56859-155-1 (alk. paper)
ISBN: 1-56859-155-1

1. Pontus—History. 2. Armenians—Pontus—History. 3. Trabzon (Turkey)—History. 4. Armenians—Turkey—Trabzon—History.
5. Armenia—History. I. Hovannisian, Richard G.
DS51.P67A76 2008
956.5—dc22
2008049385

CONTENTS

LIST OF MAPS AND ILLUSTRATIONS

Maps

Illustrations

SOURCES OF ILLUSTRATIONS

Aroyan, Armen. Personal collection.

British Library, London. Ms Or. 6555.

Bryer, Anthony and David Winfield. *The Byzantine Monuments and Topography of the Pontos.* Washington, DC: Dumbarton Oaks, 1985. Vol. 2.

Gulezian, Mark.Personal collection.

Hovakimian (Arshakuni), Hovakim. *Patmutiun Haykakan Pontosi* [History of Armenian Pontus]. Beirut: Mshak, 1967.

Hovannisian, Vartiter K. Personal collection.

Kévorkian, Raymond H. and Paul B. Paboudjian. *Les Arméniens dans l'Empire ottoman à la veille du Génocide.* Paris: Editions d'Art et d'Histoire, 1992.

Kuznetsov, Igor. Personal collection.

Mekhitarist Monastery, Vienna. Mss 119, 431.

Philadelphia Free Library. Frederick Lewis Oriental Ms 123.

Pietschmann, Victor. *Durch kurdische Berge und armenische Städte: Tagebuch der österreichischen Armenienexpedition 1914.* Vienna: Adolf Luser Verlag, 1940.

Simonian, Hovann H., ed. *The Hemshin: History, Society and Identity in the Highlands of Northeast Turkey.* London and New York: Routledge, 2007.

Torlakian, B.G., ed., *Hamshenahayeri azgagrutiune* [Ethnography of the Hamshen Armenians], as vol. 13 of *Hay azgagrutyun ev banahyusutyun* [Armenian Ethnography and Folklore]. Erevan: Armenian Academy of Sciences, 1981.

CONTRIBUTORS

BEDROSS DER MATOSSIAN is Lecturer in Middle East History at the Massachusetts Institute of Technology. A native of Jerusalem, he is a graduate of the Hebrew University of Jerusalem and completed his Ph.D. at Columbia University in 2008 in Middle East History in the Department of Middle East and Asian Languages and Cultures. His areas of interest include ethnic politics in the late Ottoman Empire, development of public sphere in the Ottoman Empire and Modern Middle East, social and economic history of the Middle East, the comparative study of ethnic groups, and ethnic conflict in the Middle East.

ROBERT H. HEWSEN is Professor Emeritus of History at Rowan University and has taught Armenian history as a visiting professor at several universities in the United States and Europe and most recently at the Hebrew University of Jerusalem. He is the co-founder of the Society for the Study of Caucasia and a contributor to the *Journal of the Society for Armenian Studies, Revue des études arménnienes*, and other publications. A specialist in the historical geography of Armenia, he has prepared *Armenia: A Historical Atlas*, contributed several maps for the *Tübingen Atlas of the Middle East*, and translated with critical commentary the *Ashkharhatsoyts*, an early geography that he attributes to Anania of Shirak.

RICHARD G. HOVANNISIAN is Holder of the Armenian Educational Foundation Chair in Modern Armenian History at the University of California, Los Angeles, and editor of this series. His numerous publications include *Armenia on the Road to Independence*, the four-volume *The Republic of Armenia*, five volumes on the Armenian Genocide, the latest being titled *The Armenian Genocide: Cultural and Ethical Legacies*, and seventeen other volumes and sixty research articles relating to Armenian, Caucasian, Middle Eastern, and Islamic studies. A Guggenheim Fellow, he has received many honors, including encyclicals from the supreme patriarchs of the Armenian Church, two honorary doctoral degrees, and election to membership in the National Academy of Sciences of Armenia. He is the initiator and six-time president of the Society for Armenian Studies (SAS).

VARTITER KOTCHOLOSIAN HOVANNISIAN is an Internist with the Kaiser-Permanente Medical Group of Southern California and a contributor to several Armenian American newspapers and journals. She is the author of an ethnographic study of her father's native village titled *Dzitogh: Dashti Karno* (Dzitogh in the Plain of Garin/Erzerum) and has engaged in extensive archival research on the Armenian Question and the first Republic of Armenia. She collaborates in editing this series as well as in translating and editing other related works in Russian, Armenian, and English.

DAVID KERTMENJIAN is Professor of Architecture at Erevan State University and Chair of Art History at the Erevan State Academy of Fine Arts. His Ph.D. thesis at Erevan Polytechnic University is titled "Planning and Architectural Features in Downtown Areas in Medieval Armenia," and his Doctor of Sciences dissertation is titled "The Medieval School of Architecture in the Lake Van Region." He is the author of numerous articles relating to Armenian city planning and architecture.

IGOR V. KUZNETSOV is Associate Professor of Anthropology at Kuban State University, South Russia. His research focuses on history of anthropological theory and Pontus and Caucasus ethnography. He is a founding member and director of the Center for Pontic and Caucasian Studies (Krasnodar), as well as an editor of its *Bulletin: Anthropology, Minorities, Multi-Culturalism*. He has also published a monograph devoted to the Hamshen Armenians and many articles on the Armenians, Hemshins, Pontic Greeks, and Meskhetian Turks in *Nationalities Papers: Ethnographic Review* and *Diaspora* (Moscow), *Gesellschaftliche Transformationen/Societal Transformations* (Berlin), and several other journals.

CHRISTINA MARANCI is Holder of the Arthur H. Dadian and Ara Oztemel Chair in Armenian Art and Architectural History at Tufts University. Her research focuses on medieval Armenia and cross-cultural relations with the Byzantine, Sasanian, and Islamic worlds, as well as issues of historiography. Her publications on Armenian art and architecture have appeared in numerous journals, including the *Art Bulletin*, *Gesta*, *Journal of the Society for Armenian Studies*, and *Journal of the Society of Architectural Historians*. Her book, *Medieval Armenian Architecture: Constructions of Race and Nation*, examines the role of Austrian art historian Josef Strzygowski in shaping the study of the field.

VARTAN MATIOSSIAN is affiliated with the School of Oriental Studies, University del Salvador, Buenos Aires. He has written extensively about Armenian history and literature, both ancient and modern, in scholarly and popular publications in Armenian, Spanish, and English. He has translated twelve books from Armenian into Spanish and has published four volumes in Armenian, among them studies on the twentieth-century writer, Kostan Zarian, and on the Armenian communities of Latin America. He has an unpublished volume in Spanish about the origins of the Armenian people.

BARBARA J. MERGUERIAN is the director of the Women's Information Center of the Armenian International Women's Association in Boston. She has been a visiting professor at Tufts University, Erevan State University, and California State University, Fresno. She is the former editor of the *Journal of Armenian Studies* and the *Armenian Mirror-Spectator* newspaper and is the co-editor of three books: *Exploring Gender Issues in the Caucasus*; *Voices of Armenian Women*; and *Armenian Women in a Changing World*. Her major research interest has been the role of the American missionaries in their work among the Armenians of the Ottoman Empire in the nineteenth and early twentieth centuries, about which she has published several articles.

CLAIRE MOURADIAN is Senior Researcher and Vice Director at the Centre d'études des mondes russe, caucasien et centre-européen of the Centre national de la recherche scientifique (CNRS-EHESS) and teaches at the Ecole des hautes études en sciences sociales (EHESS) and at the Institut national des langues et civilisations orientales (INALCO) in Paris. She is a founding member and president of the Société des études arméniennes; has published *De Staline à Gorbatchev: Histoire d'une république soviétique, l'Arménie* and many

articles on modern Armenian and Caucasian history; and is co-editor of
Le Crime de Silence: *Actualité du génocide des Arméniens*, and the
special issue of *Revue d'histoire de la Shoah* titled "Ailleurs, hier,
autrement: Connaissance et reconnaissance du génocide des Arméniens."

SIMON PAYASLIAN is Holder of the Charles and Elisabeth Ken-
osian Chair in Modern Armenian History and Literature at Boston
University and formerly Kaloosdian/Mugar Professor of Armenian
Genocide Studies and Modern Armenian History at Clark University.
He is the author of *The History of Armenia: From the Origins to the
Present*; *United States Policy toward the Armenian Question and the
Armenian Genocide*; *The Armenian Genocide, 1915-1923: A Handbook for Students and Teachers*; *U.S. Foreign Economic and Military
Aid: The Reagan and Bush Administrations*; and *International Politi-
cal Economy: Conflict and Cooperation in the Global System* (co-
author); as well as articles on the United Nations, international law and
human rights, peace studies, the Kurdish question, U.S. foreign policy,
and Armenian literature.

ANNE ELIZABETH REDGATE is Lecturer in History at the University of Newcastle upon Tyne, where she includes Armenian history
in her courses in European history and World history. Her book, *The
Armenians*, gives an account of the Armenians from the twelfth century B.C. to the late eleventh century A.D., and she is working on a
second edition to continue the account up to the present day. Her research focuses on the early medieval period and especially on comparative history and issues of identity.

HOVANN H. SIMONIAN is a Ph.D. Candidate in the Department of
Political Science at the University of Southern California. He holds
MA degrees in International Relations from the University of Southern
California and in Central Asian Studies from the School of Oriental
and African Studies of the University of London. He has edited and
contributed to *The Hemshin: History, Society and Identity in the Highlands of Northeast Turkey*; coauthored, with Richard Hrair Dekmejian,
Troubled Waters: The Geopolitics of the Caspian Region; and has published scholarly articles in several journals.

ABRAHAM TERIAN is Professor Emeritus of Early Christian Literature, including Armenian Patristics, at St. Nersess Armenian Seminary in New Rochelle, New York. He served for two decades as Professor of Intertestamental and Early Christian Literatures at Andrews University and has been a recurring Visiting Professor of Armenian Studies at the University of Chicago. A recipient of the Fulbright Distinguished Chair in the Humanities award, he has served as president of the Midwest Region of the Society of Biblical Literature, as editor *of St. Nersess Theological Review*, and as a member of the editorial boards of several scholarly journals. His publications include works on the writings of Philo of Alexandria as well as other monographs in Armenian Studies. His latest book, *Macarius of Jerusalem: Letter to the Armenians, AD 335*, establishes the authorship and date of the earliest full-length document bearing on the history of Armenian Christianity.

RICHARD WILKINSON is Head of the Department of Spanish at Winchester College in England after completing a career with the British Diplomatic Service. A graduate of Cambridge University with a degree in Classics and Archeology, he has also studied Modern and Classical Armenian in Paris, authored an occasional paper of the Society for Armenian Studies titled *An Introduction to the History of Pre-Christian Armenia,* and published articles on various aspects of Armenian archaeology in the *Revue des études arméniennes* and the *Journal of the Society of Armenian Studies*. He spent a semester attached to the Faculty of History of Erevan State University and has been Visiting Professor of Armenian History at the University of Michigan, Ann Arbor.

Preface

Armenian Pontus is based on the papers delivered in the ninth semiannual conference in the international series on *Historic Armenian Cities and Provinces* held at UCLA since 1997. Publication of the edited proceedings began with *Armenian Van/ Vaspurakan* (2000), followed by *Baghesh/Bitlis and Taron/Mush* (2001), *Tsopk/Kharpert* (2002), *Karin/Erzerum* (2003), *Sebastia/Sivas and Lesser Armenia* (2004), *Tigranakert/Diarbekir and Edessa/Urfa* (2006), and *Armenian Cilicia* (2007). Future publications in this series include Kars and Ani and the Armenian communities of Constantinople, Smyrna/Izmir, Caesarea/ Kesaria, New Julfa and Iran, Jerusalem, India, and the Northeastern Mediterranean.

The challenge of bringing consistency in style and format to a variety of essays in different disciplines is formidable, requiring of the editors great patience and much attention to detail both in form and in content. The views expressed by the individual contributors, however, are their own. In this series, a simplified system of transliteration is used to make the words and titles recognizable for persons who have proficiency in Armenian but who would find it difficult to comprehend scholarly scientific transliteration systems with diacritical marks (for example, *cʻ* representing "*ց*" (ts) as in the English word "lo<u>ts</u>" or the Armenian word "ha<u>ts</u>," meaning bread). Except for chapters in which the authors have expressed a definite preference, the transliteration of the Armenian letter "*ո*" (vo, o) in the initial position is rendered as *vo* rather than *o*, thus "vordi" instead of "ordi." The drawback of this adaptation is that it does not allow for a precise conversion from the Latin alphabet back to the original Armenian script, as, for example, the transliterated character "e" in this volume may stand for any one of three Armenian letters (*է, ֆ, ե*). In the citation of works that use diacritical marks, however, the form as it appears on the given title page has been retained. The transliteration of identical Armenian words may vary slightly depending on the orthography used in the original. Hence, the word "history" or "story" may appear as *patmutiun* (*պատմություն*) when taken from works published in traditional Armenian orthography or as *patmutyun* (պատմություն) when transliterated from the reformed orthography that was adopted in Soviet Armenia.

In this modified transliteration system, Eastern Armenian phonetic values are used in the citations, but exceptions have been made in the text in chapters using the more familiar Western Armenian forms of place names and personal names, as in Ordu rather than Ortu and Garabed instead of Karapet. Turkish names are rendered in the style commonly used before the Turkish alphabet reform of 1928—thus, for example, Jemal rather than Cemal, and Gumushkhane rather than Gümüşhane. Terms in foreign languages, such as *vilayet*, are italicized only the first time they appear in each chapter. In certain instances, the editor has not required absolute consistency when there are discrepancies in the information given or data cited by different authors.

Richard and Anne Elizabeth Elbrecht of Davis, California, have enhanced this conference series with meticulously-prepared, colorful photographic exhibits. Sadly, the death of Mr. Elbrecht in 2008 has deprived both the participants and attendees of a devotee and of the superb visual component that he and Mrs. Elbrecht presented so effectively. He is fondly remembered by all who have been enriched by their remarkable contributions.

The editor is pleased to acknowledge the assistance of Dr. Robert Hewsen, who drafted the five maps in his chapter; of Mr. Armen Aroyan, who has been a knolwedeable consultant and who supplied several photographs, including the panorama on the back cover viewed from the Amenaprkich (Kaymakli) Monastery in Trebizond; of Professor Hagop Gulludjian, who helped greatly in formatting the volume; and of Dr. A. Kamron Jabbari, the publisher of this series, who has been resourceful and accommodating. The informative conference paper by Dr. Avetis Papazian on overall aspects of the postwar Turkish court-martial proceedings, although not appearing in this volume, served as a foundational starting point from which the editor prepared the brief chapter that focuses specifically on the Trebizond trial and verdict. As has been the case with all other volumes in this series, Professor Simon Payaslian and Dr. Vartiter Kotcholosian Hovannisian have collaborated closely with the editor at each stage leading to the publication of *Armenian Pontus*.

❊ 1 ❊

THE ARMENIAN PONTUS

Richard G. Hovannisian

The great Pontic mountain range separates the lush, semitropical Black Sea littoral from the golden plains, river valleys, and mountain ribs of the Armenian Plateau or Highland to the south. Although in many places the distance from the Highland to the sea is less than 100 miles, the bounds of the historic Armenian principalities and kingdoms rarely, if ever, extended beyond the peaks of the Pontic chain. Thus, the story of Armenian Pontus is primarily one of Armenian trade and commerce through the Black Sea ports and eventually of Armenian communities dotting the long narrow corridor from Batum in the east to Samsun and Sinope in the west. Unlike the previous volumes in this series, which focus on the historic Armenian homelands from Van to Cilicia, *Armenian Pontus* begins a second level of studies, these relating to the areas neighboring or not too distant from the Armenian Highland. In the case of Pontus, aside from the small Hamshen canton and possibly the Karadere/Sev Ler valley, the Armenians never constituted a majority of the population anywhere, but they maintained a permanent presence there since medieval times with their churches and monasteries and other national institutions.

The association between Armenia and Pontus dates back at least to the era of the Persian Achaemenian Empire beginning in the sixth century B.C. The Greek general Xenophon traversed the Armenian Plateau in 401-400 B.C. as an escape route from the Persian heartlands to Trapezus (Trebizond) on the Black Sea, his account of that adventurous journey affording one of the earliest written descriptions of ancient Armenia. Much later, in the first century B.C., Mithridates VI Eupator, king of Pontus and champion of Hellenism against Roman encroachments in Western Asia, allied with the Armenian emperor Tigran II (the Great–*Mets*), not only in a political-military pact but also through the marriage of his daughter to the Armenian monarch. Before his ultimate defeat at the hands the Romans, Mithridates extended his control over

Armenia Minor or Lesser Armenia, lying to the west of Greater Armenia and southwest of Pontus. Armenians from this area apparently served in the Pontic armies.

In the early Christian era, the emperor Hadrian built up the port of Trebizond to make it a major emporium of trade and the hub of the overland caravan route to and from the Armenian Plateau and Persia. In the sixth century, the Roman/Byzantine emperor Justinian placed the Pontus in an enlarged province known as First Armenia, and in the next century, Heraclius included most of it in a reorganized military province identified as the *Armeniakon theme*. Trebizond also became a significant cultural-intellectual center, where the brilliant seventh-century Armenian scientist and geographer Anania Shirakatsi received his higher education at the feet of a master teacher.

Armenian settlement in the Pontus increased because of the sporadic persecutions during Arab dominion over the Armenian Plateau in the seventh through ninth century, as well as the continued development of Trebizond as a center of trade. It was in this period that an Armenian noble family, fleeing Arab oppression, is said to have founded the Hamshen settlements in the eastern Pontus. Later waves of Armenians moved into the Trebizond region as the result of Byzantine expansionist policies and the turmoil caused by the Turkic-Mongol-Tatar invasions from the eleventh century onward. Armenian churches in the region date back at least to the thirteenth century during the existence of the Greco-Byzantine Empire of Trebizond (1204-1461). The Armenian presence along the Black Sea developed further down through the Ottoman centuries that followed.

In the nineteenth century, the Christian Armenian population of the Pontus region numbered around 70,000, but this does not include the thousands of Hamshen people who had converted to Islam in the previous two centuries yet who still spoke an Armenian dialect and maintained identifiable Armenian customs, traditions, and transformed religious observances. Existing on or near the sea, the Pontic Armenian communities were relatively enlightened and prosperous. Armenians were represented far out of proportion to their numbers in trade and commerce, as well as in the arts and crafts. They served as professionals, representatives of foreign firms, and interpreters and aids of foreign consulates and missions. Their main economic competitors were the Greeks, who regarded themselves as the true native inhabitants of the Pontus and who constituted the largest Christian element, almost quadruple the size of the Armenian population. Nearly all the Armenian communities, both coastal and inland, maintained a church, and those on the seacoast and some inland operated schools, several of them even being coeducational. Protestant and Catholic missionaries—American, German, French—contributed to the enlightenment, and the open sea was conducive to the influx of cultural and ideological currents from Europe and Russia.

Despite the social conservatism of the Armenian Apostolic Church and the merchant classes, during the closing years of the nineteenth century, both the Hnchakian and Dashnaktsutiun revolutionary societies established footholds in Trebizond and Samsun and used the Black Sea ports to disseminate clandestine literature. It was in Trebizond that the horrific Hamidian massacres of 1895-96 began and then spread throughout the Armenian Plateau. Although Trebizond was not regarded as being part of the traditional "Turkish Armenian" provinces, its close association with the Highland was demonstrated in the fact that it was included in the Armenian reform programs that the European powers attempted to impose on Sultan Abdul Hamid (1876-1908/09) and then on the Young Turk regime after it ousted the sultan. When the world war erupted in the summer of 1914, Trebizond's location on the sea and close proximity to Russia quickly turned a major socioeconomic and cultural asset into a grave peril. The entire Armenian population was soon marked for elimination under the cover of that conflict. The year 1915 began the final chapter in the history of the Armenian communities of the Pontus, with only converted Hamshentsis—the Muslim Hemshinli—and the ruined and deserted Armenian edifices left behind.

A considerable number of studies on the Armenian communities and monuments of the Black Sea-Pontus region have been published in the Armenian language, especially by the Mekhitarist order in Vienna and Venice. The Armenian Academy of Sciences has compiled an ethnographic volume rich in information on the traditions, folklore, and dialects of the Armenian Pontus, and there are memorial volumes dedicated to the region, including the Christian Hamshen villages in the interior. In addition, the Russian Institute of Ethnography and Kuban State University have published several studies in Russian on the Hamshentsis and Hemshinli who now populate the eastern and northern shores of the Black Sea from Batum and Abkhazia to Krasnodar and the Crimean Peninsula. European and American scholars have contributed travel literature, linguistic and dialectical studies, detailed surveys of the region's monuments, and comprehensive books and articles on the Hamshen/Hemshin people. It is significant that Armenian-sponsored conferences were organized in Sochi in 2005 and in Erevan in 2008 to explore the Hamshentsi/Hemshinli connection, while in 2007 a full volume was published in modern Turkish with the apparent objective of reaching out to the Hemshinli Muslims and gradually drawing them back into the Armenian fold.

Armenian Pontus is intended to add to the literature on the region through an interdisciplinary approach that includes geography, prehistory and history, theology and religion, trade and commerce, art and architecture, education and cultural interaction, demography and ethnography, political and social developments, issues of human rights and genocide, and historical memory and transnational connections. The sixteen chapters that follow address some but certainly not all aspects of these subjects.

Robert Hewsen offers a geographic and historical survey of the Pontus and Armenian associations with the region. He demonstrates how the rugged topography and numerous parallel rivers gushing down from the mountains have influenced the political and socioeconomic history of the area. Outlining in consecutive order the powers that held sway over the Pontus and the noted figures who contributed to its colorful history, he explains the reasons for the increasing Armenian presence in the Pontus since medieval times. He uses comparative statistics from various sources to show the relative strength and standing of the several ethno-religious elements. Discussion of the modern period ends with a description of the now bustling city of Trabzon, an important gateway to former Soviet republics to the east.

The next two chapters examine whether there was an ancient association between Armenia and Pontus. Vartan Matiossian returns to the question of Armenian origins and specifically the location of the Azzi-Hayasa homeland mentioned in Hittite inscriptions. It has been suggested by some that the location was near the Black Sea, thereby decreasing the likelihood of an important linkage between Hayasa and what was or what was to become the Armenian homeland. After examining and assessing the sources, he discounts the Black Sea connection and concludes that, in fact, the location of Azzi-Hayasa was right in the center of Upper Armenia—Bardzr Hayk.

Richard Wilkinson finds no clear evidence of any association between Pontus and the Kuro-Araxes culture that spread over the Armenian Plateau (and Georgia) in prehistoric times or even the later kingdoms of Nairi and Urartu. On the other hand, there was a definite connection between Pontus and the northern shores of the Black Sea. Armenia's primary route to the sea was far to the west through Amisus (Amisos; Samsun), not through Trebizond. It was not until the time of the Artaxiad (Artashesian) dynasty and Tigran the Great's alliance with Mithridates of Pontus that communication between the two regions became steady. Armenian communities probably first appeared along the coast at the time of the Roman Empire.

This view is challenged by Babken Harutyunyan of Erevan State University, whose conference paper unfortunately does not appear in this volume. He asserts that in the first millennium B.C. the Ervandian (Orontid) Armenian rulers had possession of a long stretch of the seacoast and that this continued for a time even after Armenia became a satrapy of the Achaemenian Empire in the sixth century B.C. He contends that later in the second century B.C., the kingdom of Lesser Armenia, with the support of Artashes I of Greater Armenia, expanded to the sea until Mithridates Eupator annexed all of Lesser Armenia with the tacit assent of Tigran the Great. Trebizond, it is asserted, again came under Armenian rule for a brief time in the seventh century A.D. after the supreme commander (*sparapet*) Theodorus Rshtuni gained the favor of Mu'awiyya, the Arab governor of Damascus, and, based on inferences of the medieval historian Hovhannes Draskhanakerttsi, Armenia once more extended to the coast at the turn of the tenth century during the reign of the Bagratuni king Smbat I. Although this constructed interpretation is quite daring and not widely accepted, it is nonetheless worthy of note.

Armenian ties with medieval Trebizond are assessed by Abraham Terian, who focuses on Anania Shirakatsi as a source. In his autobiography, Shirakatsi gives much information about the cultural and religious life of Trebizond and about his learned tutor Tychicus. Armenians became widely dispersed during the Middle Ages, as aside from earthquakes and other natural disasters, the Byzantine expansion onto the Armenian Plateau was accompanied by forced or enticed population transfers toward Caesarea and Armenia Minor in the west and eventually also across the Pontus range. The establishment of a relatively small but vibrant Armenian community at Trebizond was also the result of the growth of trade and commerce at that port. Although relations between the Armenian and Greek churches were not cordial, the Armenians managed to build a number of sanctuaries and to establish a bishopric at Trebizond from the time of the Greek Comneni emperors.

Several chapters in this volume address the complex story of the Armenian Christian Hamshentsis and the Muslim Hemshinli, about whom there are strong disagreements and conflicting interpretations. According to Armenian sources, these people are the descendants of the Armenian Amatuni princes Shapuh and Hamam and 12,000 of their subjects who migrated to the Pontus from Greater Armenia in the eighth century A.D. A. Elizabeth Redgate sees in this tradition strong biblical parallels, beginning with the likely equation of the 12,000 with the 12 tribes of Israel and followed by many other comparisons. The search for a Jewish biblical lineage among the Christian Armenian noble families derived from their desire to prove their antiquity and enhance their prestige and legitimacy. Also involved were inter-princely rivalries, as between the House (*Tun*) of the Amatuni and both the Georgian and Armenian Bagratunis, the latter finally achieving the rank of royalty in the ninth century.

Claire Mouradian discusses the Islamization of the Hamshentsi Armenians, examining multilingual sources and concluding that the coercive policies leading to the ultimate conversion of this population were not a matter of Ottoman religious fanaticism but rather part and parcel of a calculated political-military strategy to consolidate the frontier areas of the empire. She considers the social and economic pressures that contributed to the conversion and characterizes the adherence of the Hamshentsi Armenians to Islam as a "safety belt" in a time of troubles. Overlapping religious and ethnic identities of this now diverse and dispersed group are examined and particular attention is drawn to the recent discourse in Turkey on what has long been a strictly taboo subject.

The last two chapters of the volume return to the Hamshentsi/Hemshinli theme. Hovann Simonian traces the transformation of the Armenian population from its solely Christian identity to becoming *kes-kes* (half and half)—externally Muslim but crypto-Christian—and then to its deeper Islamization and distancing from an Armenian connection as such associations became particularly disadvantageous in the twentieth century. Turkish nationalist scholars have now invented a new theory of origins and explain away the Hemshinli Armenian dialects by asserting that a Turkish tribe came into contact with Armenians as it gradually migrated from Iran and settled in the eastern Pontus. The underlying weaknesses of such interpretations are exposed by the author.

Igor Kuznetsov focuses on the contemporary Hamshentsi/Hemshinli communities in Abkhazia and the Krasnodar region of southern Russia. Most Christian fugitives from the Pontus found haven along the eastern and northern shores of the Black Sea, which were first under Russian imperial and then under Soviet rule. He measures the retention and changes in the dialects and identities of the Hamshen population as well as their interaction with the Muslim Hemshinli, whom Stalin deported from Georgia to Central Asia but some of whom have now moved to the vicinity of Krasnodar. The Hamshentsi–Hemshinli divide is marked by essential cultural-religious differences, yet the two groups may be drawn closer together because of widespread Russian-Cossack xenophobia and rising interethnic tensions in southern Russia.

In a related essay on art, Christina Maranci notes that while manuscript production was in sharp decline in the fifteenth and sixteenth centuries on the Armenian Plateau and in Cilicia, the Hamshentsi enclave of the Pontus enjoyed a surge of activity. Because the region was protected by a natural line of fortifications and enjoyed relative peace and autonomy, a lively community of scribes and artists continued to produce and copy illuminated manuscripts. She describes and illustrates several of the manuscripts now preserved in repositories in Erevan, Jerusalem, Vienna, London, and Philadelphia. It is of interest that this rare survival of age-old Armenian artistic traditions in the Hamshen country occurred during one of the darkest periods in Armenian history and cultural output.

David Kertmenjian contributes a chapter on Armenian architecture in the Pontus. He depicts the location and planning of the Armenian quarters, commercial centers, caravanserais, and other communal and administrative structures, as well as the layout of several monasteries and churches, which combine traditional Armenian and local architectural forms. The discussion concentrates on the city and environs of Trebizond, but it also briefly depicts other coastal towns from Sinope in the west to Rize in the east and inland settlements from Charshamba to Gumushkhane.

Treatment of the modern period begins with Bedross Der Matossian's survey of the Armenian Black Sea communities in the nineteenth century, especially after the formation of the *vilayet* of Trebizond in the provincial reorganization of 1864. The discussion covers the Apostolic, Catholic, and Evangelical schools and churches and the cultural and educational societies and periodic press, as well as Armenian participation in the local administration, trade and commerce, arts and crafts, and production and export of tobacco, filbert nuts, leather and hides, and other agricultural goods. A direct relationship is demonstrated between political and military developments in the Ottoman Empire during the latter half of the century and the fluctuating demographic picture of the Armenian Black Sea communities.

The deteriorating political situation in the nineteenth century and the cycle of demands for reform and heightened repression are reviewed by Barbara Merguerian. She assesses the impact of the Armenian political parties, especially Hnchakian, in their attempts to bring about far-reaching reforms and then describes in chilling detail the massacres and looting in the marketplace and Armenian quarters of Trebizond in October 1895. Included are vivid eyewitness accounts of the British consul, an American missionary doctor, and two hapless American diplomats who were passing through the city when they were caught in the inferno.

The final destruction of the Pontic Armenian communities is depicted by Simon Payaslian, who observes that, despite Abdul Hamid's repressive measures, the Armenian communities were able to recover and spring back by the early part of the twentieth century. Much optimism was generated by the Young Turk revolution in 1908, but this soon proved to be ephemeral. The outbreak of the world war in 1914 gave the ultranationalist wing of the Young Turk-Ittihadist party the opportunity to eliminate the Ottoman Armenian population. Widespread arrests in the Pontus in June 1915 were followed the next month by successive mass caravans of deportation and death, which set out toward Gumushkhane and the Kemakh gorge—the notorious slaughterhouse on the Upper Euphrates River. Excerpts quoted from the reports of the German, Italian, and American diplomats leave no doubt about the premeditated nature of the operations that enveloped the Pontus during the summer of 1915.

The defeat of the Ottoman Empire in October 1918 offered the Allied victors the opportunity to fulfill their wartime pledges to punish the perpetrators of the Armenian Genocide. It was, in fact, the new Turkish government which initiated the trials of war criminals but with mixed results. Richard Hovannisian turns specifically to the court-martial trial of the chief organizers of the Trebizond massacres, including the former provincial governor and the Young Turk provincial responsible secretary. The overview includes a quasi-literal rendering of the court's verdict, which reaffirmed the premeditated, wantonly cruel butchery of the men, the wholesale rape and enslavement of the women, and the drowning or dumping of countless infants and children in the Black Sea. The verdict, like those of other trials, condemned to death primarily persons who had already managed to escape. It was left to Armenian vengeance seekers to track them down and carry out the sentences.

The future of the Pontus lay in the balance at the end of World War I. The prospect of the formation of a united Armenian state encompassing both former Turkish Armenian and Russian Armenian lands raised the urgent question of affording the projected state one or more outlets on the sea. Richard Hovannisian discusses the intense competition for control of Trebizond and the Black Sea littoral between 1916, when the Russians occupied much of the area for two years, and 1922, when the Turkish Nationalists under Mustafa Kemal triumphed in their campaign against both the Allied Powers and the sultan's government in Constantinople. Meanwhile, aspirations of the substantial Greek population for a separate Pontic state were disregarded as the Paris Peace Conference created a united Armenian state, at least on paper, with outlets on the Black Sea through the Treaty of Sèvres in August 1920. In a related arbitration decision on the exact boundaries between Armenia and Turkey, United States President Woodrow Wilson awarded Trebizond and much of the Pontic seacoast as far west as Tireboli to the Republic of Armenia. It was to be a pyrrhic victory for the Armenians, however, for Kemal soon quashed the Sèvres treaty and won international recognition of that fait accompli in the Treaty of Lausanne in 1923, after first defeating the Greek armies in Anatolia and cleansing the Pontus of its Greek inhabitants in a compulsory population exchange.

Vartiter Kotcholosian Hovannisian engages historical memory as she and her sister return to their mother's birthplace, the town of Ordu, there to rediscover their murdered grandfather's home and to relive their mother's constant nightmare of chaos and confusion going back to the summer of 1915 when the Armenian quarter was surrounded by gendarmes and explosives while the men were rounded up, after which the insatiable looters ransacked the homes and storehouses and snatched away everything of value, including babes in arms. This is "a narrative of organic footprints, still very fresh, defining an ever-evolving reality." The photographic essay is supplemented with oral history accounts of four survivors—girls torn away from an idyllic youthful innocence to sudden violent separation and ceaseless traumatic memory.

Here, then, is *Armenian Pontus*—its land and people; cities, towns, and villages; trade and commerce; art and architecture; schools and churches; history and politics. Yet it is inevitable that this collective endeavor can offer only a pale and imperfect panorama of that which was.

Trebizond: Engraving, Joseph Pitton de Tournefort, 1701

Trebizond: Harbor

12

Trebizond: Giavur Meydan and Deyermen-Dere Christian Quarters

Trebizond: Amenaprkich (Kaymakli) Monastery before 1915

Trebizond: Surb Stepanos (Charkhapan) Church

Trebizond: Surb Stepanos Converted to a Theater

Trebizond: National School Teachers and Graduates, 1908

Trebizond: Regional Teachers' Conference, 1914

Trebizond: Sahak-Mesrobian School, 1922

Trebizond: Mekhitarist Academy

Trebizond: Shahen's Armenian Dramatic Troupe, 1905-1909

Trebizond: Grigor Siuni's Orchestra and Chorus

Trebizond: Kushana Village

Rize

Hamshen Armenian Family

Hamshen Armenians

The Zigana Pass to the Armenian Plateau

Le défilé d'Ardassa, Trébizonde

Ardasa and the Pontic Landscape

Gumushkhane: Before 1915

Gumushkhane: Surb Prkich (Holy Savior) Monastery

Gumushkhane: Ruins of Surb Astvatsatsin (Mother of God) Church

26

Tireboli (Tripoli): Tournefort Engraving, 1701

Tireboli: Before 1915

Kerasund/Girason/Giresun: Tournefort Engraving, 1701

Kerasund: Before 1915

Kerasund: Surb Lusavorich (Illuminator) Church

Kerasund: Armenian Educational Council

Kerasund: Cherkezia Picnic Grounds

Ordu

Ordu

Ordu: Former Armenian School

Unieh (Uniye)

Threshing of Filberts (Hazelnuts)

Samsun (Amisus)

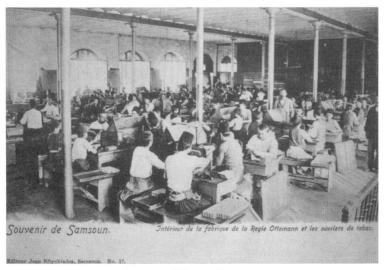

Samsun: Tobacco Factory

Samsun: Ipranossian Brothers Firm

Samsun: Armenian National School Band

Samsun: Inaugural Event of Armenian General Benevolent Union, 1911

Bafra: Armenian School and Church

Sinope

❋ 2 ❋

ARMENIANS ON THE BLACK SEA:
THE PROVINCE OF TREBIZOND

Robert H. Hewsen

> "Where can I find a little wild strawberry . . .
> that will look and smell like the wild
> strawberries of Trebizond?"
> —Leon Surmelian, *I Ask You
> Ladies and Gentlemen*, p. 308.

Although it was never considered one of the six Armenian provinces in the Ottoman Empire, the *vilayet* of Trebizond (Turkish: Trabzon)—the ancient land of Pontus—loomed large in the eyes of the Armenians for centuries, for through it lay the only convenient outlet of Greater Armenia to the sea.[1] Traditionally, Pontus or Pontos (Western Armenian: Bondos) was the name given to the northeast coast of Asia Minor or, put another way, to the southeast shore of the Black Sea. On the south it extended to the summits of the high coastal range known in antiquity as the Paryadres[2] or Parihedri Mountains,[3] and in modern times as the Pontic Mountains or occasionally as the Pontic Alps (Turkish: Anadolu Daghlari/Dağları). On the west, Pontus began at the River Halys (Kizil Irmak—Red River), where it entered the Black Sea, separating Pontus

---

[1] Close as it lay to the coast, Armenia never extended as far as the Black Sea even during the period of its greatest expansion under King Tigran the Great (circa 95-56 B.C.). Pontus, under Tigran's father-in-law and ally, Mithridates Eupator, was much too powerful and strategically vital to be challenged by Armenia.

[2] Strabo, *Geography* (Loeb Classical Library), XI.xii.4; Claudii Ptolemaei (Claudius Ptolemy), *Geographia,* ed. C.F.A. Nobbe (Leipzig: Tauschnitz, 1843-1845; reprint, Hildesheim: Georg Olms, 1966), V.xiii.5. For the origin of the term *Paryadres* and its use for other parts of the mountain chain running from northern Anatolia through northern Iran, see Cyril Toumanoff, *Studies in Christian Caucasian History* (Washington, DC: Georgetown University Press, 1963), p. 450.

[3] Pliny, *Natural History (*Loeb Classical Library), VI.ix.25, VI.xi.29.

from Paphlagonia, while on the east it extended as far as the borders of Colchis (West Georgia), both frontiers varying over the centuries. Since the mountains come close to the sea along the entire coast, the region of Pontus actually consists of a large number of small parallel valleys each carved out by one of the mountain torrents flowing down to the Black Sea.[4] The climate of Pontus is hot and humid in summer; damp and rainy in winter. In summer, the mountains are overgrown with verdure, especially wild azaleas and rhododendrons. The soil is rich and excellent for the growing of crops, and the mountains offer fine summer pasturage for flocks of sheep and goats.

There are few routes through the Pontic range, the most commonly used being the one through the Zigana Pass leading directly south of

---

[4] Beginning at Amisus (Samsun), the chief waterways of the Pontus are, from west to east with their Greek and Turkish names (in parentheses), the Lykastos (Murat), entering the Black Sea southeast of Amisos; Khadiseia (Aptal, just southwest of Khadiseia); Iris (Yeshil), at Ankon; Thermedon (Fatsa, just south of Lamyron/Herakleion); Beris (Milich); Thoaras (a tiny stream, now unnamed); Oinos/Phigamos (Jeviz, east of Oinoe); Sidenos (just southeast of Polemonion); Genetos (southeast of Boon); Malanthios (Melet, east of Kotyora); Pharmatenos (Turma, at Iskhopolis); [three nameless streams now the Ak-su, Yaghu, and Gelavar, all east of Kerasoun/Giresun]; Tripoli, (Kharshut, Armenian: Tsanakhadzor, just east of Tripoli); Philokaleia (Gorele on its lower course but called Mirkmenti and Golchekoy further upstream); Karasous (Ak-su); Pyxites (Meryamane); Hyssos (Ishan; Armenian: Ishkhan); Ophios (Solak); Kalos (Kalopotamos); Askuros (Tasli) at Islampasa, east of Rhizaion/Rize); Adienos (Kibledaghi), west of Adienos/Çaybaşi; Zagatis (Pazar), just east of Athenai/Pazar); Prytanis, Pyramos, or Pordanis (Furtuna; Firtina); Kissa (a tiny stream, now unnamed); and the Akampsis/Apsarraros or Boas (Choruh; Armenian: Akamsis; Voh; Chorokh), which enters the sea southwest of Bathys/Batum, and which marked the frontier with Colchis.

None of these waterways, except the Yeshil, the Kharshut, and the Choruh, are really rivers; the rest are, at most, large streams, and some are quite small. The Greeks came to know (and to name) them by passing their mouths as they skirted the coastline. The streams left anonymous were probably unknown because Greek (and Roman) ships cut across the shallow gulf into which they flowed and so did not notice their mouths. Greek and Roman authors (Scylax of Corianda, Strabo, Pliny, Ptolemy, Arrian) differ in their depiction of the order of these rivers and towns. Arrian is probably the most authoritative. For his account in an official report to the emperor Hadrian (117-38), see "Periplus Ponti Euxini," in Alexandre Baschmakoff, *Synthèse des périples pontiques,* no. 3 in the series *Etudes d'ethnographie et de sociologie, et d'ethnologie* (Paris: Geunthner, 1948). For the topography of Pontus, see William M. Ramsay, *The Historical Geography of Asia Minor* (London: J. Murray, 1890; reprint, Amsterdam, A. M. Hakkert, 1962); Franz and George Cumont, *Studia Pontica,* vols. 2-3 (Brussels: H. Lamertin, 1906, 1910); Anthony A. M. Bryer and David Winfield, *The Byzantine Monuments and Topography of the Pontos,* 2 vols. (Washington, DC: Dumbarton Oaks, 1985), which contains a superb bibliography.

Trebizond upwards to Armenia. Once a traveler has climbed to the top of the pass, however, there is little in the way of a descent since the mountain range buttresses the high-lying Armenian Plateau on its northern side, where both the severe climate and the harsh appearance of the terrain differ dramatically from the subtropical climate and lush greenery of the coast.[5]

Ancient Pontus

Pontus comes onto the light of history in the works of the Greek mythologists, who tell of how Jason and his crew, the Argonauts, sailed east to Colchis to find the fabled Golden Fleece.[6] This tale reflects the knowledge gained by Greek traders of the coastal waters, river mouths, maritime tribes, and local ports, whose ships increasingly plied the waters of the Black Sea. The earliest description of this coastline is found in the work of Scylax of Korianda at the end of the Urartian period in the seventh century B.C.,[7] by which time Greek colonists were settling along the coast of what they eventually came to call the Pontos Euxeinos (Welcoming Sea).[8] According to Scylax, the first major colony on

---

[5] For maps showing the lay of the mountains and their relationship to the Armenian Plateau, see H.F.B. Lynch, *Armenia: Travels and Studies,* 2. vols. (London: Longman's, 1901), vol. 1, map (citations below are to vol. 1); the more detailed and up-to-date USAF, *World Aeronautical Chart* Black Sea (324) (St. Louis: United States Air Force, 1952); and Richard Talbert, ed., *The Barrington Atlas of the Greek and Roman World* (Princeton: Princeton University Press, 2000), map 87.

[6] The classic account of the story of Jason is found in Apollonius of Rhodes, *Argonautica,* ed. Rudolf Merkel in *Corpus poetarum epicorum graecorum* (Leipzig: Teubner, 1852); trans. Edward P. Coleridge, *Apollonius of Rhodius, Argonatica, or, the Quest for the Golden Fleece* (New York: Limited Editions Club, 1957). For the pre-Greek history and ethnography of Pontus, see W.E.D. Allen's series of articles, "Ex Ponto," in *Bedi Karthlisa* 30-31 (IV-V) (1958): 39-54, 32-33 (VI-VII) (1959): 29-47, 34-35 (VIII-IX) (1960): 79-92.

[7] The *periplos* (coastal description) of Scylax of Corianda is found together with the other surviving Black Sea *periploi* from antiquity in Alexandre Baschmakoff, *Synthèse des périples pontiques* (Paris: Geunthner, 1948). See also his *Cinquante siècles d'évolution ethnique autour de la Mer Noire* (Paris: Geunthner, 1937).

[8] The original Greek name for the Black Sea is said to have been the *Axeinos* or "inhospitable to outsiders," supposedly from its sudden and dangerous storms. The Greeks are said to have changed its name to *Euxeinos* "welcoming to outsiders" after the establishment of Greek colonies along its coasts (*Encyclopedia Britannica,* 11th ed., vol. 2, p. 25n1). Actually, the name *Axeinos* was probably derived from the Old Persian word for "dark," a name preserved in that of the modern "Black" Sea, cf. *Kakamar,* the supposed Khaldian name for the same sea found in the seventh-century

the western edge of Pontus was the town of Sinope, founded by Mile-sian Greeks.[9] Later, during the Persian Achaemenian period (circa 550-330 B.C.), other colonies were founded as offshoots of the one at Sinope. Among these was Trapezous or Trapezus "the table," so-called from the flat-topped butte on which it was built.[10]

From Sinope were also founded the later colonies of Kotyora (Turk-ish: Ordu) and Kerasous (later Kerasund or Kerasunt; Armenian: Gira-son; Turkish: Giresun).[11] After the founding of Phasis (Armenian: Pasht or Poyt; Georgian: Poti) at the swampy mouth of the River Pha-sis (Georgian: Rioni) in Colchis, the Greeks came into direct contact with the Caucasian peoples, just as through Trapezus they became ac-quainted with the Urartians, whom the Greeks called Alarodioi.[12]

The territory of Pontus was officially included within the Persian Empire from the sixth or fifth centuries B.C., and the Greek colonies would have been subject to it if only as vassals.[13] When the Greek commander Xenophon passed through the region in the winter of 401-400 B.C., however, he encountered no evidence of Persian presence along the coast until he reached Paphlagonia, the coastal province to the west of Pontus, which, however, was in open rebellion against the Persians.[14]

In the northern part of the Armenian satrapy (province) were pre-sumably grouped the Proto-Caucasian Moskhians, Tibarenians, Ma-

---

Armenian *Geography.* See Ananias of Shirak (*Anania Shirakatsi*), *Ashkharhatsoyts* [Geography]; short version, ed. Ashot G. Abrahamyan, *Anania Shirakatsu matena-grutyune* [The Works of Ananias of Shirak] (Erevan: Matenadaran, 1944); long ver-sion, Arsèn Soukry and Robert Hewsen (Delmar, NY: Caravan Press, 1994); Suren T. Eremyan, *Hayastane est "Ashkharhatsoyts"-i* [Armenia According to the "Geogra-phy"]. (Erevan: Armenian Academy of Sciences, 1963), p. 78, s.v. "Pontos tsov"). According to Babken H. Harutyunyan (personal communication, 1993), the Khaldian word may have come from the Greek root *kak-* "ill," "bad" + *mar,* the Indo-European root for "sea."

[9] See note 7 above.

[10] Lynch, *Armenia,* p. 9.

[11] David Magie, *Roman Rule in Asia Minor* (Princeton: Princeton University Press, 1950), p. 183; Arnold H. M. Jones, *Cities of the Eastern Roman Provinces* (Oxford: Clarendon, 1937; 2d ed. rev., 1966), pp. 148-49.

[12] Herodotus, *The Histories,* trans. Rose Waterfield, intro. and notes Carolyn Dewald (Oxford and New York, Oxford University Press, 1998), III.93.

[13] Robert H. Hewsen, "Introduction to Armenian Historical Geography II: The Boundaries of Achaemenid 'Armina'," *Revue des études arméniennes,* n.s., 17 (1983): 134-37.

[14] Xenophon, *Anabasis* (Loeb Classical Library), V.vi.8, VII.viii.25; Hewsen, "Achaemenid 'Armina'," pp. 136-37.

krones, Mossynoikians, and Mares, all located along the northern slopes of the Armenian Highland or directly along the coast. Herodotus placed them in the same (nineteenth) satrapy as the Armenians, but Ernst Herzfeld has shown that these tribes can only be the unnamed northern neighbors of Armenia who extended up to the Black Sea,[15] a stretch of territory that Xenophon states was no longer under direct Persian control, if indeed it ever had been. Interpretation of the data of Herodotus and Xenophon is, of course, controversial.[16]

By the fourth century B.C., the former Persian province of Katpatuka in east central Anatolia had emerged as a kingdom known to the Greeks as Cappadocia.[17] At some time or another, this kingdom gained possession of the Pontic coast, the new acquisition being referred to as Cappadocia-on-the-Pontus or simply as Pontus. Thereafter, Pontus became the name of a kingdom created when this coastal part of Cappadocia was separated from the rest.[18] This new kingdom was founded by a Persian official, Mithridates (Mithradates) in about 302 B.C., but its greatest ruler was Mithridates VI Eupator (131-63 B.C.), who made Pontus a political and military force with which to be reckoned and who made his chief goal the expulsion of the Romans from Asia Minor.[19] It took the Romans three Mithridatic wars before they defeated Mithridates and annexed his kingdom to their rapidly expanding empire. Before that final defeat, however, Pontus and Armenia were allies. Mithridates annexed the kingdom of Lesser Armenia, along with

---

[15] Herodotus, *Histories*, III.93-94; Ernst Herzfeld, *The Persian Empire* (Wiesbaden: F. Steiner, 1948), p. 313.

[16] For a discussion of the data of both authors, Herodotus and Xenophon, see Herzfeld, *Persian Empire,* ch. 14.

[17] For Cappadocia, see Magie, *Roman Rule*, pp. 179, 183, 196, 377, 433, 555, 562, 621, 706; William Gwatkin, "Cappadocia as a Roman Procuratorial Province," *University of Missouri Studies* 5:14 (Oct. 1, 1930); Jones, *Cities,* ch. 7; Richard D. Sullivan, "The Dynasty of Cappadocia," in Hildegard Temporini, ed., *Aufstieg und Niedergang der römischen Welt,* vol. 2, pt. 7:1 (Berlin: De Gruyter, 1979), pp. 1125-68; Timothy B. Mitford, "Cappadocia and Armenia Minor: Historical Setting of the Limes," in Temporini, *Aufstieg,* pp. 1169-1228.

[18] For the Kingdom of Pontus, see Eduard Meyer, *Geschichte des Königreichs Pontos* (Leipzig: W. Engelmann, 1879); Theodore Reinach, *Trois royaumes d'Asie Mineur* (Paris, 1888); Michael Rostovtzeff, "Pontus and its Neighbours," in *Cambridge Ancient History*, vol. 9, ch. 5 (Cambridge: Cambridge University Press, 1994).

[19] For Mithridates the Great, see Theodore Reinach, *Mithridates Eupator Koenig von Pontos* (Leipzig: Tuebner, 1895; reprint, Hildesheim and New York: Georg Olms, 1975); Alfred L. Duggin, *He Died Old: Mithradates Eupator, King of Pontus* (London: Faber and Faber, 1958); Magie, *Roman Rule,* chs. 9, 14.

the lands of the Pontic and Colchian tribes, and married his daughter Cleopatra to the rising Armenian conqueror, Tigran the Great. The motives of these two ambitious rulers are vague, but it would appear that Mithridates saw himself as becoming master of Asia Minor, while allowing Tigran full freedom to pursue the creation of an Armenian empire by annexing Cilicia and the lowlands of Syria and Mesopotamia to the south. According to Strabo, the kingdom of Pontus was divided into a number of administrative districts, each called an *eparchy*.[20] Their names reflect their origin in the bureaucracy of a typical Hellenistic state: Phazimonitis, Megalopolitis, Gaziakene, and so forth.

Roman and Byzantine Pontus

Under Roman rule which began with the piecemeal annexation of Pontus in 64-65 A.D., the eparchies of the former kingdom were at first added to the great amalgam that was the province of Galatia.[21] In the reign of the emperor Trajan (98-117), however, these lands were separated from Galatia and added to the province of Cappadocia (annexed by the Romans in 17 A.D.), where they remained until the reforms of Diocletian in 295. There are no natural ports anywhere along the Pontic coast, and the city of Trapezus (Armenian: Trapizon; Western European: Trebizond) itself was unimportant until the second century A.D., when the emperor Hadrian (117-38) visited it and ordered the construction of an artificial port that made the city the main base for supplies serving the Roman legionary bases at Satala and Melitene on the interior plateau. Trapezus was already the naval base for the Roman Pontic fleet (first-third centuries A.D.), and in the late fourth century, the 1st Legion Pontica was posted there. From here a road led up the Pyxites River Valley to the Zigana Pass and onwards to Satala on the border of the Roman Empire and the kingdom of Greater Armenia. At about 40 miles south of Trapezus, the road divided, the one to Zigana being longer but open all winter; the other, to the vicinity of modern

---

[20] Strabo, *Geography*, XII.i.2.

[21] For Pontus under the Romans, see Arrian (2d cent. A.D.), *Periplus Ponti Euxini,* in Baschmakoff, *Synthèse des périples pontiques,* pp. 80-107; Magie, *Roman Rule,* ch. 15 *passim*; Jones, *Cities, passim*; Duggin, *He Died Old, passim;* Richard D. Sullivan, "Dynasts in Pontus," in Hildegard Temporini, ed., *Aufstieg und Niedergang der römischen Welt,* vol. 2, pt 7:2 (1980), pp. 913-30; Bryer and Winfield, *Byzantine Monuments, passim.*

Gumushkhane, further east, being shorter but only passable in the summer months.[22]

In 257 A.D., the Goths, arriving by ship, attacked and plundered Trapezus, which was then restored by the emperor Diocletian (284-305).[23] Following his policy of breaking up the large Roman provinces into smaller, more manageable units, Diocletian separated the districts of Pontus from Cappadocia and arranged them into three provinces: 1) the westernmost, Galatian Pontus, its capital set at Amisus, was later renamed Helenopontus by the emperor Constantine (307-37) in honor of his mother, (Saint) Helena, and included the towns of Sinope, Amasia, Ibora, and Zela; 2) Polemonian Pontus to the east, with its capital at Polemonium (also called Side), included Neocaesarea, Comana, and Cerasus; and 3) Cappadocian Pontus, centered at Trapezus and extending further east to the borders of the West Georgian land of Colchis, included the small ports of Rhizaeon (now Rize) and Athenae (Pazar).[24] When in 395 the Roman Empire became permanently divided into the Western Empire centered at Rome (which fell in the fifth century) and the Eastern or Byzantine Empire with its capital at Constantinople (which lasted until the fifteenth century), the three Pontic provinces remained in the Byzantine sphere. The administrative organization of the emperor Diocletian lasted until the sixth century when the emperor Justinian (527-65) reformed the borders of the provinces once again, at which time the Pontus was placed within a much larger province called First Armenia, with its capital far inland at Justinianopolis (Armenian: Vzhan, now Vijan) to the east of Erznka (Erzinjan).[25] Justinian was most solicitous of the eastern frontier of the empire and not only built or restored existing fortifications in the Pontic area but campaigned successfully there against the mountain tribe known as the Tzans (Armenian: Chaniuk), who were certainly one of

---

[22] For these routes, see Bryer and Winfield, *Byzantine Monuments*, section 22, Chaldia, and map 100 facing p. 299.

[23] Bryer and Winfield, *Byzantine Monuments*, p. 181.

[24] For Diocletian's division of the earlier provinces, see Christopher Scarre, *The Penguin Historical Atlas of Ancient Rome* (London: Penguin Books, 1995), pp. 122-23.

[25] For Justinian's rearrangement of the eastern provinces, see Nikolai Adontz, *Armeniia v epokhu Iustiniana* [Armenia in the Period of Justinian] (University of St. Petersburg, 1908; reprint, Erevan; Erevan State University, 1971); trans. and notes, Nina G. Garsoïan, *Armenia in the Period of Justinian* (Lisbon: Bertrand, 1970), ch. 7. See also Hewsen, *Geography,* map III.

44

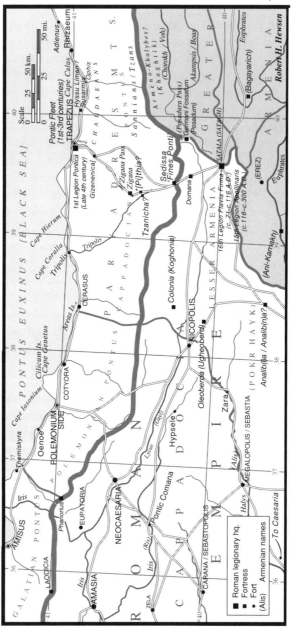

The Roman Province of Pontus

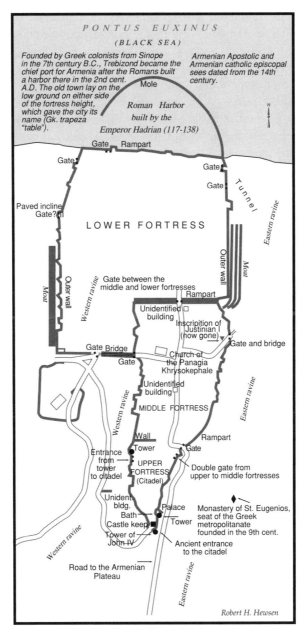

The Medieval City of Trebizond

the components of the people now known as the Laz.[26]

Under the emperor Maurice (582-602), a further reorganization was introduced in 591. Though eastern Pontus was still included in the same province centered at Justinianopolis, that province was now re-named "Greater Armenia," falsely implying Byzantine control over the whole of Armenia.[27] Soon afterward, however, Heraclius (610-42) abandoned the province altogether and introduced the thematic system whereby civil and military authority was vested in one provincial commander, the *theme* or military province under his control being de-fended by local citizen-soldiers. Under this new dispensation, Pontus became a part of the theme of Chaldia, an interesting name since the Chaldians (Armenian: Khaghtik) were one of the major tribes of the Pontic Mountains and according to an Armenian source were identical to the Chaniuk-Tzans.[28]

Despite the strategic importance of Trapezus and the desirability of its location, the Arabs, probably deterred by the unfamiliar mountain-ous terrain, made no attempt to capture the city after their arrival on the Armenian Highland in the mid-seventh century, and both Trapezus and the theme of Chaldia remained in Byzantine hands for centuries to come.

Christianity came early to the Pontic region and already by the time of the Council of Nicea in 325, there was a bishop sitting at Trapezus. Later, the seat of the metropolitan was transferred to Phasis (Poti) in Lazica (formerly Colchis, now West Georgia), while the Pontic towns of Amisus, Polemonium, Cersasus, and Trapezus were served by local bishops.[29] Trapezus itself eventually became the metropolitanate of Lazica, probably in the time of Emperor Basil I (867-86).[30]

---

[26] For Justinian's constructions, see Procopius of Caesaria, *On Buildings* (Loeb Classical Library); for Justinian's wars, Procopius of Caesaria, *History of the Wars* (Loeb Classical Library).

[27] For the provincial reforms of Emperor Maurice, see Paul Goubert, *Byzance avant l'Islam* (Paris: A. and J. Picard, 1951); Hewsen, *Geography,* map IV.

[28] For the provincial reforms of Emperor Heraclius and implementation of the so-called thematic system, see George Ostrogorsky, *The Byzantine State* (New Brunswick, NJ: Rutgers University, 1957); Romily Jenkins, *Byzantium: The Imperial Centuries* (New York: Random House, 1966), pp. 16, 17, 22-23; Walter E. Kaegi, "Al-Baladhuri and the Armeniak Theme," *Byzantion* 38 (1967): 273-77; Hewsen, *Geography,* p.100n1.

[29] Robert H. Hewsen, *A Historical Atlas of Armenia* (Chicago: University of Chi-cago, 2001), maps 62, 65, 69.

[30] Bryer and Winfield, *Byzantine Monuments,* p. 313.

Early Byzantine Trapezus was apparently a center of Classical learning, especially in the sciences. It is known, for example, that in the seventh century a native of the city, a certain Tykhikos (Tychicus), who had distinguished himself as a scholar in Constantinople, returned to his hometown where he opened a school that attracted students from a great distance. Among his disciples was the Armenian Ananias of Shirak (Anania Shirakatsi), who later became famous as a brilliant astronomer and mathematician and is now celebrated as Armenia's first scientist.[31]

The Empire of Trebizond

The Turkish occupation of central Anatolia began in the eleventh century and for a long time concerned only the arid central highlands of the plateau, lands similar to those that they had known in Central Asia. In the north, except for a brief Turkish occupation after 1071, the Byzantines retained control of the theme of Chaldia, that is, the Pontic Mountains, whose capital still lay at Trapezus, now Byzantine Trapezount (famous to European contemporaries as the storied city of Trebizond). The theme of Chaldia, governed hereditarily by the Greek Gabrades family, nominal vassals of the Comneni emperors at Constantinople, remained within the empire until 1204, when Constantinople was captured by the Crusaders, the Comnenus dynasty was deposed, and a Latin (Roman Catholic) empire was set up that lasted until 1261.[32] At that time, however, two scions of the Comneni, Alexius Comnenus and David Comnenus, managed to escape to Trapes, where, with the help of Queen Tamar of Georgia (niece of their grandmother who was the first wife of the emperor Andronicus I Comnenus, 1183-

---

[31] Tykhikos would be unknown were it not for the praise lavished on him by Ananias in his autobiography. See Abrahamyan, *Anania Shirakatsu matenagrutyune*, pp. 206-09 (complete version); English trans. (incomplete version), Frederick C. Coneybeare, "Ananias of Shirak: His Autobiography; His Tract on Easter," *Byzantinische Zeitschrift* 6 (1897): 572-74; French trans. (complete version), Haïg Berbérian, "Autobiographie d'Anania Shirakatsi," *Revue des études arméniennes*, n.s., 1 (1964):189-202. See also Hewsen, *Ashkharhatsoyts*, pp. 272-78.

[32] Michael Angold, *The Byzantine Empire: A Political History, 1025-1204*, 2d ed. (New York and London: Longman, 1997), ch. 17. Stephan W. Reinert, "Fragmentation (1204-1453)," in Cyril Mango, ed., *The Oxford History of Byzantium*, ch. 10 (Oxford and New York: Oxford University Press, 2002), pp. 248-83; *The Oxford Dictionary of Byzantium*, ed. Alexander P. Kazhdan et al., 3 vols. (New York: Oxford University Press, 1991), vol. 3, p. 2112.

85), they established the Comnenid Empire, a sort of Byzantium in exile that was to last until 1461. A Georgian vassal state at its inception and based to a great extent on the resources of its Laz hinterland, the Empire of Trebizond, as it has come to be called, may be considered to have been one of the Caucasian states, a situation strengthened by repeated intermarriages between the Comneni and the Bagratuni rulers of Georgia and by the presence of a large Georgian-speaking Laz population in the Pontic range.

The fact that the Empire of Trebizond lasted as long as it did was due in part to the enormous wealth it amassed in its capital, which became the foremost trading emporium on the south coast of the Black Sea,[33] and its rich commerce with the Genoese and Venetians.[34] In addition, its flexible and resilient foreign policy managed to keep the various Turkish emirates of Anatolia at bay. The Comneni accepted Seljuk vassalage in 1214, for example, and submitted to the Mongols in 1240, and they had no hesitation in marrying their princesses, famed for their beauty, to various Turkmen dynasts, Muslims all, when this seemed to be a judicious move.[35] During its 257-year existence as the capital of a rich mercantile empire, the city of Trebizond, protected by ramparts and towers and surrounded by gardens, orchards, and olive groves, was celebrated for the strength of its fortifications, the beauty of its cathedral and churches, the richness of its palaces and mansions, the luxury of its court, and the splendor of its ceremonial.[36] The Trebizondine emperors, known in Europe as the "Grand Comneni," were great patrons of art and learning, and their capital became the resort of numerous artists and men of letters, who gave it a considerable cultural luster. The Genoese were the major commercial partners of the city, and many Armenian merchants doubtless plied their trade within its

---

[33] Lynch, *Armenia*, p. 30.

[34] Ibid., p. 12. Despite its wealth, Trebizond was not a large city. It was located on a steep hill surrounded by walls, with a market harbor and suburbs and a number of fortified monasteries in the area. The emperor of Trebizond, Alexius II Comnenus (1297-1330), built a new wall encompassing the harbor and the lower city, formerly a suburb. Nevertheless, the city had only about 4,000 inhabitants in 1438. Turkish attacks began in 1223 but were fended off by the city's strong walls and other fortifications until 1461. See *The Oxford Dictionary of Byzantium*, vol. 3, p. 2112n35.

[35] Henry F. Tozer, *Turkish Armenia and Eastern Asia Minor* (London: Longmans Green, 1881), p. 454. For the marital relations between the Comneni and the Black Sheep Turkmen, see Cyril Toumanoff, "Comnènes et Grands Comnènes" in his *Les dynasties de la Caucasie chrétienne* (Rome: n.p., 1990), pp. 489-93.

[36] Tozer, *Turkish Armenia*, p. 453; Lynch, *Armenia*, p. 30.

walls and along its quays. With the fall of Constantinople to the Ottoman Turks in 1453, however, the days of the Comnenid state, the last remnant of the old Byzantine Empire, were obviously numbered. The Turks occupied the city and what was left of its hinterland in 1461.[37]

The Vilayet of Trebizond

The *vilayet* (civil province) of Trebizond was one of the oldest in the Ottoman Empire, having been organized as an *eyalet* (military province) immediately after the conquest in 1461. Its territory remained virtually unchanged throughout those centuries except in the east, where it bordered on the Georgian principality of Guria and then on the Russian Empire after the latter annexed Georgia at the beginning of the nineteenth century. In 1888-89, however, the *kaza*s (districts) of Shiran and Kelkit were taken from the vilayet of Erzerum and added to the *sanjak* (county) of Gumushkhane in the Trebizond vilayet.[38] Again, in 1910, the sanjak of Janik was separated from the vilayet of Trebizond and became an independent county.[39] The vilayet was 434 kilometers/270 miles long and on average about 74 kilometers/46 miles wide, covered an area of 31,300 square kilometers/12,084 square miles, and was divided into four sanjaks: Samsun, Trebizond, Lazistan, and (the only one inland) Gumushkhane. Each was named for its sanjak capital except Lazistan, whose center was at the small port of Rize. The 4 sanjaks were subdivided into 22 kazas (districts), and 24 *nahiye*s (cantons or village clusters).[40] The reason for the small number of nahiyes was that the kazas were in many cases very small themselves, often consisting of only a single valley.

The vilayet of Trebizond was extremely mountainous, and the valleys, though each well watered by its own stream, were so narrow and steep that agriculture was practiced only with difficulty and even stockraising was not easy to sustain. Grain, nuts, white beans, and tobacco pecially fine and were exported to Russia. In 1892, Vital Cuinet estimated that only about one-fifth of the land in the vilayet—the coast and

---

[37] For the fall of the Empire of Trebizond, see the works cited in note 32 above.

[38] Justin McCarthy, *Muslims and Minorities: The Population of Ottoman Anatolia and the End of the Empire* (New York: New York University Press, 1983), p. 21.

[39] Mesrob K. Krikorian, *Armenians in the Service of the Ottoman Empire, 1860-1908* (London: Routledge and Kegan Paul, 1977), p. 47.

[40] Vital Cuinet, *La Turquie d'Asie,* 4 vols. (Paris: 1890-1895), vol. 1, p. 5 (citations below are to volume 1).

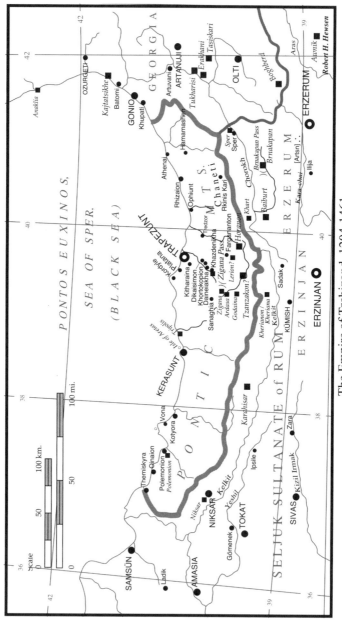

The Empire of Trebizond, 1204-1461

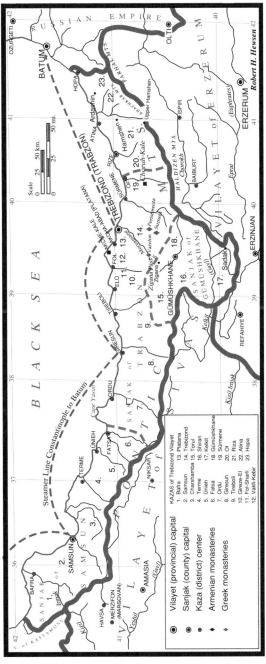

The *Vilayet* of Trebizond (Trabzon), circa 1900

tiny coastal valleys—was under cultivation and that perhaps another fifth could be put to such use. A full 60 percent of the province consisted of the abruptly rising Pontic Alps, suitable only for summer pasturage. Much of the remainder consisted of the lower mountain slopes facing the Black Sea, where the dense forests and thick undergrowth made cultivation impossible. Mining of silver and alum, once practiced extensively in the hinterland, had almost come to an end by the late nineteenth

The Trebizond vilayet was thus strikingly different geographically from those of the Armenian Highland and was not part of Armenia proper. Its proximity to Armenia, however, and its significant Armenian population, coupled with the fact that Woodrow Wilson assigned it to Armenia through provisions of the Treaty of Sèvres in 1920 so that it would have access to the sea, certainly demonstrate its association with the Armenian vilayets.

Population

Population figures for Trebizond are somewhat less uncertain than those of other provinces of Ottoman Anatolia but are still muddled by the different systems used by different authors for their calculation. There seems to be a general agreement that the total inhabitants of the vilayet numbered just over a million but the breakdown of the population into its component ethnic groups is not clear at all. The following figures are taken from the most accessible sources:

Cuinet (circa 1890)[41]

Muslim		806,700
Turk	691,700	
Laz	55,000	
Circassian	60,000	
Christian		240,600
Armenian Apostolic	44,100	
Armenian Catholic	2,300	
Armenian Protestant	800	
Greek	193,000	

---

[41] Ibid., p. 10.

Latin (Roman Catholic European)	400	
Other (Jew)		400
TOTAL		1,047,700

Malachia Ormanian
(for the vilayet's two dioceses circa 1910)[42]

Armenian		32,700
Apostolic	30,000	
Catholic	2,000	
Protestant	700	

Armenian Patriarchate
(Armenian Population, 1913-14)[43]

Sanjak of Trebizond	
Trebizond, Akchaabad, and Surmene	20,158
Gorele/Eleu	562
Tireboli	868
Girason (Kerasund)	2,335
Ordu	13,565
Sanjak of Samsun/Janik	
Samsun	5,315
Bafra	2,035
Charshamba	13,316
Terme	3,427
Unieh	7,700
Fatsa	1,330
Sanjak of Gumushkhane	2,749
Sanjak of Rize	35
TOTAL	73,395

---

[42] Malachia Ormanian, *The Church of Armenia* (2d ed.; London: Mowbray, 1954), p. 205.

[43] Raymond Kévorkian and Paul Paboudjian, *Les Arméniens dans l'Empire ottoman à la veille du Génocide* (Paris: Editions d'Art et d'Histoire, 1994), p. 57. This table also shows that Armenians lived in 118 localities in the vilayet's four sanjaks, having 106 churches and 3 monasteries, as well as 190 schools with 9,254 students. There were also 11,316 Armenian émigrés, primarily from Trebizond, Girason, and Charshamba.

Ottoman Census of 1914[44]

Muslim		921,128
Armenian (excluding Protestants)		38,899
Apostolic	37,549	
Catholic	1,350	
Protestant (mostly Armenian)		1,338
Greek		161,574
Jew		8
TOTAL		1,122,947

Justin McCarthy
(for 1911-12)[45]

Muslim	914,592
Jew	8
Armenian	39,952
Greek	160,427
TOTAL	1,114,979

As shown above, the population of Trebizond vilayet included a large number of Circassians (Cherkess) who had abandoned their ancient homeland in the North Caucasus after its final conquest by Russia in the 1860s. Fortunately for the local inhabitants of the Pontus, most of the Circassians here took readily to agriculture and trade rather than turning to brigandage, as did so many of their countrymen who immigrated to the Armenian Highland. The Circassians in the Pontus were settled primarily in the kazas of Charshamba and Bafra, where they put to good use lands that had been previously neglected.[46] A curiosity in the hinterland of Trebizond were the Kromli, the 12,000 to 15,000 Islamicized Greek inhabitants of nine villages (among them Krom, Imera, Livadia, Prdi, Alitinos, Mokhora, and Ligosti), who still spoke a Greek dialect and who were said to have remained Christians in secret.[47]

According to McCarthy's estimates, the birthrate for the vilayet was 48 per thousand per year; the death rate 29 per thousand per year; the

---

[44] Kemal Karpat, *Ottoman Population 1830-1914: Demographic and Social Characteristics* (Madison: University of Wisconsin Press, 1985), pp. 188–89.

[45] McCarthy, *Muslims and Minorities,* p 112.

[46] Cuinet, *La Turquie d'Asie*, p. 12.

[47] Ibid.

net gain being 19 per thousand per year, then far above average for Anatolia. Life expectancy was estimated at thirty-five years, which was the longest in Anatolia, reflecting the higher standard of living in the coastal provinces.[48] The population density was 48 per square kilometer. By his calculations, Armenians formed only 3.58 percent of the total population.[49]

Ecclesiastical Organization

The vilayet of Trebizond was heavily Christian, though mostly Greek Orthodox. Its Armenian population was served by an archbishop at Trebizond (presiding over 42 parishes, 35 churches, and more than 30,000 communicants). His see embraced the entire vilayet, except for the sanjak of Janik, which formed the diocese of Samsun (42 parishes, 39 churches, and about 20,000 members).[50] The Armenian Catholic Church was administered by a bishop appointed to Trebizond in 1850, but his jurisdiction extended beyond the vilayet to include the sanjaks of Amasia and Marsovan (Marzvan; Merzifon) in the vilayet of Sivas.[51] Armenian Catholics were scattered throughout the province but organized parishes existed only at Trebizond itself and at Samsun, the three other parishes of the see (Marsovan, Khavsa/Havsa, and Amasia) lying in the vilayet of Sivas.

The Greek Orthodox ecclesiastical structure was more complex, however, for the vilayet comprised three Greek dioceses, each under its own metropolitan: 1) Trapezount (including both the sanjaks of Trebizond and Lazistan); 2) Khaldia (Chaldia), comprising the sanjak of Gumushkhane; and 3) Amisos, consisting of the sanjak of Samsun or Janik minus the kazas of Fatsa, Unieh (Uniye), and Terme, which was included under the jurisdiction of the metropolitan of Neocaesaea (Niksar).[52]

---

[48] McCarthy, *Muslims and Minorities*, pp. 20-21.

[49] Ibid., p. 113.

[50] Ormanian, *Church of Armenia*, p. 205.

[51] *Dictionnaire d'histoire et géographie ecclésiastiques*, vol. 4 (Paris: Letouzey et Ané, 1930): col. 370.

[52] [Jean Naslian], *Les mémoires de Mgr. Jean Naslian, Evêque de Trébizonde, sur les événements politico-réligieux en Proche-Orient de 1914 à 1918*, 2 vols. (Vienna: Mekhitarist Press, 1951), vol. 1, ch. 3; Hewsen, *Atlas*, p. 210 and map 211.

Schools and Churches

The Trebizond vilayet had 82 schools and *medreses* (Muslim religious schools), according to Cuinet, but he does not break them down by the groups they served in the provincial capital as he does for other places.[53] There had been Franciscan and Dominican missions in Trebizond since the fourteenth century and a Jesuit mission since 1685.[54] By the end of the nineteenth century, missions of the Armenian Catholic Mekhitarist order of both Venice and Vienna, the Armenian Catholic Sisters of the Immaculate Conception, the Capuchin Fathers, the Sisters of Saint Joseph of the Apparition, and the Brothers of Christian Schools had all been opened in the city.[55] The American Board of Commissioners for Foreign Missions (Congregationalists) had established a minor mission post as early as 1834, which was expanded into a major station in 1840. The city boasted an American "college," an important Armenian private school, and a large Armenian Protestant congregation dating from 1846.[56] A commercial center of international importance, Trebizond was the seat of British, French, Russian, Austro-Hungarian, and Persian consuls; Belgian, Greek, Italian, and Spanish vice consuls; and an American consular agent.[57]

There were at least two medieval Armenian churches in the city, Surb Astvatsatsin (Holy Mother of God), first mentioned in the early fifteenth century,[58] and Surb Amenaprkich (All Savior), the latter in its earliest form also having been built before the fall of Trebizond in 1461 and being part of the monastic foundation of that name.[59] The most noteworthy institutions in the hinterland were the three important Greek monasteries of Sumela, Vazelon, and Peristereota, which owned, respectively, fifteen, twenty, and eleven villages and were in effect the spiritual guardians of the heritage of the Empire of Trebizond.[60] Of

---

[53] Cuinet is unusually terse in his description of the city of Trebizond (pp. 42-45).

[54] *Dictionnaire d'histoire et géographie écclésiastiques,* vol. 4, col. 327.

[55] Ibid., col. 370.

[56] Julius Richter. *A History of Protestant Missions in the Near East* (New York, London: Fleming H. Revell, 1910), pp. 114-15.

[57] Bryer and Winfield, *Byzantine Monuments,* pp. 207-08.

[58] Ibid., p. 208.

[59] Cuinet, *La Turquie d'Asie,* p. 7.

[60] On Sumela, see Tozer, *Turkish Armenia,* pp. 434-45; Bryer and Winfield, *Byzantine Monuments,* pp. 283-85; Sinclair, *Eastern Turkey,* pp 82-86. On Vazelon, see Bryer and Winfield, *Byzantine Monuments,* pp. 289-94; Thomas A. Sinclair, *Eastern Turkey: An Architectural and Archaeological Survey,* vol. 2 (London: Pindar, 1989),

these, Sumela, about 40 kilometers/25 miles south of Trebizond, was the most important. Located on a rock shelf of a steep cliff some 1,219 meters/4,000 feet above sea level (800 feet above the river bed), it was said to have been founded in the fourth century, but more probably it arose under the Byzantine Empire. All three monasteries were under the direct jurisdiction of the Greek patriarch of Constantinople. Armenians and Muslims, too, held all three religious centers in great reverence.

The City of Trebizond

The city of Trebizond or Trabzon lay on the gently rising slopes of a triangular plateau some 259 meters/850 feet above sea level, cut off from the land around it by deep ravines, through one of which flowed the stream still called Meryamane "Mary-Mother"—as the Muslims call the mother of the prophet "Isa" (Jesus)—the ancient river Pyxites.[61] The Mount Mithros of the Greeks, this triangle-shaped plateau not only gave the city its name "the table" but served as the platform on which was built the citadel. Here, too, was the great Cathedral of Hagia Sophia —Holy Wisdom (of God)—long before converted into the Orta Hisar Mosque and now a museum. Across the eastern ravine lay the Yeni Juma (New Friday) Mosque, once the church of the famed Monastery of Saint Eugenius, whose cult had been a major feature of the religious life of the Byzantine city.[62] Though Trebizond was increasingly modern in many respects, H.F.B. Lynch noted that in the late nineteenth century there was much that could hardly have been different in the age of the empire centuries earlier. Comparing the role

---

pp. 87-90. On Peristereota, see Bryer and Winfield, *Byzantine Monuments,* pp. 271-72; Sinclair, *Eastern Turkey,* pp. 90-91. For the present condition of Sumela and local facilities for visitation, see Bernard Mc Donagh, ed., *Blue Guide Turkey* (2d ed.; London and New York, 1995), pp. 658-59.

[61] For descriptions of Trebizond city, its topography and monuments, see Carl Ritter, *Die Erdkunde von Asien,* vol. 18 (St. Petersburg: Bezobrazova, 1895), pp. 852ff.; Tozer, *Turkish Armenia,* pp. 434, 450, 454-61; Lynch, *Armenia,* pp. 1-36, map following p. 30; Bryer and Winfield, *Byzantine Monuments,* section XX; Sinclair, *Eastern Turkey,* ch. 4, "The Pontus." For the entire vilayet, see Kévorkian and Paboudjian, *Les Arméniens dans l'Empire ottoman à la veille du Génocide,* pp. 179-206.

[62] Bryer and Winfield, *Byzantine Monuments,* section XX, "The City of Trebizond"; Sinclair, *Eastern Turkey,* pp. 48-82.

58

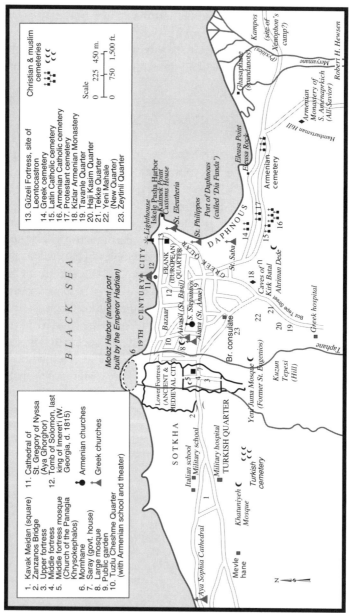

The City of Trebizond, circa 1900

1. Kavak Meidan (square)
2. Zanzanos Bridge
3. Upper fortress
4. Middle fortress
5. Middle fortress mosque (Church of the Panagia Khrysokephalos)
6. Momhane
7. Saray (govt. house)
8. Large mosque
9. Public garden
10. Tuzlu Cheshme Quarter (with Armenian school and theater)
11. Cathedral of St. Gregory of Nyssa (Aya Ghorghor)
12. Tomb of Solomon, last king of Imeret'i (W. Georgia, d. 1815)

● Armenian churches
▲ Greek churches

13. Güzeli Fortress, site of Leontocastron
14. Greek cemetery
15. Latin Catholic cemetery
16. Armenian Catholic cemetery
17. Protestant cemetery
18. Kizlar Armenian Monastery
19. Tavanle Quarter
20. Haji Kasim Quarter
21. Tekke Quarter
22. Yeni Mahale (New Quarter)
23. Zeytinli Quarter

Christian & muslim cemeteries

Scale
0   225   450 m.
0   750   1,500 ft.

of the British and French in foreign trade with that of the medieval Genoese, he observed the continued heterogeneous character of the local population. He also noted the traffic in European goods being carried to Persia along the same old routes by identical strings of camel caravans.[63]

Although much of Trebizond was still oriental, with its narrow, twisting lanes and houses surrounded by high walls presenting a totally blank exterior to the passerby, the people of the coastal towns were noticeably more advanced culturally than those of the interior. Their lives were more comfortable and more Europeanized, and their homes more of the Mediterranean type even as far inland as Gumushkhane. According to Henry Tozer, who visited Trebizond in 1878, the population of the city was 32,000, made up of 2,000 Armenians, 7,000 to 8,000 Greeks, and the rest Turks.[64] Writing shortly before 1890, Vital Cuinet gave the number of inhabitants in the city as 35,000, of whom 19,500 were Muslims, 8,200 Greek Orthodox, 6,000 Armenians (he did not specify their confession), and 1,300 foreigners.[65] Rounded as they are, of course, these figures can only be estimates.

Other Towns of the Vilayet

Armenian communities existed in all of the major coastal towns from Zonguldak and Sinope in the west to beyond the Russian frontier in the east, including Bafra, Samsun, Unieh, Fatsa, Ordu, Giresun, Tireboli, Trebizond, and Batum. At Sinope, in the vilayet of Kastamonu, there was a large Armenian community with smaller ones nearby in the villages of Kuyluji, Ali-Beyuli, Gol-Dagh, Gerze, and especially Boyabad. There were twenty Armenian villages in the kaza of Charshamba, four in Terme, ten in Unieh, and two in Fatsa. There were twenty-nine Armenian villages in the vicinity of Ordu, many of them of Hamshen origin, sixteen villages to the immediate southwest of Trebizond, and twenty more to the east of the provincial capital centered around Drona.

---

[63] Lynch, *Armenia*, p. 32.
[64] Tozer, *Turkish Armenia*, p. 450.
[65] Cuinet, *La Turquie d'Asie,* pp. 43-44.

Gumushkhane—Silver Inn

The town of Gumushkhane (Greek: Argyropolis = Silver Town or Argyrokastron = Silver Fort) lies on the main road between Trebizond and Erznka (Erzinjan) on the Armenian Plateau. The mountains that separate it from Erznka may be taken as the northeast boundary of Pontus with Armenia.[66] Gumushkhane is thus a Pontic town rather than Armenian, and the local population in the nineteenth century was composed largely of Greeks. The capital of the sanjak of that same name, Gumushkhane was once the center of a great mining industry, and many of the Greeks who were later found in Armenia and elsewhere in the Caucasus region were previously miners in the Pontus. The entire kaza was heavily Christian until the compulsory population exchanges between Greece and Turkey in 1923. Cuinet cites 95 churches there compared with 130 mosques—a very high ratio. In the town of Gumushkhane itself, there were 550 houses, of which 300 were Greek, 150 Muslim, and 100 Armenian, suggesting a population of about 3,000. Cuinet describes the people as being relatively advanced and devoted to education so much that every village possessed a school, even though a lack of resources made it impossible to establish any at the secondary level.[67] The famed silver mines were productive until the late eighteenth century, after which there was a steady decline in the industry. The land, mountainous, steep, and extremely precipitous, made agriculture and stockbreeding unfeasible to any significant degree, and the decline of mining resulted in the emigration of many of the miners—some to Russian Armenia—and the impoverishment of the rest.[68]

---

[66] Eremyan, *Hayastane est "Ashkharhatsoyts"-i*, map, indicates that Gumushkhane dated back to antiquity and that Argyrokastron was its ancient Greek name. Argyrokastron and Argyropolis were actually Greek "back formations" from the Turkish name rather than the other way around. There is no doubt, however, that Gumushkhane or a site very near it must have existed in ancient times. It is probably to be identified with the Medocia or Patara of the *Peutinger Table* (see Hewsen, *Atlas,* map 59).

[67] For the town and sanjak of Gumushkhane, see Cuinet, *La Turquie d'Asie*, pp. 123-29; for the schools, p. 126.

[68] Greeks are still encountered in the Republic of Armenia, and even in remote Karabagh and Zangezur there are descendants of Greek miners who were brought in to work in copper mines in the latter part of the nineteenth century.

Samsun, Ordu, and Giresun

A small town of only 3,000 people in 1860, Samsun (the ancient Amisos and at one time the capital of the kingdom of Pontus) had grown to some 11,000 people by 1890, approximately 2,000 of whom were Armenians.[69] The port of Ordu occupied the site of ancient Kotyora but was founded only in the late eighteenth century on the site of an Ottoman military camp established at the time of the Ottoman conquest (1397). According to Cuinet, the town consisted of five quarters, three Greek, one Turkish, and one Armenian, and had about 6,000 inhabitants, whose religious needs were served by three Greek churches, one Armenian church, and two mosques. The town was known for its port, its weekly fairs held each summer, and its Greek dialect, which was the furthest removed from standard Greek of any along the littoral.[70]

The city of Giresun (Girason; ancient Kerasous), beautifully located on the Black Sea coast, was a very small port with some 8,440 people, about an eighth of whom were Armenian, the rest divided almost evenly between Greeks and Muslims. The town possessed eleven mosques, nine Greek churches, and a large Armenian church and a stone-hewn Armenian chapel, as well as a telegraph station, a military post, oil-storage depots, and an arsenal. The Black Sea steamers stopped here once every fortnight.[71]

The Hinterland

The Laz

The most striking demographic feature of the vilayet of Trebizond was the large population of Georgian-speaking Muslims known as the Laz, an ancient people already known in the second century A.D.[72] They seized control of Colchis in the late fourth or early fifth century and established a kingdom there that was to dominate West Georgia and the

---

[69] For the sanjak of Samsun, see Cuinet, *La Turquie d'Asie*, pp. 87-118; for the city, pp. 102-06.

[70] For the town and kaza of Ordu, see Cuinet, pp. 78-86; for the Greek dialect, p. 86.

[71] For the city and sanjak of Giresun, see Cuinet, *La Turquie d'Asie,* pp. 64-78. Lynch, *Armenia,* refers to its castle-rock (p. 6) and to the fruit which received its name, cherry, from the Greek name for the city—Kerasous (p. 18).

[72] Ptolemy, *Geography,* ed. Nobbe, V.x.5: *Lazai.*

east coast of the Black Sea until the late eighth century.[73] The Laz were found chiefly in the easternmost part of the vilayet in the sanjak that bore their name, Lazistan. Their chief towns were the small ports of Atina and Rize, the latter of which, following the loss of Batum to Russia as a result of the Russo-Turkish war of 1877-78, had become the center of the kaza and had begun to grow.[74]

A Pontic curiosity was the Laz community of the small coastal town called Of (Greek: Ophios). Though Muslims by faith, they were speakers of Greek and obviously represented Greeks who had converted to Islam.[75] In the hinterland back of the Pontic Mountains were also many other speakers of Georgian besides the Laz, and now that the border has become porous since the fall of the Soviet Union, a surprisingly large number of local Muslims in northeastern Turkey—chiefly Ajars—have emerged, who not only still speak Georgian but make no secret of their Georgian identity, trading freely with the Georgian entrepreneurs who now cross the border almost at will.

The Hamshentsis

A little-known area of Lazistan was the nahiye or canton of Hemshin, a community of about 8,000 Armenian-speaking Muslims, calling themselves Hamshentsi or Homshetsi after their historic center, Hamshen. Known to the Turks as Hemshinli, these Armenians dwelled apart in their own villages in the eastern parts of the Pontic Mountains.

According to a story reported by Leontius the Priest (Ghevond Erets) in the eighth century, two Armenian princes, Shapuh Amatuni and his son Hamam, dispossessed by the Arabs of their domains in Armenia, left their homeland with some 12,000 of their people seeking lands on which to settle within the Byzantine Empire.[76] By tradition,

---

[73] Cyril Toumanoff, "Armenia and Georgia," in *The Cambridge Medieval History*, vol. 4, pt. 1: *The Byzantine Empire: Byzantium and Its Neighbours* (Cambridge: Cambridge University Press, 1966), pp. 593-94, 600-03, 605-07, 610.

[74] For the kaza of Lazistan, see Cuinet, *La Turquie d'Asie,* pp. 119-22. For the Laz, see William R. Rickmers, "Lazistan and Ajaristan," *The Geographical Journal* 84:6 (Dec. 1934): 455-80; Anthony Bryer, "Some Notes on the Laz and Tzans," *Bedi Karthlissa* 21-22 (1966): 174-95, and pt. 2, 23-24 (1967): 161-68; Anthony Bryer, "The Last Laz Risings and the Downfall of the Pontic Derebeys, 1812-1840," *Bedi Karthlisa* 26 (1969): 191-210.

[75] Lynch, *Armenia,* pp. 11-12.

[76] Ghevond Erets [Leontius the Priest], *Patmutiun Ghevondiay metsi vardapeti Hayots* [History of Ghevond, the Great Vardapet of the Armenians], ch. 42; trans.

they settled in the mountains south of Rhizaion (Rize), where Hamam founded Hamamashen. There, the Armenian immigrants prospered, the district of Hamshen at one time forming the diocese of Khachkar, with its own bishop. These hardy people maintained their quasi-independence until the nineteenth century, when they were still ruled by their own local *derebeys* (valley lords). Christians as late as the eighteenth century, they gradually converted to Islam, and except for their unique dialect they live much like the Georgian-speaking Laz who surround them. Many do not deny their Armenian origin and distinguish themselves from their neighbors as being Hamshentsi or Hemshinli. They are mostly to be found in the valley of the Firtina River between the port of Atina (now Pazar) on the coast and the great inland peak called Kachkar Dagh (Armenian: Khachkar Ler, meaning Cross-Stone Mountain), and farther west in the Karadere valley Their villages include several that bear in whole or in part the name Hemshin, together with Toroslı, Pertevan, Ayven, Tredzor (Dzimla), Yeghiovit (near which the Monastery of Surb Khachik was located), and Artashen at the mouth of the Firtina River, which was the easternmost extent of their district.

There are, in addition, Hemshinli villages in the vicinities of Artvin and Ardala whose inhabitants speak the Hamshen Armenian dialect known as Homshetsma. In the past, however, the Hamshentsis gradually spread out over a large area until there were villages speaking their dialect as far west as Samsun (as in the village of Khurchunli near the mouth of the Iris or Yeshil River) and as far east as Sukhum in Abkhazia. In Abkhazia today the Hamshentsis are still Christian and retain much of their Armenian identity. Like the Laz, the Hamshentsi/Hemshinli are noted for their rich folklore, especially in regard to proverbs, jokes, riddles, and other forms of oral literature, some of it rather ribald in nature.[77]

Zaven Arzoumanian, *History of Leontius, the Eminent Vardapet of the Armenians* (Wynnewood, PA: St. Sahag and St. Mesrop Church, 1982), ch. 42. For details of the settlement of Hamam in Pontus, see Nicholas Adontz, *Patmakan usumnasirutiunner* [Historical Studies] (Paris, 1948), p. 60; and Levon S. Khachikyan, "*Ejer Hamshina-hay patmutyunits*" [Pages from the History of the Hamshen Armenians], *Banber Erevani Hamalsarani 2* (1969): 115-20.

[77] Regarding the Hamshentsi/Hemshinli, see the chapters in this volume by Elizabeth Redgate, Claire Mouradian, Hovann Simonian, and Igor Kuznetsov.

The End of Armenian and Greek Pontus

The massacre of the Armenians under Sultan Abdul Hamid II in the 1890s actually began in Trebizond, when in October 1895 nearly 1,000 Armenians were killed in the city itself and another 200 in the nearby villages.[78] Most of the local Armenians survived, however, only to be deported along with the remainder of the Ottoman Armenian population twenty years later.[79] Mass deportations from Trebizond began in July 1915 and were accompanied by many forced conversions.[80] Shortly afterwards, a Russian military campaign aimed at seizing Trebizond took the city in 1916 but ultimately failed to hold it.[81]

At the end of World War I, there were high hopes among the Greek population of Pontus that the region would be established as a Greek state, but these aspirations were ignored by the abortive Treaty of Sèvres in 1920 by which most of Pontus (from the former Russian frontier westwards as far as Giresun) was granted to the Republic of Armenia in order to enable it to have access to the Black Sea. This treaty was never ratified, however, and instead Pontus remained a part of Turkey. In 1923, the Pontic Greeks, along with the rest of the Greek population of Anatolia, were deported to Greece in exchange for a far smaller number of Turkish inhabitants of Greece. In this way, the Greek presence in the Pontus and in Anatolia, dating back nearly 3,000 years, was virtually erased in a matter of months.

Trabzon Today

Under the administration of the Republic of Turkey, the sanjaks of the former vilayet of Trebizond have been dissolved into seven separate divisions known as the *ils* (provinces) of Trabzon, Sinop, Ordu, Gire-

---

[78] Christopher Walker, *Armenia: The Survival of a Nation* (London: St. Martin's, 1980), pp. 156-58.

[79] See the chapter by Simon Payaslian in this volume. See also [Arnold Toynbee, ed.], *Treatment of Armenians in the Ottoman Empire* (London: H.M.S.O., 1916), pp. 285-300; Naslian, *Memoires,* vol. 1, pp. 170-220, vol. 2, pp. 43-68; Walker, pp. 216-18.

[80] Naslian, *Memoires,* vol. 1, p. 171n72.

[81] For the best account in English of the campaigns of World War I in Anatolia, see Richard G. Hovannisian, *Armenia on the Road to Independence, 1918* (Berkeley and Los Angeles: University of California Press, 1967), especially chs.4, 7, 9; for the Trebizond campaign in particular, see "Trapizoni operatsia 1916," *Haykakan Sovetakan Hanragitaran* [Armenian Soviet Encyclopedia], vol. 12 (1986), p. 90.

sun, Rize, Gümüshane, and Samsun (to the last of which have been added the former kazas of Havsa, Ladik, and Vezirköpru taken from the former vilayet of Sivas).[82] The city of Trabzon has grown enormously in recent years and in the last census in the 1990s had a population of 155,960.[83] Industry has expanded, and the port has been modernized. The city has an airport and, though not on a railway line, it is connected by bus service on good roads to other coastal cities of eastern Turkey as well as to Ankara and Istanbul.[84]

The collapse of the Soviet Union in 1991 has had an enormous effect on the Black Sea towns of Turkey. With the independence of Georgia and Ukraine and the emergence of Romania and Bulgaria as truly independent states, the coastal cities of Turkey are now thronged with shipping from every direction. Ports are busy, business is booming, and new construction is visible everywhere. Contact between the Georgian elements in Turkey and Georgia is now free, and it appears that the number of Georgian speakers in northeastern Turkey, Laz, Gurians, and Ajars, is considerably larger than the Turkish government has ever cared to acknowledge.[85] The border with Georgia is open, and even Armenian "businessmen" are doing a brisk trade in Armenian brandy and other goods brought illegally into Turkey from Armenia and many Turkish goods that flow in the opposite direction.

---

[82] Hewsen, *Atlas*, p. 244.
[83] McDonagh, *Blue Guide Turkey*, p. 651.
[84] Ibid., p. 654.
[85] Personal observation, summer, 1999.

✻ 3 ✻

AZZI-HAYASA ON THE BLACK SEA?
ANOTHER PUZZLE OF ARMENIAN ORIGINS

Vartan Matiossian

There are many puzzling issues surrounding the earliest origins of the Armenians. For obvious reasons, the land mentioned either as Azzi or as Hayasa (its resemblance to the Armenian self-designation *hay*) in the Hittite inscriptions of the fourteenth-thirteenth centuries B.C. has attracted scholarly interest since the 1920s. This essay focuses on the location of Azzi-Hayasa, while briefly touching on several related issues. The location has been as controversial as the ethnic affiliation of this land. In fact, both are interrelated. If Azzi-Hayasa was in the Armenian Highlands (Plateau), then it might have some closer relationship with Armenian history. But if Azzi-Hayasa was near the Black Sea or elsewhere, its importance in the Armenian context would be sharply diminished.

The noted French scholar Louis Delaporte, in his 1938 monograph *Les Hittites*, placed Azzi-Hayasa in the region of Trebizond, a view subsequently repeated by his colleague René Grousset.[1] However, in the first volume of his unfinished and posthumously-published *Histoire d'Arménie*, Nicolas Adontz, the highly-regarded Armenian historian, had already laid the foundations to situate Azzi-Hayasa to the south of the Black Sea region, on the Armenian Highland around Erzinka (Erzinjan) and Erzerum.[2]

Igor Diakonoff, in his noted monograph *The Pre-History of the Armenian People* (1968; English translation, 1984), which is the most thorough survey on this subject so far available in Western languages, echoed and refined Delaporte's view by placing Azzi-Hayasa along the ovalleys of the rivers Kharshit (Harshit; Harşit) and Chorokh up to the

---

[1] Cf. René Grousset, *Histoire de l'Arménie* (Paris: Payot, 1947), p. 42.
[2] Nicolas Adontz, *Histoire d'Arménie* (Paris: Union Générale Arménienne de Bienfaisance, 1946), p. 28.

Black Sea. Thus, the country would have fallen within the Pontus area and outside the Armenian Highland. Notwithstanding this conclusion, the Russian scholar conceded that at some point Azzi-Hayasa could have temporarily extended its power as far as the Upper Euphrates region.[3]

Interestingly, the first volume of *History of the Armenian People*, the flagship historical project of the Soviet Armenian Academy of Sciences (8 volumes, 1967-1982), contains a chapter on Azzi-Hayasa with sections written by Diakonoff and Suren Eremyan. Here, Eremyan pursued the path set by Adontz and reinstated Azzi-Hayasa as being part of the Armenian Highland.[4] Both positions have been maintained at different times by various scholars. Before dealing with this geographical puzzle, a brief look at the historical background would be helpful.

Hittites and Azzi-Hayasa

By 2000 B.C., people of Indo-European stock had arrived in Asia Minor. Two centuries later, they had subjugated a good share of the territory without eliminating its inhabitants, the Hatti or pre-Hittites, who probably belonged to the Caucasian language family. The newcomers, the Nesites or Hittites, had been preceded by their relatives, the Luwians. Both the Hittite and Luwian languages, together with a few others of lesser importance, constitute the Anatolian branch of the Indo-European family.

Around 1400 B.C., the Hittites started a second wave of territorial expansion with imperial ambitions and became the foremost power in Western Asia for more than a century. Their two main fronts of external conflict were Egypt and the Syro-Mesopotamian realm (Mitanni and Assyria). However, the eastern borders, on the margins of the Euphrates, were in a state of permanent instability. The mountaineer Kaskas and the leaders of Azzi-Hayasa and Ishuwa did not lose an opportunity to give trouble to their powerful neighbor. They managed to keep the Hittites at bay, sometimes even going on the offensive.

---

[3] Igor Diakonoff, *The Pre-History of the Armenian People* (Delmar: Caravan Books, 1984), p. 46.

[4] Suren Eremyan and Igor Diakonoff, "Hayasa-Azzi tseghayin miutyune" [The Hayasa-Azzi Tribal Union], in *Hay zhoghovrdi patmutyun* [History of the Armenian People], vol. 1 (Erevan: Armenian Academy of Sciences, 1971), pp. 192-93.

The confrontation was apparently not strictly a military affair. James Mellaart has advanced the possibility of the Hittites trying to keep control over an alternative source of tin.[5] Although Caucasian tin may or may not have been indigenous,[6] James G. Macqueen has suggested that Azzi-Hayasa possessed rich metallic ores in the northwestern and northern sections of the Armenian Highland, which would have piqued the interest of the empire.[7] The Hittite inscriptions are practically the only written source about Azzi-Hayasa, and their disappearance after the fall of the empire (thirteenth century B.C.) also meant the end of references to this name.

Azzi or Hayasa?

Who were the people of Hayasa? It has been advanced since the 1920s that the origins of the Armenian self-designation *hay* should be searched in this neighborhood. The name appears in the Hittite annals as *Khayasa*, since the Hittite *h* is strongly aspirated, but the phonemes *h* and *kh* are interchangeable. The case is similar to some of the southern dialects of Armenian (Van and Khoi, among others), whose speakers employ a strongly aspirated *kh* as in *khay* (Armenian) or *khats* (bread).

The toponymic suffix *(a)sa*, of Hittite-Luwian origin and indicating "land," was widespread in Asia Minor (as in the names Harpasa, Mylasa, Datassa(s), and Wilusa). Therefore, *Hayasa* would have meant "land of the *hay*," a question-laden parallel to *Hayk,* the ancient self-designation of Armenia, or the modern *Hayastan,* where *k* is the Old Armenian geographical suffix and *stan* is, of course, the well-known Iranian suffix, both with the meaning of "land." This parallelism does not justify, however, the equating of Hayasa with Hayastan. The geographical borders of Azzi-Hayasa are extremely imprecise, since it is necessary to rely exclusively on the identification of the names mentioned in Hittite sources. But these sources only mention those places

---

[5] James Mellaart, "Anatolian Trade with Europe and Anatolian Geography and Culture Provinces in the Late Bronze Age," *Anatolian Studies* 18 (1968): 200-01.

[6] See Charles Burney and David M. Lang, *The Peoples of the Hills: Ancient Ararat and Caucasus* (London: Weidenfeld and Nicolson, 1971), p. 68; Jak Yakar, "Regional and Local Schools of Metalwork in Early Bronze Age Anatolia, Part II," *Anatolian Studies* 35 (1985): 31.

[7] James G. Macqueen, *The Hittites and Their Contemporaries in Asia Minor* (London: Thames & Hudson, 1996), pp. 41-43, 54.

which were part of the contact zone between the Hittite Empire and
Azzi-Hayasa. They do not give any information, for instance, about
eastern or southern borders of the country.

Diakonoff maintained that the absence of the suffix *asa* in the Armenian Highland was an indication that Hayasa had no relation either
with the great plateau or with the Armenians.[8] This view does not seem
pertinent, first of all because a name quoted in a foreign source is not
necessarily expected to retain its original form. On the other hand, it
would be more accurate to say that *asa,* at least in the case of Hayasa,
is not used as a toponymic suffix. The absence of *a(s)sa* in the Armenian realm indicates that Hayasa was not a geographic term like the
Hittite-Luwian ones, dispersed in the central and western zones of Asia
Minor.

How is this possible? In a more restricted sense, *asa* is a possessive
suffix which compounds adjectives parallel to the genitive case (cf.
Hittite *assa,* Hieroglyphic Luwian *asa,* Luwian *assi,* all of them derived from the Indo-European genitive case **osio*); for instance, Hittite
hantassa (frontal) comes from *hant* (forefront).[9] Thus, in a literal
sense, Hayasa meant "related to the hay," like *ian* (*Armen-ian* or *Iranian*), and in all likelihood it was not a toponym, but a genitive adjective. The country was seemingly called Azzi and its inhabitants, *hay.*
When a Hittite king mentioned [URU]*Hayasa* ([land of] Hayasa) without
using Azzi, he was actually referring to an ethnic concept.

The difference between the meanings of Azzi (political) and Hayasa
(ethnic) is reminiscent of the case of Mitanni during its period of de-
cay. After the dynastic quarrel in the Mitannian kingdom around 1370
B.C., the sources simultaneously mention both Mitanni and Hurri, and
it was believed for a long time that they pointed to the division of the
kingdom into two separate states. Actually, both terms were synonyms:
Mitanni translated a political situation and Hurri, an ethno-linguistic
reality. Indeed, there is no evidence that the Hittites referred to Hayasa
as encompassing the whole Armenian Highland. Rather, they apparently applied the name to one particular polity in its western area on
the basis of the dominant ethno-linguistic unit, the *hay.*

---

[8] Diakonoff, *Pre-History,* p. 114.

[9] Gevorg Jahukyan, *Hayots lezvi patmutyun: Nakhagrayin shrjan* [History of the
Armenian Language: Pre-Literate Period] (Erevan: Armenian Academy of Sciences,
1987), p. 331.

What does *hay* mean? After more than a century of speculations, the most plausible explanation of the ethnonym seems to be an old social interpretation of Indo-European names. Around the end of the nineteenth century, Friedrich Spiegel and Heinrich Kiepert had derived *hay* from I.E. *pótis (husband, lord, also chief); *hay* would have become a self-designation that immigrant Armenians adopted to differentiate themselves from autocthonous tribes.[10] In the same way, Sanskrit *aryá* became both an Indo-Iranian self-denomination with the double meaning of "lord" and "Aryan," and the basis of the toponym *Iran* (< Avestic *airyo,* genitive plural *aryanam*).

Armen Petrosyan turned his attention to this etymology in 1983-86 and then refined it in 1990 (**potiio* > *(h)eti(y)o* > *(h)ati(y)o* > *hay*). The reconstructed term **(h)eti(y)o* might have been transcribed as *Etiuni* (**etio-ni*), the name of a powerful confederation in the Ararat plain, frequently mentioned in Urartian inscriptions.[11] With its pros and cons, this hypothesis is much sounder than another old theory ingeniously revamped some decades ago. At the end of the nineteenth century, shortly before the discovery of the Hittite archives in 1907, German linguist Peter Jensen suggested identifying the still non-deciphered Hittite language with Armenian and regarded the mysterious Hittites as ancestors of the historical Armenians. He formulated a

---

[10] Cf. Hayk Zhamkochyan, Stepan Melik-Bakhshyan and Ashot G. Abrahamyan, *Hay zhoghovrdi patmutyun* [History of the Armenian People], vol. 1 (Erevan: Armenian State Educational-Pedagogical Press, 1963), p. 107.

[11] Armen Petrosyan, "Otrazhenie indoevropeiskogo kornia *uel- v armianskoi mifologii" [The Reflection of the Indo-European Root *uel- in Armenian Mythology], *Lraber hasarakakan gitutyunneri* 1 (1987): 70; idem, "Armianskie etnonimii v svete mifologicheskikh dannykh" [Armenian Ethnonyms under the Light of Mythological Data], in *Mezhdistsiplinarnye issledovaniia kul'turogeneza i etnogeneza armianskogo nagor'ia i sopredel'nykh oblastei* [Interdisciplinary Studies About Culture and Ethnogenesis in the Armenian Highland and Adjacent Regions] (Erevan: Armenian Academy of Sciences, 1990), pp. 240-41. For a recent reassessment in English, see Armen Petrosyan, "The Problem of Identification of the Proto-Armenians: A Critical Review," *Journal of the Society for Armenian Studies* 16 (2007): 32-33. Jahukyan, *Hayots lezvi patmutyun,* pp. 284-85, had also suggested **potiio* > *hay,* but with doubts (I.E. **o* is the source of Armenian *a* when there is no **o* in the following syllables). However, after 1987 he always discussed **pótis* > *hay* as the most plausible explanation. See Gevorg Jahukyan, "O sootnoshenii khayasskogo i armianskogo iazykov" [The Correlation between Hayasan and Armenian Languages], *Patmabanasirakan handes* 1 (1988): 68; Gevork Djahukian, "Did Armenians Live in Asia Anterior before the Twelfth Century B.C.?" in Thomas L. Markey and John A.C. Greppin, eds., *When Worlds Collide. Indo-Europeans and Pre-Indo-Europeans* (Ann Arbor: Karoma Publishers, 1990), pp. 26ff.

hypothetical passage *hate > hay* on the well-known model of I.E. **pater >* Armenian *hayr* (father). Diakonoff rephrased this long-outdated etymology with a different argument. He argued that long after the demise of the Hittite Empire, in Urartian times, the area to the west of the Euphrates River was known as *Hate* and its inhabitants as "Hittite" (*hattini*). Therefore, the whole population on both banks of the Upper Euphrates, without ethnic distinction, would have been labeled as Hittites, including the Armenians. When the Urartians were assimilated by the Armenians after the sixth century B.C., they would have adopted that name (in Old Armenian, **hatiyos*), which became **hayo*, root of *hay* (genitive plural *hayots*) through the above-mentioned *te > y* (*pater > hayr*) rule.[12]

Western scholars subsequently adopted Diakonoff's highly speculative view as the most plausible explanation to this issue with no further questioning.[13] However, Tamaz Gamkrelidze and Viacheslav Ivanov have rightfully observed in regard to Diakonoff's opionion that "the claim would be more plausible if evidence from other borrowings had been given showing the application of the Armenian sound law in historical times."[14] Phonological studies seem to prove otherwise. Jahukyan has shown that between the twelfth and fourth centuries B.C. the proto-Armenian predecessor of *hayr* already sounded **háyir* and the passage *t > y* was no longer functional.[15] Therefore, the whole *Hate > hay* argument in its new "packaging" comes to naught.

The absence of Hayasa or any similar name after the fall of the Hittite Empire points to the idea that it was really a genitive adjective and not the name of the country. The Hittite inscriptions put further the determinative ^{URU} (country), which could come from the existence of *Til-Hayasa* as the core of the confederation of Azzi (compare, for example, Assur, the original center of Assyria). The case of the official

---

[12] Diakonoff, *Pre-History*, pp. 126-27.

[13] Cf. James Russell, "The Formation of the Armenian Nation," in Richard G. Hovannisian, ed., *The Armenian People from Ancient to Modern Times*, vol. 1 (New York: St. Martin's Press, 1997), p. 22.

[14] Tamaz Gamkrelidze and Viacheslav Ivanov, *Indo-European and the Indo-Europeans: A Reconstruction and Historical Analysis of a Proto-Language and a Proto-Culture*, vol. 1 (Berlin: Mouton de Gruyter, 1995), p. 808.

[15] Jahukyan, *Hayots lezvi patmutyun*, p. 354. It was already a known fact that the passage *t>y* had ceased in Urartian times; around the sixth century B.C. Armenian had started to borrow from Iranian without changing the *t*. Cf. Iranian *patikara >* Armenian *patker*, "image" in Hrachia Acharyan, *Hayots lezvi patmutyun* [History of the Armenian Language], vol. 1 (Erevan: Erevan State University, 1940), p. 107.

names of the former Soviet republics is quite illustrative as a parallelism: "Russian Soviet Federative Socialist Republic," "Georgian Soviet Socialist Republic," "Armenian Soviet Socialist Republic," and not "Soviet Federative Socialist Republic of Russia", "of Georgia", "of Armenia," and so on. In Soviet times, these names had an ethnic and not politico-geographic connotation.

The Location of Azzi-Hayasa

Azzi-Hayasa has been placed both inside and outside the Armenian Highland. How have these two opposing views fared so far? The fragmentary nature of the Hittite annals, which are the basic source of knowledge about Azzi-Hayasa, have paved the way for the existing disagreement. For instance, the Hittite king Mursilis II mentioned three place-names—Ingalawa, Aripsa, and Dukkamma—in the campaign, in the tenth year of his reign, against Azzi-Hayasa. The three names are highly controversial, because the text of the annals of Mursilis II is damaged between the reference to Ingalawa and Aripsa.

Following Adontz, Diakonoff rightfully questioned the traditional identification of Ingalawa with Ingila or Angl (Anggh), on the Eastern Tigris near Diarbekir, but he did not offer an alternative.[16] However, an identification of Ingalawa with the district of Nigal would be likely if it is accepted that Mursilis II first invaded and subdued the Kaskas near the Black Sea before campaigning to the south against Azzi-Hayasa. This district is situated on the lower course of the Chorokh (by metathesis, *Nigal > Ingal/awa*) and its name might have an Armenian etymology.[17]

Aripsa is actually the key subject of the controversy, because the annals say: "I marched towards the city of Aripsa to hold battle. But

---

[16] Adontz, *Histoire,* pp. 38-39; Diakonoff, *Pre-History,* p. 150.

[17] Valeri Khachatryan, "Strana Khayk v sostave Urartu" [The Land of Hayk as Part of Urartu], *Lraber hasarakakan gitutyunneri,* 6 (1980): 110; cf. idem, *Hayastane m.t.a. XV-VII darerum (hayots hin patmutyun]* [Armenia in the 15th-7th Centuries B.C.E. (Ancient Armenian History*)*] (Erevan: Zangak-97, 1998), p. 35. He connects *Nigal* with Armenian *nig* (bolt, lock < i.e. **k'neigh*, to hold on; to close) and *al* (deep place, origin unknown); cf. Hrachia Acharyan, *Hayeren armatakan bararan* [Armenian Etymological Dictionary], vol. 1 (Erevan: Erevan State University Press, 1971), p. 96.

the said Aripsa is surrounded by water."[18] What is the meaning of "surrounded by water"? By adopting the previous hypothesis of a location on the Black Sea, Diakonoff noticed the parallel of the suffix *psa* of *Aripsa* with the *pse* of some coastal cities in the Caucasus like Tuapse.[19] However, he failed to give a convincing explanation about the fact that the inscription speaks about a city "surrounded" by water and he gave no sound proof to locate Aripsa with greater precision. In fact, it is quite implausible that, after invading the country from the Black Sea area, the Hittite king would have turned back to occupy the coastal zone. He probably would have secured his rearguard first before advancing farther into enemy lines.

What about a place with fortifications surrounded by a river? Valeri Khachatryan has suggested the fortress of Arab-kale (Arabic *kaleh* = castle, fortress), whose name has a phonetic resemblance with Aripsa. Its ruins are located to the northeast of Sper, on one of the branches of the Chorokh River.[20] In a recent work on the Hittite annals and the toponymy of the Armenian Highland, Aram Kosyan also gives almost equal attention to the previous hypotheses by Grigor Ghapantsyan (on the shore of a swamp-lake close to Erzerum, where Byzantine sources mentioned the town of Arabesson) and by Khachatryan (near Lake Tortum).[21]

According to Diakonoff, the third place under scrutiny, Dukkama, would have been located in the valley of the Gayl River (Lycus, Kelkit), or in the pass between the valleys of the Gayl and Kharshit.[22] Bearing in mind that the name comes from Hittite *dukk* (to be visible),[23] is it possible to see it as a Hittite translation of an Armenian name? Or perhaps it was translated later from Hittite into Armenian. Khachatryan points to the late medieval place-name *Hay* (Armenian *hay-el* = to look, hence, *hayeli* = mirror) in the province of *Azord,* which was also the name of one of the tributaries of the Chorokh on its

---

[18] Quoted in Ashot G. Abrahamyan and Petros Hovhannisyan, *Hay zhoghovrdi patmutyan krestomatiya* [Chrestomathy of the History of the Armenian People], vol. 1 (Erevan: Erevan State University, 1981), pp. 10-11.

[19] Diakonoff, *Pre-History,* pp. 149, 151. Cf. *pse* (water) in two Caucasian languages, Kabardinian and Adyge. See Jahukyan, *Hayots lezvi patmutyun,* p. 336.

[20] Khachatryan, *Hayastane,* p. 35.

[21] Aram Kosyan, *Haykakan lernashkharhi teghanunnere (est khetakan sepagir aghbyurneri)* [The Toponyms of the Armenian Highland (According to the Hittite Cuneiform Sources)] (Erevan: Zangak-97, 2004), p. 39.

[22] Diakonoff, *Pre-History,* p. 149.

[23] Jahukyan, *Hayots lezvi patmutyun,* p. 335.

left margin (modern Tortum River).[24] Despite this, Kosyan notes that, taking into consideration recent research, "the location of the city to the north or northeast of Erzinka appears more likely."[25]

The above-mentioned name *Azord* also points toward the location of Azzi-Hayasa being around Erzinka, in Upper Armenia, for several reasons:

a) Hittite sources called the Iris River (modern Yeshil Irmak) *Az(z)i*;[26]

b) Megalithic monuments of Upper Armenia (Bardzr Hayk) were called *Aznaberd*;[27]

c) Georgian sources of the eleventh and twelfth centuries mention the village of Tordan in Upper Armenia under the name of *Andzoreti* or *Andziandzora*.[28]

d) Seventeenth-century author Hakob Karnetsi identified Ghuruchan, the "deep and wooded land called *Azntsik*," as one of the three districts of Kamakh in Upper Armenia.[29]

Jahukyan had derived *Azzi* from the Armenian *azn*, genitive *azin* (tribe, people, relatives, from I.E. *ag'h-iio*),[30] although he later ascribed an Iranian origin (nobleman, member of the nobility) to that word.[31] It is possible to suggest the elimination of the final -*n* of *azn* in Hittite by a phonetic process called dissimilation (*Aznzi > Az[n]zi > Azzi*), and in this case the toponym *Azntsik* (land of those from *azn*) would be the "lost link" in the chain. Its association with *hay* might presume that the relation Azzi/*azn* would also reflect some feature of social organization.

---

[24] Khachatryan, "Strana Khayk," p. 110 (cf. Khachatryan, *Hayastane*, p. 35).

[25] Kosyan, *Haykakan lernashkharhi teghanunnere*, p. 99.

[26] Jahukyan, "O sootnoshenii khayasskogo i armianskogo iazykov," p. 69.

[27] Eremyan and Diakonoff, "Hayasa-Azzi," p. 194.

[28] Ibid, p. 193.

[29] Quoted by Lavrenti Barseghyan, "Hayasa-Azzii u nra mi kani bnakavayreri teghadrman hartsi shurje" [On the Question of Locating Hayasa-Azzi and Some of Its Places of Habitation], *Patma-banasirakan handes* 3 (1963): 312.

[30] Guevorg Djahukyan, "The Hayasa Language and Its Relation to the Indo-European Languages," *Archiv Orientální* 3 (1961): 364-67. Cf. Eremyan and Diakonoff, "Hayasa-Azzi," p. 194.

[31] Jahukyan, *Hayots lezvi patmutyun*, p. 512. Cf. John Greppin, "An Etymological Dictionary of the Indo-European Components of Armenian," *Bazmavep*, 1-4 (1983): 262. Following Khachatryan, Jahukyan later explained Azzi through the Armenian root *az* (dry), *azazim* (to become dry) < I.E. *az-gh* (dry). See Khachatryan, "Strana Khayk," p. 110 (cf. Khachatryan, *Hayastane*, p. 35); Djahukian, "Did Armenians Live in Asia Anterior," p. 20.

A few other places of Azzi-Hayasa can be located with considerable accuracy: Arziya (Artzn, near Erzerum),[32] Kumaha (Kamakh or Kemakh, on the sources of the Euphrates),[33] and Pittiyariga (Btarich, near Altintepe).[34] The name Arziya seems to have an Armenian origin (*artz* = shining, *artzat* = silver < I.E. **arg'* = shining).[35] Kamakh, on the other hand, was the royal pantheon in Arsacid times, and it perhaps performed a similar function in Azzi-Hayasa; the name *Kumaha* could reflect this (Armenian *kmakhk* = skeleton).[36] Suggested Armenian etymologies for Pittiyariga are much more shaky,[37] while the origin of *arich* (place) is unknown.[38] There is also Arniya, center of the cult of the storm-god of Azzi-Hayasa (cited in Hittite texts as ^{d}U, which is the ideographic way to show a name). Although there are too many homophonous names in the Armenian Highland to come to an agreement,[39] this town might be identified with Ani, in Upper Armenia (not to be confused with the medieval capital Ani in the Plain of Ararat), where Aramazd, the Armenian equivalent of Zeus, was worshipped in Arsacid times.[40] It has also been identified with Arnos, in the district of Sper.[41]

Some other names are also found far from the Black Sea, such as Ura, the main fortress of Azzi-Hayasa, which might be located near the

---

[32] Khachatryan, "Strana Khayk," p. 111 (cf. Khachatryan, *Hayastane,* p. 42); Djahukian, "Did Armenians Live in Asia Anterior," p. 26. Kosyan, *Haykakan lernashkharhi teghanunnere,* p. 43, only agrees that it was close to the Euphrates or on the upper Halys.

[33] Adontz, *Histoire,* p. 28.

[34] Grigor Ghapantsyan, *Hayots lezvi patmutyun* [History of the Armenian Language], vol. 1 (Erevan: Armenian Academy of Sciences, 1961), p. 67; Eremyan and Diakonoff, "Hayasa-Azzi," p. 191.

[35] Khachatryan, "Strana Khayk," p. 111 (cf. Khachatryan, *Hayastane,* p.42); Djahukian, "Did Armenians Live in Asia Anterior," p. 26.

[36] From Akkadian *gimmahu, kimmahu* (tomb). See Hrachia Acharyan, *Hayeren armatakan bararan,* vol. 2 (1973), p. 605.

[37] Cf. Jahukyan, "O sootnoshenii khayasskogo i armianskogo iazykov," p. 79; Khachatryan, "Strana Khayk," p. 111; Khachatryan, *Hayastane,* p. 43.

[38] Ghapantsyan, *Hayots lezvi patmutyun,* p. 67; Gevorg Jahukyan, "Hayasayi lezvi hinanatoliakan varkatse" [The Paleo-Anatolian Hypothesis of the Language of Hayasa], *Patma-banasirakan handes* 1 (1976): 105.

[39] Kosyan, *Haykakan lernashkharhi teghanunnere,* p. 41.

[40] Cf. Armen Petrosyan, *Aramazd: kerpar, pashtamunk, nakhatiper* [Aramazd: Figure, Cult, Prototypes] (Erevan: Van Aryan, 2006), pp. 71-72, who makes an interesting attempt at etymology.

[41] Khachatryan, *Hayastane,* p. 44, relates Arniya to Armenian *arn* (male wild goat). It has also been located in Arane (modern Alaca-khan), mentioned by classical sources. See Eremyan and Diakonoff, "Hayasa-Azzi," p. 192.

Gayl River[42] or correspond to Uren, to the west of Baberd (Baiburt).[43] Arhita, situated on the borderline of Azzi-Hayasa and Hatti, has been identified with Erez in the district of Khordzeank, or Eriza in the district of Hashdeank, on the Upper Euphrates.[44] Kosyan also supports a site on the Upper Euphrates in the vicinity of Kummaha and Pahhuwa, a land on river's right bank, without attempting a more specific identification.[45] The first component of the name Pahhuteia (linked to the above-mentioned Pahhuwa) and the second component of Lahirhila seem to have Hittite origin,[46] but their location in Azzi-Hayasa is not known. Some other names cannot even be located or explained in a plausible way.

One can infer from these place-names that Azzi-Hayasa was not situated in the Black Sea area, but in the Armenian Highland. Its core was around the upper courses of the Western Euphrates, Gayl, and Chorokh rivers, immediately to the south of the Pontus area. Its inhabitants, called *hay*, might have been Armenian-speakers, at least in part, as suggested by the etymologies of some of these place-names and also of a few kings[47] and gods.[48]

---

[42] Kosyan, *Haykakan lernashkharhi teghanunnere*, p. 101. Djahukyan, "The Hayasa Language," p. 397, has suggested a Hittite etymology (*ura* = big).

[43] Khachatryan, "Strana Khayk," p. 110; cf. Khachatryan, *Hayastane*, pp. 43-44, who explains the name through Armenian *ur* (sprout).

[44] Valeri Khachatryan, "Hayasa," *Haykakan Sovetakan Hanragitaran* [Soviet Armenian Encyclopedia], vol. 6 (Erevan: Soviet Armenian Encyclopedia, 1980), p. 134; Khachatryan, *Hayastane*, p. 43, who presumes a translation from Armenian *erez* (border), since Arhita is clearly related to Hittite, Luwian, and Hieroglyphic Luwian *arha* (outside); Hieroglyphic Luwian, *arha* (border). See Ghapantsyan, *Hayots lezvi patmutyun*, pp. 66-67.

[45] Kosyan, *Haykakan lernashkharhi teghanunnere*, p. 37.

[46] Jahukyan, "O sootnoshenii khayasskogo i armianskogo iazykov," pp. 76-77; Ghapantsyan, *Hayots lezvi patmutyun*, p. 66. An Armenian origin for both second components has been also suggested by Jahukyan, pp. 76-77; idem, "Did Armenians Live in Asia Anterior," p. 26.

[47] For instance, *Mariya*, from Armenian **mari* (young man < i.e. **m^briya*), among others. See Vartan Matiossian, "Hayasa erkri aradjnord Mariya ev ir arnchutiunnere" [Mariya, Leader of the Land of Hayasa, and His Connections], *Bazmavep* 1-4 (1992): 322-24.

[48] It is not far-fetched to suggest that the god-name *Baltaik* might have an Armenian origin with the meaning of "bright," as in sister Indo-European languages, despite the fact that this meaning has been lost in Armenian (cf. I.E. **bhl-to* "resplendent" > Armenian *bal* (fog, mist); Acharyan, *Hayeren armatakan bararan*, vol. 1, p. 383). In fact, the suffix *ik* has Armenian origin (cf. the Armenian goddess *Astghik*, equivalent to the Akkadian Ishtar and the Roman Venus).

❊ 4 ❊

CONTACTS BETWEEN ARMENIA AND PONTUS IN THE PRE-CHRISTIAN PERIOD

Richard Wilkinson

By the twentieth century, Armenians had come to consider Pontus—by which is meant the stretch of Black Sea coast and its hinterland from Sinope in the west round to Batum and Poti in the east—almost an integral part of their homeland. This is shown by the fact that the Armenian delegation to the Paris Peace Conference in 1919 claimed for an independent Armenia some 250 miles of Black Sea coastline extending on both sides of and including the ancient Greek city of Trebizond.

But how ancient were these links with the Black Sea coast? Were there always contacts with the peoples, whether proto-Armenian, Urartian or pre-Armenian, or Armenian, who inhabited the highland areas of geographical Armenia proper that lie to the south and southeast of Pontus? This essay explores the existence of such contacts and examines the evidence such as it is for their nature and intensity from prehistoric times down to period of the Roman Empire.

Armenia has been inhabited since the earliest times. The country possessed animals to hunt, trees and bushes from which to gather fruit and berries, and, perhaps most important of all for stone-age beings, a suitable stone from which to fashion tools and implements. Armenia has extensive deposits of the dark volcanic glass known as obsidian, a material ideal for chipping into a cutting edge. Discoveries of obsidian tools of various kinds have been made in many parts of Armenia, most abundantly on the slopes of Mount Aragats. These discoveries have established that Armenia was inhabited at all the main stages of the development of prehistoric man.[1]

---

[1] Of the many studies of Paleolithic remains in Armenia, one of the most useful and accessible is still John M. Coles and Eric S. Higgs, *The Archaeology of Early Man* (London: Faber, 1969), pp. 325-56.

With the Neolithic revolution around 10,000 B.C. man began to live a settled existence based on agriculture and pastoralism and for the first time made use of pottery. Egypt, Western Asia, the central Anatolian plateau, and Mesopotamia (modern Iraq) have all been put forward as the place where this settled existence first began, but Armenia was not far behind. The picture based on excavations near Van and from sites such as Kultepe near Nakhichevan is of an unsophisticated society, more or less keeping pace with most of the main advances of the more developed societies in Mesopotamia and Anatolia, but of no great originality or dynamism. Pottery has demonstrated that there were trading links between the Van region and northern Mesopotamia and Syria, but no clear connection has yet been established with the Black Sea region.[2]

With the advent of the Bronze Age toward the end of the fourth millennium B.C., the picture changes. Armenia is one of the places where copper, the basic material for bronze, is found, not far away from the other minerals required—tin, arsenic, and antimony. For the first time the historic land of Armenia acquired a certain cultural uniformity. The two characteristics that best illustrate this culture, called the Early Transcaucasian or the Kuro-Araxes culture, are its pottery and architecture.[3] Although the evidence is not conclusive, it is widely believed that this distinctive culture may have originated in the Araxes River Valley in the plain at the foot of Mount Ararat. It seems that this culture spread rapidly outwards to cover most of Transcaucasia, the highlands of what became known as the Armenian Plateau, as far west as modern Elazığ (Kharpert; historic Tsopk/Sophene), and northwestern Iran. A later expansion brought exponents of the Kuro-Araxes culture right down into the Levant and northern Palestine. This expansion does not, however, seem to have reached the Black Sea coast of Pontus. Discoveries of this period have been made in sites near Amisus

---

[2] For a brief account of Neolithic finds in the region, see Charles Burney and David Marshall Lang, *The Peoples of the Hills* (London: Weidenfeld and Nicolson, 1971), pp. 18-42.

[3] General surveys of this culture include Tariel N. Chubinishvili, "The Interconnections between the Caucasian ('Kura-Araxes') and the Near East Cultures in the Third Millennium B.C.," *Seventh International Congress of Anthropological and Ethnological Sciences* (Moscow, 1964); Boris B. Piotrovskii, "The Aeneolithic Culture of Transcaucasia in the Third Millennium B.C.," *Sixth International Congress of Prehistoric and Protohistoric Sciences: Reports* (Moscow, 1962); *Hay zhoghovrdi patmutyun* [History of the Armenian People], vol. 1 (Erevan: Armenian Academy of Sciences, 1971), pp. 100-56; Burney and Lang, *Peoples of the Hills*, pp. 43-85.

(Samsun), but they suggest that the cultural affinities of that region in the latter half of the third millennium B.C. (around 2,300) were with the central Anatolian plateau.[4]

More remarkable still, perhaps, is the apparent connection between Pontus and the Kuban region of southern Russia where the great burial at Maikop shows clear affinities with the burials at Alaja Huyuk in central Anatolia.[5] No evidence suggests any comparable burials on the Armenian Plateau or Transcaucasia dating from that period, so the conclusion is that even at that early period there was a maritime trade across the Black Sea, or at least over the fairly short distance between the Kuban and central Pontus.

With the breakup of the Early Transcaucasian/Kuro-Araxes culture toward the end of the third millennium B.C., the picture becomes more confused. Local traditions carried on in many places; continuity of occupation is shown, for example, by the excavations at Metsamor in the Plain of Ararat not far from Erevan. Anatolia, Armenia, and Iran in the course of the second millennium B.C. were the scene of various invasions or infiltrations of Indo-Aryan peoples, and the presence of barrows near Vanadzor (Kirovakan) as well as at Trialeti some 40 miles to the southwest of Tbilisi (Tiflis) shows that Armenia, too, was affected by these migrations—barrows being one of the most distinctive characteristics of the Indo-Aryan newcomers.[6] Yet, although there was contact with Colchis at the eastern end of the Black Sea, Pontus itself seems once again to have been isolated from significant cultural or other influences from Armenia.

Toward the end of the second millennium B.C., there are records of Assyrian campaigns against first the "Kings of the Khurri land," then "Uruatri," and then "the land of Nairi," where forty kings, it was boasted, were taken prisoner in around 1230 B.C. Assyria had become the dominant power in Western Asia, based in what is now northern Syria and northern Iraq. Nairi appears to have been situated to the

---

[4] Charles A. Burney, "Northern Anatolia before Classical Times," *Anatolian Studies* 6 (1956): 179-203.

[5] A general description of the Maikop barrow is in Franz Hančar, *Urgeschichte Kaukasiens* (Leipzig and Vienna: A. Schroll and Co., 1937), pp. 247-52.

[6] For a brief summary of discoveries at Trialeti, see David M. Lang, *The Georgians* (London: Thames and Hudson, 1966), pp. 44-50; for the Kirovakan (now Vanadzor) barrows, see Arutiun A. Martirosian, *Armeniia v epokhu Bronzy i rannego Zheleza* [Armenia in the Bronze and Early Iron Ages] (Erevan: Armenian Academy of Sciences, 1964), pp. 47-78.

south of Lake Van and Lake Urmia, as well as on the northern shore of
Van where the Assyrians campaigned against this foe some hundred
years later in around 1100 B.C. In the following century, Assyrian inscriptions revert to use of the term Uruatri and from then on that term
becomes dominant.[7]

The kingdom of Urartu was the principal and at the time the only
power in the Armenian highlands for some 350 years from the mid-
ninth century B.C. Its main centers were Van (it is sometimes identified
as the kingdom of Van) and the Plain of Ararat, now the center of the
modern Armenian republic. Westwards, it expanded as far as the Euphrates River, and eastwards, as far as Lake Urmia. To the south, the
border fluctuated as the power of Urartu's great rival, Assyria, rose and
declined. To the north, Urartu appears not to have pushed beyond the
mountains around Lake Sevan, though in the eighth century there is
mention of contact with a land called Qulha, which may be synony-
mous with Colchis. Even if this is correct, it seems fairly certain that
Urartian domination never actually reached the Black Sea coast and
that the Urartian rulers were content to shelter behind the jagged peaks
of the Pontic Mountain chain.

The Urartians were fine workers of metal, and it has long been
known that objects of Urartian manufacture made their way to the
Greek world and farther westward to Etruria in modern Italy. How did
they come? One route was undoubtedly down from Van to northern
Syria and the coast of the Levant held at that time by the Phoenicians.
But some scholars have suggested an alternative route up the Araxes
River Valley to where modern Erzerum (Karin) stands, then down
through the Pontic chain to the Greek city of Trebizond. If so, this
would be the first clear instance of regular contact between the Pontic
littoral and Armenia.[8] But its importance and indeed its existence as a
trade route have been put into question by other scholars who rely on
archaeological evidence of finds along the route to show that substantial trade was carried from the Urartian centers of Van and Karmir Blur
westward through Asia Minor to the Greek cities of the Aegean sea-

---

[7] A pioneering work on the history of Armenia is that of Nicolas Adontz, *Histoire
d'Armenie* (Paris: n.p., 1946). For a comprehensive overview of the main archaeological excavations, see Boris Piotrovsky, *The Ancient Civilization of Urartu* (London: Barrel and Rockliff, 1969).

[8] Richard D. Barnett, "Ancient Oriental Influences on Archaic Greece," in Saul S.
Weinberg, ed., *The Aegean and the Near East* (Locust Valley, NY: J.J. Augustin,
1956), pp. 228-34.

board, such as Smyrna, Ephesus, and Miletus.[9] It has in fact been generally believed—and accepted by as distinguished an authority as Hakob Manandian—that the route from Erzerum via Baiburt down to the Black Sea at Trebizond only really came into use in Roman times.[10] It may seem surprising that Trebizond, which was founded by Greek colonists from Sinope further west along the coast in 756 B.C., did not trade with its hinterland. But Trebizond, or Trapezos (Trapezus) to use its Greek name, remained an insignificant town until Roman times. Its function was largely to provide a stopping post and shelter to the Greek and other trading vessels that plied from the eastern end of the Black Sea (Phasis and Dioscurias) to the substantial cities of Amisus (Samsun) and Sinope, which had regular contact with the interior. The Greeks, intrepid and adventurous sailors in their way, preferred to hug the shore and put in for the night at a regular harbor, and thus founded a whole chain of coastal settlements from the Bosphorus along to Colchis.

Urartu succumbed to the Medes around the beginning of the sixth century B.C., and later that century the Persian Achaemenid Empire took over. This was the period during which the Armenians as such were establishing their ascendancy, at this stage probably more preponderantly in the western part of their traditional homeland. In the winter of 401/400 B.C., the Greek general Xenophon crossed Armenia from south to north and subsequently described his journey with his 10,000 soldiers in his *Anabasis*. This famous description, the first eyewitness account of life and conditions in Armenia, bears out the proposition that at that time there was little contact between Armenia and the Black Sea coast around Trebizond. The contrast between the situation Xenophon finds in Armenia and that in the lands further north in the Pontic chain behind Trebizond, is striking. Armenia itself, that is to say, the lands to the west and north of Lake Van, is prosperous and ordered. The satrap or governor, Tiribazus, is clearly in direct control. The Greeks pass by his palaces, they negotiate with him, and in one place they find horses that are being reared as tribute for the Persian king. Society as a whole is generally peaceable and ordered. Village headmen exercise authority at a local level. When a detachment of the

---

[9] See, for example, J.M. Birmingham, "The Overland Route across Anatolia in the Eighth and Seventh Centuries B.C.," *Anatolian Studies* 11 (1961): 185-95.

[10] Hakob A. Manandian, *The Trade and Cities of Armenia in Relation to Ancient World Trade*, trans. Nina G. Garsoïan (Lisbon: Calouste Gulbenkian Foundation, 1965), p. 79.

Greek force meets up with a group of women and girls at a well outside a large fortified village, the Greeks are able to converse through a
Persian-speaking interpreter. Agriculture, too, is clearly well developed
in Armenia at that time. A little further on their journey, when Xenophon and his men had probably reached the high plateau around
Erzerum, the houses had become more primitive and designed to guard
against the bitter cold.[11] Xenophon writes: "The houses here were underground, with a mouth like that of a well, but spacious below: and
while entrances were tunneled down for the beasts of burden, the human inhabitants descended by a ladder. In the houses were goats,
sheep, cattle, fowls and their young. . . . Here also were wheat, barley,
and beans and barley-wine in large bowls."[12]

When Xenophon set out with the village chief to visit his men who
were billeted in the villages around, "everywhere he found them faring
sumptuously and in fine spirits; there was no place . . . where they did
not serve on the same table lamb, kid, pork, veal and poultry, together
with many loaves of bread, some of wheat and some of barley."[13] Here,
too, Xenophon converses with the village chief through a Persian-
speaking interpreter. Although he had traveled some way since the encounter with the women by the well, he is told once more that the land
is Armenia and that the horses he had found in such number are being
reared as tribute for the king of Persia.

As Xenophon moves further north, however, the picture changes.
Once into the mountains of the Pontic chain, the tribes become wilder
and more warlike. Communication through the medium of Persian appears to become impossible: in one place it is only because by chance
there is a slave among Xenophon's forces who originally came from
that place that the Greeks are able to communicate with the fierce local
tribes barring their way. And although Xenophon and his men finally
arrive at the Greek settlement of Trapezos on the Black Sea coast, it
seems clear that there is no well-marked trade route leading down
through the mountains behind.

These mountains at that time seem to have no Armenian inhabitants, while on the coast Trebizond is described as a Greek settlement
set among Colchian neighbors. The mountains behind Trebizond of

---

[11] Xenophon, *Anabasis*, trans. Carlton L. Brownson and John Dillery (Loeb Classical Library), IV.iv-viii.
[12] Ibid., IV.v.25-26.
[13] Ibid., IV.v.30-31.

course subsequently become home to the Hamshentsi Armenians, and it has been noted that Xenophon gives an interesting description of the honey-sickness prevalent in those parts and for which the Hamshens have a special word.[14] Xenophon writes:

> The swarms of bees in the neighbourhood were numerous, and the soldiers who ate of the honey all went off their heads and suffered from vomiting and diarrhea, and not one of them could stand up, but those who had eaten a little were like people exceedingly drunk, while those who had eaten a great deal seemed like crazed, or even in some cases dying, men. So they lay there in great numbers as though the army had suffered a defeat, and great despondency prevailed. On the next day, however, no one had died, and at approximately the same hour as they had eaten the honey they began to come to their senses; and on the third or fourth day they got up, as if from a drugging.[15]

Seventy years later in 331 B.C., Alexander the Great crushed the Persian army at the battle of Gaugamela and ushered in the Hellenistic age. Armenia itself was never actually conquered; like the rest of the Persian Empire, it was deemed to have passed into the hands of Alexander and his successors after the final defeat and death of the Persian king. In fact, however, the family of the Persian satrap Orontes (Ervand) was able to maintain itself in power despite the pretensions of the Seleucid dynasty, based in Antioch in northern Syria, which considered that Armenia was a legitimate part of its inheritance from Alexander.[16]

Despite the success of the Orontid dynasty in hanging on to power, the Seleucid Antiochus III does seem to have brought Armenia under more direct control toward the end of the third century B.C. When he was defeated by the Romans in 189 B.C., his two governors, Artaxias (Artashes) and Zariadres (Zareh), who may in fact themselves have been connected to the Orontid dynasty, declared themselves independent with the title of king. Artaxias ruled over the greater part of Armenia and founded a new capital at Artaxata (Artashat) on the Araxes in

---

[14] Bert Vaux, "Hemshinli: The Forgotten Black Sea Armenians," *Journal of Armenian Studies* 6:2 (2000/2001): 48.

[15] Xenophon, *Anabasis*, IV.viii.20-21.

[16] The main historical outline in the rest of this essay is drawn from Richard D. Wilkinson, *Introduction to the History of Pre-Christian Armenia* (Society for Armenian Studies, Occasional Paper No. 3), where additional detailed references can be found.

the Plain of Ararat. Zariadres ruled over the smaller province of Sophene to the west, situated in the bend of the Euphrates River. Artaxias
was a powerful and wily ruler; the Greek geographer Strabo, who himself came from Amasia in western Pontus not far from Armenia, wrote
that Artaxias and Zariadres gradually extended their territories in all
directions and that as a result the same language, that is Armenian, became spoken from the Caspian to the west of the Euphrates.[17] At the
same time, by conquering some of the territory occupied by the tribes
of the Pontic Mountains and by pushing westwards, Artaxiad Armenia
became more closely the neighbor of the kingdom of Pontus, which
had also maintained its independence under a dynasty of Iranian origin.

The second century B.C. saw the rise of two powers in Western Asia
which were destined to dominate the region for the next 400 years and
put an end to the pattern of rival Hellenistic kingdoms which had prevailed since the death of Alexander the Great. The first of those powers
was Parthia.[18] The Parthians were a semi-nomadic Iranian people, thus
related to the Persians and Medes, who established their dominance to
the east and south of Armenia in what is present-day Iran and northern
Iraq. The second power was Rome, which in the course of the second
century after the defeat of the great Carthaginian general Hannibal
found itself without a serious rival in the Mediterranean basin. Rome
had already humbled Seleucid ambitions at the battle of Magnesia in
Asia Minor in 189 B.C. (after which Artaxias and Zariadres had established their independence). But it was only after Rome's friend and
ally Attalus III, the king of one of the most prosperous cities of western
Anatolia, Pergamum, bequeathed his kingdom to Rome in 133 B.C.,
that Roman power actually became physically established on the
mainland of Asia Minor. Italian merchants and tax-farmers poured in to
take advantage of this wealthy province of the Roman Empire, and
they soon won for themselves the bitter resentment of the local Greco-
Asiatic population.

In between these two powers, Rome and Parthia, there remained a
number of relatively small Hellenistic kingdoms—Bithynia in northwestern Asia Minor, Galatia in west-central Asia Minor, Cappadocia in
the central plateau around the modern town of Kayseri or Kesaria, and
the shrunken core of the once mighty Seleucid kingdom, then reduced

---

[17] Strabo, *Geography* (Loeb Classical Library), XI.14.5.

[18] For a useful introduction to the history and civilization of Parthia, see Malcolm
A.R. Colledge, *The Parthians* (London: Thames and Hudson, 1967).

to the coastal strip of eastern Cilicia and the lands between the Syrian desert and the Mediterranean Sea. There were also the kingdoms of Pontus, Armenia, and Sophene.

Pontus and Armenia were in some ways similar. Both were ruled by dynastic families of Iranian origin. But while Pontus contained a large number of ancient Greek cities dating from the period of extensive Greek colonization 600 years before—Amasia, Sinope, Amisus, Cerasus, Trebizond—Armenia had no Greek population and no Greek cities. The Armenian capital city, Artaxata (Artashat), had been founded for strategic reasons and for control of the overland caravan route along the Araxes River Valley. There was, as far is known, no Greek element in its population; the famous but enigmatic Greek inscriptions of Armavir seem to point to the absence of any mastery of the Greek language among the local population, and Greeks are never mentioned (unlike in many Hellenistic kingdoms) as forming part of the Armenian armies.

Perhaps this different demographic and cultural make-up influenced the orientation of the two kingdoms. Be that as it may, the two kings who emerged at the head of neighboring Pontus and Armenia at the beginning of the first century B.C. seem to have decided that though they both harbored immense ambitions for their respective realms, those ambitions need not and should not conflict. These personages were Mithridates VI Eupator of Pontus and Tigranes II (Tigran Mets) of Armenia.[19]

Both Mithridates and Tigranes began the expansion of their kingdoms by annexing an adjoining province. Mithridates subdued Lesser Armenia, roughly speaking the region lying to the west of modern Erzinjan (Erznka). It may be an interesting correction, incidentally, to any tendency to ascribe too much in the way of modern nationalist feeling to Tigranes to reflect that he seems to have had little or no objection to this annexation by the king of Pontus even though the evidence suggests that the region of Lesser Armenia was inhabited largely by Armenians, who apparently contributed a contingent to Mithridates' armies. Tigranes, for his part, conquered the neighboring Armenian kingdom of Sophene, probably reducing its rulers to vassalage. Then,

---

[19] Probably the two most informative and readable biographical accounts of Mithridates and Tigranes remain Theodore Reinach, *Mithridate Eupator* (Paris: Firmin-Didot, 1890), and Hagop A. Manandian, *Tigrane II et Rome*, trans. Hranth Thorossian (Lisbon: Calouste Gulbenkian Foundation, 1963).

in around 93 B.C., Mithridates and Tigranes made their famous treaty which was to set the pattern for the future relationship between themselves and their kingdoms. The treaty was solemnized by the marriage of Tigranes to Mithridates' daughter Cleopatra.

The first fruit of this treaty was an agreement to make war jointly on the kingdom of Cappadocia. The terms of the agreement were that Tigranes would keep the prisoners and the booty while Mithridates would occupy and annex the territory, and they show the degree of confidence in each other that the two monarchs already enjoyed. At the same time, Mithridates and Tigranes seem to have agreed, or come to a tacit understanding, that their ambitions would lie in different directions. Mithridates was drawn to the west, to Asia Minor and beyond that to the Aegean and the Greek mainland. Tigranes for his part sought to expand above all to the south and to the east. He profited from a temporary eclipse in the power of Parthia to restore his eastern frontiers and then invaded the Seleucid lands lying in what is now southeast Turkey, northern Iraq, and Syria.

This difference in their ambitions finds fascinating reflection in the coinage of the two emperors. Mithridates was clearly modeling himself on Alexander the Great and wished to be seen as the heir and protector of Hellenic civilization. There is even a statue in the Louvre which was long thought to be a statue of Alexander and only more recently was identified as being of Mithridates Eupator. His coin portraits are deliberately reminiscent of the stylized features of Alexander—the curly disheveled hair, the strong neck and jaw, the slightly parted lips and upturned gaze are all characteristic features of the Hellenistic portraits of Alexander the Great. This is surely designed to suggest to those handling the coins that Mithridates' conquests, like those of Alexander, would be followed by a flowering of Greek civilization and a happy fusion of Greek and Asiatic peoples in a harmonious empire.

The portraits of Tigranes, though struck in a Greek city (Antioch) and by Greek die-cutters, give a very different impresssion. The expression is hard and stern, the ceremonial headdress and armor emphasize the official position of the monarch. The whole feeling is Oriental and recalls Parthian coinage of the period. Someone handling these coins would not conclude that the Hellenistic empire of Alexander or of the Seleucids is to be restored, but that the Parthians have been supplanted and that echoes of the archetypal Persian Achaemenid Empire will be found in Tigranes' ambitions and policies.

If Tigranes remained largely immune to the more cultural aspects of Hellenistic civilization, the close alliance with Pontus and above all perhaps the presence at court of Cleopatra, Mithridates' daughter and Tigranes' wife, did have influence. The evidence suggests that she encouraged the use of the Greek language among the king's entourage. The Greek historian Plutarch tells us that Cleopatra became the patron of the Greek philosopher Amphicrates whom she invited to court, and when he died it was she who arranged a suitably honorable burial.[20] Tigranes' successor Artavasdes (Artavazd), who was presumably the son of Cleopatra, was also a master of the Greek language and may have owed this to his mother and the education she encouraged. Plutarch again writes that Artavasdes actually composed tragedies in Greek and wrote orations and histories, some of which had survived down to his own day (toward the end of the first century A.D.), some 150 years later.[21]

Tigranes' alliance with Mithridates, however, though it strengthened Armenian links with Pontus and may have contributed to the introduction of Hellenistic fashions into Armenia, also brought conflict with Rome. Mithridates' expansion westward inevitably clashed with Rome's interests in Asia Minor and Greece. Mithridates was ultimately defeated and took refuge with his son-in-law Tigranes. In the ensuing wars with the Roman generals Lucullus and Pompey, Tigranes, too, was defeated and stripped of his conquests. Unlike Pontus, however, where the Romans drove Mithridates out of his kingdom and to his death by suicide, Tigranes was allowed to retain the core of his kingdom, and his dynasty continued to rule as "friend and ally" of Rome after his death in 55 B.C.

The next hundred years present a picture of instability and confusion as Armenia was torn between the rival ambitions of Rome and Parthia and sought to retain some form of independence. While the Artaxiad dynasty continued to supply a succession of kings and princes, rulers from elsewhere also at various times briefly occupied the throne, including a Pontic prince Zeno, who appears to have reigned from 18 to 34 A.D. Zeno had, according to the Roman historian Tacitus, endeared himself to the Armenian nobility by adopting Armenian customs and dress from his youth, and when the Armenians were sum-

---

[20] Plutarch, *Lucullus* (Loeb Classical Library), XXII.
[21] Plutarch, *Crassus* (Loeb Classical Library), XXXIII.

moned by the Roman general Germanicus to choose a king or suffer invasion they selected him.[22]

Pompey's policy for the eastern frontier had been to keep a circle of client states beyond the boundary of the empire proper which would act as a buffer to the power of Parthia. These client kingdoms included Iberia (on the territory of present-day Georgia), Albania to its east, Pontus, Cappadocia, and Commagene to the south. But the most problematic was Armenia whose strategic location meant that neither Rome nor Parthia was prepared to see it dominated by the other power. So when in 53 A.D. the Parthian king Vologeses (Vagharsh) installed his brother Tiridates (Trdat; Drtad) on the throne of Armenia, the tutors and guardians of the young emperor Nero decided that decisive military action should be taken.

The tough and experienced general Corbulo was sent to the east. He found the state of the troops at his disposal lamentable. Two years of training were required to bring the army up to scratch, and then for the next eight years or so Corbulo fought to achieve a settlement with Parthia. Two full-scale invasions of Armenia were required, including the occupation of Tigranocerta (Tigranakert) and Artaxata, before Vologeses and Tiridates finally accepted Rome's terms for peace. These required Tiridates to travel to Rome and receive the diadem of Armenia from the emperor Nero himself, and there to do obeisance and declare himself the vassal of Rome.

The difficulties faced by Corbulo in campaigning in the east led to a reorganization of the frontier. The Roman Empire was pushed forward to the line of the Euphrates, and Pontus was formally annexed to the empire. Two great legionary camps were set up: one at Melitene on the Euphrates in eastern Cappadocia (today's Malatia) which became the headquarters of the XII Legion Fulminata, and the other at Satala, in Lesser Armenia to the north, which seems to have been situated at the site today called Satak, near Kelkit some 50 miles north of Erzinjan. This became the headquarters of the XV Legion Apollinaris.

The establishment of direct Roman rule in this part of Anatolia seems finally to have opened up the eastern Black Sea region around Trebizond to contact with the hinterland. Up until then, contact between Armenia and Pontus seems to have taken place along the ancient caravan road that ran up the Araxes River Valley then past Erzerum, Erzinjan, and Sivas (Sebastia) to Amasia, the principal town of inland

---

[22] Tacitus, *Annals* (Loeb Classical Library), II.56.

Pontus, and thence down to the Greek coastal cities of Amisus and Sinope.[23] That such contact was well-established is attested by the Greek geographer Strabo in the first century A.D. He describes Comana, situated near the modern town of Tokat, halfway between Sebastia and Amasia, as "a populous city and a notable emporium for the people from Armenia." Strabo was himself from Amasia and obviously knew Comana well.[24]

But the Roman garrison at Satala required more direct access to the sea. It seems almost certain therefore that it was Roman military engineers, either in the period following the campaigns of Corbulo in the first century A.D. or under the reigns of the emperors Trajan and Hadrian in the first half of the second century A.D., who finally laid a proper road through the wild Alpine landscape north of Satala, over the Zigana Pass, and down to the ancient Greek city of Trebizond.[25] The emperor Hadrian also ordered the building of an enlarged modern harbor there. Not only was it now possible to supply by sea the garrisons of Rome's northeastern frontier, but trade was at last able to cross the Pontic chain and conditions were established for the first regular interchange between Armenia and the Black Sea coast around Trebizond. It was probably during the second century A.D., a period of relative peace and prosperity when the power of Rome was at its zenith, that the first Armenian communities became established in Trebizond.

---

[23] Manandian, *Trade and Cities*, pp. 51-52, 79.

[24] Strabo, *Geography*, XII.3.36.

[25] Franz and Eugène Cumont, *Studia Pontica* II (Brussels, 1906), paragraph 36.

❊ 5 ❊

THE ARMENIAN TIES
TO MEDIEVAL TREBIZOND

Abraham Terian

The initial fame of Trebizond goes back to Xenophon and his wearied "Ten Thousand" warriors who, upon reaching the Black Sea after their long and perilous march through Armenia, joyously shouted *"Thalatta! Thalatta!"* when they sighted the water.[1] It is beyond the scope of this study to discuss either the possible route taken by Xenophon in 401/400 B.C. on his retreat from Persian territory or the various networks of roads in northwestern Armenia in ancient times.[2] By virtue of its fine harbor built by the emperor Hadrian (117-38 A.D.), Trebizond became a commercial gateway to the interior, situated as it was at the head of the best trade routes to Greater Armenia and on to Persia. The importance of the port city to the interior is manifested by the Armenian campaigns of Justinian I (527-65), which were waged from there after the city had been restored and assigned by him to the province called First Armenia. According to the sixth-century historian Procopius of Caesarea in Palestine, who spent his adult life in Constantinople and accompanied the campaigns of Justinian under Belisarius, the

---

[1] Xenophon, *Anabasis,* 4.7.24, trans. Carlton L. Brownson and John Dillery (Loeb Classical Library) (Cambridge, MA and London: Harvard University Press, 1998), p. 365.

[2] See Robert H. Hewsen, *Armenia: A Historical Atlas* (Chicago and London: University of Chicago Press, 2001), pp. 29-30, for the likely route taken by Xenophon, and pp. 50-52, for the Roman roads in the region. For the Byzantine trade routes, see Hakob A. Manandian, *The Trade and Cities of Armenia in Relation to Ancient World Trade,* trans. Nina G. Garsoïan (Lisbon: Calouste Gulbenkian Foundation, 1965), pp. 67-116; Speros Vryonis, Jr., *The Decline of Medieval Hellenism in Asia Minor and the Process of Islamization from the Eleventh through the Fifteenth Century* (Berkeley, Los Angeles, London: University of California Press, 1971), pp. 6-24; and, for a most comprehensive coverage, Anthony Bryer and David Winfield, *The Byzantine Monuments and Topography of the Pontos,* 2 vols. (Washington, DC: Dumbarton Oaks, 1985), vol. 1, pp. 17-65.

old road led south of Trebizond to the fortress of Horonon. Three roads separated from there: to Roman Armenia, to Persian Armenia, and to Tzanika, identified as the land of the marauding Tzans north of the Parhar range.[3] The location of Horonon remains elusive, though several possible sites have been suggested for the place where the east-west road and the route south of Trebizond converged. Of these, the village of Varzahan, east of the watershed between the Lykos and the Akampsis rivers in the Baberd (Baiburt) plain (one stage west of Baberd), seems to be the more likely location. "Here stood a group of Armenian churches, perhaps on the site of a halting place."[4]

A century later, possibly as early as before 622, the city was assigned to the *Armeniakon theme* of Asia Minor. The theme encompassed eastern Anatolia, from Cappadocia to the Black Sea and the Euphrates River. In the ninth century, the theme was divided into several parts, at which time the region of Trebizond was given its older name of Chaldia.[5] The city became its capital and the bishopric, in existence since the third century, became an archbishopric. Then in the early tenth century, it became the metropolitanate of seven bishoprics. According to Emperor Constantine VII Porphyrogenitus (945-59), the original Armeniakon theme was so called not simply for its proximity to Armenian territories but more especially for its large Armenian population.[6]

---

[3] Procopius, *On Buildings,* 3.6.15-16, trans. Henry B. Dewing with Glanville Downey (Loeb Classical Library) (Cambridge, MA and London: Harvard University Press, 1940), p. 209. Bryer and Winfield, *Pontos,* p. 35 and n169, have rightly rejected the identification of the site with the village of Halane by Nicolas Adontz, *Armenia in the Period of Justinian: The Political Conditions Based on the Naxarar System,* trans. Nina G. Garsoïan (Lisbon: Calouste Gulbenkian Foundation, 1970), p. 51 (cf. p. 398 and n31a).

[4] Bryer and Winfield, *Pontos,* p. 35. Elsewhere they elaborate: "A celebrated eleventh- or twelfth-century Armenian church, associated structures, and tombstones in the form of sculptured rams, stood at Varzahan until this [twentieth] century. Since 1957 there is no trace of them. But, as Varzahan lies one stage west of Baibert, nineteenth-century travelers regularly recorded the site" (p. 355 and n24 for the various travelers' records). This was the All Savior or the Ascension monastery, also known as Varzents.

[5] Ibid., p. 278. Adontz, *Armenia,* p. 53, gives the date as the eighth century.

[6] Agostino Pertusi, ed., *Constantino Porfyrogenito: De Thematibus,* Studi e Testi 160 (Vatican: Biblioteca apostolica vaticana, 1952), p. 63; cited by Peter Charanis, *The Armenians in the Byzantine Empire* (Lisbon: Calouste Gulbenkian Foundation, 1963), p. 19 and n46 (repr. of "The Armenians in the Byzantine Empire," *Byzantinoslavica* 22 (1961): 196-240, preface by Sirarpie Der Nersessian). The emperor himself was of Armenian descent.

In the ancient geographical source on Greater Armenia which was utilized in the seventh century by Anania Shirakatsi in his *Ashkharha-tsoyts,* the name Eger is used not only for the province west of Georgia but also for the entire eastern shore of the Black Sea, from Trebizond to Abkhazia.[7] In later sources, as in Greek, the name Khaghtik (Chaldia) is used for the Pontus region.[8] In much later Armenian sources, the name Trapizon appears not only for the city but also for the Pontic coastal region as a whole, as seen in a colophon of the year 1464 from Daranaghik (Kemakh): "And ten years later [following the fall of Constantinople], more or less, Pontos, that is, Trapizon," was captured "by the lawless Tachiks."[9] The name Trapizon is used more loosely at times, as in sweeping territorial descriptions that include the Black Sea, the Pontus Euxinus in general. A colophon of the year 1449, possibly from Amid/Amida (Diarbekir) describes the domain of Shah Kara Yuluk 'Uthman (d. 1435), leader of the Turkmen or Turko-man (Bayundur) emirs of Amida and the real founder of the Ak-Koyunlu dynasty, as stretching from Harran to the Pontic Sea "which is Trapizon."[10] Another colophon, of the year 1470 from Kharpert (Khar-berd), describes the territory controlled by 'Uthman's grandson, Uzun Hasan Beg (d. 1478), as extending from Babylon in the south to Trapi-zon in the north and to Shiraz in the east.[11] Such sweeping references

---

[7] Ashot G. Abrahamyan, ed., *Anania Shirakatsu matenagrutyune* [The Bibliogra-phy of Anania Shirakatsi] (Erevan: Matenadaran, 1944), pp. 340, 348, 350. For a translation of Anania's Geography, see Robert H. Hewsen, *The Geography of Ananias of Sirak (Asxarhac`oyc`): The Long and the Short Recensions* (Wiesbaden: Reichert, 1992), pp. 55, 57, 57A, 59. Cf. Adontz, *Armenia,* p. 23.

[8] As in Tovma Artsruni; Vrezh M. Vardanyan, ed., *Tovma Artsruni ev Ananun, Patmutyun Artsrunyats Tan* (Erevan: Armenian Academy of Sciences, 1978), pp. 65, 81; trans. Robert W. Thomson, *Thomas Artsruni, History of the House of the Arts-runik'* (Detroit: Wayne State University Press, 1985), pp. 130, 147. See also Heinrich Hübschmann, *Die altarmenische Ortsnamen* (Strassburg: Trübner, 1904; repr. Am-sterdam: Oriental Press, 1969), p. 432.

[9] Avedis K. Sanjian, *Colophons of Armenian Manuscripts, 1301-1480* (Cam-bridge, MA: Harvard University Press, 1969), pp. 282-83 (1464, no. 1). The reference is to the final Turkish attack on the city by Mehmed II (1458-81) in 1461.

[10] Ibid., p. 210 (1449, no. 1). A similarly compounded appellation is found in Stepanos Orbelian's *Patmutiun nahangin Sisakan* (History of the Province of Sisakan [Siunik]), 2 vols. (Paris: Shahnazariants, 1859), vol. 2, p. 148; modern Eastern Ar-menian trans. Ashot A. Abrahamyan, *Stepanos Orbelyan: Syuniki patmutyun* [History of Siunik] (Erevan: Sovetakan Grogh, 1986), p. 323.

[11] Sanjian, *Colophons,* p. 298 (1470, no. 1). Uzun Hasan suffered a decisive de-feat at the hands of Mehmed II at Otluq Beli in 1473. See Vryonis, *Decline,* pp. 141-42, 263-64, on Uzun Hasan's forces.

and allusions are comparable to the biblical phrase "from Dan to Beer-sheba" and are illusive when it comes to historical or geographical specificity.

Anania Shirakatsi as a Source

Armenian references to medieval Trebizond are few, as are the Greek references to the Armenian presence there. Foremost of the Armenian sources is the autobiography of Anania Shirakatsi, a seventh-century sage and prolific author who wrote some twenty treatises covering nearly all the sciences known in the early Middle Ages (corresponding to the second division or the *Quadrivium* of the classical curriculum).[12] Trebizond looms large in Anania's autobiography, as it was the cradle of his higher education. His plans to study in Constantinople were forgone after he learned about a distinguished teacher named Tychicus in Trebizond, to whom students from even the Patriarchal School in Constantinople were being sent. He hurried there and found the master at the shrine of Saint Eugenius, the patron saint of the city. It must have been love at first sight. Anania spent eight memorable years with Tychicus and availed himself of all that the teacher had to offer, as may be gathered from this laudatory description of the man and his personal library:

> I familiarized myself with several other branches of learning and be-
> came knowledgeable in many books which were not translated into

---

[12] This seventh-century account survives in two recensions. The shorter recension was first published by Kerovbe Patkanian, *Ananiayi Shirakunvoy mnatsordk banits* [The Rest of the Works of Anania of Shirak] (St. Petersburg: Imperial Academy of Sciences, 1877), pp. 1-4, then by Ghevond Alishan, *Hayapatum* [Armenian History] (Venice: Mekhitarist Press, 1901), pp. 232-33, and is also available in an English translation by Frederick C. Conybeare, "Ananias of Shirak (A.D. 600-650 c.)," *Byzantinische Zeitschrift* 6 (1897): 572-84 (esp. 572-74). The longer version was first published by Hakovbos Tashian [Jacobus Dashian], *Tsutsak hayeren dzeragrats Matenadaranin Mkhitariants i Vienna/Catalog der armenischen Handschriften der Mechitharisten-Bibliothek zu Wien* (Vienna: Mekhitarist Press, 1895-1896), pp. 174-76, then by Abrahamyan, *Anania Shirakatsu matenagrutyune*, pp. 206-09, and is available in a French translation by Haïg Berbérian, "Autobiographie d'Anania Širakac'i," *Revue des études arméniennes*, n.s., 1 (1964): 189-94, and, in the same volume, Paul Lemerle, "Note sur les donnees historiques de l'Autobiographie d'Anania de Shirak": 195-202. The longer version is generally preferred. Further bibliography is found in Hakob S. Anasyan, *Haykakan matenagitutyun* [Armenian Bibliology], 2 vols. (Erevan: Armenian Academy of Sciences, 1959-1976), vol. 1, pp. 731-74.

our language. For he had them all: exoteric and esoteric, secular [and religious], scientific and historical, medical and chronological. And why should I name them one by one? For there is no book which was not found with him. And in translating he had such grace as bestowed by the Holy Spirit. For when he desired to translate from books written in Greek, he never hesitated like other translators; it was as if he was reading in the Armenian tongue from writings in Armenian. I do not wish to leave you uninformed about the goodness of this most knowledgeable man, but I shall inform you by telling his history, how he came to know our language and the extent to which he was trained in the various disciplines.

He was from the land of Pontus, from the city of Trebizond. In his younger years, he had been in the service of Emperor Tiberius [578-82], under the commander John, who was in Armenia for several years until the time of Emperor Maurice [582-602]. And he learned our language and literature. But when the Persian army attacked the Greek army in the vicinity of Antioch, it so happened that he was wounded and fled to Antioch, and all his belongings were taken among the spoils. As he fell ill for many days, sorrowful also for the loss of his belongings, he prayed to God to be healed of his wounds and made a vow, saying: "If you will bestow upon me life and health, I will not hoard treasures that pass away; but I will pursue the treasures of knowledge."[13]

Anania's encounter with an Armenian-speaking Greek scholar with whom he studied may not have been all that unique, at least in those parts of Armenia under Byzantine control. What is more important is the information he provides on Byzantine education in the seventh century and on the presence of Armenian students in Byzantine schools.

The old University of Constantinople founded by Emperor Theodosius II in 425 was apparently taken over by the Patriarchal School in Constantinople, and it remained a center for the study of theology at a time when Christianity had rejected ancient civilization as being permeated with falsehood. The best education was not in monasteries, not even in the Patriarchal School, as Anania found out. His autobiography provides additional proof that the classical curriculum of Greco-Roman times was still alive, albeit in private schools. The scholarly curiosity of youth had to be satisfied by private teachers. The closest parallel to Anania's experience in Byzantium is that of Leo the Mathematician (circa 790-870), who found a "wise man" on Andros to teach him

---

[13] Abrahamyan, *Anania Shirakatsu matenagrutyune*, p. 27 (my translation).

rhetoric, philosophy, and arithmetic. The educational decline was halted in the middle of the ninth century, when Caesar Bardas (d. 866), an Armenian from Paphlagonia and brother of the empress Theodora and the patrician Petronas, organized the Magnaura School in Constantinople to revive the "external" or secular learning and patronized scholars such as Leo the Mathematician. It took another two centuries for the re-establishment of the University of Constantinople as a center of higher learning by Emperor Constantine IX in 1047.[14]

The reliability of Anania's claims is substantiated in part by the considerable number of works he has left behind, aside from his lost works for which there is fragmentary evidence. Together, his autobiography and the corpus of his writings may give a tangible picture of Byzantine education in the age of Heraclius—a momentous period in the history of the Byzantine Empire which witnessed protracted wars with the Persians and also the rise of Islam. The autobiography is the only known source on the Byzantine scholar Tychicus, Anania's teacher, and the place of Trebizond in Byzantine education, especially in preserving and transmitting secular education in the classical tradition. Given the scarcity of Byzantine sources on the history of education in this period, the document is deemed highly significant. It helps fill substantial lacunae in the early history of this most prominent city and its bequest to subsequent Armenian learning through the works of Anania.

The Armenian Presence in Trebizond

The beginnings of the Armenian presence in Trebizond cannot be separated from the early Armenian settlements in Byzantine Asia Minor. Given the Byzantine emperors' general practice of transplanting populations, for centuries (up to the tenth century at least) there were Armenian communities in central Anatolia.[15] While Armenians were originally brought for military purposes and settled in various parts of Asia

---

[14] Alexander P. Kazhdan and Robert Browning, "Education," in Alexander P. Kazhdan et al., eds., *The Oxford Dictionary of Byzantium,* 3 vols. (New York and Oxford: Oxford University Press, 1991), vol. 1, pp. 677-78; cf. Charanis, *Armenians,* p. 27.

[15] Peter Charanis, "Ethnic Changes in the Byzantine Empire in the Seventh Century," *Dumbarton Oaks Papers* 13 (1959): 25-44; idem, "The Transfer of Population as a Policy in the Byzantine Empire," *Comparative Studies in Society and History* 3 (1961): 140-54.

Minor, including the western coast and beyond,[16] they kept coming as refugees from Greater Armenia and from the eastern borders, territories under the control of the empire which the Byzantines deemed as a buffer against the Persians, then the Arabs, and after the tenth century the peoples of Central Asia. Their numbers increased, especially from Caesarea in the south to Neocaesarea in the north, as many more of those who fled the Arab conquest of Armenia took refuge in Greek territories, including the Pontic cities. The late eighth-century historian Ghevond attests to such migrations in his time and to settlements in Eger (Egeria).[17] Even the heretical "Armenian Paulicians, driven from their homes sometime before 662, settled in the Empire, especially in the region of the junction of the Iris and the Lycus rivers in the territories of the Pontus."[18]

The anonymous collection of Byzantine chronicles from the ninth and tenth centuries, named after Theophanes the Confessor, accounts for the territorial expansion of the Byzantine Empire eastward. Much of this was achieved by annexing territories and giving land elsewhere in the empire to the rulers whose lands were taken. The continuator of the chronicles tells of the ceding of the region of Tekis (the area around Chemishgezek, east of the Euphrates River and north of the Arsanias or Aratsani River) by its Armenian chieftain Manuel to the empire during the reign of Emperor Leo VI (886-912), in return for which he and two of his sons were vested with important commands and two other sons were given lands in the vicinity of Trebizond.[19]

The settlement in and around Trebizond grew as trade to the interior increased. Emperor Constantine VII Porphyrogenitus (945-59) describes the flow of commerce from Trebizond to Armenia along two

---

[16] Basil I (867-86), the founder of the so-called Macedonian dynasty (867-1025) "was an Armenian, born in Macedonia where numerous Armenians were settled." See Charanis, *Armenians,* p. 34.

[17] *History of Lewond the Eminent Vardapet of the Armenians,* trans. Zaven Arzoumanian (Wynnewood, PA: St. Sahag and St. Mesrop Church, 1982); esp. chs. 10, 34, 42 (pp. 66, 130, 149). On Armenian immigration into the Sebastia region with Byzantine encouragement, see Friedrich Hild and Marcell Restle, *Kappadokien* (Vienna: Austrian Academy of Sciences, 1981), esp. pp. 177, 274.

[18] Charanis, *Armenians,* p. 13.; cf. Nina G. Garsoïan, *The Paulician Heresy: A Study of the Origin and Development of Paulicianism in Armenia and the Eastern Provinces of the Byzantine Empire* (The Hague and Paris: Mouton, 1967), pp. 85, 136-38, 146.

[19] Charanis, *Armenians,* pp. 29, 48, citing Theophanes Continuatus, *Chronographia,* p. 268 (ed. Bekker), and Cedrenus, *Historiarum Compendium,* 2.207 (ed. Bekker).

ways: through the town of Artze, located southeast of Trebizond and inhabited by local Armenian and Syrian merchants who conducted the caravans through Karin (Erzerum), and through the Georgian town of Adranoutzi, where shipments were brought first by sea and then overland, before being moved by Armenian and other ethnic merchants through the Caucasus.[20] Others describe the lively harbor, the energetic international commerce and the local industry, the ethnic mix of seamen and merchants both at the harbor and in the khans, and the pilgrims of similar ethnic mix looking for cures at the shrine of Saint Eugenius. The city also had mining works in the vicinity and silos for the grain from "the golden prairies" of the region. Armenians were involved not only in the international trade but also in the local industry. In the tenth century, Trebizond was at the height of its prosperity, deriving much of its wealth from exporting its own products as well as imports from Constantinople, from various other Black Sea ports, especially Cherson on the Crimean peninsula, and from the interior regions. It was a commercial hub in the full sense of the word.[21]

Armenian sources about Trebizond in the two centuries after Anania are scarce. The community must have had its origin in the commerce associated with the city and grew after humble beginnings like other Armenian communities along the trade routes. Whatever its origin, the Armenian community on the Black Sea must have shared the common experiences of Armenians living under Byzantine rule near the end of the first millennium A.D. For most, it meant submission to Chalcedonian (duophysite) Christology and the Chalcedonian episcopal sees (at times headed by native Armenians) under the jurisdiction of the Greek metropolitan archbishop.

The expansionist policies of Byzantium, especially in the eleventh century, did not sit well with the Armenians, who were at odds with the Greeks for both political and religious reasons. The bitter Christological controversies surrounding the Council of Chalcedon (451) had reached their peak when Emperor Basil II (976-1025) annexed the Kingdom of Vaspurakan in 1021 and made arrangements that the other major Armenian state, Ani, should be handed over to the empire upon the death of its king. This was accomplished in 1045, when the last

---

[20] *De Administrando Imperio* (ed. Moravcsik), trans. Romily J.H. Jenkins (Washington, DC: Dumbarton Oaks, 1967), pp. 208, 214, 216-17. On the Armenian merchants of Artze, see Cedrenus, *Historiarum Compendium,* 2.577 (ed. Bekker), cited by Vryonis, *Decline,* pp. 16-17 and notes 86, 94, 96.

[21] Vryonis, *Decline,* pp. 15-17, cites several other primary sources.

king of the native Bagratuni dynasty, Gagik II (1042-45, d.1079/80), was coerced into abdicating and settling in Lykandos and the extensive lands of Charsianon in Cappadocia. The Catholicos Petros I Getadardz (1019-58) relocated to Sebastia/Sebasteia (modern Sivas), the old metropolis of First Armenia and a historical Greek metropolitanate with several episcopal sees in northeastern Cappadocia. Twenty years later, just when Ani fell to Seljuk Sultan Alp Arslan in 1064, one of the last independent Armenian princes, Gagik of Kars (1029-64), was pressured to move to Tzamandos. Many of his subjects, who feared living along a border under attack by the Seljuk Turks, accompanied him. They settled in the surrounding lands and in between the new domains of the Bagratunis. These lands, long settled by Armenians, had once belonged to the Armenian chieftain Mleh (Melias in Greek, d. 934), who built the fortress of Tzamandos and rebuilt that of Lykandos.[22] Such migrations helped to swell the Armenian population not only in Cappadocia but also in Pontus to the north and more so in Cilicia to the south—especially after the decisive victory of the Seljuks over the Byzantines at the Battle of Manzikert in 1071.

Centuries later, when Timur (Tamerlane) sacked the substantially Armenian city of Sebastia in 1400, many refugees poured into Trebizond. Ruy Gonzales de Clavijo, the ambassador of Henry III of Castile to Timur, writing in 1404, was struck by the number of destitute Armenian newcomers in Trebizond, adding that they "are not greatly liked in these parts."[23] Further waves of Armenian refugees are accounted for in 1414, 1429, and 1431. "On 11 February 1414 an Armenian of Trebizond petitioned the Senate of Venice on behalf of eighty Armenian families of Sebastia and elsewhere to be allowed to emigrate from Trebizond to Crete."[24] Others probably made their way to the Crimea.

It must have been during such an influx from Sebastia to Trebizond, whether in the eleventh or fifteenth century, that the so-called "Trapizon Gospel" appeared in the city. One of the most prized Armenian Gospel manuscripts, dating from the eleventh century and of an as-yet-unknown place of origin, became part of the Venetian Mekhi-

---

[22] Charanis, *Armenians*, p. 30.

[23] Ruy Gonzalez de Clavijo, *Embassy to Tamerlane, 1403-1406*, trans. Guy Le Strange (London: Routledge, 1928), pp. 108, 113.

[24] Freddy Thiriet, ed., *Regestes des deliberations du Senat de Venise concernant la Romanie*, 3 vols. (Paris: Mouton, 1958-1961), vol. 2: no. 1516 of February 11, 1414, cited by Bryer and Winfield, *Pontos*, p. 210 and n204.

tarist collection soon after the establishment of the library in 1717 (Ms 1400, their largest manuscript in folio size, 37 by 46 centimeters). The Gospel was probably among the possessions of the royal Bagratunis, if not of a ranking churchman. It shares some common features with Erevan Matenadaran manuscripts 275 and 10434, which are known to have come from Kars and to be the work of a certain scribe named Hovhannes.

Relations of the Armenian and Greek Churches

Local traditions suggest that the relocated Armenian magnates—Catholicos Petros in particular—were not confined to their estates but that they traveled north to the coastal cities, besides visiting the various pilgrimage centers in the region of Sebastia. Several of the scores of Armenian monasteries in the northeastern regions of the empire are said, rightly or wrongly, to have been founded by the exiled catholicos whose image loomed larger than life. He was buried at Varagavank in Van.

By contrast, the treatment of Catholicos Khachik II Anetsi (1058-65), a nephew of Petros, was deplorable. Apprehended in 1059 with several bishops in Sebastia, where Petros had moved with the treasures of the Catholicosate, Khachik was taken to Constantinople and detained for three years by Emperor Constantine X Doukas (1059-67) in an effort to force him to agree to a Chalcedonian profession of faith and to hand over the treasures. His Church was despoiled and taxed heavily, and as a matter of course Greek or Chalcedonian bishops were installed in the annexed provinces. Khachik was eventually released to retire to the Monastery of Tavblur at Taranta in a district of Sebastia, where he remained until his death.[25]

Generally treated as untrustworthy subjects and heretical Christians, Armenians were fit subjects for either persecution or conversion. Thus, the perplexing theological reality with its increasingly strained relations gave rise to disturbing socio-religious issues affecting the lives of Armenians vis-à-vis their Greek neighbors. The Greek Church discouraged fellowship in all its forms with Armenians, Saracens, and

---

[25] The primary source for the period is the contemporaneous history of Aristakes of Lastivert, *Patmutiun Aristakeay Vardapeti Lastiverttsvoy* (Venice: Mekhitarist Press, 1844), which was repeatedly quoted by subsequent historians. For the preceding decades, see Stepanos Taronetsi (Asoghik), *Patmutiun Tiezerakan* [Universal History], ed. Stepan Malkhasiants (St. Petersburg: Skorokhodov, 1885).

Jews. Regarding Armenians, however, the negative attitudes were based on religious rather than ethnic biases. The Greeks considered the two primary sacraments of the Armenian Church, Baptism and the Eucharist, unacceptable. They demanded the rebaptism of Armenian converts and, as corollary, denied the Eucharist to those who did not embrace Chalcedonian Christology. The strongest Armenian denunciation of the Greek Church is found in Sahak Vardapet's ninth century comparatively mild *Batsahaytutiun*,[26] and the worst Greek portrayal of Armenians is in the *Panoplia dogmatike* of Euthymios Zigabenos (circa 1100).[27] Such notions as the untrustworthiness of the Armenians were rekindled at the time when Emperor John II Comnenus (1118-43) retook Cilician Armenia in 1137 and nearly put an end to the Rubenian barony.

Illustrative of the tensions of the times is the variously reported encounter between Emperor Basil II and Catholicos Petros I Getadardz in 1023 to negotiate the promised surrender of Ani. The earliest report, by Aristakes Lastiverttsi (d. 1071), describes how Catholicos Petros paid the emperor a visit on Christmas day while the latter was wintering on the Pontic coast in the province of Chaldia. Basil, by virtue of his ecclesiastical privilege, invited the catholicos to join in the Epiphany service alongside the Greeks. When they stepped into the water, the emperor asked Petros to bless it in the Armenian tradition while the Greeks did the blessing in their tradition. The catholicos amazed the

---

[26] Sahak Vardapet [Mrut], *Batsahaytutiun* [Exposition] (Jerusalem: St. James Press, 1994). This exposition is not to be confused with Sahak's earlier response, written at the behest of the first Bagratuni king, Ashot I "The Great" (Prince of Princes, 855-84, King, 884-90), in reply to a letter from Photios, Patriarch of Constantinople (858-67, 877-86). From what is left of that correspondence, see Norayr Pogharian, ed., *Girk Tghtots* [Book of Letters] (Jerusalem: St. James Press, 1994), pp. 515-39. The *Elegxos kai anathrope* [Examination and Refutation] by Nicetas of Constantinople (Niketas Byzantios) is likely a response to Mrut (*Patrologia Graeca* 105: 587-666).

[27] See especially ch. 23, "Adversus Armenios," in *Patrologia Graeca* 130: 1173-90. On Zigabenos' sources, see Erich Trapp, "Die Quellen von Zigabenos' Panoplia, Tit. 23 (Gegen die Armenier)," *Jahrbuch der Osterreichischen Byzantinistik* 29 (1980): 159-64. See also Hratch M. Bartikian, "The Religious Diplomacy of Byzantium in Armenia during the Tenth and Eleventh Centuries," in Dickran Kouymjian, ed., *Etudes arméniennes/Armenian Studies: In Memoriam Haïg Berbérian* (Lisbon: Calouste Gulbenkian Foundation, 1986), pp. 56-62; Speros Vryonis, Jr., "Byzantine Images of the Armenians," in Richard G. Hovannisian, ed., *The Armenian Image in History and Literature* (Malibu, CA: Undena Publications, 1981), pp. 65-81, esp. pp. 77-81.

people with a miracle of luminous bubbles emanating from the water when he poured out the sacred *miuron* (holy prism).[28]

While Aristakes is not specific about the location of the event, naming neither the city nor the river, later chroniclers such as Kirakos Gandzaketsi consistently place the showdown in the city of Trebizond, implying that it was at the delta of the Pyxites, where an Armenian chapel was later built to commemorate the event.[29] Gandzaketsi goes on to tell that the Greeks of the city had asked the Armenians to hold their service upstream while they held theirs downstream, thus indicating that the Armenian service was deficient and that the water blessed by the Armenians stood in need of being blessed by the Greeks. Moreover, the Greeks had trained a white dove to dip into the water at their site during the service and to take off, so as "to deceive" simpletons that it was the Holy Spirit that descended in the likeness of a dove. No sooner had Catholicos Petros stepped into the water than the stream of the river changed course and began to flow in the opposite direction.[30] An overwhelming light accompanied the miracle, surpassing the brightness of the sun. As for the white dove of the Greeks, it was snatched away by an eagle while descending on the water. Gandzaketsi concludes: "The Greeks, one and all, were greatly embarrassed and they praised the faith of the Armenians with reluctance." Furthermore, he wrongly deduces that it was for this reason that Basil asked Petros to move his Holy See to Sebastia and to shepherd his flock from there.

The embellishments of Kirakos Gandzaketsi and those of the other elaborators on the story by Aristakes Lastiverttsi, including their attempts at revising the meaning of the nickname of the Catholicos Getadardz as "one who made the river to turn around," are but a commentary on the religious tensions of the times. The catholicos seems to have derived his nickname on his return from a journey, perhaps his ill-omened meeting with the emperor Basil regarding the fate of Ani (the original meaning of "Getadardz" being "one who returned from

---

[28] *Patmutiun Aristakeay Vardapeti Lastiverttsvoy,* pp. 11-12.

[29] Karapet A. Melik-Ohanjanyan, ed., *Kirakos Gandzaketsi. Patmutyun Hayots* [Kirakos Gandzaketsi: History of the Armenians] (Erevan: Armenian Academy of Sciences, 1961), pp. 94-95; trans. Robert Bedrosian, *Kirakos Gandzakets`i's History of the Armenians* (New York: Sources of the Armenian Tradition, 1986), pp. 85-86.

[30] According to Smbat the Constable (d. 1276), Mkhitar Ayrivanetsi (d. circa. 1290), and Arakel Tabrizetsi (d. 1454), Catholicos Petros held up the stream with a relic of the True Cross, an event memorialized in the Armenian *Haysmavurk* (Synaxarion) in the reading for January 6 (Kaghots 29).

across the river," clearly alluding to the border between Armenia and Byzantium).[31]

Later developments within the Armenian community in Trebizond are invariably related to historical events in the eleventh and subsequent centuries. The Armenian population of Byzantine Asia Minor, already on the rise since the seventh century, kept growing by leaps and bounds as of the eleventh century.[32] The demographic and ethnographic picture in the Trebizond region was not unlike that in the rest of the eastern part of the Byzantine Empire. However, sharp increases in the population of the city are doubtful, for the city was visited by occasional Turkmen raids—the imperial protection notwithstanding— and regular plagues kept the population growth in check, as was usual in coastal cities.[33] It is difficult to determine the size of the Armenian community of the city during these centuries. "In spite of its monuments, Trebizond was surprisingly small, with only about 4,000 inhabitants in 1438."[34] It would be fair to assume that the city's ethnic composition remained constant during the Middle Ages. In rural areas, however, where Armenians were very numerous, the picture must have been different.[35] According to early Ottoman tax registers, the district of Trebizond had 199 villages in the sixteenth century, with 13,730 households, of which nearly a tenth was Muslim.[36] No data are available on the proportions of Greeks and Armenians among the Christian majority of the Trebizond state. Discussing eleventh-century Anatolia, Speros Vryonis notes:

> The dominant language of western, central, and eastern Anatolia to the confines of Cappadocia was Greek, and the dominant religion was that of the Greek or Byzantine church. In the regions of Anatolia east

---

[31] Maghakia Ormanian, *Azgapatum* [National History], 3 vols. (rep. Beirut: Sevan, 1959-1961), vol. 1, pp. 1200-07 (§§ 826-30).

[32] On the ethnography of the Byzantine Empire in this period, see Vryonis, *Decline*, pp. 42-55.

[33] There is sparse documentation of the plagues in Trebizond. Their regularity is suggested by the record of occurrences in the years 1341, 1348, 1362, 1382 (Vryonis, *Decline*, pp. 256-57 and n706).

[34] Clive F.W. Foss, "Trebizond," in *The Oxford Dictionary of Byzantium*, vol. 3, p. 2112.

[35] Charanis, *Armenians*, p. 20.

[36] Vryonis, *Decline*, pp. 354-55; cf. the nineteenth-century statistics on p. 447, reflecting Greek emigration to Asia Minor during Ottoman rule.

of Cappadocia this Greek element, though present, was very weak in comparison with the non-Greek elements.[37]

The Empire of Trebizond

The eleventh century marks a new era in Trebizond in several other ways. Shortly after the city fell briefly to the Turks in 1071, it revived under the Gabrades—a branch of the Comneni who created a kingdom at Trebizond. The Gabrades were nominally subject to the Comneni, thanks to a palace revolution in Constantinople that had brought Isaac, the first of the Comneni, to the throne in 1057. The local industry at this time came to include textiles, especially silk, and was competing with the silk production in Constantinople, only to be surpassed by Andros and Salonika in the twelfth century. After the fall of Constantinople to the Latins in 1204, Salonika, Nicea, and Trebizond issued coins of their own. In 1204, Alexius and David Comnenus established the Empire of Trebizond and ushered in another era of relative peace and boom. The stability of the city during these turbulent centuries may be explained by the marriage alliances between the Comneni of Trebizond and the Turkmen princes of northern Anatolia. Christian merchants were thus able to pursue their trade in the expanding Muslim portion of Anatolia where commerce, industry, and agriculture continued to flourish, the occasional raids notwithstanding. The late thirteenth-century account of the Venetian traveler Marco Polo reflects this reality: "The other two classes are the Armenians and the Greeks, who live mixed with the former [Turkmen] in towns and villages, occupying themselves with trades and handicrafts."[38]

Indicative of the relative peace and prosperity in the Empire of Trebizond under the Comneni dynasty is the construction of the Hagia Sophia Church about 2 kilometers west of the walled city. The church was built by Emperor Manuel I Comnenus of Trebizond (1238-63) and was almost totally rebuilt in the early fifteenth century. The external sculptures on this church, considered to be from the original construction, mark the first such features on churches in Byzantium. There is reason to believe that the sculptures are of Armenian influence. Com-

---

[37] Ibid., p. 42.

[38] Ibid., p. 235 and n553, quoting Marco Polo 1.43 (ed. Yule) and 1.95 (ed. Moule-Pelliot).

menting on the Saint Sophia sculptures, Tamara Talbot Rice remarks: "But in Byzantium their role was never so important, nor their number so great as in the Caucasus."[39]

Many of the Armenian refugees fleeing the Mongol advance on Ani in 1239, and other inhabitants after the fall of the city, settled in Trebizond. When a devastating earthquake shook Ani exactly a century later, in 1339, many of the homeless joined their compatriots in Trebizond who by this time had their own quarter in the heavily built commercial and industrial eastern part of the city.[40] There was the Armenian bishopric, at the Church of Surb Astvatsamayr (Holy Mother of God). The archaeological evidence points to another period of local prosperity at the beginning of the fifteenth century, when some of the local churches were restored and others built next to them. Greek and Armenian craftsmen thrived alongside merchants of various ethnic groups. An example of the Armenian jewelers' fame may be gathered from a testimonial about the achievements of Mkrtich Naghash, the multi-talented archbishop of Amida who imported numerous vessels for the new cathedral he had built in his metropolis in 1447: "And he adorned the church with all kinds of furnishings and ornaments. And he brought [berial] from Trebizond the large chalice [zmets skihn] made in various combinations, gold-plated and precious. Such a glorious chalice could be found nowhere, elegant and out of this world [gerashkharhik]; 182 msghal[41] of cast silver, gold-plated and adorned with gems."[42] Aside from "brought," the word "berial" could also mean "imported," and this seems to be the contextual meaning here rather than that of having a gift transferred. The archbishop's native city was renowned for its jewelry, yet Trebizond, which he had once visited, surpassed it in this industry.[43] This passage antedates two later

---

[39] Tamara Talbot Rice, *Everyday Life in Byzantium* (New York: Barnes and Noble, 1967), p. 218.

[40] Grigor Avagyan and Ashot Melkonyan, "Trapizon," in *Haykakan Sovetakan Hanragitaran* [Armenian Soviet Encyclopedia], 13 vols. (Erevan: Armenian Academy of Sciences, 1974-1987), vol. 12, p. 87. Emperor Alexius II Comnenus of Trebizond (1297-1330) had just enlarged the city with a new wall that encompassed the harbor and lower city. See Foss, "Trebizond," p. 2112.

[41] A weight unit of slightly over five grams, better known as *miskal,* so that the chalice weighed about a kilogram.

[42] Text cited by Harutiun Kiurtian [Kurdian], "Aknark me Trapizoni hay arvesti hishatakutiants vray" [An Observation on the Testimonials Regarding the Armenian Art of Trebizond] *Hask* 30 (1961): 298.

[43] Ormanian, *Azgapatum*, vol. 2, p. 2136 (§ 1474).

attestations that underscore the city's fame in this industry: one claims that a Greek goldsmith of Trebizond taught jewelry making to Sultan Selim I (1512-20), and the other, that the sultan's successor, Sultan Suleiman I (1520-65), learned the craft in Trebizond from the Greek goldsmith Constantine.[44]

Churches and Monasteries

Of the ninety-five churches and monasteries accounted for in and around Trebizond by Bryer and Winfield, six are identified as Armenian.[45] Oskian and Thierry include only two of these six as they go on to list ten others in the city and the district.[46]

Surb Astvatsamayr (Bryer and Winfield, no. 46; Oskian, no. 9; Thierry, no. 436; cf. Bzhshkian, no. 127), conceivably the oldest Armenian church in the city, stood in the eastern suburb and had a cemetery all around. It was the cathedral of the Armenian churches in the district and the seat of the bishopric until the nineteenth century, when the seat was moved to Saint Auxentios (Surb Oksent/Okhsent). Surb Astvatsamayr may have been built as early as 1204 and, in any case, long before the year 1345, when its bishop, Stepanos, attended the Council of Sis convened by Catholicos Mkhitar Grnertsi (1341-55) to formulate a strong rebuttal to papal emissaries who had sent to the pope a letter unfavorable to Armenian interests.[47] The church had five altars and a forecourt. The site is mentioned in several colophons, the oldest of which is from the year 1383.[48] Clavijo, the ambassador of

---

[44] Cited by Vryonis, *Decline,* p. 239 and n576.

[45] Bryer and Winfield, *Pontos,* pp. 178-250.

[46] Hamazasp Oskian [Voskian], "Trapizoni nahangin vankere/Die Klöster der Provinz Trapezunt," *Handes Amsorya* 75 *(*1961): 273-81; repr. in *Sebastiayi, Kharberdi, Tiarpekiri ev Trapizoni nahangneru vankere* [The Monasteries in the Provinces of Sebastia, Kharberd, Diarbekir, and Trebizond] (Vienna: Mekhitarist Press, 1962), pp. 225-39 (subsequent citations, *Vankere,* are to the latter edition). See also Michel Thierry, *Repertoire des monasteres arméniens* (Turnhout: Brepols, 1993), pp. 80-82. Foremost of the earlier Armenian sources is Minas Bzhshkian, *Patmutiun Pontosi or e Sev Tsov* (History of the Pontus on the Black Sea) (Venice: Mekhitarist Press, 1819), esp. pp. 79-86.

[47] For a list of the participants at the Council of Sis, see Ormanian, *Azgapatum,* vol. 2, pp. 1868-72 (§ 1291). Cf. Aloysius L. Tautu, *Acta Benedicti XII* (Rome: Typis Pontificiae Universitatis Gregorianae, 1955), p. 160. Oskian, *Vankere,* p. 228, refers to a list of the Armenian bishops of Trebizond prepared by Khosrov Pehrikian at the end of the nineteenth century.

[48] Kiurtian, "Aknark," p. 350. Several manuscripts were penned there in the fif-

Henry III of Castile to Timur, refers to this church in his memoirs of 1404: "The Armenians have a bishop and a church of their own tongue in Trebizond."[49] Two inscriptions from 1414 refer to the dedication of the altars of Saint James and Saint Stephen, respectively, and another from 1429 refers to the dedication of the dome donated by Melik Hovhannes and Khoja Stepanos. These inscriptions exist in publications only, for since 1915 nothing is left of the church or of the small monastery attached to it.[50]

The most prominent monastery in the region is that of the All Savior or Holy Savior (Amenaprkich or Surb Prkich vank), outside the city to the east, on the eastern slopes of Mount Minthrion, 2 kilometers south of the Daphnous harbor (Bryer and Winfield, no. 48; Oskian, no. 1; Thierry, no. 433; cf. Bzhshkian, no. 130). The monastery is also known by two other later names: Kaymakli or Kaymakhli vank, because of its large dairy, or Shamshadli (Shemshedli) vank, after Khoja Stepanos Shamshadli (the "Oriental"), previously mentioned. He was a local magnate, originally from Hamadan, who rebuilt the church in 1421, restored the monastery and purchased the vast lands around for its upkeep, according to a marble inscription above the main entrance of the church. The lengthy inscription adds that the restoration continued under the patronage of the son of Khoja Stepanos, Baron Mkrtich, who also restored one of the chapels which was named after his namesake, Surb Karapet (The Forerunner or Saint John the Baptist, Surb Hovhannes Mkrtich). Baron Mkrtich also erected the cross and rebuilt the outer walls of the monastery (30 by 45 meters/98.5 by 147.5 feet). It was an attractive site with its stone-built church, a vaulted basilica with a single apse. Of this freestanding church only the walls remain (it was roofed with wood in 1961 to be used as a fodder store).

The compound had two other chapels—Surb Errordutiun (Holy Trinity) and Surb Astvatsatsin (Holy Theotokos). An imposing belfry once adorned the monastery. An inscription among the ruins names Khoja Paghtasar (Baghdasar) as its builder; another names the celibate priest (*vardapet*) Astvatsatur as the one who adorned the narthex or the *zhamatun,* built against the western wall of the church. Astvatsatur's wall paintings or frescoes are substantially discussed by various researchers, as are also those of the chapel in the southeast corner of the

---

teenth century and thereafter.

[49] Clavijo, p. 113; cited by Bryer and Winfield, *Pontos,* p. 219 and n276.
[50] Bzhshkian, *Patmutiun Pontosi,* pp. 79-80.

compound.[51] There were several rooms for the local monks and for visitors, and a special residence for the abbot, built by Khoja Ghara according to a dateless inscription. Other inscriptions were at the beautiful fountain. These structures appear to be of the same period, constructed at a slightly later time than the dated buildings. Some manuscripts were copied there in the fifteenth century, as attested by a few otherwise insignificant colophons of the same century.[52]

The monastery had its heyday in the fifteenth century, especially during the reign of Alexius IV Comnenus of Trebizond (1416-29). It was sacked and partially destroyed by the Turks in 1461 and a few times thereafter. It recovered some of its former viability as it was restored time and again. Tradition has it that Sultan Murad III (1574-95) was once entertained there with a meal consisting entirely of local dairy products. The monastery remained the center of Armenian religious life in Trebizond until 1915, when it became a detention camp for the soon to be drowned or deported Armenians.[53]

Catholicos Petros Getadardz is considered the founder of the monastery as well as most other monasteries in the region. This is unlikely since the earliest archeological remains seem to be from the thirteenth century: the externally pentagonal apse of the main church, which is in Greek style, and the few older *khachkars* (cross stones) utilized in the 1421 construction.[54] Thus, it is extremely difficult to determine the origin of the site. It remains to suggest that the church was probably of Chalcedonian Armenian origin, hence the initial Greek architecture. There is reason to believe that before the influx of Armenians into the region following the fall of Ani, the local Armenians were predominantly Chalcedonian and some of their churches appear to have been constructed in the Greek style. Following the migrations after the fall of Ani, non-Chalcedonian Armenians became a majority; hence the numerical increase of churches and monasteries and—in certain

---

[51] D. Talbot Rice, "Notice on Some Religious Buildings in the City and Vilayet of Trebizond," *Byzantion* 5 (1930): 47-81. See also Kiurtian's report on Talbot Rice's work in "Aknark," pp. 298-302, 347-50. Much of what Talbot Rice cleaned in the southeastern chapel, recorded, and published in the year following has since disappeared. For what is left, see Bryer and Winfield, *Pontos,* Plates 155b-159b.

[52] List in Oskian, *Vankere,* pp. 229-30; none included in Sanjian.

[53] A description of the tragic days is found in Christopher J. Walker, *Armenia: The Survival of a Nation* (London: Croom Helm, 1980), pp. 216-18. See also the chapter by Simon Payaslian in this volume.

[54] Rice, "Notice on Some Religious Buildings," pp. 63-64; Oskian, *Vankere,* p. 228.

places—possible takeovers from Chalcedonians, as indicated by architectural replacements and restorations.

Four other churches and monasteries of varying significance are listed and briefly described by Bryer and Winfield and by Bzhshkian (but not by Oskian or Thierry). Surb Astvatsatsin (called Nativity of God by Bryer and Winfield, no. 54; cf. Bzhshkian, no. 128) was a cruciform church, known also as Charkhapan (Warder Off of Evil), in the eastern suburbs. It was restored in 1431, according to a now lost inscription naming Khoja Shamshadin as the benefactor. There was a small cemetery adjoining the church of which no trace is left. A much older church, that of Surb Oksent or Auxentios (Bryer and Winfield, no. 62; cf. Bzhshkian, no. 129a), the only other Armenian church with a monastery in the city, also located in the eastern part, became the cathedral bishopric as of the nineteenth century.[55] Both churches survived until 1915. Saint John (Hovhannes) Church in Saint John's Square (Bryer and Winfield, no. 90; cf. Bzhshkian, no. 129b) and Saint Mamas on the east side of Mount Minthrion (Bryer and Winfield, no. 99; cf. Bzhshkian, no. 131b) were in ruins before the nineteenth century. The latter church was considered an extension of the Kaymakhli monastery; an inscription referred to Khoja Mirijan as a benefactor.

Oskian names two other local monasteries: Hambardzman (Ascension) vank (Oskian, no. 6), presumably on Boz Tepe between Kaymakhli and Trebizond, and a smaller (Surb Petros) Getadardz vank (Oskian, no. 2; cf. no. 8, Gedargel Surb Nshani vank; Thierry, nos. 434 and 435), presumably on the site of the miracle reported above, on the Pyxites. Both of these churches are now completely destroyed.

Oskian (followed by Thierry) mentions other monasteries in the district of Trebizond. In the village of Kohana, the Monastery of Saint George/Surb Gevorg (Oskian, no. 3; Thierry, no. 437) and that of Saint Luke/Surb Ghukas (Oskian, no. 7; Thierry, no. 438); in the village of Kelkit, the Monastery of Surb (Grigor) Lusavorich/Holy Illuminator (Oskian, no. 4; Thierry, no. 267) and that of Surb Sargis (Oskian, no. 10; Thierry, no. 268)[56]; in Asamut, that of the Holy Cross/Surb Khach and perhaps another by the same name elsewhere in the district (Oskian, no. 5; Thierry, no. 440); in the village of Surmene, that of Surb Vardan (Oskian, no. 11; Thierry, no. 439); and at Varzahan, in the

---

[55] Leon Z. Surmelian, *I Ask You, Ladies and Gentlemen* (New York: Dutton, 1945), pp. 26-28, gives a brief description of the church.

[56] Bzhshkian, *Patmutiun Pontosi,* p. 90, mentions another monastery by this name, an hour's walk from Gumushkhane.

Gumushkhane-Baiburt region where most likely the ancient trade route south of Trebizond crossed the east-west road, that of the All Savior or the Ascension monastery, known also as Varzents (Oskian, no. 12; Thierry, no. 252). Oskian also mentions the Holy Savior or All Savior Church (Surb Prkich) with its monastery, an hour's walk north of Gumushkhane (Oskian, no. 13; Thierry, no. 241). The domed church had three apses, a baptistry, and a loft. The monastery had a scriptorium, attested in colophons of the eighteenth century. While one or two of these monasteries were in ruins before the calamities of 1915 and stood as markers of the gradual decline, most were in existence as late as the middle of the twentieth century, as at Varzahan, but this is no longer the case.

The Armenians of Trebizond, like the rest of the population of the city, experienced the horrors that preceded and followed its fall to the Turks in 1461.[57] In a colophon of the year 1464 the scribe Stepanos, writing from the Monastery of Avag in the province of Daranaghik (Kemakh), described as follows the atrocities in Trebizond "some ten years after" the fall of Constantinople in 1453:

> Trapizon was captured; and much damage was done there, for they separated sons and daughters from their mothers and fathers, and brothers from brothers. The weeping and lamentation were so heart-rending that I cannot describe them in writing. And who can estimate the damage done to the churches and the sacred effects![58]

In conclusion, the textual and archaeological evidence for the Armenian ties to medieval Trebizond and the state of Trebizond bespeak a vibrant and widespread Armenian presence, its occasional setbacks notwithstanding. The deliberate eradication of substantial archeological evidence, however, remains a matter of grave concern not just to Armenians but to the civilized world in general.

---

[57] "It was a panic-stricken Armenian woman who nearly burnt down the walled city when Sheikh Cuneyd was besieging it in the 1450s." Bryer and Winfield, *Pontos*, p. 210 (no ancient source given).

[58] Sanjian, *Colophons*, p. 283 (1464, no. 1).

✻ 6 ✻

THE FOUNDATION OF HAMSHEN AND ARMENIAN DESCENT MYTHS:
PARALLELS AND INTERCONNECTIONS

Anne Elizabeth Redgate

According to tradition, the Armenian community of Hamshen was founded by two nobles (*nakharar*s) of the Amatuni family, Shapuh and his son Hamam. The *History* written by the learned clergyman, Ghevond (Leontius) *vardapet,* relates that they led a part of their people into the territory of the Byzantine Empire, near the Georgian frontier, to escape Arab oppression. The emperor, whose name is given as Constantine, subsequently welcomed Shapuh, Hamam, and the several other noblemen with honors, and accorded to the lower orders of the population good and fertile land on which to settle. The entirety of Ghevond's account of the actual migration and settlement is unfortunately brief:

> Left without property and food, naked and barefoot, [the inhabitants of Armenia] were exposed to the horrors of famine. They left their country and fled to the Greek territory to seek refuge. The mass of the population, over twelve thousand men, women, and children, as we were told, migrated from their land under the leadership of Shapuh from the house of Amatunik', Hamam his son, and other Armenian nobles with their cavalry. The lawless and brutal enemy then persecuted the fugitives with the help of his troops and reached the districts of Kol, near the Georgian frontier, where a battle took place. Some of the enemy troops perished and others fled, while [the emigrants] crossed the river Akampsis.
>
> The sources of this river are found in the province of Tayk' and it flows in a northwesterly direction, irrigating the country of Eger and ultimately flowing into the Pontus (Sea). As they crossed the river, the Greek emperor Constantine (VI) was immediately notified [about their arrival]. He called them unto him and gave the nobles and their

cavalry high honors. [The emperor] accommodated the bulk of the lower class people on good fertile lands. The other half of the population [of Armenia], on the other hand, remained there in the servitude of [the Arabs] and lived in extreme poverty; they were either woodcutters or water-carriers like the Gebeonites.[1]

The date of these events is almost certainly circa 790. This date is suggested first of all by the names that Ghevond gives for the Caliph (Harun al-Rashid, 786-809) and for his brother the *ostikan* or governor ('Ubaid-ullah, 788-90), as well as the brother's appointee as co-governor (Suleiman), who were responsible for the oppression. Ghevond follows his account of the emigration with a couple of instances of Arab spoliation of the Armenian Church following the death, "in those days," of the Catholicos Isaiah (788) and the accession of his successor Stepanos (788-90).[2] This allows Zaven Arzoumanian, Ghevond's English translator, to date the exodus to 789-90.[3] Peter Charanis had deduced the date of "about 790,"[4] and Joseph Laurent, 791.[5]

The Date of the Migration

The dating of these events to around 790 is crucial to the final conclusion of this chapter. But the date as implied by Ghevond's account is not itself indisputable. A different version of events is given by the eleventh-century Stepanos Asoghik of Taron. The reliability of Ghevond must therefore be examined. The *History* contains no information about its author other than that supplied by the copyist who worked some time between 1279 and 1311. This copyist placed his colophon, with which the text (as it has survived) ends and in which he

---

[1] Ghevond, *Patmutiun* [History], ed. Karapet Eziants (St. Petersburg: I.N. Skorokhodov, 1887). I have not been able to locate and consult this edition and therefore cite the chapter numbers as used by Zaven Arzoumanian in his translation, *History of Lewond, The Eminent Vardapet of the Armenians* (Wynnewood, PA: St. Sahag and St. Mesrob Armenian Church, 1982), ch. 42, p. 149.

[2] Ibid. chs. 41-42, pp. 147-50.

[3] Ibid., p. 195, notes to ch. 42.

[4] Peter Charanis, "The Armenians in the Byzantine Empire," *Byzantinoslavica* 22 (1961): 196-240 (reprinted as Study VI of Peter Charanis, *Studies on the Demography of the Byzantine Empire* (London: Variorum Reprints, 1972), p. 2.

[5] Joseph Laurent, *L'Arménie entre Byzance et l'Islam depuis la Conquête Arabe jusqu'en 886* (Paris: Fontemoing [E. de Boccard], 1919), pp. 184n4, 193n2, 194n9.

identifies himself, immediately after the accession of Catholicos Stepanos in 788. He also names Ghevond's patron as one Shapuh Bagratuni.[6] The natural inferences to be drawn from the colophon are first that it was shortly after 788 that Ghevond, a contemporary or so he claims,[7] of recent events, had composed or finished his work, and second, that he had written it for the Shapuh Bagratuni (died 824), who was the son of one presiding prince of Armenia (Smbat, 761-75) and brother of another (Ashot, 806-26).[8] It has generally been agreed that the text has not survived in its "original" state, since it seems that the initial chapters are missing, but that a late-eighth-century date for the composition of the text is correct. Stephen Gero has argued, however, that the extant version, although incorporating—with extensive remodeling—an earlier version, was in fact written much later, namely after the eleventh-century *History* of Stepanos Asoghik and in part based upon it.[9]

Asoghik's account of the Amatuni migration and the subsequent Arab spoliation of the Church does indeed read very much like Ghevond's, but there is a crucial difference in what precedes it. In Asoghik's text, as in Ghevond's, the exodus is followed by the death of Catholicos Isaiah, preceding the accession of Stepanos, and it follows oppression, from which the migrants flee. But in Asoghik's text the oppression that led to the migration occurred not in the 780s, but in the early 750s, the work of the Caliph Abul Abbas (750-54) and his brother rather than the responsibility of Harun al-Rashid and his brother.[10] Ghevond's *History* records this oppression of the 750s as well as that of the late 780s and describes them in very similar terms.[11] Asoghik's description of the miseries of the 750s is much the same as Ghevond's. There are three possible explanations for the discrepancy

---

[6] Ghevond, *History*, "Colophon" = Arzoumanian, *History of Lewond*, p. 150.

[7] Ghevond, *History*, ch. 34 = Arzoumanian, *History of Lewond*, p. 137.

[8] Arzoumanian, *History of Lewond*, p. 196n3.

[9] Stephen Gero, *Byzantine Iconoclasm during the Reign of Leo III with Particular Attention to the Oriental Sources* (Louvain: Secrétariat du Corpus SCO, 1973), pp. 137, 140.

[10] Stepanos Asoghik of Taron, *Patmutiun Tiezerakan* [Universal History], ed. Stepan Malkhasiants (St. Petersburg: I.N. Skorokhodov, 1885); French trans. of part I by Edouard Dulaurier, *Histoire Universelle par Etienne Açoghᶜig de Daron, Première partie* (Paris: Ecole Spéciale des Langues Orientales Vivantes, 1883), Bk II, ch. 4, pp. 161-62.

[11] Ghevond, *History*, chs. 28, 41 = Arzoumanian, *History of Lewond*, pp. 122-23, 147-48.

between the two accounts regarding the date of the migration to Hamshen. One is that Ghevond, using Asoghik as his source, for some reason duplicated Asoghik's single account of one episode of oppression to make two. A second possibility is that Asoghik, using Ghevond as a source for eighth-century history, had a version of the *History* that lacked the lengthy section that covers the period from 755 to 788. A third is that Asoghik simply failed, by mistake or by design, to summarize this section.

This conundrum seems to have attracted little if any attention from scholars.[12] René Grousset, in his *Histoire de l'Arménie*, followed both Asoghik and Ghevond, in that he recounted the same migration twice, once as an event in the 750s and again as one in 791, apparently without noticing (he certainly makes no comment about the duplication or the discrepancy between the sources).[13] His response cannot therefore be regarded as representing a considered case for one date or the other. It is quite easy to imagine how "Ghevond," if he was indeed writing not in the late eighth century, but much later, could have misdated the episode, in view of another chronological discrepancy regarding another dramatic tale, that of the spoliation, with carnage, of the Monastery of Saint Gregory (Surb Grigor Lusavorich). Ghevond dates this calamity to the turn of the eighth century, that is, about a century earlier than dated by the early-tenth-century historian Hovhannes Catholicos.[14] Jean-Pierre Mahé has suggested that the memory of this event may have derived from oral tradition, in which time and place were vague, thereby requiring an author to undertake the task of locating it chronologically.[15] The same could apply to the Amatuni migration.

---

[12] This fact has been pointed out by Hovann Simonian.

[13] René Grousset, *Histoire de l'Arménie* (Paris: Payot, 1947; reprinted, 1973), p. 320 (citing Asoghik), 338 (citing Ghevond, Asoghik, and Laurent).

[14] Ghevond, *History*, ch. 7 = Arzoumanian, *History of Lewond*, pp. 57-58. Hovhannes Catholicos, *Patmutiun Hayots* [History of the Armenians], ed. Nikolai Osipovich [Mkrtich] Emin (Moscow, 1853; reprinted, Tiflis: N. Aghaniants, 1912, and in Classical Armenian Text Reprint Series, ed. John Greppin [Delmar, New York, 1980]), p. 61 (this edition does not divide the text into chapters); *Yovhannēs Drasxanakertc̣i. History of Armenia*, trans. Krikor H. Maksoudian (Atlanta: Scholars Press, 1987), ch. 24, sections 1-9, pp. 114-15.

[15] Jean-Pierre Mahé, "Le problème de l'authenticité et de la valeur de la chronique de Łewond," in *L'Arménie et Byzance: Histoire et Culture* (Paris: Publications de la Sorbonne, 1996), pp. 119-26 (pp. 122-23 for the story of the Monastery of Saint Gregory).

There is no enlightenment about the date of the migration to be gained from a consideration of any other sources. The *History of Taron* attributed to Hovhannes Mamikonian, which is, as Levon Avdoyan has shown, a late-tenth-century composition,[16] includes a story which Robert Edwards regards as a tale concerning the second generation of the Amatuni settlement. In this account, a prince called Hamam is attacked by the prince of Georgia, as punishment for Hamam's warning another prince, who was an ally of the Byzantine emperor, against the Georgian prince. The author records that Hamam's city, Tambur, was struck with sword and fire but that Hamam rebuilt it and then called it Hamamashen, after himself:

> . . . [the Persian king] Xosrov . . . adopted Tiran and made him *marzpan* of Armenia. [Tiran] took many troops and went against the Greeks, as if in battle, but he sent [a message] to the emperor:
> "Do not be afraid. . . ." Then [Heraclius] concluded a treaty of friendship with him . . . . When Vašdean, prince of Georgia, learned of this, he sent [word] to Xosrov that "Tiran has deceived you . . . send eight thousand men and horses . . . and I shall deliver [Tiran] into your hands."
> Then the king . . . sent an army of five thousand to Vašdean.
> Now Vašdean had written a letter to Tiran: ". . . come, let us plan something together against the king [of Persia]." After [Tiran] had received the letter and read it, there came on that same day a letter from Hamam, the son of Vašdean's sister, which revealed the deceit among the troops coming from Persia. And [Tiran] immediately wrote a letter to Vašdean putting him to shame on account of these secretive affairs.
> And the enraged Vašdean had Hamam fetched and his hands and feet cut off. And he took the Persian [soldiers], passed along the Čorox [Chorokh] River, and went into Hamam's *k'ałak'*, which is called Tambur, which [Vašdean] struck both with the sword and with fire and he enslaved the *k'ałak'*'s [inhabitants].
> Now the holy bishop of the *k'ałak'*, Manknos, vehemently cursed the prince. And [Vašdean] ordered the Persians to slaughter the priests in the church which was called Holy Siovn. The bishop then silently prayed to God . . . [Vašdean's men] sacrificed [him] on the day of Pentecost . . . .

---

[16] Hovhannes Mamikonian, *Patmutiun Taronoy* [The History of Taron], ed. Ashot Abrahamyan (Erevan: Matenadaran, 1941); trans. and comm. Levon Avdoyan, *Pseudo-Yovhannēs Mamikonean. The History of Tarōn [Patmutʿiwn Tarōnoy]* (Atlanta: Scholars Press, 1993), esp. pp. 25-48 for the dating. I have been unable to consult the Armenian edition and cite hereafter only the translation.

And two days later clouds from heaven burst, and consumed [Vašdean] in fire while he was sitting at the gate of the *k'aĺak'* of Tambur. After this Hamam built it again and called it by his own name, Hamamašēn. . . .

Then in this year Heraclius went out and killed Xosrov.[17]

This story suggests to Edwards that the Byzantine emperor had not enjoyed an undisputed right to the lands that he had granted to the Amatunis and that the Georgians subsequently tried to reassert a claim to them, their attempt being remembered, in a garbled form, in the tale of Prince Hamam.[18] Even if this interpretation is correct, however, it reveals nothing about the date of the migration. The whole story of Hamam is set in the seventh century, at the time of the emperor Heraclius (610-41), eight years before even the beginnings of Arab expansion, and long before the time of Arab rule over Armenia.

The dating of the Amatuni migration to the late eighth century depends entirely on acceptance that Ghevond's *History* is indeed a contemporary work. The main problem about the acceptance of an eighth-century date, in general, is the exchange of letters that the text contains, purportedly between the Caliph Umar II (712-20) and the Byzantine emperor Leo III (717-41). This section and its problems do not, however, necessarily seem to affect the authenticity of the rest of the work. Since there is within the rest some internal evidence for a late-eighth-century date and none for a later one, it is reasonable to accept its authenticity, as Mahé has argued, even though it cannot be proved by reference to other evidence.[19]

The Number of the Migrants

It was thus around 790 that Shapuh and Hamam Amatuni are believed to have led some other nakharars, their cavalry, and a mass of people from misery and oppression to a new land. Ghevond wrote that he had heard that more than 12,000 people went. It is not clear whether by 12,000 Ghevond meant 12,000 men plus their women and children, as

---

[17] Avdoyan, *Pseudo-Yovhannēs*, pp. 159-60.

[18] Robert W. Edwards, "Hamšēn: An Armenian Enclave in the Byzanto-Georgian Pontos. A Survey of Literary and Nonliterary Sources," *Le Muséon* 101 (1988): 403-22 (405-06 for this story).

[19] Mahé, "Le problème," esp. pp. 120, 124-25, for the correspondence.

his French translator, Garabed Chahnazarian, has it, or 12,000 in total, as Arzoumanian's English translation suggests.[20] The accuracy or inaccuracy of Ghevond's number is not a concern here. The existence and reliability of various accounting methods, from the "primitive," such as requiring everyone to deposit a pebble and then requiring someone to count the pebbles, to the more sophisticated, like the census and the records that lay behind the taxation demands of the Abbasid caliphs and their governors which Ghevond complains about, will not be explored.[21] Nor will the statistics in the famous Armenian *Military List* that was composed at some date between the mid-sixth and mid-seventh century be utilized. That source records conditions from the period of the Arshakuni/Arsacid kingdom, that is, from the first century to the fifth century A.D., and lists the number of cavalry each nakharar family or "prince" was apparently meant to make available to the king.[22]

What is important is that Ghevond is asserting that the migrants constituted a large group of people. Twelve thousand is not, after all, a small number in comparison with either the 120,000 that the *Military List* says was the total of the Armenian cavalry in the Arshakuni period or the 14,000 that was the number of the men of Vaspurakan who, in the early eleventh century, migrated with their king to Byzantium as part of the famous Byzantine annexations of the Armenian realms.[23] The French and English translators of Ghevond differ slightly in their rendering, but according to the latter, Ghevond terms the migrants "the mass of the population," and the people who stayed in Armenia "the other half of the population."[24] The French translation is less mathe-

---

[20] Garabed V. Chahnazarian, *Histoire des guerres et des conquêtes des Arabes en Arménie, par l'éminent Ghévond, Vartabed arménien* (Paris: Benjamin Duprat, 1856), p. 162; Arzoumanian, *History of Lewond*, p. 149.

[21] Ghevond, *History*, chs. 28, 41 = Arzoumanian, *History of Lewond*, pp. 122-23, 148.

[22] For discussion of the contents and dating, see Nicholas Adontz, *Armenia in the Period of Justinian: The Political Conditions Based on the Naxarar System*, trans. and comm. Nina G. Garsoïan (Lisbon: Calouste Gulbenkian Foundation, 1970), pp. 193-98, 206-10, 218-24, 232-34; Cyril Toumanoff, *Studies in Christian Caucasian History* (Georgetown: Georgetown University Press, 1963), pp. 135-36, 229-41.

[23] Tovma Artsruni, *Patmutiun Tann Artsruniats* [History of the House of the Artsrunis], ed. Kerovbe Patkanian (St. Petersburg: I.N. Skorokhodov, 1887), Continuator Bk IV, ch. 12; trans. and comm. Robert W. Thomson, *Thomas Artsruni, History of the House of the Artsrunik'* (Detroit: Wayne State University Press, 1985), pp. 370-71.

[24] Arzoumanian, *History of Lewond*, p. 149.

matically precise,[25] but both versions show that Ghevond's words imply that in making these remarks he had in mind the population of Armenia as a whole and not simply that of the Amatuni domains.

Although the statistical accuracy of the number that Ghevond states is of no importance in the argument of this chapter, in another respect this number is crucial and very revealing. It is not a random number, because it has a major symbolic importance. The number 12,000 was of great significance in God's ordering of the world in the Bible as a whole and in His ordering of history in the Old Testament in particular. Its application by a medieval author to recent events is a device that enables such a writer to assert that these events are important in God's plan, and perhaps something even more precise than this. Robert Thomson has summarized what early Armenian writers say about number symbolism. Regarding the number twelve they point, among other things, to the twelve hours each of the day and night, the twelve baskets in Christ's feeding of the 5,000, the twelve apostles in the New Testament; the twelve stones of the temple, and various other groups of twelve in the Old Testament.[26]

The most important of such groups is the twelve tribes of Israel. In the New Testament, The Revelation of St. John the Divine records that Saint John, in his vision of the end of the world, "heard the number" of the foreheads of the servants of God "which were sealed." The text lists 12,000 from each of the twelve tribes and states that those who lacked the seal were given up to torment by locusts. Subsequently, it records that the Heavenly City, the Holy Jerusalem, has twelve gates, with twelve angels at the gates, and the names of the twelve tribes written on them; that it is square, measuring 12,000 by 12,000 furlongs, with a wall with twelve foundations; that it is 144 (that is twelve by twelve) cubits high, the height of the city being equal to the length and breadth. The inhabitants of the city are implied to be the 144,000 persons whom Saint John apparently saw with the Lamb on Mount Sion, the redeemed, with His Father's name written on their foreheads.[27] It is

---

[25] Chahnazarian, *Histoire*, p. 162, "Quant au reste des habitants qui demeurèrent en Arménie."

[26] Robert W. Thomson, "Number Symbolism and Patristic Exegesis in Some Early Armenian Writers," *Handes Amsorya* 90 (1976): cols. 117-38 (132-33 for the number twelve).

[27] Revelation, ch. 7, verses 4-8; ch. 9, verses 1-11; ch. 21, verses 10-17; ch. 14, verses 1-4; biblical references are to the King James English translation.

not explicitly stated, though it is implied, that some people of each tribe were not marked as servants of God. It is not clear exactly what number of people the author of Revelation envisaged as comprising each of the tribes of the children of Israel. Yet 12,000 is implied to constitute as well as to represent a tribe. Likewise in the Old Testament, The Book of Joshua states that when Joshua conquered and destroyed the men of Ai, "all that fell . . . , both of men and women, were twelve thousand, even all the men of Ai."[28] The Book of Numbers records that after the Lord told Moses to avenge the children of Israel, Moses told them to arm some of themselves, "of every tribe a thousand," and "so there were delivered out of the thousands of Israel . . . twelve thousand armed for war."[29]

The number 12,000, therefore, has connotations both of constituting a people and of being a (larger) people's defenders and also of being chosen by God or by His agents and of being saved. Christian writers everywhere were impressed by number symbolism and commonly attempted to connect their own subject matter to biblical references in order to give it meaning. The Armenian historian Bishop Sebeos, who wrote, perhaps but not for certain, in the second half of the seventh century, did this in his account of Jewish participation in the origins of Islam and the rise of the Arabs to the status of a world power.[30] Sebeos states that the twelve tribes of the Jews went to Arabia from Edessa, and their 12,000 were there divided, 1,000 per tribe, to guide the Ar-

---

[28] The Book of Joshua, ch. 8, verse 25.

[29] Numbers, ch. 31, verses 1-5.

[30] The text which has traditionally, since 1837, been regarded as the *History of Heraclius* by Bishop Sebeos is most probably not that work. The surviving text is generally regarded as having been compiled, or finished, not very long after 661 (since it ends with an account of the Arab civil war of 656-61), using earlier compositions as sources. It is, however, possible that the compilation was done later still, in the eighth century.

The text is translated and discussed in Robert W. Thomson and James Howard-Johnston, *The Armenian History Attributed to Sebeos*, 2 vols. (Liverpool: Liverpool University Press, 1999). In part I, pp. xxxi-xxxix, Thomson surveys the issues of attribution, authorship, and date but does not explicitly consider an eighth-century date, for which see Anne E. Redgate, *The Armenians* (Oxford: Blackwell, 1998), pp. 189-90. Timothy W. Greenwood, "Sasanian Echoes and Apocalyptic Expectations: A Reevaluation of the Armenian History Attributed to Sebeos," *Le Muséon* 115 (2002): 323-97, offers an extensive discussion of the author/compiler's sources but does not consider his date to be a problem, having "no doubt that it was compiled in the mid-seventh century," about 655 with three updates added that bring the coverage to 661, probably by a senior cleric, and for Prince Hamazasp Mamikonian (pp. 334, 389-94).

abs, who themselves were constituted into twelve tribes, to the land of Israel.[31] Likewise, but more strikingly, Nennius, an early-ninth-century British writer, states that the achievements of Saint Patrick, the evangelizer of Ireland, included the following: he preached to foreign nations for forty years; he wrote 365 or more alphabets; he founded 365 churches; he consecrated 365 or more bishops; he baptized on one day seven kings; he made three petitions to God for the Christian Irish; and, in one day, he converted and baptized 12,000 men in a single region, Connacht.[32] The truth of such assertions for their authors is not literal but moral.

Old Testament Parallels

Ghevond's reference to 12,000 was meant as a statement to his audience about the migrants, but this statement was not an assertion regarding how many people an observer could have counted. If the number of migrants really was 12,000, this was a coincidence, perhaps (even probably) a contrived one, but it was not the ultimate cause of this very number being stated in the text. Ghevond offers his audience a further coded message. The people who stayed behind, in servitude to the Arabs and in poverty, "were either woodcutters or water-carriers like the Gebeonites."[33] Again, the literal statement may be disregarded. It is af-

---

[31] Sebeos, *Patmutiun Sebeosi* [History of Sebeos], ed. Georg V. Abgaryan (Erevan: Armenian Academy of Sciences, 1979), pp. 134-35 (ch. 42); trans. Robert Thomson, in Thomson and Howard-Johnston, *The Armenian History Attributed to Sebeos*, pt. 1, pp. 95-96; French trans. Frédéric Macler, *Histoire d'Héraclius par l'évêque Sébéos* (Paris: Imp. Nationale, 1904), pp. 94-96. Macler's translation explicitly identifies as Israelites the 12,000 who were divided; Thomson's translation states that these 12,000 were divided "like the sons of Israel." Howard-Johnston, *Sebeos*, pt. II, pp. 238-40, regards this Jewish contribution as a spurious account, reaching Sebeos conjoined with authentic material. Robert G. Hoyland gives it more credence and thinks that Sebeos had two reports about Jewish activity which he himself put together. See his chapter, "Sebeos, the Jews and the Rise of Islam," in Ronald L. Nettler, ed., *Medieval and Modern Perspectives on Muslim-Jewish Relations* (Luxembourg: Harwood Academic Publishers, in co-operation with the Oxford Centre for Postgraduate Hebrew Studies, 1995), pp. 89-102.

[32] John Morris, ed. and trans., *Nennius. British History and the Welsh Annals* (London and Chichester: Phillimore, and Totowa, NJ: Rowman and Littlefield, 1980), ch. 54 of *Historia Brittonum* [History of the British], English trans., pp. 34-35; Latin text, p. 75.

[33] Ghevond, *History*, ch. 42 = Arzoumanian, *History of Lewond*, p. 149.

ter all scarcely possible either that there were no other occupations available or that all practitioners of all other occupations had migrated. It is the comparison that counts. The Old Testament Book of Joshua relates the story of the Gibeonites. The Gibeonites hear that Joshua and the Israelites have destroyed Jericho and Ai, realize that they are likely to be treated similarly, and are afraid. Some of them disguise themselves as ambassadors and travelers and seek Joshua out, pretending to have come from a far country and asking for an agreement "to let them live." Their request is granted. When the Israelites subsequently realize that they have been tricked, they keep to the agreement but Joshua tells the Gibeonites that they will henceforth be bondmen, woodcutters, and water carriers for the congregation and altar of the Lord.[34] The Gibeonites had previously been very powerful and their agreement with the Israelites precipitates an alliance of five kings against them. To meet this, they seek Joshua's help. During the campaign, Joshua works the great miracle of causing sun and moon to stand still at his command while the people take vengeance.[35]

So Ghevond's comparison of the non-migrant Armenians with the Gibeonites is relatively complimentary, and certainly not insulting. The Bible after all implies that the Gibeonites, though wily and enslaved, nevertheless enjoy some favor of the Lord. They are the only people to make peace and survive, whereas the others' hearts are hardened, by the Lord, so that they fight the Israelites and are painfully destroyed.[36] The Lord subsequently inflicts a three-year famine on Israel as punishment for the Israelite King Saul's hostility to the Gibeonites, and King David delivers two sons and five grandsons of Saul to the Gibeonites to be hanged as atonement.[37]

Ghevond and his audience, even the laity, were of course much more familiar with the Bible and with biblical stories than most people today. Unlike some educated scholars in the early twenty-first century, eighth-century clerics would not have had to do any research about the Gibeonites in order to be aware of their story. Nor would their audience have been mystified by the allusion. Ghevond and almost all other early medieval Armenian historians (an exception being Sebeos) wrote for patrons and to advance causes.[38] Certainly they took pains to pre-

---

[34] Joshua, ch. 9.
[35] Ibid., ch. 10, verses 1-14.
[36] Ibid., ch. 11, verses 19-20.
[37] The Second Book of Samuel (or The Second Book of Kings), ch. 21-22.
[38] Thomson and Howard-Johnston, *The Armenian History Attributed to Sebeos,*

sent their patrons and causes in a particular light and to interpret the past in a way that explained and justified their present circumstances and policies and which would inspire right conduct in the future. In so doing, they selected and molded their material, and the very fact that they sought to communicate particular messages reveals that in their works they were not simply reflecting current circumstances and ideas; rather, they were seeking to influence them. Nevertheless, it is not plausible that the authors' mentalities and representations were divorced from the ideas and aspirations of their audience. They drew on memories in their accounts of recent history. They wanted their accounts to be accepted and must have realized that if these accounts were unrecognizable they would not be well received.

Ghevond's representation of eighth-century Armenian politics as involving Christian martyrdom, death for the Christian faith and fighting for it, clerical exhortation and angelic participation must have been both intelligible and credible.[39] His audience will have been cognizant of other Armenian texts that had biblical content and inspiration. It will have been familiar with the religious art of Armenia that, of course, incorporated biblical themes and references. It will have had access to monasteries (for monasteries were not extinct; some of them even flourished in the eighth century),[40] and, at the aristocratic level, to family bishops. It will therefore not have been unlike the contemporary elites in the new warrior kingdoms that were located in territories that had formerly been part of the Roman Empire, for whose states the Old Testament provided a political model and guidance.[41] Such an audience

---

pt. 1, pp. xliv-xlvii (Thomson's introduction).

[39] Ghevond, *History,* ch. 34 = Arzoumanian, *History of Lewond,* pp. 131-32, 136-38.

[40] Redgate, *The Armenians,* pp. 186-88.

[41] Adrian Hastings, "Christianity and Nationhood: Congruity or Antipathy?" *Journal of Religious History* 25:3 (2001): 247-60; idem, *The Construction of Nationhood: Ethnicity, Religion and Nationalism* (Cambridge and New York: Cambridge University Press, 1997), p. 14, and ch. 8, esp. pp. 195, 198. The attractions for rulers and aristocracies of an Old Testament self-image are shown in John Michael Wallace-Hadrill, *Early Germanic Kingship in England and on the Continent* (Oxford: Clarendon, 1971), chs. 3-6. Nicholas Howe, *Migration and Mythmaking in Anglo-Saxon England* (New Haven and London: Yale University Press, 1989), argues that one of the factors which enabled the Anglo-Saxons to conceive of themselves as a common people was their belief in an ancestral migration (from the Continent to Britain) that they envisaged as a re-enactment of the biblical exodus and which allowed them to see their experiences in Britain as those of a chosen people in a Promised Land, part

would have been alert to the implications of the Armenian "12,000" and of the "Gibeonites." Any member of his audience who appreciated Ghevond's reference to the Gibeonites must have immediately thought of Joshua, to whom the Gibeonites submitted. Joshua, favored by God, was a ruthless destroyer of those who did not submit. It is conceivable that a parallel between Joshua and the Israelites on the one hand and the Arab governor and the Arabs on the other is being implied by the comparison. In eighth-century Armenia, the Arabs were certainly ruthless and might have been perceived as favored by God in that God was allowing them to oppress the Armenians. But it is hard to think that Ghevond meant, and wanted his audience to feel, that the hero Joshua and an Arab Muslim ruler were equivalents; an alternative, more attractive parallel is easily identifiable. In the Old Testament, Joshua is the successor, though not the son, of Moses. After Moses' death, Joshua takes over the leadership of the Israelites, continuing the exodus from servitude in Egypt to the Promised Land, achieving the crossing of the River Jordan and conquering thirty-one kings who stood in the way of their taking over the Promised Land.[42]

It is most likely that Ghevond's audience will have been meant to think that Shapuh Amatuni and his son Hamam were modern Moses and Joshua figures. The fact that Ghevond left this comparison implicit rather than explicit is easily explained: first, because such a comparison would not have been welcomed by his Bagratuni (Bagratid) patrons, since the Bagratunis as non-migrants are implicitly compared with the Gibeonites, and second, because allusion, reliance on the audience to notice references and to meditate on them, seems to have been a common and preferred usage by writers in early medieval Christendom. Two Western analogies illustrate this tendency. The famous Anglo-Saxon epic poem *Beowulf,* composed perhaps at about the same time as Ghevond's *History,* was once generally regarded by scholars as an essentially and originally pagan composition, on the grounds of its plot and other superficialities.[43] But it has now been

---

of God's plan, and, in some cases, to identify themselves with the Israelites. See also notes 44 and 61 below.

[42] Joshua, ch. 1, 3, 12.

[43] See the translation into modern English by Seamus Heaney, *Beowulf* (London: Faber, 1999). The literature about *Beowulf* is extensive. Suggestions as to its date range from the sixth to the tenth century. For a late-eighth-century date and context, see C. Patrick Wormald, "Bede, Beowulf and the Conversion of the Anglo-Saxon Aristocracy," in Robert T. Farrell, ed., *Bede and Anglo-Saxon England* (Oxford: British

demonstrated to be not only essentially and originally a Christian text but also one that was directed at an audience that had significant knowledge of the Bible.[44] The work of the early-ninth-century British writer Nennius is an important source of evidence about the figure known in later medieval European literature as King Arthur and the vexed question of his historical reality. According to Nicholas Higham, Nennius' account is designed to present Arthur as a British Joshua figure, successor to the British Moses figure who was Saint Patrick. Whereas Nennius explicitly compares Patrick to Moses, he only implicitly compares Arthur to Joshua. Nevertheless an evocation of Joshua is present in the text, deliberate and effective. Nennius draws a parallel between Arthur and Joshua by his use of the number twelve, in his list of Arthur's (twelve) battles, and by his use of a particular phrase in referring to Arthur, *dux bellorum*, meaning leader of battles. This phrase is reminiscent of *dux belli*, leader of battle, which is used in the Vulgate, the Latin version of the Bible, in The Book of Judges where the death of Joshua has left the leadership of the Israelites vacant.[45]

It is more probable than not that Ghevond's perception of parallels between the two Amatuni leaders and Moses and Joshua was not only intelligible to his audience but also fairly widely shared, especially among the Amatunis and the migrants whom they led. It is likely that the leaders, and so perhaps the followers, knew where they were going, that there had been advance negotiations with the Byzantine authorities, and that the travelers therefore had an expectation that the enterprise was practicable. But even if this was the case, and certainly if it

---

Archaeological Reports, 1978), pp. 32-95.

[44] Dorothy Whitelock, *The Audience of Beowulf* (Oxford: Clarendon Press, 1951). The Old English poem *Exodus* (like *Beowulf* difficult to date) also depends on allusion, though rather differently. Howe, *Migration*, pp. 72-107, shows that the poet identifies the Anglo-Saxons with the Israelites entirely allusively, through his use of language and imagery; essentially Anglo-Saxon sea and sail imagery is applied, and the story of the exodus is limited to the Red Sea crossing.

[45] *History of the British*, chs. 55-56, in Morris, *Nennius*; English trans., p. 35, Latin text, p. 76; The Book of Judges, ch. 1, verse 1 (the phrase is rendered "to fight against them" in the King James English translation). This argument was put forward in Nicholas J. Higham's "Arthur, Joshua and the Israelites: History and Its Purposes in Early Ninth-Century North Wales," unpublished paper delivered to EMERGE (Early Medieval Europe Research Group), Edinburgh, Oct. 22, 2001. See also his *King Arthur: Myth-Making and History* (London: Routledge, 2002), pp. 136-57, esp. pp. 141-43.

was not, the migrants must have anticipated the possibility of what actually happened, that is, Arab pursuit and the necessity of battle, so their journey must have been both physically challenging and psychologically stressful. It is inconceivable that there was neither need nor occasion for the boosting of morale and confidence. There are three obvious mechanisms, not exclusive of each other, by which this could have been undertaken. One is the production and dissemination of prophesy, perhaps something comparable to the encouragement of the visionary monk who had exhorted the nakharars day after day during the middle stages of the Armenian rebellion against the Arabs in 774-75.[46] Another method is the telling of inspirational tales of ancient heroes, preferably kinsmen of the migrants themselves and of their leaders—perhaps tales comparable to the Mamikonian traditions recorded in the fifth-century Epic Histories (*Buzandaran Patmutiunk)*[47] and the Bagratuni traditions in the surviving *History* that is attributed to Sebeos.[48] Such activity was an important function of minstrels, in Parthian Iran and in many other societies.[49] The reminiscence and underlining of biblical parallels would have been a third method of encouraging fortitude and optimism.

The Historical Context

Both the Amatuni migration and the perception of its leaders as a new Moses and a new Joshua fit easily into the historical context and must have posed a challenge to the aristocratic families, the new Gibeonites, who stayed behind. The eighth century was a period of oppression and decline. Incorporated into an Arab province, with a governor and military garrisons, Armenians suffered heavy and intensified taxation (especially after the Abbasids took over the Caliphate in 750); increasing Arab settlement; invasions by the Khazars from the north; disruption of trade routes; Arab domination of the declining urban life; a diminution in intellectual vivacity and productivity; a near cessation of art and

---

[46] Ghevond, *History,* ch. 34 = Arzoumanian, *History of Lewond,* pp. 131-32.

[47] Nina G. Garsoïan, trans. and comm., *The Epic Histories Attributed to Pᶜawstos Buzand, Buzandaran Patmutᶜiwnkᶜ* (Cambridge, MA: Harvard University Press, 1989), pp. 6-11, 30-35.

[48] Howard-Johnston, in Thomson and Howard-Johnston, *Sebeos,* pt. I, pp. lxvii-lxviii.

[49] Mary Boyce, "The Parthian Gōsān and Iranian Minstrel Tradition," *Journal of the Royal Asiatic Society* (1957): 10-45.

architecture; and intermittent religious oppression and attempts at forced conversion to Islam. The consequences of these developments were economic decline, depopulation, and poverty, a series of rebellions (the most serious being those of 747-48 and 774-75, both ultimately unsuccessful), heavy casualties, seizure by the Arabs of the estates of rebels and refugees, and westward migration, though, except in the case of the Amatunis, this was an aristocratic rather than a mass phenomenon.[50]

Behind these outcomes lay differences in policy and debates, some of which Ghevond records. There were negotiations with the Byzantine emperor for military aid and for places to settle. Catholicoses in the hope of toleration and peace offered the caliphs submission. A rebellion nearly erupted in 745, fomented by some Bagratunis in collusion with two Mamikonians, Grigor (Gregory) and David, who had been exiled for opposition when the Arabs made Ashot Bagratuni presiding prince over the Armenians in 732.[51] The rebellion that broke out in 747 was led not by this Ashot but by Grigor Mamikonian. Ashot participated reluctantly but then deserted, for which he was blinded.[52] Another Ashot Bagratuni later spoke repeatedly against the 774-75 Mamikonian revolt. His view, "useful advice" according to Ghevond, was disregarded "as words of treason" by the others. This rising began well with the killing of Arab officials, a great victory, the nakharars swearing an oath to live and die together, and with the siege of the city of Karin (Erzerum), but it ended badly, with two disastrous defeats.[53]

Although Ghevond does not report any debate in this particular case, the option of the Amatunis to migrate must nevertheless have been discussed before being undertaken. Behind the decisions of various individuals and groups, to leave or not to leave, must have been reasoning and explanations, not simply bravado or inertia. The departure of 12,000 people reveals a major difference in policy between the

---

[50] Redgate, *The Armenians*, pp. 170-73, 188-92, 195-96.

[51] For negotiations with the emperor, see Ghevond, *History*, chs. 8, 26, 29 = Arzoumanian, *History of Lewond*, pp. 59-60, 120, 124; for the Catholicos, Ghevond, *History*, ch. 9 = Arzoumanian, *History of Lewond*, pp. 62-63; for the events of 745, Ghevond, *History*, ch. 25 = Arzoumanian, *History of Lewond*, pp. 117-19, 177n4: for the exile of the Mamikonians, Ghevond, *History*, ch. 21 = Arzoumanian, *The History of Lewond*, pp. 113-14.

[52] Ghevond, *History*, ch. 26 = Arzoumanian, *History of Lewond*, pp. 119-21.

[53] Ghevond, *History*, ch. 34 = Arzoumanian, *History of Lewond*, pp. 129-33.

leaders of Armenian society which must have involved ideological issues and assertions, claims and counterclaims.

By the last years of the eighth century, the internal power structure both of Armenia (since it now included areas dominated by Arab settlement and power) and of Armenian aristocratic society was very different indeed from what it had been a century earlier.[54] The Mamikonians, previously the most preeminent of the Armenian dynasties, had throughout the century suffered the rivalry of the Bagratunis, and the failure of their rebellions proved to be catastrophic for their fortunes. Politically, they were eclipsed by the end of the century. Others, too, had declined drastically. Cyril Toumanoff estimates that in about 800 A.D. there were only twenty aristocratic "houses" (*tun*; families) left, which could be grouped (since some were offshoots or junior lines of others) into twelve "dynasties," in contrast to the thirty-five princely houses from twenty-two dynasties in around 500 A.D.[55]

In the ninth century, instead of comprising a multiplicity of powerful families, political society was dominated by three or four tuns.. These included the family that held Siunik. There were also the Artsrunis, who in the middle and later parts of the eighth century had been prominent in resisting Arab invasion, two of their leaders being killed in 762 and two more martyred in 786. The Artsrunis had expanded their land holdings, were the only magnates who apparently did not engage in migration, and were perhaps the most powerful and secure family by 800.[56] There were also, of course, the now preeminent Bagratunis. The Bagratunis themselves had split into two branches. A nephew of Ashot the Blind had departed to the borderlands of Klarjk in Iberia (western Georgia), where in the last quarter of the eighth century his family became well entrenched and through marriage to an Iberian princess and acquisition of estates was to replace the reigning dynasty in 813.[57]

---

[54] Redgate, *The Armenians,* pp. 175-77, 182.

[55] Toumanoff, *Studies,* pp. 227-29.

[56] Ghevond, *History,* chs. 30, 40 = Arzoumanian, *History of Lewond,* pp. 124-25, 144-47, 194n7; Toumanoff, *Studies,* pp. 199-200 and notes; Redgate, *The Armenians,* pp. 175, 177-83.

[57] Arzoumanian, *History of Lewond,* p. 177n4. Robert W. Thomson, trans., intro., comm., *Rewriting Caucasian History: The Medieval Armenian Adaptation of the Georgian Chronicles: The Original Georgian Text and the Armenian Adaptation* (Oxford: Clarendon Press, 1996), p. 248 and n47.

Political Challenges and Responses:
The Use of Descent Myths

By the late eighth century, the old certainties had gone and in a changed political landscape the future must have seemed fraught with questions, especially of where, under whose leadership, and on what foundations Armenian fortunes could or would revive. Those families and their leaders who survived remained capable, retained ambition, and will have felt it necessary to compete for prestige and hence for respect and power. It was traditional in Armenia, as it has been in many other societies, for those aspiring to or exercising leadership to have their ideological stall, as it were, set out in a work of history. Some scholars regard the famous *History of the Armenians* by Movses Khorenatsi as a work of the eighth century rather than the fifth, despite Movses' own claim that he was writing in the fifth century. They assert that one of Khorenatsi's main purposes was to explain, to justify, and hence to ensure the new preeminence of the Bagratunis. He did this by portraying them as having been not only meritorious in the past, consistently loyal to friends and steadfast in religion, but also the most illustrious family in the pre-fifth-century past.[58] The Mamikonians, the family which in reality had enjoyed this position, are effectively written out.

More particularly, Khorenatsi is the first writer to represent the ancient origins of the Bagratunis as Jewish. For him, they were originally a family prominent in Israel, one of whose members was among the people taken captive by Nebuchadnezzar, king of Babylon, and was settled in Armenia at the request of the then Armenian king.[59] It is most

---

[58] The crucial reason for rejecting Movses Khorenatsi's assertion about when he wrote is that he seems to have known and used texts that are themselves of a date later than the period which he claimed as his own lifetime. In addition, though less important, some of his interests and attitudes seem anachronistic to a fifth-century date. See Toumanoff, *Studies*, pp. 330-34; Robert W. Thomson, trans. and comm., *Moses Khorenats^{c}i: History of the Armenians* (Cambridge, MA and London: Harvard University Press, 1978), pp. 1-61 for Khorenatsi as historian (pp. 58-61 for a summary of the dating issue). The traditional fifth-century date is still maintained by a number of scholars and is broadly accepted in Armenia.

[59] Movses Khorenatsi, *Patmutiun Hayots* [History of the Armenians], ed. Manuk Abeghian and Set Harutiunian (Tiflis: Mnatsakan Martirosiants, 1913); reprinted in Classical Armenian Text Reprint Series, ed. John Greppin (Delmar, New York: Caravan Books, 1981), Bk I, ch. 22; Thomson, *Moses Khorenats^{c}i* , pp. 110-11.

likely that the Bagratunis were descended from the ancient Armenian royal Ervandian (Orontid) dynasty, so their asserted Jewish descent was neither a historical discovery nor a memory.[60] Khorenatsi actually explicitly criticizes a view that linked the Bagratunis to the founder of the Armenian race, Hayk, an opinion that is much closer to historical reality than is his own. The Jewish descent of the Bagratunis is an invention, even if it was believed to be true. The Old Testament, as has been noted, had a great appeal in Western Christendom as a political inspiration for the new Germanic kingdoms there, and its appeal was not limited to the West. Throughout Christendom, states and societies developed Old Testament self-images in varying respects, seeing themselves as a new chosen people, enjoying the same close relationship with God—with its perils and its perquisites—that the Israelites had possessed. Eighth-century echoes of this imagining are to be found, for example, in the Byzantine emperor Leo III's iconoclastic policies and in the Western emperor Charlemagne's assuming the nickname of David.[61] To claim biological descent from the Jews was merely to take one step further along a well-trodden path.

This path was not, however, without some disadvantages. In Western societies, the physical presence of Jewish communities was an embarrassing reminder that the Christian claims to be Israelites was, in a literal sense, not true, and this fact contributed to Western anti-Semitic feelings and policies.[62] In Armenia, too, there must have remained Jewish communities, remnants of those that are attested with large numbers in the cities of the fourth century in the *Buzandaran Patmutiunk*.[63]

---

[60] Toumanoff, *Studies*, pp. 201, 306, 320-24.

[61] Redgate, *The Armenians*, pp. 245-46. For iconoclasm, see Peter Brown "A Dark Age Crisis: Aspects of the Iconoclastic Controversy," *English Historical Review* 88 (1973):1-34. For Old Testament influence and self-image involving war, Byzantium, Spain, and for Frankish parallels, see Michael McCormick, *Eternal Victory: Triumphal Rulership in Late Antiquity, Byzantium and the Early Medieval West* (Cambridge and New York: Cambridge University Press, 1986), pp. 245-52, 308, 344, 347, 357-58, 385. See Howe, *Migration*, in notes 41 and 44 above, for some Anglo-Saxon parallels.

[62] Their causes are, however, complex. For increasingly hostile Christian attitudes to and treatment of Jews and Judaism in eleventh- and twelfth-century Europe, bedeviled by the claim of the clerks of the Latin Church to be the custodians and interpreters of classical scholarship and of the biblical prophets (despite the traditions of scholarship of other Christian churches, the Arabs, and the Jews), see Robert I. Moore, *The First European Revolution, c. 970-1215* (Oxford: Blackwell, 2000), pp. 146-59.

[63] Garsoïan, *The Epic Histories*, Bk IV, ch. lv, pp. 173-76, 380-81. As Garsoïan

And in Western Asia in the seventh and eighth centuries, Jewish-Christian tension would not have been simply a matter of rival self-images. There was an upsurge of Christian hostility toward Jews, in part because Islam was considered to have been Jewish-inspired and because the Muslim conquests, perhaps with some truth, were attributed partly to Jewish participation. Local Christians could not, however, deal with their Jews as contemporary Byzantium or Visigothic Spain could.[64] In Byzantium, for example, Judaizing was a crime, and Jews were under pressure to become Christian, whereas in places like Armenia, which were under Arab Muslim rule, Jews and Christians were on equal footing with each other. This is a period in which Jews took the opportunity to go on the offensive, producing a number of anti-Christian tracts.[65] In this general context, the Jewish descent of the Bagratunis seems like a neat way out of these ideological minefields.

Movses Khorenatsi extends the privilege of Jewish ancestry to the Amatunis. He reports two versions of their origins: that their family was an ancient Iranian one, a claim that Toumanoff takes to be correct,

---

notes, the exact "figures given in BP for the number of deported Jewish families, as for the Armenian ones, are patently fantastic; nevertheless, they show almost invariably that the Jews composed the majority of the early Armenian urban population." The assertions in the text that everyone was deported and the cities demolished should likewise be taken to indicate severity of treatment rather than total destruction.

[64] Jews were treated much more harshly in later medieval Western Europe and possibly in Visigothic Spain than they were in Byzantium, where they only had an inferior legal status and paid extra taxation. See Joshua Starr, *The Jews in the Byzantine Empire, 641-1204* (Athens: Verlag der Byzantinisch-Neugriechischen Jahrbücher, 1939), pp. 11-12, 18-23; Andrew Sharf, *Byzantine Jewry from Justinian to the Fourth Crusade* (London: Routledge and Kegan Paul, 1971) pp. 61-67, 189-200. See also Averil Cameron, "Byzantines and Jews: Some Recent Work on Early Byzantium," *Byzantine and Modern Greek Studies* 20 (1996): 249-74. The emperor Heraclius in the 630s decreed a forced conversion. A century later, Leo III did the same in 721 or 722 but probably no longer after 726. See Sharf, *Byzantine Jewry*, pp. 47-57, 61-67; Kenneth R. Stow, *Alienated Minority: The Jews of Medieval Latin Europe* (Cambridge, MA and London: Harvard University Press, 1992), pp. 28-29; Starr, *The Jews*, pp. 2-3. There has been debate about the true extent of persecution by the Visigothic regime in Spain, but it seems to have spent 98 years (613-711) following the decree of King Sisebut that Jews be forcibly baptized in continuing to attack Judaism. Stow, *Alienated Minority*, pp. 47-54, discusses the problems and differing interpretations of this policy. See also Bernard Bachrach "A Reassessment of Visigothic Jewish Policy," *American Historical Review* 78 (1973): 11-54.

[65] Robert G. Hoyland, *Seeing Islam as Others Saw It: A Survey and Evaluation of Christian, Jewish and Zoroastrian Writings on Early Islam* (Princeton: Darwin Press, 1997), pp. 538-40.

and that they were descended from Manue, the father of Samson. It is this latter version that Movses prefers.[66] Toumanoff's explanation of the story of Manue is that Movses was confusing some ancient names, putting two and two together and making five. Acceptance of this interpretation involves no speculation about Amatuni traditions as a factor in Movses' account.[67] A different explanation suggested by Jacob Neusner, however, is that the Amatunis were indeed of Jewish descent, that they were descendants of the royal and Jewish house of the ancient kingdom of Adiabene.[68] This interpretation would allow the possibility that Movses was actually drawing on Amatuni traditions when he wrote about their origins.

There must surely have been some Amatuni traditions, for the Amatunis were a family distinguished in Armenian history. Ranked among the greatest of the nobles in the fourth century, they were demoted to the lesser ranks in the fifth, having offended the Persian king. They held the office of *hazarapet* (including possibly supervision of the peasantry) in the fifth century.[69] They participated honorably in the mid-fifth-century rebellion (led by Vardan Mamikonian) against Persia. Vahan Amatuni was one of the princes who, after being summoned to and imprisoned in Persia, feigned apostasy in order to return home only to rebel (though a lesser Amatuni noble was on the side of the sincere apostate Vasak of Siunik). Arandzar Amatuni, a junior noble, threw back marauding Persian forces to the joy of the Armenian army. Both, with a third, Arnak, were among the "princes by birth" and "citizens of heaven by spiritual virtue" who subsequently "gave themselves up to holy bonds, and torture,"[70] that is, to imprisonment for the sake of their faith. Amatuni nobles were active, in association with the Artsruni princes, in the failed 774-75 rebellion,[71] which is why they lost most of

---

[66] Movses Khorenatsi, *History*, Bk II, ch. 57; Thomson, *Moses Khorenats⁽ᶜ⁾i*, pp. 199-200.

[67] Toumanoff, *Studies*, p. 198n223.

[68] Jacob Neusner, "The Conversion of Adiabene to Christianity," *Numen* 13 (1966): 144-50.

[69] Garsoïan, *The Epic Histories*, pp. 346-47, 531.

[70] Eghishe, *Vasn Vardanay ev Hayots Paterazmin* [On Vardan and the Armenian War], ed. Ervand Ter-Minasian (Erevan: Armenian Academy of Sciences, 1957; also Classical Armenian Text Reprint Series, ed. John Greppin [Delmar, NY: Caravan Books, 1993]), Bk I, ch. 22; trans. and comm., Robert W. Thomson, *Elishē. History of Vardan and the Armenian War* (Cambridge, MA, and London: Harvard University Press, 1982), pp. 94-102, 144, 158, 237-38.

[71] Ghevond, *History*, ch. 34 = Arzoumanian, *History of Lewond*, pp. 133-34.

their domains in the north to the Arabs and presumably why in the 780s they contemplated and decided upon migration.

If the Amatunis were in the 780s cognizant of and developing a tradition that they were descended from Manue, this would have been ideologically and psychologically useful to them in their exodus. For Manue's wife, according to the Bible, was told by an angel that her forthcoming child, Samson, would begin to liberate Israel from the Philistines (Israel having been delivered to the Philistines as punishment for evildoing).[72]

Amatuni claims in the 790s to the status of Samson, Moses, and Joshua must have been embarrassing to the Bagratunis, the most eminent of the non-migrants, the "Gibeonites." They must also have revealed and emphasized an ideological weakness in the position of those Bagratunis who were then establishing themselves in Iberia, east-northeast of the new Amatuni settlement. And the Bagratunis might well have wondered what might come of that new Amatuni settlement, given that it had Byzantine imperial support. The implications of the biblical parallels were not auspicious for the Bagratunis. In the Bible, the Gibeonites (the Bagratuni equivalent) have to appeal to Joshua (Hamam Amatuni's equivalent) for help against five kings, and thereby provide the opportunity for him to demonstrate his power by successfully commanding sun and moon to stand still.

That the Amatunis in exile were indeed a power to be reckoned with is suggested by Edwards' interpretation of the mixed-up tale recounted in the *History of Taron* by Hovhannes Mamikonian. If Edwards is right, it seems that early in the ninth century the Georgians to the east of Hamshen were concerned about Amatuni power and independence, tried to destroy it, but failed. The prince of Hamshen is a dominant figure in this tale, involved in politics at the very highest level. In view of the fact that the Amatunis were an embarrassment to the Bagratunis in the 790s, Movses Khorenatsi's choice not only to record but also to endorse the Amatuni-Samson link points towards a date for his *History of the Armenians* of before 790. Several scholars have deduced a date that is before the end of the eighth century from his failure to assert that the Bagratunis were descended from the Old Testament King David.[73]

---

[72] Judges, ch. 13, verses 1-5.
[73] Toumanoff, *Studies*, p. 334; Thomson, *Moses Khorenats^ci*, p. 59.

This particular Bagratuni claim is first reported in a Georgian history which scholars date to about 800. The claim is mentioned with reference to Adarnase, or Ashot, the nephew of that Ashot who had been blinded for deserting the 747 rebellion. It was Adarnase's son, also called Ashot, who became prince of Iberia in 813 and his claim to Davidic descent was emphasized in stone during his lifetime.[74] There is a sculptured relief from the Georgian church of Opiza, which traditionally has been regarded as contemporary with Ashot, depicting him as a patron of the church. This interpretation is still convincing, despite a recent re-dating. If the traditional date is correct, then this relief portrays David acting as intercessor for Ashot with Christ and in this portrayal is alluding to the Davidic claim of the Bagratunis.[75] In the tenth century, this claim entered mainstream historical tradition, being reported by the Armenian historian Hovhannes Catholicos and known to the Byzantine emperor Constantine VII Porphyrogenitus.[76]

The dates of these allusions to the Bagratuni claim to Davidic descent suggest that the claim itself was first made very late in the eighth century. It fits into the claim of Jewish descent, which had been made for them by Movses Khorenatsi. But it was nevertheless a novel and somewhat bold assertion. Something must have provoked it and made it seem desirable, even necessary. It seems likely that the stimulus was the particular context of the Amatuni migration, the Davidic claim being an assertion and insurance of Bagratuni superiority in prestige over other Armenian families. The Amatunis could be warrior leaders, but the Bagratunis would be kings.

---

[74] Toumanoff, *Studies*, pp. 328, 353 and n4; Thomson, *Rewriting Caucasian History*, p. 248 (the reference is from Juansher, *The History of King Vaxtang Gorgasali*).
[75] Toumanoff, *Studies*, p. 328. The reasons for re-dating the relief to 923-937 are summarized by Antony Eastmond, *Royal Imagery in Medieval Georgia* (University Park: Pennsylvania State University Press, 1998), pp. 222-24. If it is a tenth-century relief, it depicts a later Ashot, namely Ashot IV, son of the first Bagratuni king of Georgia with this Ashot's elder brother, King David, and commemorates remodeling of the church. The depiction of David is, however, curious if David is Ashot's brother. It would make more sense if this David is Ashot's ancestor. This is because David appears on the same side of the relief as Christ, rather than with Ashot. The pairing suggests that the two men, David and Ashot, were perceived as being on different planes.
[76] Toumanoff, *Studies*, p. 329; Maksoudian, *Yovhannēs Drasxanakertc͑i*, p. 73; Constantine Porphyrogenitus, *De Administrando Imperio*, Greek text, ed. Gy. Moravcsik and Engl. trans. Romilly J.H. Jenkins (Washington, DC: Dumbarton Oaks, 1967), ch. 45, lines 1-12 (pp. 204-05).

Conclusion

The reading presented here of Ghevond's account of the Amatuni migration and of Movses Khorenatsi's assertions about the Jewish descent of two Armenian families leads to four conclusions. First, that Ghevond and his audience not only perceived Shapuh and Hamam Amatuni as being related to, and as emulating, Samson, who had begun the delivery of the Israelites from the Philistines, but they also perceived these two Amatunis and their followers as a new Moses and a new Joshua, and as a new people of Israel following them to a new promised land. Second, that the migrants shared these interpretations and drew on them to boost their morale and cohesion. Third, that the new Amatuni settlement and its ideological and psychological strength were an embarrassment and a potential threat to the Bagratunis. Fourth, that the Bagratunis responded to the challenge posed by the Amatunis by revising their own ancient genealogy. The contribution of the foundation of Hamshen to Armenian history was thus twofold: directly, the establishment of a community remarkable in itself, and, indirectly, the establishment of a powerful and enduring Bagratuni royal descent myth.

❋ 7 ❋

ISLAMIZATION OF ARMENIANS
IN THE OTTOMAN EMPIRE:
THE HAMSHENTSI/HEMSHINLI CASE

Claire Mouradian

This survey of the Islamized Armenians of the district of Hamshen or Hemshin is an outgrowth of a request of the late Alexandre Bennigsen for information on Armenian sources about members of a particular population he had encountered in Soviet Central Asia.[1] These were the Hemshinli/Hemşinli, who had been deported from the Caucasus, especially Ajaria, on Stalin's orders in 1944. They were "a punished people," along with their neighbors the Meskhs/Meskhetians (Turkish-speaking Georgians), the Chechens, and other Caucasian Muslims. The Hemshinli and Meskhetians were punished, not for having collaborated with the Germans, as Hitler's armies did not reach the South Caucasus, but rather for preemptive reasons stemming from fear of their eventual collusion with compatriots living across the border in Turkey.[2]

In their book on Muslims in the USSR, Alexandre Bennigsen and Chantal Lemercier-Quelquejay estimated the number of Hemshinli in the 1970s to be 1,500 to 2,000.[3] In fact, they are far more numerous,

---

[1] A version of this paper was first published as "Aperçu sur l'Islamisation des Arméniens dans l'Empire ottoman: Le cas des *Hamchentsi/Hemşinli*," in Mercedès Garcia-Arenal, ed., *Conversions islamiques: Identités religieuses en Islam méditerranéen/Islamic Conversions: Religious Identities in Mediterranean Islam* (Paris: Maisonneuve et Larose, 2002), pp. 399-418. I wish to thank Professors Nina Garsoïan and Richard Hovannisian for their assistance in translating and editing this chapter.

[2] See Aleksandr M. Nekrich, *The Punished Peoples* (New York: Norton, 1978); Jacques Kayaloff, "The Khemshels: Another Deported Nationality," *Armenian Review* 33:2 (1980): 216-17; Jean-Jacques Marie, *Les peuples déportés d'Union soviétique* (Brussels: Complexe, 1995). Hovann H. Simonian, "The Vanished Khemshins: Return from the Brink," *Journal of Genocide Research* 4:3 (Sept. 2002): 375-85.

[3] Alexandre Bennigsen and Chantal Lemercier-Quelquejay, *Les musulmans oub-*

the figures varying from 50,000 to 100,000 and much higher when including the Hemshinli in Turkey. In the Soviet Union, most people of Hamshen/Hemshin origins are Armenian Christians identified as Hamshentsi or Hamshetsi (Russian: Khemshin/Khemshil/Khemshel), who decades earlier fled to Russia to avoid conversion or who reverted to their original religion after having emigrated. Many of the Christian Hamshentsis who settled in the Crimea were also deported by Stalin in 1944 (with local Tatars, Bulgars, and Greeks) for allegedly having collaborated with the Germans or assisting the German-sponsored "Armenian Legion."

The paucity of sources makes a scientific study difficult, especially as Armenian conversion to Islam has been a taboo subject. The Armenians pride themselves on their ancient Christianity, their autocephalous national church, which separated from the rest of Christianity in the Oriental schism following the Council of Chalcedon in 451,[4] and their cultural specificity resulting from the creation of a distinct alphabet in the fifth century. Their identity was forged in the tradition of heroic martyrdom for the Christian faith at the battle of Avarair also in 451) against Zoroastrian Persia, in the resistance to Orthodox Byzantium and to the Muslim Arabs and Turks, and in the continuing struggle for self-preservation until the genocide of 1915. Witnesses and survivors of the genocide often mention offers of conversion to Islam— usually rejected—as the only way to escape deportation and death.

The fusion of national and religious sentiment was intensified by the Ottoman confessional-based *millet* system of administration. The conversion of some Armenians to Catholicism since the seventeenth century and the establishment of a de-facto separate Catholic millet in 1831 or else the conversion to Protestantism since the nineteenth century and the formation of the Protestant millet in 1850 were long viewed as betrayal of the national community. A fortiori, any conversion to Islam and the impossibility of apostasy and return to Christianity became a radical breach within the Armenian corpus that was preferably forgotten. A nineteenth-century article in Armenian dealing with the Muslim Hemshinli was appropriately titled "Lost and Forgotten

---

liés: L'Islam en URSS aujourd'hui (Paris: François Maspéro, 1981). See also Alexandre Bennigsen and S. Enders Wimbush, *Muslims of the Soviet Empire: A Guide* (Bloomington: Indiana University Press, 1986).

[4] Cf. Nina Garsoïan, *L'Eglise arménienne et le grand schisme d'Orient* (Louvain: Peeters, 1999).

Armenians."[5] The conversion of members of this group to Islam is explained only as the result of coercion. Spiritual or opportunistic conversions are not easily acknowledged except as individual acts that are heavily stigmatized. The case of the Hamshentsi Armenians, who long preserved their original language and even a form of crypto-Christianity, is fraught with a still more perplexing problem—that of maintenance of national identity even after having "turned" from Christianity. The Hamshentsi case is the only relatively well-known and recognized one, although this phenomenon is far more extensive and concerns the entire Ottoman Empire.[6] There is, however, no general reference work on the Islamization of Armenians.

For the Turks or for Muslims in general, as well as for certain Orientalists who are committed to the rehabilitation of Islam and the Ottoman Empire, the concept of forced conversion is rejected or questioned. In *Histoire de l'Empire ottoman*, edited by Robert Mantran, authors such as Nicoarae Baldiceanu and Gilles Veinstein consider forced conversion as rare, since it was not favored by the state for fear of losing the benefit of special taxes such as the *jizye*. Islam, they maintain, was tolerant as demonstrated by the case of the Jews driven from Spain and the spiritual and cultural freedom granted to "peoples of the Book" who "enjoyed" the status of protected clients or *dhimmi*. Nor were the dhimmi displeased with the *devshirme* (child levy)—although this was one of the most overt means of forcible conversion—as many families, it is said, may have used this practice that entailed the transformation of Christian children into Muslim officials and soldiers as a means of social and economic advancement.[7]

It may be argued, of course, that the jizye could always be obtained under various guises and through new taxes and that the status of dhimmi was both discriminatory and humiliating. Although the dhimmi status allowed the Christian and Jewish communities to main-

---

[5] Sargis Haykuni, "Korats ev moratsvats hayer: Sev getatsik" [Lost and Forgotten Armenians. The Armenians of the Black River], *Ararat* (Echmiadzin) (July-August 1895): 239-43, 293-97.

[6] See, for example, Garegin Amatuni [Karekin Amadian], *Dareru entatskin trkatsats hayer, krdatsats hayer* [Down through the Centuries, Turkified Armenians, Kurdified Armenians] (Beirut: Shirak, 1980).

[7] Robert Mantran, ed., *Histoire de l'Empire ottoman* (Paris: Fayard, 1989). See especially Nicoarae Baldiceanu, "L'organisation de l'Empire ottoman, XIVe-XVe siècles," pp. 117-38, and Gilles Veinstein, "L'empire dans sa grandeur, XVIe siècle," pp. 159-226.

tain a semi-autonomous religious and cultural life, it nevertheless also implied that the discriminatory fiscal and social pressures could be surmounted only through conversion to Islam or to one of the foreign "protected" religions (Catholicism and Protestantism). It is also possible to cite as many prescriptions to intolerance as to tolerance in the tenets of Islam. Indeed, the practices of Muslim governments toward the conversion of infidels were uniform neither in time nor in space.

Clearly, the process of Islamization and Turkification of Asia Minor between the eleventh and sixteenth century was not merely the result of migrations and demographic growth of the conquerors but primarily because of widespread conversion or at least external adhesion to the faith of those holding military superiority or political power. Contemporary minimizing of the phenomenon of forced conversion may be regarded as an indication of a certain Western patronizing attitude toward Christian peoples in the Near East who were unable to preserve their sovereignty and instead had to settle for an inferior tolerated status.

Since the end of World War II and the beginning of the Cold War in the 1940s, the Western objective of safeguarding the territorial integrity and secularism of Turkey against Soviet pressure, Muslim fundamentalism, and Kurdish separatism have led certain powers to defend implicitly the myth of Turkish unity—a myth that might burst were there recognition of forcible conversion or the continuing existence of various non-Turkish ethnic (especially Muslim) groups. The debate between the nation-state and the mosaic-state theory regarding Turkey has gone on for a long time and its bloody results have been seen in the suppression of the Kurds and Alevis just as previously they were manifested in the elimination of the Armenian and Greek elements.

This discussion does not focus so much on the spiritual and religious aspects of conversion, which apply more to the individual than to collective cases, as it does on the political and social pressures on the inhabitants in contested border regions. From a national point of view, this implies a reassessment not only of Armenian identity but also of the composition of the modern Turkish nation-state. Despite the Turkish government's firm stand on a unified ideology, questions arise about religious syncretism and crypto-Christianity equivalent to that of the Marranos in the Iberian Peninsula. These seem to entail strategies devised by national and/or religious minorities through camouflage or overlaying of identities.

The Sources

Armenian sources on the first waves of Islamization of the Hamshentsis in the seventeenth century are virtually non-existent because of the destruction of monasteries and other Armenian institutions with archives. In addition to research *in situ* or studies of comparable cases, especially with Greek-speaking Muslims or Georgian Muslims, other types of repositories must be consulted:

1) State archives, primarily Ottoman; Russian/Soviet archives, which are now more accessible; diplomatic archives of countries having a presence in the area;

2) Religious archives, both Muslim and Christian, especially those of the Armenian Church housed in the Patriarchate of Constantinople and the Catholicosate of Echmiadzin; the archives of Catholic missions (there was an Armenian Catholic See at Trebizond).[8]

In addition to general works on Islam, the Ottoman Empire, the minorities and the status of dhimmis, travel accounts, and a few recent Western works, this discussion relies primarily on published sources and ethnographic works of the nineteenth and twentieth centuries.[9] For the origins and history of the principality of Hamshen, references may

---

[8] Les *mémoires de Mgr.Jean Naslian, évêque de Trébizonde, sur les événements politico-religieux en Proche-Orient de 1914 à 1918*, 2 vols. (Vienna: Mekhitarist Press, 1951).

[9] See, for instance, Robert Mantran, *Histoire de l'Empire ottoman;* Speros Vryonis, Jr., *The Decline of Medieval Hellenism in Asia Minor and the Process of Islamization from the 11th through the 15th Century* (Berkeley, Los Angeles, London: University of California Press, 1971); Benjamin Braude and Bernard Lewis, eds., *Christians and Jews in the Ottoman Empire* (New York: Holmes & Meier, 1982), 2 vols; Laurent and Annie Chabry, *Politiques et minorités au Proche-Orient: Les raisons d'une explosion* (Paris: Maisonneuve et Larose, 1987); Antoine Fattal, *Le statut légal des non-musulmans en pays d'Islam* (Beirut: Imp. catholique, 1958); Bat Ye'or, *The Dhimmi: Jews and Christians under Islam*, trans. David Maisel, Paul Fenton, and David Littman (Cranbury, NJ: Fairleigh Dickinson University Press/Associated University Presses, and London: AUP, 1985; 6th printing, 2003); idem, *The Decline of Eastern Christianity under Islam: From Jihad to Dhimmitude, 7th-20th Century*, foreword by Jacques Ellul, trans. from French by Miriam Kochan and David Littman (Cranbury, NJ: Fairleigh Dickinson University Press/Associated University Presses, and London: AUP, 1996; 5th printing, 2003); Nehemia Levtzion, ed., *Conversion to Islam* (New York and London: Holmes & Meier, 1979); Yousseff Courbage and Philippe Fargues, *Chrétiens et Juifs dans l'Islam arabe et turc* (Paris: Payot, 1997); Gérard Dédeyan, ed., *Histoire du peuple arménien* (Toulouse: Privat, 2007); Raymond H. Kévorkian and Michel Paboudjian, *Les Arméniens dans l'Empire ottoman à la veille du génocide* (Paris: Editions d'Arts et d'Histoire, 1992).

be sought in chronicles up to the fifteenth century and even as late as the seventeenth century,[10] as well as traveler accounts, such as those of the Armenian Hetum (fourteenth century)[11] and the Spanish Ruy González de Clavijo (fifteenth century).[12] Issues of conversion are raised only in nineteenth-century travel accounts, especially those of Protestant missionaries Eli Smith and H.G.D. Dwight (1830-31)[13] and of German botanist Karl Koch (1844),[14] as well as in the studies of the Armenian Catholic Mekhitarist fathers Ghukas Inchichian (Injijian),[15] Minas Bzhshkian (Pzhishgian),[16] and especially Hakovbos Tashian (Hagop Dashian),[17] who prepared a monumental work on the region, of which he himself was a native. Ethnographic and ethno-linguistic studies appeared from the end of the nineteenth century, among them being those of Sargis Haykuni (research done in the 1860s and published in 1895),[18] P. Tumayian (written 1870s and published in

---

[10] See, for instance, one of the rare surviving chronicles of the seventeenth century by Hakovb Karnetsi (Jacob of Karin [Erzerum]). There exists a French translation: "Erzeroum ou la topographie de la Haute-Arménie," trans. Frédéric Macler, *Journal Asiatique* (March-April 1919): 153-257. Medieval texts have been edited and analyzed by Levon Khachikyan, "Ejer hamshenahayeri patmutyunits" [Pages from the History of the Hamshen Armenians], *Banber Erevani Hamalsarani* [Herald of Erevan University] 2 (1969): 115-44.

[11] Héthoum l'historien [Het'um Lambronac'i], *Les Fleurs des Hystoires de la terre d'Orient* (Paris: Denis Janot, n.d.); *A Lyttel cronycle: Richard Pyson's translation (c. 1520) of "La Fleur des Histoires de la terre d'Orient" (c. 1307)*, ed. Glenn Burger (Toronto: Toronto University Press, 1988).

[12] Ruy González de Clavijo, *Narrative of the Embassy to Tamerlane, 1403-1406*, trans. Guy Le Strange (London: Routledge, 1928).

[13] Among the reports sent to the emissaries of the American Board of Commissioners for Foreign Missions in Armenia and Persia, those of Eli Smith and Harrison Gray Otis Dwight have been published under the title, *Missionary Research in Armenia*, 2 vols. (London: G. Wightmann, 1834).

[14] Karl Koch, *Wanderungen im Oriente während der Jahre 1843 und 1844*, vol. 2: *Reise im pontischen Gebirge und türkischen Armenien* (Weimar: Druck und Verlag des Landes Industrie Comptoirs, 1846).

[15] Ghukas Inchichian, *Ashkharhagrutiun chorits masants ashkharhi* [Geography of the Four Parts of the World] (Venice: Mekhitarist Press, 1802-1806).

[16] Minas Bzhshkian, *Patmutiun Pontosi or e Sev Tsov* [History of Pontus on the Black Sea] (Venice: Mekhitarist Press, 1819).

[17] Jacobus Dashian [Hakovbos Tashian], *La population arménienne de la région comprise entre la mer Noire et Karin (Erzeroum): Rapide coup d'œil historique et ethnographique*, trans. Frédéric Macler from Armenian, *Hay bnakchutiune Sev tsoven minchev Karin* (Vienna: Mekhitarist Press, 1921).

[18] See note 5 above, and Sargis Haykuni, "Hay Gaspare" [The Armenian Gaspar], *Ararat* (Oct. 1895): 397-400.

1899),[19] Hakob Muradiants (1898-1900), Hakob Manandian (1903),[20] Hrachia Acharian (Ajarian, 1911),[21] and Georges Dumézil (1960s). There are also publications from the Soviet period,[22] original monographs of a commemorative nature published in the Diaspora,[23] and the Armenian press.[24] Rüdiger Benninghaus lists the Turkish sources with critical analyses in a collaborative work intended to give a comprehensive inventory of the various ethnic groups making up present-day Turkey.[25]

---

[19] See P. Tumaian, "Pontosi Hayere: Ashkharhagrakan ev kaghakakan vichak Trabizoni" [The Pontic Armenians. Geographical and Political Situation of Trebizond], *Luma* (Tiflis) 2 (1899): 144-92.

[20] Hakob Manandian, "Hayots nor vkaner: Ter Karapet kahana Torosletsi" [New Armenian Martyrs: Father Karapet the Priest of Torosli], *Ararat* (1903): 702-09.

[21] Hrachia Acharian, "Haykakan barbaragitutiun: Hamsheni barbar" [Armenian Dialectology: The Dialect of Hamshen], *Eminian azgagrakan zhoghovatsu* [Eminian Ethnographic Anthology] (Moscow, 1911), pp. 184-98.

[22] See Levon Khachikyan, "Ejer hamshinahay patmutyunits" [Pages from the History of Armenians of Hamshen], *Banber Erevani Hamalsarani* 2 (1969): 115-44; Barunak K. Torlakyan, "Hamshenahayeri masin" [About Hamshen Armenians] *Banber Erevani Hamalsarani* 2 (1970): 197-202; idem, "Hamshenahayeri bnakaranayin hamalire" [The Residential Complex of Hamshen Armenians], *Patma-banasirakan handes* [Historico-Philological Journal] 2 (1970): 93-104; idem, "Hamshenahayeri ev pontahayeri bnakavayrere u tvakanake 1914 tvakanin" [The Location and Number of Hamshen Armenians and Pontic Armenians in 1914], *Patma-banasirakan handes* 2 (1970): 202-15. See also N.G. Volkova, *Etnicheskii sostav naseleniia Severnogo Kavkaza v XVII–nachale XX veka* [Ethnic Structure of the North-Caucasus Population from Eighteenth to the Beginning of Twentieth Century] (Moscow, 1974); L. Petrosyan, "Hamshen," in *Haykakan Sovetakan hanragitaran* [Armenian Soviet Encyclopedia], vol. 6 (Erevan: Armenian Academy of Sciences, 1980), p. 119.

[23] Hovakim Hovakimian, *Patmutiun Haykakan Pontosi* [History of Armenian Pontus] (Beirut: Mshak Press, 1967), pp. 54-71 and *passim.*

[24] Sergei Vardanyan, "Hamshentsiner tsanot ev antsanot" [Hamshentsis, Known and Unknown], *Garun* [Spring] (Erevan), 11 (1982): 60-73; republished in *Haratch* [Forward] (Paris), Feb. 12-13, 1983; Sero Khanzadyan, "Ejer chambordakan oragrits" [Pages from (My) Travel Diary], *Sovetakan Hayastan* [Soviet Armenia] (Erevan) 10 (1986): 23-25; Vardan Grigoryan, "Hamshenahayeri mshakutayin tone," [The Cultural Festival of Hamshen Armenians], *Hayreniki dzayn* [Voice of the Fatherland] (Erevan), Jan. 28, 1987, p. 4; Alvard Ghazinyan, "Nshkharner Hamsheni ev Trabizoni banahyusutyan" [Relics of the Folklore of Hamshen and Trebizond], *Hayreniki dzayn*, March 25, 1987.

[25] Rüdiger Benninghaus, "Zur Herkunft und Identität der Hemşinli," in Peter A. Andrews, ed., *Ethnic Groups in Turkey* (Wiesbaden: Ludwig Reichert, 1989), pp. 475-87. For comparative purposes, see Alexandre Toumarkine, *Les Lazes en Turquie (XVIIᵉ-XXᵉ siècles)* (Istanbul: Isis, 1995); Neal Ascherson, *Black Sea* (New York: Hill & Wang, 1995); Uwe Bläsing, *Armenisches Lehngut im Türkeitürkischen: Am*

The Historical Dimension

The term Hamshen in Armenian or Hemshin/Hemşin in Turkish desig-
nates a geographic region, a district in the Laz back country overlapping the provinces of Rize and Artvin to the Chorokh River, which
marks its eastern border. As in the case of the Pontic Mountains, which
form a barrier rising to 3,700 meters/12,100 feet above sea level at
Mount Kachkar, this district offers a compartmentalized landscape
made up of isolated valleys and forested slopes. Access is very difficult. Although the barrier of the Pontic Alps and its extension to the
Caucasus Mountains is the northern limit of the Armenian Plateau or
Highland, an Armenian presence on the Pontic coast since antiquity is
attested by classical Greek writers. Under the Roman/Byzantine Justinian emperors in the sixth century A.D., parts of Armenia Minor or
Lesser Armenia (lying to the northwest of Greater Armenia) reached
the Black Sea as far as Batum, even though the coastal regions were
peopled primarily by Greeks and by Laz and other Georgian tribes.
According to Armenian chroniclers, among them Ghevond,[26] the province of Hamshen takes its name from Prince Hamam Amatuni. With
his father, Shapuh, other princes, and some 12,000 men (perhaps families), he had fled from his original domain in the land of Ararat (west
of Lake Sevan) at the end of the eighth century to escape the increasingly heavy military and fiscal pressures of the Arab governors (*ostikan*) of Armenia, especially 'Ubaidulla-ibn-Al and his Greek renegade
son-in-law. Seeking refuge in the "world of the Greeks"—ancient
Chaldia—in 788-90, the Armenians encountered and fought the Georgian army of Prince Vashdean, an uncle of Prince Hamam. The city of
Tambur, destroyed during the combat, was reconstructed by Hamam,
whence its name of *Hamamashen* (shen = constructed or built), in time
the name contracting into "Hamshen." There are, of course, other hypotheses on the origin of this toponym, whether they be the Armenian
popular etymology referring to the brothers Ham and Shem of the Bible or the Turkish etymology deriving the name from the aggregation
of the Turkish words *hem* = really and shen = prosperous, or *emshen* =
lamb skin, as the cloth material of a certain Turkish tribe, or again the

---

Beispiel von Hemşin (Amsterdam and Atlanta: Rodopi, 1992). Hovann Simonian has
published a collection of articles under the title, *The Hemshin* (London and New
York: Routledge, 2007).
    [26] Ghevond, *Histoire des guerres et des conquêtes des Arabes*, trans. G. Chahna-
zarian (Paris, 1857).

Iranian *hemnishin*, meaning "living in common" as an Oghuz tribe. The latter are the theories cited by Benninghaus which seek a Turkish genealogy for almost every group in Turkey as propagated by the Turkish Institute of History since its creation in the 1930s. According to Fahrettin M. Kirzioğlu, the Hemshinli were either a Balkar tribe (a Turkish people of the Caucasus whose language belongs to the Kipchak group) or an Oghuz tribe whose ancestors had come with the Iranian Arsacids, first to Khorasan, then to Hamadan, where they assumed the name of Hamatuni, before settling in the region of Hamshen around 620 A.D.

Medieval Armenian sources bear witness to currents of migration to this refuge, "a dark country, with high summits and deep valleys hidden in fog" as the result of Arab-Byzantine wars or internal disorder. According to these sources, some of the people stayed in the mountains, while others pushed to the coast where Armenian princes from the House of Amatuni allied themselves with the rulers of Lazistan. The fall of Ani, capital of the Armenian Bagratuni (Bagratid) kingdom, to the Byzantines in 1045 and to the Seljuks in 1064, prompted a new flow of migration toward Trebizond and the Black Sea. The Christian Hamshentsis of Russia, for instance, claim to be the descendants of Ani, having crossed the sea in search of safe haven. In fact, there is little information on the medieval period except in some rare manuscripts, mostly in colophons. The borders of the Hamshen principality may have reached as far as Sper, one of the bastions of the Bagratunis. In the ninth and tenth centuries, the influence of the Bagratunis was predominant through the interaction of military and matrimonial alliances, though not without contests between the Armenian and Georgian branches of the dynasty. It is likely that the construction of Ardashen on the coast was linked to these princely rivalries. In the thirteenth century, after the sack of Constantinople by the Fourth Crusade, two fleeing Comneni princes founded the Empire of Trebizond, which encompassed Greek, Georgian, and Armenian lands. The principality of Hamshen in the theme of Chaldia apparently became a vassal of Trebizond but preserved a semi-independent existence in its mountainous stronghold.

After the decline of the Empire of Trebizond, Hamshen passed successively under the suzerainty of the emir of Baiburt, then the fearsome Jelalis, and finally, in the 1360s, to Leng Timur (Tamerlane). De Clavijo, who passed through the region at the beginning of the fifteenth century on his return from Samarkand, mentions the replacement of the Armenian prince Arakel by a Muslim governor and then the restoration of Arakel, possibly as the result of strong popular discontent. The relative autonomy that is evident in this episode is based on the district's strategic role as guardian of the transit routes granted to local princes, who occasionally even refused to pay tribute to their overlords.

Like Armenia and Iran, the Hamshen district passed under the control of the Turkmen Kara-Koyunlu (Black Sheep) confederation at the beginning of the fifteenth century until the successors of Prince Arakel, the barons Davit and Vard, assumed power in 1420-22. They were able to rule semi-independently while maintaining good relations with the Kara-Koyunlu. Following the Ottoman conquest of Constantinople (1453) and of Trebizond (1461), continued Turkish expansion put an end to the principality in around 1489, after as many as eight centuries of existence. Set in an area disputed between the Ottomans and the Persians, the Hamshen would not pass finally under Ottoman control until the middle of the seventeenth century. Some lords or their children who had not died in combat or fled converted to Islam and continued to rule their local domains.

Except for Hakovb, a priest from Karin/Erzerum who describes the region bordering on the Pontus and chronicles events from 1622 to 1662,[27] there are no other Armenian sources on the situation until the beginning of the nineteenth century when the Mekhitarist Father Ghukas Inchichian (1806) and Father Minas Bzhshkian (1819) wrote on the events of the seventeenth and eighteenth centuries—particularly the conversion to Islam—on the basis of locally-gathered oral accounts. Much of this information found its way into subsequent Armenian and Western sources.

The Conversion

The narratives, all more or less similar, place the first conversions to Islam toward the middle of the seventeenth century, starting first among Chalcedonian Armenians affiliated with the Georgian Orthodox Church. This may be an interesting index of the lesser resistance by a group that no longer belonged to the national Armenian Apostolic Church and adhered to another Christian faith.[28] These Armenians of

---

[27] Hakovb Karnetsi, "Erzeroum."

[28] It would be interesting to check whether conversion zones are the same as those

the Orthodox rite seem to have followed the example of their Georgian Meskh neighbors who, in order to escape heavy taxation, converted to Islam in about 1635. In the Armenian case, a census ordered by Jafar Mullah of Erzerum in 1642-43 set a new pattern of taxation and increased pressure on the Armenians of Tortum and elsewhere, becoming a significant factor in their opting for collective conversion.[29] This process increased in the late-seventeenth century and early-eighteenth century, reaching a climax in 1708-10 but still continuing until the 1780s.

In the Armenian accounts, Islamization is described as forced conversion through terrorization in which recent Laz and Greek converts actively participated. The fanaticism of the Greek-speaking mullahs of Of is especially underscored. It is interesting to note that in the period when Of was Christian, the Chalcedonian Orthodox clergy of the town were already notorious for their vigorous proselytism of non-Chalcedonian Armenians. There was also the auxiliary role of Laz brigands of Surmene and then of the Janissaries of Trebizond who accused the Armenians of apostasy and rebellion. The fate of the largest village, Torosli, noted by Sargis Haykuni, appears to be characteristic. A mullah from Surmene named Ghuruf oghlu Mehmed with a few disciples succeeded in winning several converts after years of preaching, but he was expelled by the Hamshentsis after proposing an official registration of the conversions. He returned with a fanatic mob and Janissaries, accusing the inhabitants of apostasy. Torosli was taken by surprise and attacked on the Saturday before Easter while the entire population was at church. The priest Karapet was beaten to death, together with many of his parishioners. Survivors who were unable to flee to the forests toward Baiburt or Trebizond were forced to convert on Easter Sunday. Haykuni comments bitterly on the story spread by the mullahs of Of, according to which the Armenians had been converted by a miracle, an apparition of Mohammed which unleashed a torrent of blood.[30] The example of Torosli soon spread to other parts of the Karadere valley.

---

of sectarian movements such as those of the Paulicians or the Tondrakians, who fled to areas not too distant from Hamshen to escape persecutions by the Byzantine and Armenian churches.

[29] Hakovb Karnetsi, "Erzeroum," p. 177.

[30] Sargis Haykuni, "Korats ev moratsvats hayer," p. 243.

Islam as a Safety Belt in a Time of Trouble

In contrast with Anatolia where Islamization had begun much earlier, the region of Trebizond was still overwhelmingly Christian at the time of the Ottoman conquest.[31] This picture had already changed by the end of the sixteenth century, as from 1520 to 1585 the proportion of Muslims reportedly rose from 15 to 54 percent.[32] Islamization seems to have begun among the Laz of the coastal areas around 1580. It continued with the Pontic Greeks before extending into the mountain valleys. During the first half of the seventeenth century, however, the Ottoman Empire began to crack as evidenced in the decline of state institutions, the first execution of a sultan in 1622, the power plays by the mothers of sultans and the grand viziers, the intensification of court intrigue, the system of clientelism, the spread of corruption, the military decline with ruinous wars which in turn increased fiscal pressure, and the deterioration of the Janissary system paralleled by the defeat before Vienna (1683) and the first retreat marked by the peace of Karlowicz (1699).

Simultaneously, starting with the first capture of Azov by the Russians (1696), the subsequent expansion of the "Great Neighbor of the North" toward the Black Sea, the Caucasus, and the Caspian Sea appears to have been inevitable. The Pontic coast and its back country became once more strategic zones as they were at the time of the Ottoman and Persian conflicts, but this time facing a Christian power. The systematic Islamization of the region may be seen, therefore, in practical and imperial terms as a means of bolstering both the damaged prestige of the state and the security of the frontier, through the creation of a human safety belt similar to the Russian practice with the Cossacks. External conquest would be replaced by internal conquest. Among political considerations, the local ambitions of the Janissaries of Trebizond, eager to show their power, may have played a role. Ancient national rivalries also contributed as there was an important proselytizing role of recent Greek and Laz converts. The restoration of religious orthodoxy in Islam toward the end of the seventeenth century and the growing role of the clergy must be studied further, but the

---

[31] V.L. Menage, "The Islamization of Anatolia," in Levtzion, *Conversion to Islam*, pp. 52-67. The author gives estimates by O.L. Barkan for the years 1520-25 of 1,094 Muslim families and 12,632 Christian families.

[32] Cf. Cem Behar, *Osmanli Imparatorlugu'nun ve Türkiye'nin nüfüsu, 1500-1927* [The Population of the Ottoman Empire and Turkey, 1500-1927] (Ankara: T.C. Başbakanlik Devlet Istatistik Enstitüsü, 1996).

purely religious factor was probably secondary, since the Islamization of the Hamshen seems to have been superficial.

Armenian Marranos?

In Armenian sources, Islamization is indicated either by the simple *kronapokhutiun* (religious conversion) or more often by *tajkatsum* (Turkification), "Tajik" being used in the current sense for "Turk" derived from the Turkmen of Central Asia who came by way of Iran.[33] Thus, to convert to Islam meant to become a Turk, entailing a sense of allegiance and assimilation to the dominant element. In the case of Hamshen, however, converts preserved traces of their earlier religious identity which coincided with the national one. All accounts of nineteenth-century travelers, especially Armenian travelers, stress the crypto-Christianity of the population, which professed Islam only outwardly. In fact, they were called *kes-kes* ("half-half"), a nickname also used derisively by their Laz neighbors.

This phenomenon is most visible among the women, both because they are the main vectors of transmission of moral and religious values and because being isolated from public life and going rarely out of their village, their Christian practices carry fewer consequences than in the case of men. According to early-nineteenth-century Armenian travelers, village women called themselves Armenian as though this were self-evident. They gave as proof the fact that they went to former churches three times a week, lit candles and made offerings, observed the religious holidays and injunctions against sewing and housework on Saturday evenings, made the sign of the Cross on the dough before cutting it, and went on pilgrimages to nearby monasteries and performed the *madagh* (ritual animal sacrifice), actually a vestige from pagan times. Finally, they placed the Bible at the head of the bed of the sick and used *miuron* (holy oil) for the unction of the newborn. Even at the end of the nineteenth century, travelers reported the search by the women for miuron for the baptism of babies and blessed soil to pour over the dead at the funerals. They also noted clandestine visits of priests such as Father Karapet, the son of the priest of the same name

---

[33] In Persian, *Tajik* is a term used for Arabs, but subsequently used by Armenian authors for all Muslims and eventually Turks. See, for example, *The Epic Histories Attributed to P'awstos Buzand (Buzandaran Patmut'iwnk')*, trans. and comm. Nina G. Garsoïan (Cambridge, MA: Harvard University Press, 1989).

killed at Torosli, who took an oath to return to his village every year until the extinction of his line, an oath that would be honored until 1820, then renewed around 1840 by another family of priests. In his unpublished memoirs, an Armenian priest of the end of the nineteenth century also mentions that several local mullahs were great-grandsons of priests and had kept the ecclesiastical vestments of their Christian predecessors. Still-standing churches and the perpetuation of pilgrimages to ancient monasteries and the commemoration of religious feasts, particularly those of Transfiguration and Assumption, a practice still attested among the Hemshinli of Turkey, are all noted as indices of crypto-Christianity.

Other elements that indicate a sense of national identity included the maintenance of patronymics often with double names (for example, Ali-Sarkis, Karapet-oglu, Mahmo-Hovannes), a powerful if not exclusive endogamy, and the persistence beyond conversion of prejudices against rival groups through insults such as "sandal-eating Greeks," "crappy Armenians," and "converted Mingrels." Armenians sometimes referred to the Hamshentsis derogatorily as *Hay-Laz* (Armenian Laz). Father Dashian observed:

> To my often repeated question at Tortum or elsewhere to know who they really were, they always answered by the stereotyped formula of the Islamized: "We are Islam." But these Islam knew that they were various races of Islam. When we asked them: Are you Turks, Laz, or others, they answered categorically no, adding that they were neither Turks, nor Laz, nor Gurji [Georgians], nor Kurds, nor Cherkess, in other words, neither one nation nor one race specific to the country. But neither can they say, "We are Armenians," because Armenians and Christians have become synonyms. The same is true in many other places. "Our forefathers have found the true religion [Islam], and that is enough for us." Such is their final answer. On the other hand, they often boasted that their ancestors had built the magnificent churches, both those still standing and transformed into mosques and those in ruins. It goes without saying that here the Armenian Muslim woman has preserved better her dialect and Christian ways.[34]

Use of the Armenian language, openly by the women, more cautiously by the men, a practice attested until the present in Turkey, is taken by

---

[34] Dashian, *La population arménienne*, pp. 80-81.

Armenian observers as solid evidence of the true identity of the Hamshentsis.

From the Completion of Islamization
to Ethnic Cleansing

Nineteenth-century authors mention a second wave of Islamization between 1840 and 1844. This time, attacks against the Armenian language (as well as Georgian and Greek), banned as "the language of infidels" carrying heavy fines, were added to the forcible conversion. This prohibition was coupled with the implementation of Islamic education and establishment of religious schools or *medreses,* which increased in the reign of Sultan Abdul Hamid II. Once more, the greater resistance of women was noted. They are said to have chased the mullahs out of the villages on many occasions. Since they had less contact with the outside world, the women often spoke only Armenian. Haykuni reported that in the 1860s, some of them secretly placed their child in the Christian families in the cities, telling their husband that the child had drowned or been eaten by wolves. By contrast, for men the seasonal exit from villages for work and conscription for military service led to more rapid assimilation.

From a political point of view, there is a context of international tensions and military and institutional crisis in the nineteenth century: Greek independence; trouble with Mehmed Ali of Egypt; wars with Russia; European pressure in favor of Christian minorities; creation of a Catholic millet under French patronage, and so on. The *Tanzimat* reforms beginning in 1839 all appear as being coerced by external powers or as efforts to neutralize European pretexts for interference. To nineteenth-century territorial losses were added religious losses through the growing conversion of Oriental Christians to Catholicism or Protestantism, implying a diminution of Ottoman control and authority.

In this period and especially after the Treaty of Paris (1856) ending the Crimean War and the accompanying *Hatt-i Humayun* reform edict, there was a significant increase in apostasy back to Christianity among Greek converts to Islam. Thus, 2,000 to 3,000 Pontic Greek-speaking Muslims were able to reclaim their Christian faith and, with the encouragement of the Athens government, resettled in Greece. Without external support, however, the Armenian converts who sought to follow this example did not succeed. Many were forced to emigrate for fear of retaliation. They fled to the coastal regions of the Black Sea, either westward to Trebizond, Samson, and Sinope, which were more protected from arbitrary action, or eastward and northward to the Caucasus and the Crimea—from Batum to Sukhum, Gadauta, Novyi-Afion, Sochi, and as far as Ekaterinodar (Krasnodar) and other towns in the Kuban. The pressure on those who remained only increased, especially after the completion of the Russian conquest of the Caucasus (surrender of Shamil, 1859, and of Abkhazia, 1864), when countless thousands of Mountaineers from the North Caucasus fled to the Ottoman Empire. Exchanges of populations between the Caucasus, the Balkans, and Anatolia would take place once again during and immediately after the Russo-Turkish war of 1877-78.

The pan-Islamism of the Hamidian period, during which an attempt was made to use Islam as the ultimate mortar to hold the empire together, unleashed a new wave of forced conversion. Selim Deringil has studied the organization of Muslim missions on the model of and against the increasingly active Protestant missions.[35] The Armenian massacres of 1895-96, a bloody response (with up to 200,000 victims) to Armenian and European demands for reforms, were also accompanied by Islamization. In this period, there was important emigration not only of the Christian Hamshentsis but also of the Muslim Hemshinli who took refuge along the Caucasian coastline from Batum to Sukhum. This combined group was made up of 15,000 to 20,000 persons, according to the research published in the Armenian ethnographic journal *Azgagrakan handes* in Tiflis.[36] The author, who does not mention the religion of the Hamshetsis as though it went without saying that they were Christians or had reconverted to Christianity, nevertheless noted their particularism based on place of origin and their distinct social and religious practices. The Hamshentsis who remained in Turkey also served as migratory seasonal agricultural workers, thus main-

---

[35] Selim Deringil, "L'Empire contre-attaque: les missionnaires ottomans à la fin du XIXe siècle," oral communication at François Georgeon seminar, Paris, EHESS, January 1995. See also his *The Well-Protected Domains: Ideology and the Legitimation of Power in the Ottoman Empire, 1876-1909* (London and New York: I.B. Tauris, 1998).

[36] Hakob Muratiants, "Hamsheni hayere," *Azgagrakan handes* [Ethnographical Review], vol. 4 (1898): 17-143, vol. 5 (1899): 361-406, vol. 6 (1900): 109-58. For a study of this journal, see Claire Mouradian, "La revue ethnographique arménienne *Azgagrakan Handès* (1895-1916)," *Cahiers du Monde russe et soviétique* 31:2/3 (1990): 295-314.

taining links with their compatriots who had crossed into the Russian Empire.

It is difficult to estimate the actual size of the Hamshen population because of insufficient census data and conflicting Armenian and Turkish sources. Aside from the numerical aspect, there were also the shifting of state and administrative boundaries and problems of identifying the various groups. Thus in the case of the Laz, for example, the ethnonym can designate either a precise ethnic group or the whole population of much of the Pontic coastline. Hamshentsi and Pontic Armenians are sometimes used synonymously in nineteenth-century sources. An Armenian researcher in Sochi (himself a native of Hamshen) who compared several Armenian, Russian, and Turkish statistics, gave the number of Pontic Armenians in the Ottoman Empire in 1914 as 160,00, of whom 81,000 were Hamshentsis, half of these being Muslim. Large numbers of Hamshetsis had already emigrated to Russian territory after the 1895 massacres.[37]

Communal life in the vilayet of Trebizond seems to have been fairly active despite the relatively small number of Armenians. The Armenian element undoubtedly benefited from the presence of the large Greek population and of a number of Catholic institutions. According to a monograph on the Armenians of Pontus, there were 155 schools and 145 churches, monasteries, and chapels in the region on the eve of World War I, not counting Catholic establishments. Some fifteen newspapers or bulletins likewise bore witness to the revival of political life during the euphoric period following the Young Turk revolution in 1908. There were attempts to return to Christianity at this time, as, for example, Ali Bey (an orphan of 1895) who reclaimed his Christian name of Harutiun but who soon was compelled to flee to Russia.[38]

In 1915, the region shared in the common Armenian agony of death marches, massacres, and drownings. Monsignor Hovhannes Nazlian (Jean Naslian), the Armenian Catholic bishop of Trebizond, has shown that the Catholics and Protestants were not spared any more than the Apostolic Armenians. Even though conversion to Islam, which was sometimes offered to women and children as an alternative to death, did not always guarantee protection, the period nonetheless witnessed one of the largest surges of conversion. The fate of the long-converted Hemshenli population was apparently better, albeit there is little pre-

---

[37] Torlakyan, "Hamshenahayeri ev pontahayeri bnakavayrere," p. 208.
[38] Hovakimian, *Patmutiun Haykakan Pontosi*, p. 168.

cise evidence concerning them. At the time of the entrance of the Russian troops into Trebizond in 1916, a number of Armenian families were still found in the region. They would vanish, however, through massacre or flight during the Kemalist "War of Independence," which was supported by the notoriously cruel Topal Osman Pasha and other Laz bandits.

For both Turkey and Russia, the chaos of World War I continued in the following years. In the Caucasus, political changes brought about short-lived independent nation states and the advances and retreats of the Red and White armies. After the Sovietization of the Caucasus region in 1920-21, Armenian Hamshentsi communal life resurfaced. In Abkhazia, Ajaria, and Krasnodar, the Hamshentsis were allowed to have newspapers, schools, theaters, and dance groups until the 1930s when they were subjected to the Stalinist terror, and then during the closing months of World War II, some Hamshentsis were deported to Central Asia. Like the Meskhs, they were not rehabilitated until 1968. Several historical studies and collections of poetry relating to the Hamshetsis date from this period of the "Thaw."[39] At the time of the *perestroika* under Gorbachev in the 1980s, there was an active press campaign in Erevan, Krasnodar, and Moscow to revive the Hamshentsi community through educational and cultural activities and compatriotic societies supported by the Soviet Armenian government and these endeavors have continued in the post-Soviet period.

The Hemshinli of Turkey: An Ethnic Group?

The Hemshinli or Hemşinli continue to define themselves today according to the name of their district. Since the 1950s, those who have migrated to cities have created compatriotic associations for mutual help or for the promotion of tourism and cultural development of their native villages. The characterization of these people as an ethnic group is occasionally accepted by some Turkish authors. All of this is carefully hidden, however, by the members of the group because of the risks involved, as can be seen by the difficulty of approach by Ben-

---

[39] See several volumes of poetry, *Hamshena Dzayn* [Voice of Hamshen] edited in Krasnodar or Erevan in 1971, 1979, 1989, and folklore in 1981 and 1986. As a first, an international conference on the Hamshen Armenians was organized in Adler/Sochi, October 13-15, 2005.

ninghaus and others during their fieldwork.[40] In fact, Benninghaus was questioned by the security services after his conversation with a Hemshinli informant at Ankara.

Benninghaus divides the Hemshinli population in Turkey into two groups, in addition to migrants scattered in large metropolitan areas such as Ankara, Istanbul, Izmir, and Izmit: 1) In the west, in the province of Rize around Camlihemşin (Jamlihemshin), an estimated 15,000 to 29,000 persons in 1975; 2) In the east, in the district of Hopa near Artvin, around 25,000 persons. Those in the west speak a Turkish dialect, while those in the east use an Armenian dialect, Hemşince (Hemshinje) or Homshetsma, with a mixture of Turkish and Laz vocabulary. Members of the eastern group identify themselves by the Armenian ethnonym "Hamshetsi." or "Homshetsi." They did not indicate this dialect as a second language in the Turkish census of 1965, the only one in the Turkish republic since 1927 which collected data relating to national identity through questions about the use of a first or second non-Turkish language. Nevertheless, the use of Armenian in the 1960s was attested by Georges Dumézil. During his stay in Istanbul, the famous linguist-anthropologist collected and translated tales in this dialect from young men native to the region.[41] Yet the dialect or Armenian words used together with Turkish were not perceived (or acknowledged) as such by the speakers. It is clear that numerous, slightly distorted Armenian toponyms survive in the Hamshen country, such as Mount Kachkar or that of a monastery, the site of popular pilgrimages, Khazenavank (Khachik vank). Similarly, before the compulsory adoption of surnames in 1934, the onomasticon had preserved Armenian patronymics: Abeloghlu, Artinoghlu, Avedoghlu, Kirkoroghlu, and so forth.

Benninghaus notes a discrepancy between history, culture, memory, and perception, or at least acknowledged perception. The repression of Armenian origin seems much stronger since the resurgence of the Ar-

---

[40] Cf. Benninghaus, "Zur Herkunft und Identität der Hemşinli," p. 486. Neal Ascherson also wrote about the arrest and jailing by Turkish authorities of the German researcher Wolfang Feurstein in the 1960s because of his interest in the Laz language. See Neal Ascherson, *Black Sea*, pp. 203-04.

[41] Cf. Georges Dumézil, *Notes sur le parler d'un Arménien musulman de Hemshin* (Brussels: Académie royale, 1964); "Trois récits dans le parler des Arméniens de Hemshin," *Revue des études arméniennes*, n.s., 2 (1965): 19-35; "Notes sur le parler d'un Arménien musulman d'Ardala (vilâyet de Rize)," *Revue des études arméniennes*, n.s., 4 (1967): 135-42.

menian question and the demands for recognition of the genocide, which occasionally assumed a violent form during the decade of 1975-85. Benninghaus reported that his informants were offended that the Hemshin could be considered to be Armenians, since their Hemshinli "compatriots" had the reputation of being very peaceful while "the Armenians are terrorists and fanatic Christians, who would never have given up their faith."

As in the preceding century, the Hemshinli have entrenched themselves behind a Muslim or regional identity. Kirzioğlu's theories of Turkic origins have gained wide acceptance. The Hemshinli identity is also defined by their dispersion and homesickness (also found among the Armenians of the Diaspora). The sense of belonging to the group is maintained by the return to the village in summer and through various compatriotic associations. The first of these associations was founded in 1949 in Ankara by a group of Western Hemshinli, that is to say, by Turkish speakers who were more urbanized and educated. This is only a seeming paradox, since Armenian speakers probably did not feel the same need of offsetting acculturation. The activities of the two groups were likewise different. In the west, they are often found in the food trade (bakers, confectioners), restaurants, and hotels. In the east, they tend to be in trades connected with transportation (a reminder of their ancient role of guardians of the roads).

Traditional costumes inspired by the Laz dress, particular headgear, and folk music with the characteristic use of bagpipes (*tulum*) are some of the outward signs of separate identity in the east, especially in rural districts. Wooden dwellings with special shapes, particularly the roofs whose peculiarity has been noted by ethnographers, have been perpetuated by émigrés in Russia and the Caucasus. In the past, even the churches of this region were made of wood. The most interesting aspect without a doubt is the celebration of Christian feasts such as Vardavar (Transfiguration), identified by its Armenian name and the occasion for annual gatherings in the latter part of July. This is one of the most popular holidays with a national character, prominent in the Armenian liturgical calendar. After the Christianization of the country, this pagan feast, in which the temple of the goddess of love Astghik was adorned with roses and other flowers (whence the erroneous folk etymology of the name *vardavar* = adorned with roses), continued to be marked by important pilgrimages and festivities, in which the participants tossed water on each other. This is probably the feast most easily redefined as "folkloric" while at the same time bearing witness to the attachment to Armenian traditions.

Endogamy remains strong and desirable. Marriages with neighboring Laz occasionally take place, but they are avoided when possible, citing linguistic differences or the unpleasant character of the Laz and their tendency to blood feuds. Might these be memories of ancient conflicts between "valley lords" and the oppressive role played by the Laz *begs* as in the case of Kurdish begs in other regions? The Laz especially seek to marry Hemshinli girls but do not give their own in exchange, since locally, where their respective identities are clear, the more-recently-converted Hemshinli always remain suspect of being crypto-Christians.

In their publications, the Hemshinli hold themselves to be Turks. There probably is no reason to doubt this belief, but they also consider themselves to be a group apart with strong internal cohesion. The Hemshinli regional identity appears as a substitute for ethnic identity. It may also be stronger than is observed by outsiders. Some Turkish Armenians having performed their military service in this region have related that when they met Hemshinli the latter secretly prided themselves on their Armenian origin. The repression of national identity would then be explained here more by the psychology of conversion than by the taboo of the national question and of the Armenian Genocide in present-day Turkey. Is it a strategy of disguise by a threatened and isolated minority or the superposition of several identities? Similarly, there is the question of knowing whether the Islam of the Hemshinli is a superficial adhesion to the state religion as the result of forced conversion or whether their formerly admitted crypto-Christianity corresponds as well to an attempted syncretism of two faiths and to a form of "popular Islam" found in other parts of Asia Minor. To seek answers to questions relating to ethnic and religious minorities, new paths must be opened. Archival research and field investigations as well as comparative studies in a more dispassionate political context than the prevailing one will be required.

❋ 8 ❋

THE DARK AGES ON THE BLACK SEA?
MANUSCRIPT PAINTING OF HAMSHEN

Christina Maranci

In the scholarship on Armenian manuscript painting, certain traditions are typically celebrated as cultural high points: for example, Bagratuni (Bagratid) illumination of the tenth and eleventh centuries in Greater Armenia and particularly thirteenth-and fourteenth-century manuscripts of the Armenian kingdom of Cilicia. In contrast, it is striking to consider the reception of the manuscript illumination of Hamshen, an Armenian enclave on the Black Sea coast. Few scholars mention the area, and its manuscript art has been hitherto neglected.[1] Admittedly, the area did not produce the kind of sumptuous codices for which the Bagratuni and Cilician traditions are famous; yet it was home to a lively community of scribes and artists, whose manuscripts are today housed in the Matenadaran in Erevan,[2] the British Library, the Armenian Patriarchate of Jerusalem,[3] the Mekhitarist monastery in Vienna,

---

[1] An earlier version of this paper is published in Hovann H. Simonian, ed., *The Hemshin: History, Society and Identity in the Highlands of Northeast Turkey* (London and New York: Routledge, 2007), pp. 42-51. The most up-to-date study of the topography, archaeology, and history of the area is Robert Edwards, "Hamšen: An Armenian Enclave in the Byzanto-Georgian Pontos: A Survey of Literary and Non-Literary Sources," *Le Muséon*, 101 (1988):403-42. See also his earlier studies on the fortification architecture of the Pontus: "The Fortress of Šebinkarahisar (Koloneia)," *Corso di cultura sull'arte ravennate e bizantina* 32 (1985): 23-64, and "The Garrison Forts of the Pontos: A Case for the Diffusion of the Armenian Paradigm," *Revue des études arméniennes*, n.s., 19 (1985): 181-284. For a critical review of Edwards' works on fortification architecture, see Christina Maranci, *Medieval Armenian Architecture: Constructions of Race and Nation* (Louvain: Peeters, 2001).

[2] Among the Hamshen manuscripts in the Matenadaran are Ms 7056, which was copied in 1506 by Hayrapet, "a religious man from *Hamamashen*" (Edwards, "Hamšen," p. 410), and Ms 218, dated to 1240 (Edwards, p. 408).

[3] Among these is a collection of the writings of Grigor Tatevatsi, produced at the Monastery of Koshtents, catalogued as Ms 1617. See N. Bogharyan [Norayr Poghar-

and the Philadelphia Free Library. Furthermore, the Hamshen manuscripts were produced during the sixteenth century, a period in which book production declined sharply in Greater Armenia. Hence, the codices present a challenge, if modest, to the theory of a "Dark Age" in medieval Armenian manuscript illumination.

This essay explores a sample of Hamshen manuscript illumination and attempts to locate it within the broader context of Armenian illumination, as well as to determine whether a specific Hamshen style of painting can be identified—a reasonable supposition given the geographical insularity of the region. Such endeavors are difficult, however, because of the small number of illustrated manuscripts that survive and the paucity of their imagery. Furthermore, most of the extant manuscripts are difficult to access, and even of those that are published, their illustrations typically are neither described nor reproduced. The work of Robert Edwards and a few library and exhibit catalogues constitute the sum of the literature.

Edwards has rightly noted that evidence for a rich manuscript tradition in Hamshen extends from the thirteenth century to the seventeenth century. In 1240, a certain scribe Stepanos, who was born and possibly trained in Hamshen, copied manuscripts in Rome while in residence with the Armenian community there.[4] Further testimony to scribal activity appears with a miscellany dated to the fifteenth century, of which the first part was produced in 1422 at the Koshtents monastery of Hamshen.[5] In 1499, a certain Karapet reportedly copied a book on medicine in the region of Hamshen at the village of Eghnovit. From the following century, an anthology of the poetical works of Nerses Shnorhali survives, as well as texts by other authors such as Grigor Tatevatsi.[6] Scribal activity continued into the seventeenth century and also attracted distant clerics to the district, as in 1637 when a certain Karapet Jughayetsi came to Hamshen for the purpose of copying The Book of Psalms.[7]

The variety of texts is significant. Ranging from service books to poetical and scientific works, the surviving manuscripts demonstrate

---

ian] *Mayr tsutsak dzeragrats Srbots Hakobiants* [Grand Catalogue of Manuscripts of Saint James] (Jerusalem: St. James Press, 1971), vol. 5, pp. 417-18.

[4] Edwards, "Hamšen," p. 408.

[5] Ibid., p. 409. See also note 2 above.

[6] The work of Nerses Shnorhali is preserved in the Philadelphia Ms 123, and that of Grigor Tatevatsi appears in Jerusalem Ms 1917 and Vienna Ms 119.

[7] See Edwards, "Hamšen," p. 413 and note 36. This Psalter was also illustrated.

that, despite its isolated location, Hamshen hosted an intellectual and scientific center of some significance. The excellence of its scriptoria and libraries is further attested by the visit of Karapet Jughayetsi, among others. The mobility of local scribes is also noteworthy; in addition to the work of Hamshen Armenians in Rome, a number of colophons identify scribes with the surname Hamshentsi, leading Edwards to the conclusion that "the clerics of Hamshen not only had well-established traditions by religious training and scribal production at home, but their scholars were respected abroad."[8]

Frederick Lewis Oriental Ms 123

The first manuscript to be considered is located in the Philadelphia Free Library.[9] A copy of the poetical works of Nerses Shnorhali and other writers, it was produced, according to the colophon, at the churches of Surb Astvatsatsin and Surb Sion, "in the monastery where the relics of the father St. Khatchik and St. Vardan . . . have been placed for the glory and protection of our *gawar* of Hamshen."[10] The colophon also offers other valuable details. Relating that the codex was completed June 9, 1528, the colophon gives a number of significant historical synchronisms: the production of the manuscript took place during the sultanate of Suleiman I (1520-66) and during the reign of Skandar Pasha in Trebizond (Trabzon), "when our fortresses were controlled by the Aghas, Darshevali and Siminaws."[11] The name of the illuminator is not mentioned; however, the scribes are identified as Priest Karapet, Karapet the Younger, and Vahram.

In general, the manuscript is in a good state of preservation. The 256 folios are made of vellum (rather than paper, as was also used by this time) and are fairly large.[12] Neat lines of *bolorgir* (miniscule) script are arranged in single columns on the page, and the folios, punc-

---

[8] Ibid, p. 411.

[9] This codex is published in Avedis K. Sanjian, *A Catalogue of Medieval Armenian Manuscripts in the United States* (Berkeley and Los Angeles: University of California Press, 1976), p. 675. More up-to-date commentary and bibliography appear in *Treasures in Heaven: Armenian Illuminated Manuscripts*, ed. Thomas F. Mathews and Roger S. Wieck (New York: Pierpont Morgan Library, 1994), pp. 198-99 (cat. no. 72).

[10] Edwards, "Hamšen," p. 412.

[11] Ibid, p. 413.

[12] The folios are 14.7 by 10.7 centimeters (5.8 x 4.2 inches).

tured with V-shaped notches at the spine, are fastened to the binding with knotted cord, and the top of the spine features a raised end-band of multicolored silk thread (Fig. 1). The text block is bound with traditional Armenian leather covers, which appear to be original.[13] The design of the binding is particularly striking: decorated with blind tooling of guilloche and interlace patterns, the front and back covers feature two varieties of interlaced rectangle designs (Figs. 2 and 3). The characteristic fore-edge flap is also blind-tooled with an interlaced rectangle, framed by a border of punches, florets, and a concentric almond-shaped stamp (Fig. 4). Sylvie Merian has pointed out that there is evidence for the traditional leather strap fastenings.[14]

The ornamentation, which occurs at intervals throughout the text, is also typical of Armenian manuscript illumination, featuring decorated incipit letters, marginal arabesques, and headpieces. Light blues and pinks predominate, but their lack of intensity is most likely the product of fading. The artist has also made use of the neutral color of the background vellum in building the design; the arabesque on folio 61 (Fig. 5), for example, is defined through narrow outlines, rather than positive forms. The result is not a carpet of decoration, but rather, delicate, interlocking bands woven through empty spaces.

The headpieces that crown the text most often feature stylized plant forms, or palmettes. On folio 107, such forms are framed by half palmettes. At the base of the motif, the stem bifurcates and weaves together into an intricate band, which divides and frames the vegetal forms in box-shaped frames. The background color is blue, while the palmettes themselves are accented with rose at the base of their leaves. The decorated incipit letters (starting the page), like the headpiece, are also typical of medieval Armenian painting. In the *nomina sacra* of Christ, each letter is divided into zones which alternate between rose and blue, and bear a foliate motif at their terminations. The marginal ornament at the right of the text is also of the characteristic arabesque type, in which pointed floral forms undulate gracefully in and out of knots, creating a series of loops that end in pointed leaves.[15]

Another kind of headpiece design appears on folio 61r (Fig. 5). Again rectangular, the outline is filled with a succession of stylized

---

[13] The boards are arranged, as is usual for Armenian manuscripts, with the woodgrain running horizontally, rather than vertically as in other cultures. For further discussion, see Mathews and Wieck, *Treasures in Heaven*, pp. 130-34.

[14] Mathews and Wieck, *Treasures in Heaven*, p. 199.

[15] The marginal ornament is almost identical to that of folio 7.

acanthus leaves, oriented alternately up and down, and the spaces between them are filled with softly curving leaves. On this page, the
decorated initial is figural, consisting of a bird-like creature with a
long, thin, knotted neck and a protruding tongue. More striking decorations in the same vein occur on folio 107v (Fig. 6), where the capital-
ized letter Պ (P) has been conceived as a pair of birds, ornamented with
multicolored horizontal strips. One longer, larger bird, again with a
knotted neck creates the curved portion of the letter, while a smaller,
standing bird forms the central upright and appears to be piercing the
stomach of its partner. Next to the letter is an unusual flourish in the
margin. Unlike the standard arabesque ornamentation, this form resembles a bow and arrow, which gradually narrows into an elegant line
with spiral terminations. The central leaves are also adorned with small
circular forms, possibly a reference to berries. Both the letter and the
marginal ornament of this folio employ an unusual color scheme; the
forms are painted in deep navy blue and a light green, rather than rose
and light blue. Despite this discrepancy, the motifs display the same
interest in linear design and multicolored patterns evident in the other
ornaments of the manuscript.

Vienna, Mekhitarist Monastery Ms 119

Two additional illustrated manuscripts from Hamshen are located in
the Mekhitarist Library in Vienna,[16] of which the first to be discussed
is a collection of the writings of Grigor Tatevatsi. The manuscript is
large, measuring 18 by 13 centimeters on its exterior, and is written in
bolorgir of medium size.[17] The binding consists of wooden boards
covered with ornamented leather,[18] and the present state of the manuscript is poor.[19] The colophon, which lacks information regarding the
date, location, and scribes of the manuscript, remembers "the brave

---

[16] The two manuscripts from Hamshen to be discussed below are housed in the
Vienna Mekhitarist monastery, catalogued as Ms 119 and Ms 431, and published in
Hakob Tashian [Hakovbos/Jacobus Dashian], *Tsutsak hayeren dzeragrats/Catalog
der Armenischen Handschriften* (Vienna: Mekhitarist Press, 1891), pp. 400-02 and
882-83, respectively.

[17] The manuscript contains 163 folios.

[18] Unfortunately, this author was not able to view the Vienna manuscripts and
hence is unable to comment on issues of codicological construction.

[19] Almost every page, according to Tashian, shows signs of wear, age, and restoration.

hretor [orator] of Hamshen, and also excellent *vartabed*' who was knowledgeable and always prepared to answer scriptural or theological questions.[20] Although no date is provided, the codex most likely dates between the fifteenth and sixteenth centuries.

While full-page images are absent, as with the previous example, most of the chapter headings feature headpieces, and many pages bear marginal ornaments. Folios 14v-15 (Fig. 7) provide a representative example of the page layout of text and image. The typical arabesque-style ornament is somewhat smaller here than in the Philadelphia manuscript. The marginalia of the Vienna manuscript, however, is striking for its variety; on folio 15 is the first and most standard arabesque type, with pointed leaf terminations; however, a number of interesting variations occur, as on folio 39, where a bird appears in the margin, standing on a decorative leaf and biting a tendril (Fig. 8), and on folio 45, in which the artist has broadened the base of the arabesque form, creating a triangular effect highlighted with a wash of light blue (Fig. 9).

The most elaborate decoration of the manuscript occurs on folio 5 (Fig. 10). The page is dominated by a detailed arched headpiece, which features a series of vine-scroll rinceaux of rose and white, backed in light blue. The profile of the interior "arch" of the headpiece is particularly notable, bearing a complex profile of lobes and, near to the base, pointed horizontal cutouts. Such elaboration on the arched design of the headpiece can be found beginning in the thirteenth century onward in both Cilicia and Greater Armenia, and has been connected, as Priscilla Soucek has discussed, to Islamic and Mongol art.[21] In the fifteenth-century manuscript of Boladzor, also in Vienna and dated 1484,[22] there is the same interest in elaborating on the headpiece with the creation of pointed segments.[23]

---

[20] See Edwards, "Hamšen," p. 411; Tashian, *Tsutsak hayeren dzeragrats,* p. 402.

[21] See Priscilla Soucek, "Armenian and Islamic Manuscript Painting: A Visual Dialogue," *Treasures in Heaven: Armenian Art, Religion, and Society,* ed. Thomas F. Mathews and Roger S. Wieck (New York: Pierpont Morgan Library, 1998). Soucek notes the profiled niche head in the Cilician Gospel of Marshal Oshin, dated to 1274, and connects it to Islamic tomb portals and ceramics. Her argument is interesting in the context considered here, although one cannot rule out that such lobed forms could have also reached Cilicia from the West. The predominance of the pointed trefoil in both Cilician painting and in the Gothic style raises this question.

[22] Ms 403.

[23] See Heidi and Helmut Buschhausen, *Die illuminierten armenischen Handschriften der Mechitaristen-Congregation in Wien* (Vienna: Mekhitarist Press, 1976),

Vienna, Mekhitarist Monastery Ms 431

Another manuscript from Hamshen contains a collection of apotropaic (warding off of evil) prayers, some of them authored by Cyprian, the fifth-century bishop of Carthage. The colophon, which refers to the codex as a medical prayer book, states that the text was written in 1517, "under the sign of the ram, May 12, from a good and worthy copy, by the hands of the worthless Hovannes Malghi, in the land of Hamshen at the monastery of Surb Khatchik, the spiritual overseer of the monasteries of Surb Astvatsatsin and Surb Vartanants, at the behest of the deacon Stepanos, for the enjoyment of him, and in memory of himself and his parents Davit and Eghisabet." Now in poor condition, the manuscript is quite small, measuring only 9 by 6.5 centimeters (3.55 x 2.55 inches) in its exterior proportions. With its diminutive size, the manuscript would have been particularly appropriate for the frequent travels of the professional of Hamshen, and it is particularly tempting to imagine that it accompanied a local cleric on house visits. Several of the folios contain marginal ornaments and headpieces of the standard type. The chapter heading on folio 67 (Fig. 11) features three standing palmettes which bear a resemblance to the headpiece of the Philadelphia manuscript (Fig. 6). Most interesting, however, is a motif occurring on folio 82, featuring a long-necked bird which forms the Armenian letter Հ (Ho) (Fig. 12). Its lower body faces to the left, while its long neck twists to the right, forming the upper diagonal of the letter.

British Library Ms Or. 6555

Another manuscript connected to the region of Hamshen presents more striking marginalia, in this case involving figural scenes.[24] A menologium (collection of lives of the saints arranged according to the calendar), the codex, housed today in the British Library, measures externally 15 by 10.5 inches (38 by 26.7 centimeters). The colophon relates that it was completed in 1488, at the request of the "divinely honored and gentle Nerses the priest . . . in memory of himself and his parents, and his wife Eranuhi, and of his issue by her, Step'anos the priest."[25]

---

plate 65, Fig. 188. An abridged English translation was published in 1977.

[24] Frederick C. Conybeare, *A Catalogue of the Armenian Manuscripts in the British Museum* (London: Longman's, 1913), pp. 165-67.

[25] Ibid., p. 166.

The colophon also indicates those involved with preparation of the manuscript. A certain Nerses Malaz smoothed the vellum[26] and helped in copying of the text, but the majority of writing was undertaken by the "sin-stained and unintelligent" monk Movses. An illustrator is not mentioned, and presumably in this case, as with other manuscripts with less ambitious pictorial cycles, the scribe also painted the images.

Movses is of the district of Hamshen, and the manuscript was produced in "the canton of Khakhtik', which is now called Babert', in the monastery called Bertak."[27] A town in the vicinity of Erzerum, Baberd (Baiburt) lies outside the district of Hamshen, but the two areas seemed to have enjoyed frequent relations, particularly in the domain of book production.[28] It is unfortunate that the place of Movses' training was not mentioned in the colophon. However, considering the apparently high reputation of the scriptoria of Hamshen in the late medieval era, it is quite likely that he received his scribal training in the area of his birthplace.

The manuscript's margins are copiously illustrated with vegetal and figural ornament. Appearing either singly or in groups, the figures possess regular proportions, if sometimes rather elongated limbs. Often bearded, the faces are represented in outline, and the eyes are particularly notable, for at their outer corner the bottom and top lids join in a single line extending outward. This feature is commonly found in fifteenth-century manuscript painting in Greater Armenia, occurring both in Vaspurakan and in the north, as in a manuscript produced in Erznka (Erzinjan) in 1449, now located in the library of Princeton University.[29] The main color scheme consists of red, orange, and several tones of blue, including silver blue, light blue, and navy.

The marginalia often consist of narrative scenes, and a few representative examples have been chosen here for description. The first

---

[26] This was presumably done with a pumice stone. See Syvlie L Merian and Mary V. Orna, "The Making of an Armenian Manuscript," in Mathews and Wieck, *Treasures in Heaven* (1994), pp. 125-26.

[27] Conybeare, *Catalogue*, p. 166. The colophon also mentions a certain Melik, the steward, and his daughter Emin, "who took great pains to minister to us while we were writing this book."

[28] For example, Edwards relates that in 1637, a certain Ter Hakob Hamshentsi purchased a manuscript from Baberd and probably brought it with him to Hamshen. See Edwards, "Hamšen," p. 413, and "Šebinkarahisar," p. 39.

[29] Garret Ms 18. For a representative illustration, see folio 15v, the dedication page of the manuscript, reproduced in Mathews and Wieck, *Treasures in Heaven* (1994), plate 28.

figural scenes occur on folio 41v (Fig. 13), in which is seen the standing figure of Gregory the Illuminator (Grigor Lusavorich). The bearded saint glances and gestures to the text at right and wears a pointed hood. He is dressed in a voluminous episcopal robe of red, hemmed in blue and decorated with blue crosses at the breast. Certain features of the costume deserve special note: instead of the usual open, skirted toga typical of earlier medieval images of saints, Gregory wears red trousers, and traditional sandals are replaced with pointed boots. Similar iconography can be found in contemporary Armenian manuscript illumination of the Lake Van area and suggests contact—if only indirect—with Islamic and Mongol visual culture. The same style of costume, with trousers and pointed boots, appears, for example, in the Gospels of Khachatur Khizantsi of 1455.[30]

The treatment of the drapery allows only a vague sense of the body underneath. Gregory's right elbow can be discerned among the folds at left, and the artist has carefully observed the gatherings of drapery at his wrist, from where the cloth cascades down in a series of rhythmic curves. These curves, as well as the drapery on his left side, completely obscure the figure down to the lower legs. The abstraction of drapery into linear patterns is also evident in the presence of diagonal strokes at the hem of the cloak and trousers.

On folio 195v (Fig. 14), another protagonist of the conversion story appears: the pagan king Trdat (Tiridates) III. It is particularly interesting to note how a fifteenth-century Armenian envisioned the fourth-century ruler. Large-headed and stocky in figure, Trdat wears a nimbus and crown, the familiar pointed boots, and an elaborate cloak which falls in complex folds over his left arm. He holds a cross in his left hand, on which he also wears a large ring, and in the right hand he carries a long staff, whose top takes the form of the head of a bridled donkey or horse. Unlike Gregory, Trdat appears with a mustache and curled shoulder-length hair.

One of the most interesting scenes occurs on folio 231r (Fig. 15) depicting the vision of Gregory. According to the *History of the Armenians* by Agathangelos, the pagan Trdat cast Gregory into a deep pit, where he experienced a heavenly vision.[31] Located at the bottom of the

---

[30] Examples may be found in the scene of the Raising of Lazarus or the Marriage at Cana. Illustrations of these images are reproduced in Sirarpie Der Nersessian, *Armenian Manuscripts in the Walters Art Gallery* (Baltimore: Walters Art Gallery, 1973).

[31] Robert W. Thomson, trans. and comm., *Agathangelos: History of the Armeni-*

page, the composition features Gregory, seated in three-quarter's position on a curvilinear, amorphous form which is undoubtedly meant to
represent his rocky prison. With closed eyes and hunched shoulders,
Gregory leans forward, head in hand, lost in his dream. An angel, depicted only in half-length, descends towards him holding a scroll. His
wings are particularly striking, decorated with pink tips and horizontal
blue lines. Gregory's form is also noteworthy. Although shown in
three-quarters view, he is depicted with only one arm and leg (and it is
the left leg, rather than the right, that is shown). This indifference to
anatomy is, once again, a typical feature of late medieval Armenian
manuscript illumination, as in the Khizan Gospels of 1455 and the
Vaspurakan Gospels of 1457.[32] No shading models the figures, who are
articulated principally through line. As in the earlier figure of Trdat, the
artist reveals here a greater interest in patterns of drapery than in the
figure itself.

Gregory reappears on folio 242v (Fig. 16), here in conversation
with an angel. Although again in clerical costume, Gregory is now
barefoot. The most drastic change involves his proportions, however,
which have become extremely elongated; the saint occupies more than
half of the length of text column. The artist, however, has not chosen to
lengthen Gregory's arms, and thus his elbows reach only to chest level.
His visible hand again reveals a lack of interest in anatomy: not only is
it unnaturally large with attenuated fingers, it also appears to be a left
hand, although attached to his right arm.[33] Gregory gestures to the angel depicted at right, who appears only in bust form[34] and is actually

---

ans (Albany: New York: State University of New York Press, 1976).

[32] See, for example, the figure of Christ in the Baptism scene of a Van Gospels,
now in the Manoogian Museum in Southfield, Michigan, reproduced in Mathews and
Wieck, *Treasures in Heaven* (1994), plate 27.

[33] One must wonder here whether it is fair to impose such preconceptions on the
images. Speaking broadly, the representation of correct and lifelike proportions was
of course not often the main goal of medieval art. Yet, there is a difference between
the abstraction of the human figure, so common to the tradition, and what appears to
be very pronounced anatomical distortions. Along with the reversed hands of Gregory, one may also note the figures of John and Prochoros in the Gospels of 1211
(Matenadaran Ms 4823) by Princess Vaneni, in which one witnesses not only a "na-
ïve" canon of the figure, but also what seems to be a very deliberate alteration to it,
namely, the placement of both ears on the right side of the figures' heads! As with the
manuscript of 1211, it would be difficult to attribute Gregory's reversed hands simply
to the lack of training, and hence one wonders whether such changes held some special significance.

[34] The image is smudged in this area.

positioned within the column of text next to the uncial letter of the new chapter. The placement of the images is noteworthy, as it calls attention to the relationship between the margins and the text.

Folio 441 (Fig. 17) presents a different kind of marginal image. It illustrates a reading for the fifteenth of March, featuring a scene of the prophet Daniel, Anania, Misayel, and Azarya (of which the latter three were renamed as the famous Shadrach, Mishach, and Abednego).[35] The four young men kneel within a lobed frame, wearing draperies of red and blue. While the two central figures are obscured for the most part, the flanking figures are in full view. They wear tunics, and the excess drapery has been drawn up to expose the lower legs. This is particularly evident in the leftmost figure, who sits with his right leg folded beneath him and his left leg bent upright before him. At the far right, the figure holds his leg bent in front of him, and, in a naturalistic movement, grasps it with his hand.

The single headpiece that adorns the manuscript is located on folio 288 (Fig. 18). Large and richly ornamented, it is rectangular in form, featuring a central lobed, profiled arch, filled with decorative motifs. They consist of a repeating interlaced floral design, in which the forms are united to each other by the interweaving of leaves and stems. In its general design and the use of shading at the base of the flowers, the headpiece finds similarities with that of the Philadelphia manuscript, as with many others of fifteenth century Armenia. Above the headpiece, two birds confront a central vessel, although both, interestingly, glance to the right. A marginal ornament appears to the right of the headpiece, composed of a floral motif. Below, the first line of text consists of large decorated uncials, featuring a typically compartmentalized design of alternating red, blue, and white bands.[36] As with the Philadelphia manuscript, red, spiky lines emanate from the central motifs, perhaps meant to indicate the sections of leaves.

Conclusion

The manuscripts produced by the scribes of Hamshen testify to a lively artistic tradition, evident in the marginalia and ornamental decorations. The complex interlace designs of the arabesques and chapter headings can be compared with fifteenth-century examples from Greater Arme-

---

[35] From *The Book of Daniel*, 1:6.
[36] They are non-figural, but at the same time have an almost bird-like appearance.

nia, as can the faces and figures of the British Library manuscript. The leather binding of the Philadelphia manuscript, with its intricate patterns, is also suggestive of a developed tradition of book production in the area. Such evidence for artistic contact is all the more noteworthy when one considers the state of manuscript painting in Greater Armenia in the same era.

With the increase in Ottoman power by the sixteenth century, the internal feudal system of Armenia had virtually disappeared, and many Armenians left their homelands for the imperial capital of Constantinople. As a result of this pattern of migration, the Armenian population in Trebizond dropped by 50 percent.[37] The Ottoman-Safavid wars of this era also wreaked havoc; in 1523, Erzerum, one of the Ottoman army's staging points for attack, stood empty and in ruins. The political and economic decline of Armenians in the Ottoman Empire had deleterious consequences for artistic and architectural production. Regarding monastic complexes, little is known of construction other than repairs during this period. Manuscript illumination met a similar fate; far fewer manuscripts survive from the sixteenth than from the fifteenth century, and almost no manuscripts were known from the 1520s to the early 1540s.[38] At this very time, however, the region of Hamshen, protected by a natural line of fortifications, continued to enjoy relative political autonomy and an enduring tradition of manuscript production. The painting in the region thus testifies to the survival of the arts of the book during one of the darkest periods in the history of medieval Armenia.

---

[37] Dickran Kouymjian, "Armenia from the Fall of the Cilician Kingdom (1375) to the Forced Emigration under Shah Abbas (1604)," in *The Armenian People from Ancient to Modern Times*, ed. Richard G. Hovannisian, 2 vols. (New York: St. Martin's Press, 1996), vol. 1, pp. 28-29.

[38] Ibid, p. 43.

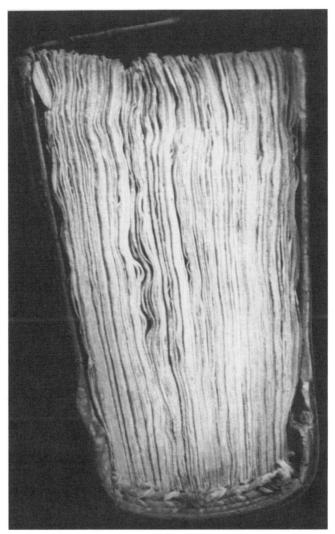

Fig. 1. Raised End-Band, Frederick Lewis Oriental Ms 123,
Philadelphia Free Library

Fig. 2. Front Binding, Ms 123

Fig. 3. Back Binding, Ms 123

174

Fig. 4. Fore-Edge Flap, Ms 123

Fig. 5. Headpiece and Marginal Ornament, Ms 123

Fig. 6. Marginal Ornament and Zoomorphic Letter, Ms 123

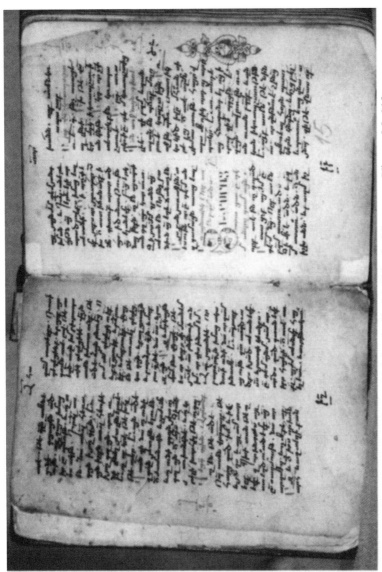

Fig. 7. Text Page with Marginalia, Mekhitarist Monastery, Vienna, Ms 119

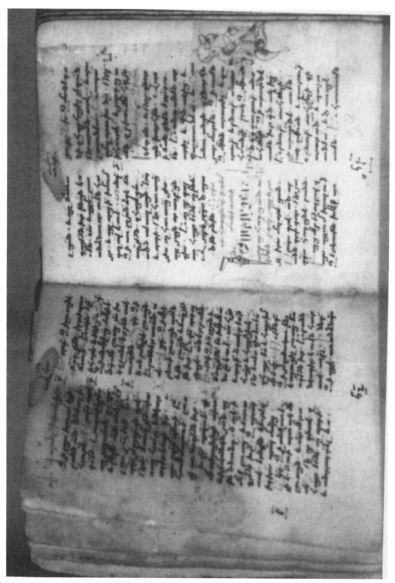

Fig. 8. Text Page with Zoomorphic Ornament, Ms 119

Fig. 9. Bifolio with Marginalia, Ms 119

Fig. 10. Headpiece, Ms 119

Figs. 11-12. Bifolio with Headpiece and Marginal Ornament,
Vienna, Ms 431

Fig. 13. Gregory the Illuminator, British Library, Or. 6555

Fig. 14. King Trdat, Ms Or. 6555

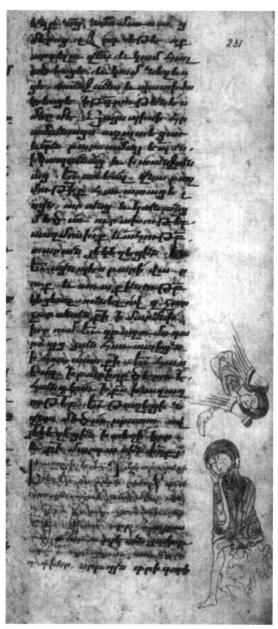

Fig. 15. Gregory the Illuminator's Vision, Ms Or. 6555

Fig. 16. Gregory the Illuminator and an Angel,
Ms Or. 6555

Fig. 17. Marginal Scene of Daniel, Anania, Misayel,
and Azarya, Ms Or. 6555

Fig. 18. Headpiece, Ms Or. 6555

❋ 9 ❋

ARMENIAN CITY QUARTERS
AND THE ARCHITECTURAL LEGACY
OF THE PONTUS

David Kertmenjian

For Armenian merchants from medieval times to the twentieth century, Pontus was the northern outlet to Europe. The ancient cities of the region such as Sinope, Samsun, Charshamba, Unieh, Fatsa, Ordu, Kerasund (Giresun; Girason), Tireboli (Tripoli), Trebizond (Trabzon), Gumushkhane, Rize, Athina (Pazar), and others were important commercial centers. Pontus had a population of various ethnic groups. While Armenians were present from ancient times until the deportations and massacres of 1915, only the remnants of a few churches and other communal structures now exist. Information on these buildings comes mostly from past Armenian publications. Among these are Minas Bzhshkian's history of the Pontus; Bishop Abel Mkhitarian's study of Armenian immigration to Trebizond; Ghukas Inchichian's geography of Armenia; Hakovbos Tashian's survey of the Armenian population from the Black Sea to Karin (Erzerum); and Hamazasp Oskian's descriptions of the monasteries of Trebizond and three other provinces.[1]

---

[1] Minas Bzhshkian, *Patmutiun Pontosi or e Sev Tsov* [History of Pontus on the Black Sea] (Venice: Mekhitarist Press, 1819); Abel Mkhitarian, *Vep gaghtakanutian Hayots Trapizoni* [Story of Immigration of the Armenians of Trebizond] (Constantinople: "Masis," 1857); Ghukas Inchichian, *Ashkharhagrutiun chorits masants ashkharhi* [Geography of the Four Parts of the World] (Venice: Mekhitarist Press, 1802-1806); Hakovbos Tashian [Dashian], *Hay bnakchutiune Sev tsoven minchev Karin* [The Armenian Population from the Black Sea to Karin], *Handes Amsoria* 1-2, 3-4 (1921): 52-62, 181-220, and his *Hay azgi ev hatkapes Karno taregrutiune germaneren vaveragreru hamemat* [The Annals of the Armenian People and Particularly of Karin According to German Documents] *Handes Amsoria* 5-6, 7-8 (1921): 315-31, 395-403; Hamazasp Oskian [Voskian], *Sebastiayi, Kharberdi, Diarbekiri ev Trapizoni nahangneru vankere* [The Monasteries of the Provinces of Sebastia, Kharberd, Diarbekir, and Trebizond] (Vienna: Mekhitarist Press, 1962), and his *Bardzr Hayki*

In addition, there are descriptive materials in the travelogues of Evliya Chelebi (seventeenth century) and Karl Koch (nineteenth century) and the valuable topographic surveys of H.F.B. Lynch at the turn of the twentieth century.[2] There are also the documents of the Russian Central Military Archives in Moscow as well as in military publications in Russian by specialists such as N.G. Korsun, S.R. Mintslov, V.T. Maevskii, and N.V. Novikov.[3] These publications have been utilized in this study to explore the Armenian architectural styles in Trebizond, other coastal towns, and the inland region between the Pontus and the Armenian Highland.

The City of Trebizond

Before the great massacres in 1915, there were eight Armenian quarters in Trebizond with several Armenian schools and four churches as well a national caravanserai (inn) and other commercial buildings (Fig. 1).[4] Around Trebizond were some ten Armenian monasteries and many Armenian villages, such as Zefanos, Sovuksu, Kropin, Pariam, and Platana. The city of Trebizond slopes down from Boz Tepe to the Black Sea, forming an amphitheater with the two neighboring valleys to the east and west. According to Lynch's survey, its layout consisted

---

vankere [The Monasteries of Upper Armenia] (Vienna: Mekhitarist Press, 1951).

[2] Evliya Chelebi, *Siahat-Name* [Travels], selected passages translated by Arshak Safrastyan in the series *Otar aghbyurnere Hayastani ev hayeri masin* [Foreign Sources about Armenia and Armenians], vol. 4: *Turkakan aghbyurner, III* [Turkish Sources, III] (Erevan: Armenian Academy of Sciences, 1967); Karl Koch, *Reise im pontischen Gebirge und türkischen Armenien* (Weimar: Druck und Verlag des Landes Industrie Comptoires, 1846); H.F.B. Lynch, *Armenia: Travels and Studies*, vol.1: *Russian Provinces* (London: Longmans, Green: 1901).

[3] Nikolai G. Korsun, *Pervaia mirovaia voina na Kavkazskom fronte* [The First World War on the Caucasus Front] (Moscow: Voenizdat, 1946); Sergei R. Mintslov, *Statisticheskii ocherk Trapizondskago okruga noiabr' 1916 goda* [Statistical Notes of the Trebizond District in November 1916] (Trebizond: Izd. Shtab-okruga, 1916); V.T. Maevskii, *Puti Maloi Azii v rayone mezhdu Samsunom i Aleksandretskim zalivom: Rekognostsirovka provedennaia rossiiskim Imperatorskim Vitse-Konsulom v Rize* [Routes of Asia Minor in the Region between Samsun and the Gulf of Alexandretta: Reconnaisance of the Russian Imperial Vice Consul at Rize (Tiflis: Tip. Shtaba Zakavkazskago voennago okruga, 1903); Nikolai V. Novikov, *Operatsiia flota protiv berega na Chernom more v 1914-17* [Naval Operation against the Coastline of the Black Sea, 1914-17] (Moscow: Mor-Akad RKKA, 1937).

[4] Trebizond is also rendered in the sources as Trapizon, Trapzun, Trapezon, Trapezos, Trabzon, and other variants. Western Armenians pronounce it as Drabizon.

of three main parts with seven individual zones. The citadel was the most important landmark. To the north toward the sea were the middle and the lower fortresses overlooking the skillfully-designed harbor. On both sides of the citadel and walled city were the suburbs, which were spread over the eastern and western slopes. Ottoman regulations required the Christian inhabitants to live outside the walled city.[5] Thus, most commercial buildings were in the suburbs, whereas the cemeteries were located on the southern bounds of the city.

The citadel, Kuli Hisar, has antique features of military architecture. It was an ensemble made up of the citadel itself, an open theater, and a hippodrome on the south side. The citadel covers around 2 hectares (5 acres). The entrance is from the south, beside the historic tower of Ioannes (John) IV. At the center of the citadel is the ceremonial courtyard, from which an extended *dromos* (passageway) leads to the inner courtyard. Nearby is the palace with a beautiful *thermae* (bath). The palace is triangular in shape, the base opening toward the city and the sea. The triangle is an isosceles (two sides of equal length): the base is 140 meters (394 feet) and the height is 200 meters (656 feet). In its composition and distribution, the palace resembles many medieval castles of Armenia such as those at Dvin, Ani, Smbataberd, and Sis. At every corner of the citadel there are high towers. The eastern tower of the palace is adjacent to the eastern gate of the walled city, hence the name Tower Gate.

The fortress or the walled city is located below the citadel to the north and is divided into the Middle Town and the Lower Town. The Middle Town, by its network of streets and the arrangement of the gates, is obviously of an antique tradition. According to Lynch's map,[6] the center of the Middle Town consisted of two perpendicularly-crossed streets, around which are the remains of an ancient *agora* (central marketplace). The site of the city in planning principles is analogous to Greek and Byzantine cities, as well Armenian cities such as Ani, Lori Berd, and Baghesh. The area of the Middle Town is 8 hectares (20 acres). It is 200 meters (656 feet) long east to west and 400 meters (1312 feet) north to south.

The Middle Town is almost rectangular in shape. The northern gate opens toward the Lower Town. The eastern and the western gates open toward the suburbs and accordingly are called "Prison Gate" and "Gate

---

[5] Inchichian, *Ashkharhagrutiun*, p. 387.
[6] Lynch, *Armenia*, vol.1, map facing p. 15.

of Dye Shops." The gates are also adjacent to the bridges entering the city from the Guzgun and Ishkale valleys on either side of the city. At the crossing of the two main streets and around the *tetrapylon* (entrance) of the ancient agora is the old palace or *serai*, not far from the Greek Church of Saint Ioannes, which was converted to a mosque after the Ottoman conquest of Trebizond.[7] At the other end of this square are two baths, a *medrese* (Islamic religious school) in an old Greek structure, a school, and other buildings.[8] Evliya Chelebi described the place in the seventeenth century as follows: "The Middle Town's fortification is a long and strong wall. Here, on the east, beside the Castle Gate is the New Jumaa [Friday] Gate."[9] Comparing this information with other sources, it becomes obvious that the medieval downtown extended from the antique agora and spread from the gates toward the suburbs.

The Lower Town was built later than the Middle Town. This fact is evident from the different masonry style and features of military architecture as well from the inscriptions of the emperors Justinian and Alexius on the old city walls. The Lower Town was constructed in the period of the Comnenus dynasty of the Empire of Trebizond (thirteenth-fifteenth centuries). According to Lynch's map, the area of the Lower Town was almost three times larger than that of the Middle Town. It extended from the north and northwest of the Middle Town to the coast, terminating at the sea next to the fortified harbor. There were eight gates in the walls of the Lower Town. Public and commercial buildings were located on the both sides of the streets extending from the gates to the center of the city.

The changes caused by the construction of the Lower Town altered the role of the agora, as the Lower Town replaced it as the center of commercial activity. Only the artisan lanes which used raw materials from the surrounding mines remained in their original place adjacent to the gates of the Middle Town. The names of the gates conveyed the make-up of the Lower Town: on the north, "Gate of the Sea"; on the east, "Bazaar Gate" and "Candle-Makers Gate"; on the west, "Gate of the Sothk Suburb" and "Palace Gate." The fortifications of the Lower Town were more regular than those of the Middle Town. Ghukas Inchichian describes the lower fortifications as being so high and wide

---

[7] Inchichian, *Ashkharhagrutiun*, p. 385.
[8] Ibid.
[9] Evliya Chelebi, *Siahat-Name*, p. 44.

that a cart could be driven on the wall, "which was built over the ruins of an older wall bearing Greek inscriptions on the huge stones scattered here and there."[10] According to the measurements of Evliya Chelebi, the length of the city walls was 9,000 steps (23,240 feet).[11] The harbor was designed to serve fifty ships. According to Lynch's second map, it was a semicircular area with a perimeter of neatly arranged shops.[12] The radius of the harbor was 140 meters (460 feet).[13] There were seven other unprotected harbors facing the suburbs on either side of the main harbor.

The suburbs lay on the east and west sides of the city. On the same city map by Lynch, these were typical medieval urban additions. Actually, their planning was based on the principle of one parochial church per quarter. This fact is obvious from the distribution of the churches (indicated on the map) as Saint Grigorios, Georgi, Christos, Ciryacus, Vasil, Farros, Stefanos, Philippo, as well as Chomlekji.[14] The eastern sector in the nineteenth century was five times larger than the fortified town. It had an open harbor along the seaside. According to Lynch's city map, near the gate of the eastern suburb were two Greek churches—Saint Vasil and Saint Anna. Not far from them was the central market or *bedestan* and the Great Mosque. Other travel documentation indicates that there were also ten caravanserais or inns.[15] The eastern suburb of Trebizond formed a city into itself. Aside from the commercial center, there was a carefully designed square named Giavur Meydan (Infidel Square).[16] Inchichian notes: "On the eastern edge of the suburb is an expansive square as a stopping place for the caravans, which is called Giavur Meydan."[17]

According to Lynch's description, on the northern side of the eastern suburb were many places belonging to Franks and Genoese. On his second map under numbers 10 and 11 are shown Guzel Serai (Beautiful Palace), built on the former Greek dwellings adjacent to a promon-

---

[10] Inchichian, *Ashkharhagrutiun*, p. 386.

[11] Evliya Chelebi, *Siahat-Name*, p. 44.

[12] Lynch, *Armenia*, vol.1, map facing p. 30.

[13] Bzhshkian, *Patmutiun Pontosi*, p. 75.

[14] Ibid, pp. 76-77.

[15] Inchichian, *Ashkharhagrutiun*, p. 389.

[16] *Giavur* means infidel or non-believer and was the name given to Christians in the Ottoman Empire, indicating Armenians or Greeks.

[17] Inchichian, *Ashkharhagrutiun*, p. 389.

tory on top of which there was a lighthouse and a church.[18] Regarding
the same part of the city, Minas Bzhshkian has written:

> On both sides of the fortress there are two suburbs, each having a
> square. The square of the western suburb is called Kabak Meydan,[19]
> the center of the eastern suburb is called Giavur Meydan, which is 278
> steps [720 feet] long and 180 [415 feet] wide.[20] The notables of the
> city often used the square for horsemanship. All around the perimeter
> of the squares are shops and some residential buildings; to the east
> side are the Great Mosque and a fountain; at the south side are the
> houses of the Armenian inhabitants with their bountiful gardens.[21]

Away from the square toward the coast were also numerous shops.
There was a customs house beside the lighthouse. Beyond were the
cemeteries of the Christians, belonging to the Armenian Apostolic,
Catholic, and Evangelical communities and to the Latins, and Greeks.

About this commercial part of the city, Evliya Chelebi observed:
"The best of the commercial lanes is the part neighboring the Candle-
Makers Gate. These are beautiful and rich shops extending from the
gate to the coast. Here is a bedestan; the owners of the shops are
mainly rich foreigners. At the Orta Hisar [Middle Town], there are
various guilds having 70 to 80 shops, all together called by the inhabitants as 'the small marketplace'."[22]

The western suburb reached out in the opposite direction from the
walled city. According to the layout published by Lynch, the northern
part of the western suburb was the Turkish "Sothk quarter." At the center of this sector were many public buildings, including a gymnasium,
an alms house, and a hospital. From here to the shore was a long street
passing through Armenian and Greek quarters from the southwest but
also interspersed by parts of the Turkish quarters. Kersam Aharonian
has asserted that many Turkish houses were placed in such a way as to
fragment the Armenian and Greek neighborhoods.[23] Otherwise that
sector would have had a purely Christian population.

---

[18] Lynch, *Armenia*, vol.1, map of "Trebizond and Surroundings" and pp. 30-31.

[19] Lynch, p. 24, mentions the name of the square as "Kavak" or "Plane Tree."

[20] One step is equal to 80 centimeters. Thus, the dimension of the square is 222.5 by 144 meters.

[21] Bzhshkian, *Patmutiun Pontosi*, p. 75.

[22] Evliya Chelebi, *Siahat-Name*, p. 45.

[23] Kersam Aharonian, *Hushamatian Mets Egherni, 1915-1965* [Memorial Volume of the Great Crime, 1915-1965] (Beirut: Atlas, 1965), pp. 466-71.

Thus, there were thirty-six quarters in Trebizond of which eight were Armenian.[24] There was only one Armenian quarter in the western suburb, the other seven being on the eastern side. Hence, about one-sixth of Trebizond's inhabitants were Armenian. In the eighteenth and nineteenth centuries, they resided primarily near the eastern gates of the Middle Town and Lower Town. Without doubt, the Armenian community had lived within the walled city in Byzantine times. Like other Christians under Ottoman rule, however, they had to move into the suburbs. Until the tragic events of 1915, there were between 14,000 to 15,000 Armenians residing in the city and around 22,000 in the district as a whole.[25] The Armenian community institutions in the city included four churches, both public national (*azgayin*) and private schools, a prelacy, clubhouses and halls, marketplaces, and caravanserais. Around 1800, the community established its first school. Then in 1817, a second school was opened by Minas Bzhshkian. Eventually, there were also coeducational and girls' schools.[26] An Armenian theater operated regularly between 1855 and 1860. In addition, the local press reported on activities of the prelacy, library, and so forth. These were adjacent to the Church of Surb Oksent/Okhsent (Auxentios), which was in the downtown quarter of Duzlu Cheshme.[27]

Armenian Churches of Trebizond

There were four working Armenian churches in Trebizond (Figs. 2-1, 2-2, 2-3, 2-4). There were also a number of public buildings such as

---

[24] Cf. Inchichian, *Ashkharhagrutiun*, p. 387.

[25] T.Kh. Hakobyan, St.T. Melik-Bakhshyan, and H.Kh. Barseghyan, *Hayastani ev harakits shrjanneri teghanunneri bararan* [Dictionary of Place-Names of Armenia and Adjacent Territories], 5 vols. (Erevan: Erevan State University, 1988-2001), vol. 5, p. 128.

[26] See Barsegh Sargisian, *Erk-hariuramia grakan gortsuneutiun ev nshanavor gortsichner Venediko miabanutian* [Two Centuries of Literary Activity and Noted Figures of the Brotherhood of Venice] (Venice: Mekhitarist Press, 1905), p. 40; Mesrop Chanashian (Janashian), "Arevmtahay bem ev anor glkhavor nerkayatsutsichnere" [The Western Armenian Stage and Its Foremost Representatives], *Bazmavep* 7-8 (1950): 145.

[27] Arman Gotikian, "Dprotsa-taterakan kyanke Trapizonum, 1815-1915 tverin". [School and Theatrical Life in Trebizond, 1815-1915], *Teghekagir: Hasarakakan gitutyunner* 7 (1962): 45, 50-51.

196

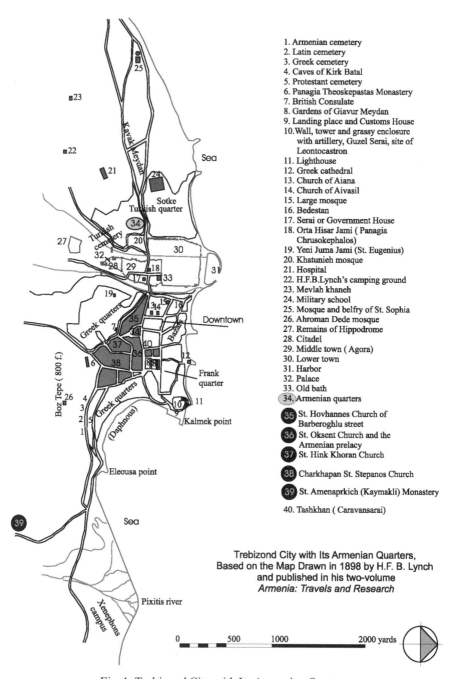

1. Armenian cemetery
2. Latin cemetery
3. Greek cemetery
4. Caves of Kirk Batal
5. Protestant cemetery
6. Panagia Theoskepastas Monastery
7. British Consulate
8. Gardens of Giavur Meydan
9. Landing place and Customs House
10. Wall, tower and grassy enclosure with artillery, Guzel Serai, site of Leontocastron
11. Lighthouse
12. Greek cathedral
13. Church of Aiana
14. Church of Aivasil
15. Large mosque
16. Bedestan
17. Serai or Government House
18. Orta Hisar Jami (Panagia Chrusokephalos)
19. Yeni Juma Jami (St. Eugenius)
20. Khatunieh mosque
21. Hospital
22. H.F.B.Lynch's camping ground
23. Mevlah khaneh
24. Military school
25. Mosque and belfry of St. Sophia
26. Ahroman Dede mosque
27. Remains of Hippodrome
28. Citadel
29. Middle town (Agora)
30. Lower town
31. Harbor
32. Palace
33. Old bath
34. Armenian quarters

35. St. Hovhannes Church of Barberoghlu street
36. St. Oksent Church and the Armenian prelacy
37. St. Hink Khoran Church

38. Charkhapan St. Stepanos Church

39. St. Amenaprkich (Kaymakli) Monastery

40. Tashkhan (Caravansarai)

Trebizond City with Its Armenian Quarters, Based on the Map Drawn in 1898 by H.F. B. Lynch and published in his two-volume *Armenia: Travels and Research*

0   500   1000   2000 yards

Fig. 1. Trebizond City with Its Armenian Quarters

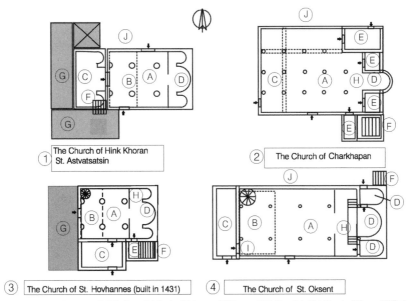

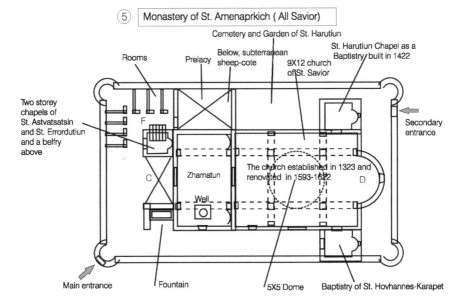

THE ARMENIAN CHURCHES OF TREBIZOND (reconstruction)

Fig. 2. The Armenian Churches of Trebizond

the bath known as the Giavur Hamam and the Dashkhan caravanserai.[28] The Armenian churches of Trebizond were built in Byzantine
times. They were Hing Khoran Surb Astvatsatsin, Charkhapan Surb
Stepanos, Surb Hovhannes, and Surb Oksent.

The Church of Hing Khoran Surb Astvatsatsin

The name of the monument translates to "Holy Mother of God Church
with Five Altars" (Fig. 2-1). Surb Astvatsatsin was built in an extensive space in the Armenian quarters near the commercial buildings adjacent to the eastern suburb. This was one of the oldest sites of Armenian habitation in Trebizond. The Hing Khoran church belonged to the
Catholic minority of the Armenian community. The complex consisted
of the main church, *gavit* (antechamber), *zhamatun* (oratorium; narthex), vestry, and a medieval cemetery. Bzhshkian states that the bell
tower was built solidly above the gavit and supported by the apses of
its altars, which were likewise solid and arched.[29] An inscription over
Surb Hakob apse at the northeast of the gavit read: "The Church of
Surb Hakob built for the memory of Aghribash and his parents in
1414."On the southern apse of the gavit, another inscription read:
"Built this luminous altar of Surb Stepan to the glory of God by the
priests Grigor, Hohan [sic], Sargis, and all the people who labored here
during the reign of Kir Manuel and Kir Alexius in 1414, Amen."
Bzhshkian noted: "All around the church are tombs. There are some
recently built houses in the southwest part of the area. Actually the
well in the former courtyard of the complex is now inside the houses. .
. . The church has two entrances, one from the north and the other from
the south. The triforium [*vernatun*] for the women is accessible from
the south."

Surb Astvatsatsin, a traditional church composition of the Trebizond region, consisted of a gavit having two altars and a small tri-
apsidal church, the apses being arranged in a linear order on the east
side. The church was of the four-column basilica type. On the western
side there was a wooden triforium for women attending the Divine Lit-
urgy. The altars of the gavit and the zhamatun were at the northeast and

---

[28] There were many public baths in Trebizond, among the most noted of which
were Kule, Imaret, Chifte (subterranean), and Pasha. See Bzhshkian, *Patmutiun Pontosi*, pp. 65-68, 79.

[29] Ibid., p. 79.

northwest corners and named after Surb Stepanos and Surb Hakob. There were two vestries on both sides of the gavit as auxiliary rooms. In its original design the church had a well at the entrance court which played the role of an atrium (courtyard).

On the basis of fifteenth-century inscriptions, one may conclude that the gavit was an extension to an already-existing building. Thus, the complex dates back at least to the times of the Comneni emperors in Trebizond, where the size of the Armenian community was large enough to have four priests in one church. Moreover, the foundational Church of Surb Astvatsatsin was clearly in place by the first decade of the fifteenth century.

The Church of Charkhapan Surb Stepanos

The name of the church translates to "Warder-off-of-Evil Saint Stephen" (Fig. 2-2). According to local tradition, the name derived from the fact that one of the builders fell from a great height without being hurt. The church was a three-nave basilica with ceiling vaults. There reportedly was a bell tower on the southeast corner. Adjacent to the church was the Holy Cross cemetery.[30]

According to the description of Abel Mkhitarian, Charkhapan Surb Stepanos was a stone-built three-nave-basilica church vaulted from the inside. Externally, its roof was sloped and covered with tiles. The altar consisted of three apses, the main one projecting out in a semicircular form from the plane of the eastern facade. The two-storey bell tower was placed over the southern apse. In its initial form, the church was small, but in 1829 it was much enlarged as the bequest of the Elmasian family.

The original building consisted of the church and gavit separated by a transversal wall. They were connected by a passageway having two symmetric windows on either side. In order to increase the space, the wall was demolished and a wooden triforium added on the western side of the sanctuary. Later, two vestries were added on the northeast and southeast corners for use as a baptistery and as dressing rooms. Both of the vestries extended along the corresponding facades. The church was 18.2 meters (60 feet) long and 10.9 meters (36 feet) wide. The entrance of the women's gallery (*gynaeceum*) was from the southwest. To the south was an ancient Greek church called Holy Trin-

---

[30] Inchichian, *Ashkharhagrutiun*, p. 387.

ity and a cemetery.[31] Among the tombstones of the cemetery there were two bearing the dates 1605 and 1703.[32] Bzhshkian has written: "This church is built a little deep, so that the women's side and the triforium are not very light. Behind the altar, there is the memorial inscription, 'The last time the church [*tajar*] was rebuilt as a gift of Khoja Shamshadin (Shemshedin) and his wife [*koghakits*] Zono . . . in the year 1431'."[33]

Surb Hovhannes (Saint John) Church

Surb Hovhannes is believed originally to have been a Greek Orthodox church (Fig. 2-3).[34] Its chronology is not yet fully detailed. The oldest tombstone in its cemetery dates to 1434. There is also information that the church was renovated in 1805.[35] Surb Hovhannes was located in the Berberoghlu quarter of the city's eastern suburb. It had three apses on the eastern side with a vestry on the southeastern corner. The smallest Armenian church of the city, the sanctuary's design was typical of the three-nave-basilica with four central columns. The church had two entrances, one from the south and the other from the west for the gynaeceum, which had a wooden triforium above.[36] The courtyard was occupied by houses belonging to Armenians and Greeks.[37] The complex also had a ruined bell tower and a wooden gavit, which for the lack of space was built on the south side.

The Church of Surb Oksent or Sulu (Having Water) Monastery

The earliest evidence about Surb Oksent or Auxentios is from 1378 (Fig. 2-4). The complex included the main church, a small baptistery, a wooden gavit, and a cemetery. The internal dimensions of the church were 20 by 7.8 meters (67 by 26 feet) and the external dimensions were 24 by 10 meters (79 by 33 feet). It was the community's largest church. Surb Oksent was of the three-nave-basilica style, with the central nave being 4.5 meters (15 feet) wide. As was usual, the church had

---

[31] Mkhitarian, *Vep gaghtakanutian*, pp. 129-34.
[32] Ibid., pp. 132-33.
[33] Bzhshkian, *Patmutiun Pontosi*, p. 81.
[34] Inchichian, *Ashkharhagrutiun*, p. 387.
[35] Mkhitarian, *Vep gaghtakanutian*, p. 138.
[36] Ibid.
[37] Bzhshkian, *Patmutiun Pontosi*, p. 82.

two entrances, one of them for the gynaeceum. There was an internal
wooden triforium built in 1842 at the northwest corner. The altar had
three apses. The baptistery was in a vestry adjacent to the northern
apse. The bell tower was over the corner room from where an intermediate entrance led to the administrative rooms of the prelate on the
northwest side of the complex.[38] The complex was renovated in 1838.
There is a *khachkar* (memorial cross stone) in the cemetery bearing the
date 1478.[39]

In addition to the above-mentioned churches, there were small
chapels in the surrounding Armenian villages. Many of these were a
particular kind of structure that was called *Khachatur*. These were
usually small cruciform domed churches or mono-nave basilicas. The
erection of Khachaturs was a local tradition thought to have been
brought by the Armenians who had migrated from the medieval Armenian capital of Ani.[40]

The Armenian Monasteries of Trebizond

There were several Armenian monasteries in the vicinity of Trebizond,
among them Surb Gevorg of Kohana, Surb Grigor Lusavorich and
Surb Sargis of Kelkit, Surb Khach of Asamut, and Surb Vardan of Surmene.[41] The most renowned monasteries were Surb Amenaprkich, in
the eastern hills outside Trebizond, and Surb Prkich, in the vicinity of
Gumushkhane.

The Monastery of Amenaprkich (All Savior)

Amenaprkich vank was popularly known as Khaymakli or Kaymakli
monastir or Shamshadli (Shemshedli), referring to the sponsor of its
restoration, Stepan of Hamadan, a native of Shamshadin (Fig. 2-5). All
Savior monastery served as the prelacy headquarters of the Trebizond
diocese. It was located on a hillside to the east of the city near the village of Aghjabad. Amenaprkich was established by Catholicos Petros
Getadardz in 1020.[42] The complex consisted of the church, a gavit,

---

[38] Mkhitarian, *Vep gaghtakanutian*, pp. 134-37.

[39] Ibid., pp. 136-37.

[40] Bzhshkian, *Patmutiun Pontosi*, p. 82.

[41] See T. Palian, "Hay vanorayk" [Armenian Monasteries], *Biuzantion* (Constantinople), 1900, nos. 1067, 1074, 1078, 1148, 1158.

[42] Oskian, *Vankere*, p. 228.

three chapels dedicated to Surb Harutiun, Surb Hovhannes, and Surb Astvatsatsin, a bell tower, prelacy offices, and, on the south, a fountain dating to 1489 (Fig. 3). There were also a stable, a garden, rooms for pilgrims, cells for the monks, a kitchen, external post, a fence, and, on the northern side, a cemetery.

All Savior Church was a small stone structure. According to the inscription carved on the entrance, it was rebuilt by Stepan of Shamshadin on the foundation of an existing church from the year 1324. Another inscription read: "I am Mkrtich, son of Khoja Stepanos, who by the command of the God built the chapel of Surb Karapet [Hovhannes Karapet—John the Precursor], with the surrounding fence of the monastery, in memory of my parents and all relatives."[43] Bishop Abel Mkhitarian has written: 'The Church of All Savior is a common-stone-built rectangular edifice having a recessed altar at the east. The building has an internal dimension of 9.1 meters (30 feet) from the entrance to the front of the apse and an internal width of 7.2 meters (23.5 feet). The external length of the church is 11.8 meters (39 feet). The roof is built of stone, too."[44] This means that the main church of the monastery was a 9 by 12 meters (29 by 39.3 feet) domed basilica with four central columns. The diameter of the dome was 5 meters (16.4 feet). The church had two entrances, from west and south. The interior, including the semicircular wall of the apse, was decorated with flower images. The design work was carried out under the patronage of Bishop Hakob and the Prelate Avetik in the years 1593-1622. There were three windows in the interior, two on the south and the other on the main axis of the altar.[45] According to the description of Bzhshkian, the church had a triforium adjacent to the main entrance.[46] The zhamatun was located in front of the western entrance as an auxiliary structure leading to the church. It was built later than the main church. Bishop Mkhitarian had noted: "The masonry of the zhamatun is primitive and the roof is gabled. There is a sacred well inside. As usual, the entrance is from the west."[47]

The Chapel of Surb Astvatsatsin was the oldest of the monastery's three sanctuaries. It was located at the west end of the northern wall of

[43] Palian, "Hay vanorayk," 1900, nos. 1067, 1078.

[44] Mkhitarian, *Vep gaghtakanutian*, p. 117.

[45] Ibid., p. 118.

[46] Bzhshkian, *Patmutiun Pontosi*, p. 82.

[47] Ibid, pp. 118, 121.

the main church. The circumference of the church was square in proportion. The Chapel of Surb Hovhannes served as the monastery's baptistery. It was located at the eastern end of the northern facade. Adjacent to the main entrance was an administrative room. The fence of the
monastery passed by the northern wall of the chapel. Here was a separate passage leading to a subterranean sheep fold under the administrative room. The chapel was located at the southeast corner of the main
church. It, too, was built by Stepanos of Shamshadin in 1422. Actually
all three chapels were not more than vestries located at the corners of
the main church. Only the southwest corner had a special entrance for
the gynaeceum. The bell tower was originally a three storey building,
but the upper storey was cut away at the behest of the Ottoman authorities. In 1648, Khoja Astvatsatur converted the second floor into the
Surb Errordutiun (Holy Trinity) chapel and built the wooden belfry.[48]

The rooms for pilgrims and the cells for the monks were adjacent to
the fence of the monastery at the southwest corner of the main entrance
and to the northwest. The cells for royalty were also on the northern
extension.[49] The external post or *drsi-tun* was on the road leading from
the monastery to the city. It was a small complex including a chapel
called Surb Mamas (which was in ruins in the nineteenth century) and
a post-house with other auxiliary rooms for temporary use. According
to Bzhshkian, there was a subterranean passage connecting Surb Mamas with the altar of the main church of Amenaprkich.[50]

The Monastery of Surb Prkich (Saint Savior)

Surb Prkich vank, located near Gumushkhane to the south of Trebizond, consisted of a small church and a gavit (Fig. 4). Its famous
door was decorated with flower motives carved on walnut wood.
Oskian states that this monastery and the Monastery of Hovakim and
Anna of Tokat were built by the same masters. Fortunately, Oskian has
published a picture of the door of the Hovakim and Anna vank (Fig.
5), which helps to give an idea about what must have been the splen-
dorous entrance to Surb Prkich.[51] The main church of the monastery

---

[48] Mkhitarian, *Vep gaghtakanutian*, p. 116.
[49] Oskian, *Vankere*, p. 227.
[50] Bzhshkian, *Patmutiun Pontosi*, p. 85.
[51] Oskian, *Vankere*, picture on the backside of the cover page.

204

Fig. 3. Trebizond: Amenaprkich (Kaymakli) Monastery

Fig. 4. Gumushkhane: Rendition of Surb Prkich Monastery

Fig. 5. Door of the Church of Saints Hovakim and
Anna Monastery, Tokat

was located in the left corner of the complex and was surrounded by a metal fence. The entrance was framed by a stone arch. Oskian states that the church, designed by the goldsmith Zugimian, was glorious.[52] Saint Savior had three apses. The interior included a dressing cabinet, a baptistery alcove, and at the right of the entrance a stone staircase leading to the triforium. The church was domed, the calotte (internal cavity) of which was tiled.

The National Caravanserai—Dashkhan

The single identifiable secular monument of Trebizond's Armenian community is the national caravanserai called *Dashkhan,* which dates to the thirteenth or fourteenth century. Minas Bzhshkian states: "Dashkhan is one of remarkable buildings of the bazaar. It is a two-storied arcaded building of stone."[53] Although there is scarce evidence about the building, its features can be reconstructed by examining similar type structures in the area. As a two-storied caravanserai, it would have had an inner courtyard with four towers at the corners. This parallels Kurt Erdemann's descriptions of other caravanserais: Thahdopa, Khatun, Durak, Chakalli, and Chinchinli khans, for example.[54] This was also true of the dashkhans in most of the Armenian towns neighboring the Pontus area, such as the one in Erznka (Turkish: Erzinjan; Erzincan).

Armenian Communities of the Coastal Towns

There were also Armenian communities in other towns of the Pontus region (Fig. 6). They may be divided into coastal and continental towns. As the Pontus was a crossroad of world trade, the important towns were on the Black Sea littoral. Among those inhabited by Armenians were Sinope, Samsun, Unieh, Fatsa, Ordu, Kerasund, Tireboli, and Rize, as well as many surrounding villages.

---

[52] *Jeride i Sharkie* [Oriental Gazette], 1899, no. 4303, as cited by Oskian, *Vankere,* pp. 237-38.

[53] Bzhshkian, *Patmutiun Pontosi,* p. 79.

[54] Kurt Erdmann, *Das anatolische Karavansaray des 13. Jahrhunderts,* pt. 1 (Berlin: Gebr. Mann Verlag, 1961), illustration nos. 13, 14, 20, 22, 37.

Sinope and Samsun

Sinope is at the extreme west end of the Pontus.[55] The town has ancient origins, reportedly established by the Miletians (seventh century
B.C.). Bzhshkian observed: "The Christian inhabitants are residing
outside the fortress in the suburbs. Most of the inhabitants are brave
Greeks. Armenians here are few and grouped by their houses around a
small church in the vicinity of the Greek quarters."[56] Samsun (Samson)
is located to the east of Sinope. Straddling the Charshamba River, it
has curvilinear layout around the harbor. Evliya Chelebi noted: "The
strong castle constructed of stone is beside the beach. Parts of it were
ruined by Russian invasions but reconstructed again. The castle has 70
ramparts and 2,000 battlements. The roofs of the houses are tiled; all
over the city are scattered green woods. There are seven schools in the
town."[57] The statistics given by V.T. Maevskii at the beginning of the
twentieth century show that 20 percent of Samsun's population was
Armenian, making up 400 families.[58] Bzhshkian reported that the Armenian quarters were mainly on the coastline near the bazaars. There
were four Armenian quarters on the northeastern skirts of the citadel
where other Christian inhabitants also resided. The quarters were clus-
tered around two churches, each having an elementary school. The
Armenian homes with their small gardens sloped from the north to the
east of the city.[59] Depending on the source, the Armenian population at
the beginning of the twentieth century ranged from 3,000 to 6,000 inhabitants. In the *sanjak* or county as a whole there were approximately
20,000 Armenians.[60]

Unieh and Fatsa

Unieh (Greek: Inion)[61] neighbors Samsun to the east. The semicircular
harbor of the town is on its western side. The town being located on a
slope, the houses were arranged densely in terraced order. The layout

---

[55] The town is also referred to as Sinap, Karabi, Corifi.

[56] Bzhshkian, *Patmutiun Pontosi*, p. 45.

[57] Evliya Chelebi, *Siahat-Name*, pp. 37-38.

[58] Maevskii, *Puti Maloy Azii*, p. 85.

[59] Bzhshkian, *Patmutiun Pontosi,* pp. 46-47.

[60] Hakobyan, Melik-Bakhshyan, Barseghyan, *Hayastani teghanunneri bararan,*
vol. 4, p. 489.

[61] Also Unia, Unie, Uniye, Yunie, Yunia.

of the town faced the sea as an amphitheater around the harbor. The town had antique features in its four-tiered fortification with a gate on each side of its rectangular perimeter.[62] It was arranged around a *Cardo* (north-south street) and *Decumanus Maximus* (east-west street). The Armenian quarter was next to the Greek quarters on the northwest side of the town. The Armenian minority, consisting of forty families, concentrated around the Aramian school and Surb Minas Church. According to an inscription on the tympanum of the church's entrance, the structure was built in 1831. Its composition was like others in the region—a simple church with a gavit. It included a wooden triforium and gynaeceum accessed from a separate entrance. The church was rebuilt after a fire in 1840. All the walls were made of stone but the roof remained wooden and was tiled. Another Armenian church existed in a Greek quarter to the south of the town, demonstrating that Armenians had lived here since medieval times.[63] The Armenian population in the town in 1915 numbered 1,000, and, in the kaza (district) as a whole, 10,769 inhabitants.[64]

Fatsa[65] is a short distance to the east of Unieh. The placement is a green promontory with the Polaman River flowing from the east and the Elekjie River from the west. The Armenian Surb Astvatsatsin Church was a small edifice built over the promontory in 1809. Ten or more Armenian families lived around the church at the skirt of the hillside. The structure was tiled and had a foundation inscription over the tympanum of its entrance.[66] At the beginning of the twentieth century. there were about 1,800 Armenians in the town.[67]

Ordu, Kerasund, and Tireboli

Ordu[68] is some distance to the east of Fatsa toward the Yoroz promontory. The town stretches out to the shore and forms a harbor on the south beyond the promontory. Around the harbor are the shops, lanes,

---

[62] Bzhshkian, *Patmutiun Pontosi*, p. 51.

[63] Mkhitarian, *Vep gaghtakanutian*, pp. 144-49.

[64] Hakobyan, Melik-Bakhshyan, Barseghyan, *Hayastani teghanunneri bararan*, vol. 3, p. 939, and vol. 5, p. 192.

[65] Also Fathsa, Fatisa, Fatisane, Fathsos.

[66] Mkhitarian, *Vep gaghtakanutian*, pp. 149-52.

[67] Hakobyan, Melik-Bakhshyan, Barseghyan. *Hayastani teghanunneri bararan*, vol. 5, p. 510.

[68] Also Kotyora, Ordu.

and other commercial buildings adjacent to the former Greek quarters. To the east, at a meeting place of three rivers, lies a beautiful plain. The Armenian quarter, made up of some 130 families, was on the western side of the town. Some of these families had Hamshen origins or were immigrants from neighboring Kerasund. The community's Church of Surb Astvatsatsin, standing in the heart of the Armenian quarter, was rebuilt over a preexisting structure in 1852.[69] The Armenian population of the town in 1915 was about 5,000.[70]

Kerasund or Giresun[71] lies between Ordu and Trebizond city. The location of the town is at the meeting place of two valleys. Its layout was centered around a citadel at the bottom of which were the residential quarters along the shoreline. The harbor was divided by the castle into two parts, the eastern harbor or Demir Kapu liman and the western harbor or Lonja liman. Both of the harbors lay behind the castle (constructed by the Greek Comneni emperors) so that they were sheltered from the sea.[72] All the commercial buildings of the town ranged around the harbor, as did the customs house, the quarantine area, and the courthouse to the east of the castle. The citadel was in a state of ruin in the nineteenth century, with only the walls standing. The population of the city and its region from the medieval times consisted of Greeks and Armenians. At the beginning of the twentieth century, there were 1,500 Armenian inhabitants in their quarters below the citadel. They had a church with two rock-hewn altars dedicated to Surb Astvatsatsin and to Surb Sargis.[73] According to Bzhshkian, the church had been converted from a Greek Orthodox sanctuary.[74] There was an inscription over the northern apse bearing the date of 1702. In the southern apse was a khachkar from the year 1751.[75] While Bzhshkian was there (second decade of the nineteenth century), the Armenian community bought land to build another church on the southern outskirts of the town.[76] According to the Armenian dictionary of place-names, there were two

---

[69] Mkhitarian, *Vep gaghtakanutian*, pp. 152-55.

[70] Hakobyan, Melik-Bakhshyan, Barseghyan, *Hayastani teghanunneri bararan*, vol. 5, p. 496.

[71] Also Gerasia, Girasun, Giresunt, Gerason, Girason, Kerasond, Kerasos, Kerason, Kirason, Kirasos, Kirisin, Pharnagia.

[72] Bzhshkian, *Patmutiun Pontosi*, p. 54.

[73] Inchichian, *Ashkharhagrutiun*, p. 400; cf. Hakobyan, Melik-Bakhshyan, Barseghyan, *Hayastani teghanunneri bararan*, vol. 3, p. 103.

[74] Inchichian, *Ashkharhagrutiun*, p. 400.

[75] Mkhitarian, *Vep gaghtakanutian*, pp. 158-59.

[76] Ibid., p. 160.

Armenian churches in the city. The old church dedicated to Surb Grigor Lusavorich (Gregory the Illuminator) was built in 1269, while the later Surb Sargis was rock hewn and located at the skirt of the citadel. Until the deportations in 1915, there was an Armenian school next to Saint Gregory Church.[77]

Tireboli or Tripoli[78] is a small town located on a promontory west of Trebizond. According to tradition the city originally consisted of three individual towns or fortresses bearing the names Guruje Kale, Castle of the Hill, and Bedroma.[79] It was divided into two main parts called the eastern town and the western town. The Turkish population lived next to the castle; the Greek inhabitants were concentrated to the north of the Turkish quarter; and the Armenian community was located near the commercial center on the coast. Tireboli had two harbors, one facing each town. As usual, the Armenian quarter, which consisted of about fifty families, was arranged around the church and a community administration building. At the beginning of the twentieth century, there were 1,500 Armenian inhabitants.[80]

Rize

Rize lies to the east of Trebizond at the far end of the Pontus.[81] The town is located around a gulf and has a linear layout spread along the harbor. The town planning principle was the same as in other places, with a citadel on the hill and a sheltered harbor beyond the castle and city quarters. A river passing through the bazaar divided the city into two parts. The Armenian community of some twenty families had a church in the Rosh quarter.[82] According to Vital Cuinet's statistics at the end of the nineteenth century, there were 5,100 Armenians in the Rize district.[83]

---

[77] Hakobyan, Melik-Bakhshyan, Barseghyan, *Hayastani teghanunneri bararan*, vol. 3, p. 103.

[78] Also Dribol, Dripolis, Kentrenos, Thirepolu, Tirebolu.

[79] Bzhshkian, *Patmutiun Pontosi*, p. 155.

[80] Hakobyan, Melik-Bakhshyan, Barseghyan, *Hayastani teghanunneri bararan*, vol. 5, p. 130; Mkhitarian, *Vep gaghtakanutian*, pp. 161-63.

[81] Also Irize, Emporion, Riza, Rizon, Rizos, Rizus.

[82] Bzhshkian, *Patmutiun Pontosi*, p. 94.

[83] Vital Cuinet, *La Turquie d'Asie: Géographie administrative, statistique, descriptive et raisonnée de chaque province de l'Asie-Mineure*, vol. 1 (Paris: Ernest Leroux, 1892), p. 119. [Editor's note: Cuinet may have based this figure on statistics compiled at a time when Artvin was included administratively in the Rize district].

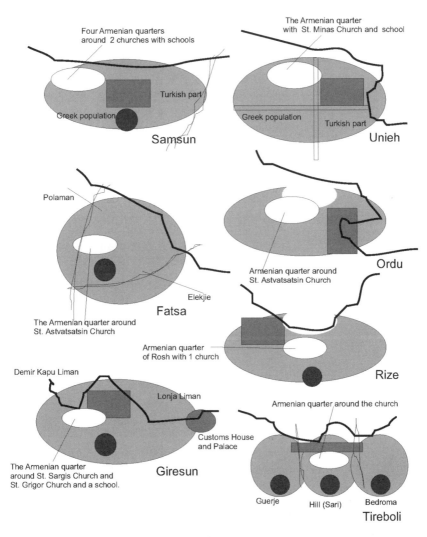

Location of Armenian Quarters in the Towns of the Pontus Region

Legend ▮ The Downtown ⬭ The Armenian Quarters ⬤ The Citadel ⌐ Coastline

Fig. 6. Location of Armenian Quarters in the Towns of the Pontus Region

Inland Armenian Communities

The inland towns of the Pontus inhabited by Armenians were Charshamba and Gumushkhane. Charshamba is in the hinterland of Samsun, situated in a low-lying plain. The town is divided into eastern and western halves by the Charshamba (Yeshil Irmak) River. In the larger eastern half were the bazaar and other commercial buildings, as well as the city hall (*serai*) and mayor's residence. The Armenian quarter, together with the Greek quarters, was in the Christian western sector. According to travel descriptions, the houses were attractive, with gardens and other amenities. Many members of the Armenian community of 150 families were bread merchants. The Mamikonian-Shushanian school was established in 1871. Surb Astvatsatsin Church (built in 1790 and rebuilt in 1816) had four altars. The semicircular eastern side of the church was built of stone, while the other parts and the roof were wooden.[84] A nearby village called Khurshunlu was populated entirely by Hamshen Armenians.[85]

The Armenian inhabitants of Charshamba in the first decade of the twentieth century numbered 5,000 and with the surrounding seventeen villages, 10,000. In 1950, there were still 560 Armenians in Charshamba.[86] Gumushkhane was one of the main towns southeast of Trebizond. Of the 1,600 families, there, 200 were Armenian in the nineteenth century. Aside from Surb Astvatsatsin Church, built in 1269, the prelate's seat was in the Monastery of Surb Sargis, a few kilometers from the city. In this mountainous district, there were some villages populated by Hamshen Armenians.[87]

Gumushkhane was the Turkish name of the city, the original Greek name of which was the Greek form Argyroupolis (Latin: Argyropolis), meaning place or mine of silver. Of a population of 40,000 in the district, the Armenians numbered 12,500 before the calamity of 1915. They maintained two schools. Earlier, much of the Armenian population had moved to neighboring regions such as Baberd (Baiburt), Erznka (Erzinjan), Trebizond, Sebastia (Sivas) and more distant places

---

[84] Mkhitarian, *Vep gaghtakanutian*, pp. 140-44.

[85] Bzhshkian, *Patmutiun Pontosi*, p. 49.

[86] Hakobyan, Melik-Bakhshyan, Barseghyan, *Hayastani teghanunneri bararan*, vol. 4, p. 224.

[87] Bzhshkian, *Patmutiun Pontosi*, pp. 92-93.

such as Constantinople, Russia, and France. In 1970, 360 Armenians still remained in Gumushkhane.[88]

Other Armenian Monuments
of the Pontus and Surrounding Areas

The architecture of Armenian monuments of the Pontus had special features because of Greek-Armenian interrelations. Neighboring Armenian sites had certain monuments that were similar to those of the Pontus. Examples were the Monastery of Hovakim and Anna of Tokat, Chordvan, Barkhar, Hohu, Oshk and others of the Tortum area; Varzahan of Baberd; Goguba (Surb Gevorg) and Surb Sargis of Ardahan; Karmir vank and Surb Astvatsatsin of Karin (Erzerum); as well as many churches of Constantinople (Surb Teodoros, Surb Astvatsatsin of the Ayub quarter, Surb Karapet of the Iskudar quarter). For this survey, it is sufficient to consider the eight-apsed church of Varzahan bordering on the area.

The eight-apsed church is located near the village of Varzahan on the Trebizond-Erzerum road, about 10 kilometers from Baiburt. At the beginning of the twentieth century, there were many other Armenian churches, many in a semi-ruined condition, in and around Varzahan. The church was octagonal. According to the measurements done by Walter Bachmann at the beginning of the twentieth century, the church had the following features: every side of the conches was 4.70 meters (15.75 feet) long, and the thickness of the wall was about 95 centimeters (38 inches).[89] The internal diameter of the church was 9.4 meters (31 feet). On every corner of the octagon were six-sided and eight-sided polyhedral columns with a diameter of almost 1.4 meters (4.6 feet). From the inside the columns stood free of the walls. The area for prayer was circular, the diameter being 5.7 meters (18.7 feet). The three entrances on the northern, southern, and western sides measured 1.15 meters (3.8 feet) in width on the northern, southern, and western sides, were designed without tympanum, and were bordered by rectangular frames as is still seen, for example, in Surb Hovhannes Church of Avan near Erevan.

---

[88] Hakobyan, Melik-Bakhshyan, Barseghyan, *Hayastani teghanunneri bararan*, vol. 1, pp. 916-17.

[89] Walter Bachmann, *Kirchen und Moschen in Armenien und Kurdistan* (Vienna: J.C. Hinrichs'sche Buchhandlung, 1913), pp. 49-53.

The high quality of the masonry on the walls and columns of the church shown in the pictures convey a skilled technique. Little is now left of the arches of the conches, and the floor of the church is under broken stones and a layer of soil 2 meters deep. The church was built of yellowish limestone. The surface of the walls was hewn with great care and skill. The masonry was of the Armenian *midis* type, having stone rows on the external and internal sides joined by a layer of compound mortar called *khipar*. The walls were in polychromatic manner treated by fascias on certain levels. The stones were quite large, especially at the lower tiers. The transition from the apsidiole of the conches to the dome was by means of squinch archs. The composition of the church was an intermediate solution between the Armenian Aghtamar type and Greek churches backed by eight supports. Actually, the design of the bearing columns resembles the sixth-century church of Surb Echmiadzin of Soradir, the prototype of Aghtamar. The axial window of the altar was a combination of three openings. The axis was emphasized by a circular window over the central opening of three windows, a design usually seen in certain Armenian monuments from early medieval times.[90] The interior of the church was covered with wall paintings. All the external angles were designed by alcoves divided into two parts as in Aghtamar, Surb Zoravar of Eghvard, Irind, and other churches.

Conclusion

Pontus is an elongated land that stretches along the southern coast of the Black Sea and lies between the sea and the historic Armenian Highland. It was a bridge connecting Armenia to Europe, so that many of the coastal towns had Armenian communities. The Armenian population was made up largely of merchants and shopkeepers who lived in their own quarters near the city centers. Typically, the Armenian quarters were grouped around the community's churches. Down through the centuries, the Armenian communities formed their own style of art and architecture which combined Armenian traditional with local

---

[90] See Nikolai M. Tokarskii, *Iz istorii srednevekovogo stroitel'stva v Taykskom kniazhestve* [From the History of Medieval Construction Activity in Tayk Principality] (Erevan: Hayastan, 1988), illustration nos. 14, 28-30, 46-48. See also Tiran Marutyan, *Tayki chartarapetakan hushardzannere* [The Architectural Monuments of Tayk] (Erevan: Hayastan, 1972), illustration nos. 4-6, 32.

forms. This was evident in the architecture of the churches, schools, prelacies, and residences. Only remnants of these structures remain, making it all the more important for careful studies based on archival materials, the Russian military surveys, and other documentation. Study of the community traditions of the Pontus Armenians has not only historical importance but also immediate relevance to understanding the Armenian architecture and planning of past centuries.

In conclusion, one may state that some of main features of Armenian architecture of the Pontus region are as follows:

1. The Armenian churches examined are of the medium-sized-basilica and domed-basilica types. There are also some instances of multi-apsidal composition which are analogous to Varzahan, to Goguba and Surb Sargis of the Ardahan region, and to other churches.

2. The functionality of the churches is based on compounds that include beside the church itself, gavits, gynaeceums, bell towers, side-chapels, baptistery alcoves or vestries, wells and fountains, courtyards, and cemeteries.

3. The main entrances of the churches are surrounded by molded rectangular frames in order to give a monumental impression.

4. The gavits are vaulted and single-naved, having apses on the western or southern sides.

5. Without exception, the churches have two entrances, one for general use and the other for the gynaeceums or the women's gallery. This is a vital Armenian-Byzantine typological correlation specific to the region.

6. The altar, consisting of three apses arranged in linear order, is a favorite composition for all of the churches.

7. Two-storied or three-storied bell towers are common.

8. Most of the churches are built of limestone in their supporting parts. In the other parts, light-weight materials are used. The roofs are mainly gabled of wood and are tiled.

9. The openings of the structures are vertical and narrow. The windows are in traditional Armenian style.

❧ 10 ❧

THE PONTIC ARMENIAN COMMUNITIES IN THE NINETEENTH CENTURY

Bedross Der Matossian

The Pontic Armenian communities of the nineteenth century were distinguished from those of previous centuries in that they were exposed to major social, economic, and political transformations. Social transformation entailed enlightenment of an emerging middle class and revival of Armenian national consciousness; economic transformation was characterized by advancement in the standard of living and growing prosperity; and political transformation entailed participation in the local administration, the adoption in Constantinople of an Armenian "National Constitution," which broadened the administration of the confessional-based Armenian *millet* to include the middle class, and in the latter part of the century the emergence of Armenian political parties calling for self-defense and national emancipation.

By the Ottoman provincial reform act of 1864, Trebizond, as other provinces, was divided into administrative units and subunits: *vilayet* (province), *sanjak* (county), *kaza* (district), and *nahiye* (village cluster). The Trebizond vilayet was made up of 4 sanjaks, 22 kazas, and 24 nahiyes.[1]

Based on Ottoman, European, and Armenian sources, this survey focuses on the changing demographics of these communities and the impact of those changes viewed in a broader context. Such an analysis raises questions about the role and position of the Armenians as historical agents in the economic, social, cultural, and political transformations that were taking place in the Black Sea region during the nineteenth century.

---

[1] The four sanjaks were Trebizond (Trabzon), Samsun, Lazistan, and Gumushkhane. For more information about the sanjaks, kazas, and nahiyes, see Appendix I.

The Armenian Population

The population of the Pontic Armenian communities varied during the course of the nineteenth century. In the closing decades, approximately 60,000 Armenians lived in the vilayet: some 15,000 in the city of Trebizond, 10,000 in Samsun, 5,000 in Ordu, 2,500 in Gumushkhane, 2,000 in Unieh (Uniye), 1,500 in Kerasund (Giresun), 800 in Tireboli (Tripoli), and the remainder in small coastal towns and numerous rural villages in the interior. The most significant factors that had a direct impact on the number of Armenian inhabitants were the political and socioeconomic conditions of the Black Sea area, particularly as influenced by time of war and peace. During the Crimean War of 1854-56, for example, there was large-scale emigration from the peripheries and from neighboring provinces to Trebizond, Samsun, Ordu, and other coastal towns. The presence in Trebizond of French and the British forces (allies of the Ottoman Empire in that war) created new job opportunities for the native inhabitants and newcomers.

The available information about the Armenian population during the first half of the nineteenth century comes primarily from foreign, primarily European, travelers. These statistics, however, concentrate on the city of Trebizond itself and do not include the entire coastal area. For example, the German traveler Jakob Philipp Fallmerayer, who visited Trebizond in 1840, indicated that the city had between 28,000 and 30,000 inhabitants, composed of 5,000 Turkish, 400 Greek, 300 Armenian, and 98 Catholic households.[2] Dr. Perunak Feruhan, who traveled through the area in 1848, estimated that there were 3,987 Armenian men and women in the city.[3] The Trebizond region was then made up of a large administrative unit known an *eyalet* with

---

[2] Ihan Pinar, "Alman gezgini Fallmerayer'in gözüyle 19. yüzyılda Trabzon" [Nineteenth-Century Trebizond According to the German Traveler Fallmerayer] *Tarih ve Toplum* 27, no. 159 (March 1997): 10.

[3] In 1847 Sultan Abdul Mejid sent Ragip Bey, the second *mabeynji* (the go-between officer of the Imperial Palace), to Baghdad for an expedition journey. He was accompanied by Dr. Perunak Feruhan, who stopped in Trebizond where he recorded important information about the history, neighborhoods, population, and daily life of the city. See Usta Veysel, *Anabasis'ten Atatürk'e seyahatnamelerde Trabzon* [Trebizond in Travel Literature from Anabasis to Ataturk] (Trabzon: Serander Publications, 1999), p. 130.

somewhat different boundaries from the Trebizond vilayet that was created in 1864.[4]

Ottoman sources, too, provide little information about the population of these communities in the first half of the century. The census of 1831, for example, indicates that there were 11,431 *raya* (the term used for non-Muslims) living in Trebizond.[5] The next Ottoman general census was not conducted until more than fifty years later in 1893. That census, which provides a more detailed picture of the distribution of the Armenians along the Black Sea coast, shows that there were 41,786 Armenians in the vilayet of Trebizond.[6] The four subsequent censuses in the four succeeding years actually reflect an increase in the Armenian population.[7] Another Ottoman source, the *Salname*s or Yearbooks of the vilayet, provide the following figures for the province's Armenian population.[8]

---

[4] The largest administrative division at the time of the 1831 census was the eyalet and its most important subdivision was the sanjak, which was headed by a sanjakbey (a *liva* was the equivalent of a sanjak). The kaza was the main judiciary district, for which a qadi or judge was responsible, while the nahiye was the rural district or village clusters of a kaza. See Kemal Karpat, *Ottoman Population, 1830-1914: Demographic and Social Characteristics* (Madison: University of Wisconsin Press, 1985), p. 114.

[5] In the nineteenth century, the term *raya or reaya* was applied to Christians living in the Ottoman Empire. The census of 1831, according to Karpat, for the first time distinguished the Bulgarians, occasionally referring them by their ethnic name. The census takers also referred to non-Muslims collectively as *"rayay-i milel-i selase,"* that is, subjects of three nations—Orthodox, Armenian, and Jewish. Karpat, *Ottoman Population*, p. 114.

[6] Karpat, *Ottoman Population*, p. 138. See Appendix I at the end of this chapter. According to Ahmet Karaçavuş, the most successful census in the Ottoman Empire was the one that began in 1882-84 and ended in 1890. The decision to conduct that census was taken in 1871 by the reform-minded official Midhat Pasha, but because of the Russo-Turkish war of 1877-78 the census was delayed until 1882 and completed only in 1890. See Ahmet Karaçavuş, "XIX.yüzyılında Trabzon nüfusu," [Trabzon's Population during the Nineteenth Century], in *Trabzon tarihi sempozyumu* [Trabzon History Symposium] (Trabzon: Trabzon Municipality Cultural Publications, 1999), p. 431.

[7] In he four censuses conducted between 1894 and 1897, the number of Armenians rose from 41,780 in 1894 to 47,196 in 1897. In these censuses, the Armenians are identified as "Gregorian." The categories of Catholic Armenian and Protestant Armenian were not shown separately. They were subsumed, however, under the categories of Catholic and Protestant.

[8] In this survey, the *Salname*s for 1869 to 1881 are also used to assess the degree of Armenian participation in the local administration.

**Gregorian (Apostolic) Armenian Population
of Trebizond Vilayet[9]**

Publication Date of *Salname*	Armenian Population
1869-70	32,798
1870-71	35,784
1871-72	35,510
1878-79	38,958
1887-88	40,887
1893-94	41,849
1895-96	42,349
1900-01	49,535
1902-03	50,678
1903-04	51,639
1904-05	51,639
1905-06	51,483

The figures given in the provincial yearbook show that the Armenian population was steadily rising, but they do not reflect the negative demographic effects of the Russo-Turkish war (1877-78) and the Hamidian massacres (1894-96).[10] Justin McCarthy, by relying on these problematic figures, argues that, despite the deteriorating Armeno-Turkish relationship, the Ottoman statistics reflect a steady rise in the Armenian population, a point that has been used to support the position that the impact of the upheavals during the reign of Sultan Abdul Hamid was not great.[11]

---

[9] The first *Salname* in Trebizond was published in 1869.

[10] As a result of these destabilizing events, there was massive Armenian emigration from the Black Sea area to the Caucasus and Russia. Simultaneously, massive immigration of Circassians from the Caucasus and Russia to the Black Sea region took place. This resulted in significant demographic changes. According to Karpat, the 1877-78 war gave new momentum to Circassian immigration. The Circassians who landed in the Trebizond area were drafted into the Ottoman army. When the war erupted, there were already about 3,000 Circassians in Trebizond who joined the Ottoman army to fight against Russia. Karpat, *Ottoman Population*, p. 69, states that the numbers involved in the Circassian immigration ranged from 700,000 to more than 1 million.

[11] Justin McCarthy, *Muslim and Minorities: The Population of Ottoman Anatolia*

Another Ottoman source from the closing decade of the century estimates the Armenians of Trebizond province to be 52,349.[12] At about the same time, Vital Cuinet placed the figure at 47,200.[13] According to Sarkis Karayan, however, the Cuinet work has serious errors and deficiencies, especially regarding the statistics for Armenians in the central and eastern vilayets of Asiatic Turkey.[14] He points out that Cuinet's figures in many instances appear to have drawn on incomplete and highly questionable Ottoman official figures. According to statistics of the Armenian Patriarchate in 1882, on the other hand, there were 120,000 Armenians in the vilayet of Trebizond.[15] The patriarchate's figures are more than twice as high as those of the European and the Ottoman sources. In his study of Armenian Pontus, Hovakim Hovakimian cites a similar number—125,000, suggesting that he has relied on the patriarchate's statistics.[16] By contrast, Teodik's *Everybody's Almanac* shows the size of the Armenian community as 65,000, while Maghakia Ormanian, followed by Johannes Lepsius, gives 53,500.[17] The figures provided by Ormanian and Teodik are the closest to those cited in Ottoman and European sources.

Caution is required in dealing with these two sources, however, because they pertain to the beginning of the twentieth century,

---

and the End of the Empire (New York: New York University Press, 1983), p. 60.

[12] Sami Frasheri, ed., *Qamus ül-A'lâm* [Dictionaire universel d'histoire et de géographie], vol. 3, (Constantinople: Mihran Press, 1891), p. 3005. Frasheri also gives information about the population of certain kazas and sanjaks. His figures approximate those of the census of 1881-82/1893. This is true, for example, for the kazas of Gorele, Fatsa, and Tireboli.

[13] Vital Cuinet, *La Turquie d'Asie: Géographie administrative, statistique, descriptive et raisonée de chaque province de l'Asie-Mineure*, vol.1 (Paris: E. Leroux, 1892), p. 10.

[14] Sarkis Karayan, "Vital Cuinet's *La Turquie d'Asie*: A Critical Evaluation of Cuinet's Information about Armenians," *Journal of the Society for Armenian Studies* 11 (2000): 53.

[15] Marcel Léart, *Population arménienne de la Turqiue avant la guerre: Statistiques établis par le Partiarcat Arménien de Constantinople* (Paris: A. Challamel, 1913), p. 59.

[16] Hovakim Hovakimian, *Patmutiun Haykakan Pontosi* [History of Armenian Pontus] (Beirut: Mshak Press, 1967), p. 20.

[17] Teodik [Lapjinian], *Amenun Taretsoytse* [Everybody's Almanac] (Constantinople: M. Hovakimian Press, 1922), p. 262. Maghakia Ormanian, *The Church of Armenia* (3d rev. ed., New York: St. Vartan Press, 1988), p. 205; Johannes Lepsius, *Der Todesgang des armenischen Volkes: Bericht über das Schicksal des armenischen Volkes in der Türkei während des Weltkrieges* (Potsdam: Missionshandlung, 1919), pp. 304-05.

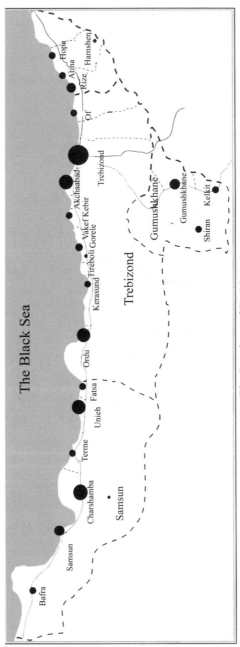

The Province of Trebizond

not the nineteenth century. Additionally, the patriarchate's statistics may be inflated because they apparently do not take into consideration the Russo-Turkish war of 1877-78 and the Hamidian massacres of 1894-96, both of which had a profound negative impact on the size of the Armenian population. Through examining the available statistics, it becomes possible to suggest a middle ground synthesizing the Ottoman, European, and Armenian sources. This would give an Armenian population of between 60,000 to 70,000 toward the end of the nineteenth century.

Map of the Pontic Armenian Communities in the Nineteenth Century

The Armenians were dispersed throughout the coastal areas of the Black Sea but were more concentrated in sanjak centers, especially in the city of Trebizond. The map shows the dispersion of the Armenians in the vilayet of Trebizond based on the 1881 Ottoman census.[18] Large circles indicate major Armenian concentrations, as in Trebizond, Ordu, Charshamba, Unieh, and Akchaabad. The Armenian population in these large circles varied between 4,000 and 14,000, whereas the population represented by the small circles represent between 700 and 1,500 Armenian inhabitants, as in Bafra, Samsun, Terme, Fatsa, Kerasund, Tireboli, Gorele, Vakef Kebir, Akchaabad, Shiran, Kelkit, Gumushkhane, Of, Rize, Atina, and Hopa.[19] As stated, during the Crimean War there was an increase in the population of Trebizond. Many

---

[18] See Appendix I. "Ottoman General Census of 1881-1882/93, *Armenians*" Source: BA (Başbakanlık Archive) Istanbul, (Y)/(P)/11s311, no. 215, cited by Karpat, *Ottoman Population*, pp. 122-51.

[19] Ibid. See also Hovakimian, *Patmutiun Haykakan Pontosi*, p. 20. Armenians also lived in the peripheral areas of the vilayet and were mostly occupied in agriculture. Thus, it is possible to differentiate between two Armenian social classes in the province: the urban class which was occupied primarily in trade and commerce, and the agricultural rural class. According to S.M. Tsotsikian, Armenians were found in the following villages: Rize, Gromi, Vikor, Of, Surmene, Kadahar, Kendi, Platana, Elevi, Sheyran, Kaylaked, Hadekoy, Mezrud, Baltaji-Dere, Solakle-Dere, Ivan, Ishkenaz, Sekahunruk, Sizene, Zeduka, Yomra, Joshara, Minasli, Afians, Major and Minor Samaruksa, Skafia, Dingils, Ferinzud, Kushana, Bashı-Dere, Samera, Galafga, Abian, Sefter, Kian, Mevrandu, Ulia, Silnas, Halman, Ziska, Ashagi Mavrant, Zisino, Cheno, Fotihos, Vesire, and Khamsi. The Armenians lived alongside the Turks and the Laz. See S.M. Tsotsikian, *Arevmtahay ashkharh* [Western Armenian World] (New York: S.M. Tsotsikian Centinental Committee, 1947), p. 783.

Armenians moved there from Tamzara, Shabin-Karahisar, and Gurun in the vilayet of Sivas/Sebastia, from Karin (Erzerum), and from Caesarea (Kesaria).[20] Substantial numbers of Muslims also migrated to the city. When the war ended, however, the population began to decrease.

The size of the Black Sea Armenian population declined during the second half of the nineteenth century as the result of the Turkish-Russian war of 1877-78, the massive immigration of Muslim refugees from the Caucasus to the Trebizond region, and the Hamidian massacres and subsequent large-scale Armenian emigration.[21] Despite these historical events, the *Salnames* of the vilayet show a steady rise in the Armenian population.[22]

Religious Life and Institutions

Much as in other Armenian communities, churches were a central institution around which schools and educational-cultural societies were formed.[23] In the nineteenth century, Trebizond had two dioceses: Trebizond and Samsun. Both were under the jurisdiction of the Armenian Patriarchate of Constantinople. The diocese of Trebizond encompassed the sanjaks of Trebizond, Gumushkhane, and Lazistan, while the diocese of Samsun was limited to the sanjak of Samsun (Janik).[24]

The Armenian churches and monasteries found in and around Trebizond dated back to as early as the fourteenth century, during the period of the Greek Comnenus Empire of Trebizond.[25] At the beginning of the twentieth century, there were three functioning Armenian Apostolic churches in Trebizond: Surb Oksent (Auxentios), Charkhapan

---

[20] Tsotsikian, *Arevmtahay ashkharh,* p. 773.

[21] As a result of the Hamidian massacres, many Armenians immigrated to the Caucasus and southern Russia. They settled especially in Batum, Sukhum, Gudaudi, Sochi, Kerch, Simferopol, Ekaterinodar, Tiflis, and Baku. See Tsotsikian, *Arevmtahay ashkharh,* p. 773.

[22] The province of Trebizond was not part of the traditional six Armenian vilayets for which Armenians were seeking reforms and a degree of administrative autonomy. Ottoman officials did not seem to regard the large number of Armenians in Trebizond as a political-geographic threat, unlike the case of the six vilayets.

[23] For more information about the Armenian churches and monasteries in Trebizond, see in this volume David Kertmenjian's "Armenian City Quarters and the Architectural Legacy of the Pontus."

[24] Ormanian, *Church of Armenia,* p. 238.

[25] Hovakimian, *Patmutiun Haykakan Pontosi,* p. 76.

(Warder Off of Evil) Surb Stepanos, and Surb Hovhannes (John), an Armenian Catholic church, and an Armenian Evangelical church or *zhoghovaran*. Minas Bzhshkian describes these monasteries and churches in considerable detail in his history of Pontus. He explains that Surb Amenaprkich (All Savior) Monastery on the eastern outskirts of the city was restored and embellished by Khoja Stepanos Shamshadli, a wealthy merchant from Persia, in the fifteenth century. Surb Oksent/Okhsent, known as Sulu (Having Water), was named after an early Christian martyr. Surb Hovhannes was a small church with an adjacent cemetery near the marketplace. The Hing Khoran Surb Astvatsatsin (Holy Mother of God with Five Altars) Catholic Church was a large edifice dedicated to the Holy Virgin.[26] The Armenian communities of Samsun and Ordu each possessed an Apostolic and an Evangelical church,[27] and the communities of Unieh, Fatsa, Giresun, Tireboli, and Rize each maintained an Apostolic church. There were also small chapels in many of the surrounding villages [28]

Armenian Participation
in the Local Administration

During the first half of the nineteenth century, the Armenian communities of the Black Sea did not play an important role in the civil administration or the governmental departments, simply because these positions were held almost exclusively by the ruling classes of the empire. Several reforms in the second half of the century made it possible for Armenians to serve in the provincial administration. The relevant statistics are based on the *Salnames* for Trebizond for the years 1869 to 1881.[29]

The vilayet of Trebizond was the only place in the eastern Ottoman provinces where the Greek presence in public life was a bit stronger than the Armenian representation. This was not surprising in view of the fact that the Greeks constituted the majority of the Christian popu-

---

[26] Minas Bzhshkian, *Patmutiun Pontosi or e Sev tzov* [History of Pontus on the Black Sea] (Venice: Mekhitarist Press, 1819), pp. 79-83.

[27] Tsotsikian, *Arevmtahay ashkharh*, pp. 623, 811-12.

[28] Ibid., p. 813. For more information about the properties of the churches in Trebizond province, see Hovakimian, *Patmutiun Haykakan Pontosi*, p. 83.

[29] Despite the fact that the population figures in the *Salnames* are problematic, the same cannot be said about the role of the Armenians in the local administration, as the names of the Armenian members in the administrative councils are listed.

lation and outnumbered the Armenians by a ratio of at least three to one.[30] The following table based on the provincial *Salname*s gives the number of Armenians and Greeks from among the approximately 900 officials in the civic administration during this period.[31]

Number of Armenians and Greeks
in the Administration of Trebizond Province
(1869-1881)

Year	Armenians	Greeks
1869	31	43
1870	58	65
1871	58	66
1872	63	68
1873	41	48
1874	45	49
1875	42	47
1876	36	45
1877	42	43
1878	50	43
1879	70	63
1881	62	67

This table reflects the increase of Armenians in the administration from 1869 to 1872; the figure fluctuates in subsequent years but reaches an apex in 1879. No major difference is apparent between Armenian and Greek participation. The chart indicates that despite the significant disparity between the size of the Greek and Armenian elements, their participation in the local administration was almost equal. In fact, in 1878 and 1879, more Armenians than Greeks were so employed.[32]

---

[30] For example, according to Cuinet, *La Turquie d'Asie*, p. 10, the Greek population of the vilayet was 193,000, whereas the Armenian population was estimated to be 47,200. In the Ottoman general census of 1881/1882-83, the Greek population was shown to be 155,039. See McCarthy, *Muslims and Minorities,* p. 93. Greek sources give a very different picture

[31] Nmes of the individuals have been used to identify the Armenians and Greeks in the administration. There are occasional cases in which the ethnic background based on the name is not conclusive, therefore leaving room for a margin of error.

[32] *Salname*s of the vilayet of Trebizond, 1870-1881.

The main fields of Armenian service were in civil administration, justice, and finance. In the administrative councils, there were one or two Armenian members at any given time.[33] The following table gives the names and dates of the Armenian elected members of the Trebizond administrative council:

Armenians in the Administrative Council
of Trebizond (1870-1881)[34]

Name	Year
Anasoghlu, Poghos Agha	1870-71
Mazlumian, Artin Effendi	1872-74
Grekian, Ohannes Effendi	1875-77
Fetvajian, Simon	1878-79
Haji Artin Agha	1881

Based on this information, it is evident that each Armenian representative served in his position for two years or more. In the provincial center at Trebizond, as well as in the kazas of Ordu, Gorele, Kerasund, Akchaabad, and Samsun, there was also an ex-officio member. In the nahiyes, an Armenian was usually included in the local administrative council.[35]

Mesrob Krikorian argues that the Armenian contribution to the judiciary was considerable. Usually in the sanjak centers of Trebizond, Samsun, and Gumushkhane, one or two Armenians served in the courts of first instance, of appeal, and of commerce. In the kazas, an Armenian normally served in the courts of first instance. Armenians in Trebizond were found in the public notary and the trial committee (*enjumen-i adliye*) as assistants to the inspectors. There were also Armenians in the commercial courts of the sanjaks.[36] The following table demonstrates participation of Armenians in the commercial courts.

---

[33] There were ex officio (*aza-i tabiye*) members and elected member (*aza-i münteheb*) of the council. Ex officio members participated by virtue of their office. At the kaza level, the ex officio members might include the governor, the deputy judge, the mufti, the head of the financial department, and the chief secretary. Usually two Christians and two Muslim members were elected by their respective communities.

[34] The *Salname*s of vilayet of Trebizond, 1870-1881.

[35] Mesrob Krikorian, *Armenians in the Service of the Ottoman Empire, 1860-1908* (London and Boston: Routledge and Kegan Paul, 1977), p.49.

[36] Ibid.

Armenians in the Commercial Courts
of the Sanjak of Trebizond (1873-1881)[37]

Name	Sanjak	Year
Gulbenkoghlu, Karabet, and Noriyanoghlu	Trebizond	1873
Ohannes and Garabet	Trebizond	1874
Krikor and Aramya Agha	Kerasund	1874
Ohannes and Vartan	Trebizond	1875-77
Gulbenkzade Karabet Effendi; Karabet Agha; and Barkend-kapanzade, Kevork Agha	Trebizond	1878
Ohannes and Vartan	Trebizond	1879
Ohannes and Vartan	Trebizond	1881

Armenians were also active in the financial affairs of the provincial government. They were employees of the taxation department and of revenue and expenditure control, the estimates committee, the Ottoman and Agricultural banks, and the chambers of commerce and agriculture.[38] According to Krikorian, many Armenians held responsible positions in the tobacco Régie and in managing the public debt.[39] Other fields of public life in which they were active were engineering, the postal and telegraphic services, the press service, and agricultural affairs.[40] In the kazas of Trebizond and in the sanjak of Samsun, Armenians were included on the agricultural and forestry board, in the municipality as advisory members and doctors, in public works, postal and telegraphic services, and in the chief secretariat.[41]

The Armenian role in local administration increased as the result of the Ottoman reforms, which were intended to strengthen the empire by unifying the various ethnic and religious elements and increasing their loyalty to the central government. The beginning of attempts at ethnic

---

[37] The *Salname*s of the vilayet of Trebizond, 1873-1881.

[38] Krikorian, *Armenians*, p. 49.

[39] Ibid.

[40] For example, Artin Cherkesian (1871) and Shirag Boynajian (1872) were the provincial engineers, and Artin Effendi (1869) and Boghos Effendi (1870) were telegraph operators of Arhavi.

[41] Krikorian, *Armenians*, p. 50.

integration in the second half of the nineteenth century occurred within the larger context of Ottomanism, a concept that originated with the so-called Young Ottomans and developed during the first constitutional period (1876-78). In principle, it maintained that all subjects of the sultan, regardless of ethnic and religious affiliation, were equal before the law. As a result, the millet system, in which the several ethno-religious groups had been given a degree of internal social and religious autonomy, was not dismantled but was liberalized through the establishment of secular assemblies.

In addition, these reforms resulted in the participation of secular elements in the local administration and in the affairs of the community while simultaneously decreasing the power of the more subservient elements, that is, the Armenian Patriarchate and the privileged *amira* class of bankers and state officials. The participation of secular elements in both areas led to the rise of new interest groups, comprised primarily of men from the middle class, the renaissance generation of intellectuals, and merchants who demanded more reforms and autonomy. Thus, the government's attempts to incorporate and Ottomanize the various ethno-religious groups indirectly paved the ground for the emergence of new elements, which demanded greater autonomy.[42]

The Role of the Armenian Communities in the Economy of the Black Sea

European trade which expanded rapidly into the Black Sea in the nineteenth century was the main factor affecting Trebizond's economic development. The Anglo-Ottoman Convention of 1838 and various other commercial agreements with European powers led to a dramatic increase in European access to Ottoman markets. In the eighteenth century, the trade in the Black Sea ports was controlled by Muslim merchants and only a few Greeks, Armenians, and Jews. As trade with Europe increased, however, the balance shifted. European companies and merchants preferred to establish commercial contacts with non-Muslim Ottoman merchants, using them as intermediaries in their trade with the Ottoman state. Gradually, Greek and Armenian merchants began to acquire an upper hand in the Black Sea trade. Some of them

---

[42] On the Armenian constitutional movement, see Vartan Artinian, *The Armenian Constitutional System in the Ottoman Empire 1839-1863: A Study of Its Historical Development* (Istanbul: Isis, 1988).

even established branches in other cities and in Russian coastal towns.[43]

According to Üner Turgay, the Crimean War was responsible for important demographic changes in Trebizond.[44] The war period transformed Trebizond into a more powerful commercial center, which primarily benefited the Armenian and Greek merchants who dominated the city's trade. As a result of this development, the economic gap between the Muslims and the non-Muslims became greater. The volume of trade and commerce increased dramatically. Many people moved to the city from towns and villages near and far. By the end of 1856, the population of Trebizond had grown to about 70,000.[45] The immigrants included Armenians and Greeks, as well as a substantial number of Turks. The economic boom created by the war gave rise to a rich class of non-Muslim merchants, while most Turks continued to be employed at minimal wages.[46] In the 1860s and 1870s, Trebizond's volume of trade decreased and then leveled out before gradually continuing to decline until the end of the century.[47] Despite this downward turn, the Armenian merchants were able to maintain their strong economic position.

During the second half of the nineteenth century, the major exported goods from the vilayet were filberts, tobacco, wood, beans, maize, and dried foods, as well as porpoise oil, minerals, wool, and hides and leather. The following table indicates the number of Armenian merchants and craftsmen in several urban centers.[48]

---

[43] Üner Turgay, "Trade Merchants in Nineteenth-Century Trabzon: Elements of Ethnic Conflict," in Benjamin Braude and Bernard Lewis, eds. *Christians and Jews in the Ottoman Empire: The Functioning of a Plural Society*, 2 vols. (New York: Holmes and Meier Publishers, 1981), vol. 1, pp. 287-89.

[44] The war had a positive impact both on the economy of the Black Sea region and on daily life. According to Turgay, the concentration of the population and wealth in the city permitted the investment in income-producing public buildings and resulted in the establishment of new religious and educational institutions. See Üner Turgay, "Trabzon," *Review: Fernard Braudel Centre* 16:4 (Fall 1993): 459.

[45] Turgay, "Trade Merchants in Nineteenth-Century Trabzon," p. 291.

[46] Ibid., p. 293.

[47] See Charles Issawi, "The Tabriz-Trabzon Trade, 1830-1900: Rise and Decline of a Route," *International Journal of Middle East Studies* 1 (1970): 18-27.

[48] Hovakimian, *Patmutiun Haykakan Pontosi*, p. 25.

The Number of Armenian Merchants
and Craftsmen in Trebizond

Place	Merchants	Craftsmen
Kerasund	50	25
Samsun	55	20
Trebizond	60	25
Ordu	30	40
Fatsa	10	5

The table shows that Trebizond had the largest number of Armenian merchants, whereas Ordu had the greatest number of Armenian craftsmen. The Armenian merchants of Trebizond were competitors with the Greeks and had an important influence on the city's commerce.[49] They entered into major trade agreements, and some of them had representatives and branches in foreign countries. Samsun, too, was an important trading center.[50]

According to a British document from the end of 1884, the foreign trade of Trebizond had clearly come under the domination of Greek and Armenian merchants. As the following table illustrates, five out of fourteen commission agents were Armenian. The majority of these served in Anatolia and the remainder in Persia.

List of Trebizond Merchants Dealing in Foreign Trade
(as of December 1884)[51]

Ballassarian	Anatolia
Constantinoff, D.J.	Persia
Hadji Mirza Baba	Persia
Dernersessian, M.	Anatolia
Hadji Djavid	Persia

---

[49] Examples of the wealthy Armenian households in Trebizond were those of Elmasian, Tiriakian, Fetvajian, Gureghian, Marimian, Nurikhanian, Hekimian, Anushian, and Turkian. Though the Khubessians were the first class commissioners/agents, they still had serious competitors such as the Gureghians, Makhokhians, Maranians, Marimanians, and Meserians. See Hovakimian, *Patmutiun Haykakan Pontosi*, p. 22.

[50] Tsotsikian, *Arevmtahay ashkharh*, p. 776.

[51] Great Britain, Foreign Office Archives, FO 526/10, cited by Turgay, "Trade Merchants in Nineteenth-Century Trabzon."

Hadji Mehmet Hassan	Persia
Hochtrasse and Co.	Anatolia; Agent for Lloyd's, Imperial Ottoman Bank, etc.
Inebeoghlu fils	Persia
Khedechian and Khoubesserian	Persia; Agent for Reliance Insurance Company of New York
Makhokhian, A.	Anatolia and Persia
Mirimian, B.O.	Persia; Agent for Manheimer Insurance Company, etc.
Triandaphilides, A.	Anatolia; Agent for La Fonciere Insurance Company, etc.
Efremides, A.C.	Lawyer
Kedikoglou Lazar Effendi	Lawyer

Another British document lists the Trebizond merchants engaged in foreign trade, both import and export.[52] It reveals that only 3 of the 32 exporters were Turks, whereas 16 were Armenians, and 14 were Greeks. The breakdown is similar among the 63 importers, of whom only 10 were Turks, whereas 20 were Armenians, and 33 Greeks.[53] Imported items included various colonial wares, bags, leather goods, metals, silk and woolen stuff, and raw cotton. Some Armenian merchants imported goods from as distant as Aleppo and Manchester.[54] Armenians were also agents at the other ports.[55] When the Europeans

---

[52] See Appendix II: "List of Trebizond Merchants Dealing in Foreign Trade as of December 1884—Exporters and Importers," from Turgay, "Trade Merchants in Nineteenth-Century Trabzon," pp. 308-10.

[53] Ibid.

[54] During this period, Aleppo and Manchester were important trade centers. In both cities Armenians had a substantial economic presence. For Aleppo, see Krikorian, *Armenians*, pp. 80-91. On the history of the Armenians of Manchester, see Mushegh Seropian, *Manchesteri hay gaghute* [The Armenian Community of Manchester] (Boston: Azg, 1911); Joan George, *Merchants in Exile: The Armenians in Manchester, England, 1835-1935* (London: Gomidas Institute, 2002).

[55] At Samsun, the agents included the following: Theodore J. Arzoglou, Algardi, Henri Coranze, I.J. Marcopoli, J. Joannides, J. Hekimian, and Y.A. Dervichian. At this port, the *Idare-i Mahsusa* (Ottoman State Shipping Company) was also represented by a Greek resident, M. Sevastikoglou. At Kerasund, Georges Mavrides, E. Pappadopolou, T. Genna, M. Pysolian, Alexi Kypriotti, S.C. Papadopoulos, G. Pisani; at Ordu, Afendul Pouloulides, D. Gregoriades, M. Vostanik, G.P. Coucoulidis, Pandeli Ionnidis, Boghos Tchildjian, Agop and Hrand Kubdjian; at Tireboli, G.P. Mavrides and H. Boyadjian as representatives of various steamship companies. See Raphael César Cervati, ed., *Annuaire Oriental du commerce, de l'industrie, de*

left Trebizond for Smyrna/Izmir and Constantinople in search of better economic opportunities, ownership of the insurance agencies passed to their local partners. By mid-1894, half of the fourteen insurance companies in Trebizond belonged to Armenians.[56]

Insurance Companies in Trebizond

Marine Insurance Company of London	J. Enepekoglou & Sons
North British Mercantile and Northern Company	Agop Shavarsh
The Patriotic Insurance Company	A. Sciandaphylidis
The New York Life Insurance Company	S. Ekmedjian
Gie.Gle. de Dresden	A. Makhokhian
Manheimer Transport Versicherungs	Boghos O. Marimian
La Fonciere et Union de Paris	A. Sciandaphylidis
Ottoman Insurance Company	Imperial Ottoman Bank
Helvetia	Hochstrasse & Company
Lloyd Suisse	Hochstrasse & Company
British Llyod	Hochstrasse & Company
La Badoise	Nourian Brothers
Le Maritime Belge	Boghos O. Marimian
Cie. Francfortaise	Boghos O. Marimian

The prominent merchants of the sanjak of Trebizond were Boghos Arabian, Gaydzag Arabian, Ipranossian, Maranian, H. Tahmazian, A. Minassian, Gureghian, Aslanian, and the Aznavourian brothers, who controlled almost the entire filbert business in the vilayet.[57] In the kaza of Samsun, Armenians excelled in the cultivation and production of tobacco. The noted Armenian merchants and tobacco producers of Samsun were, among others, the family firms of Ipekian, Kherian, Ipranossian, Gudugian, Meserian, Aprahamian, Bahchegulian, and Chekmeyan.[58]

Thus, despite their minority position within the region, Armenians were highly influential in all the fields of the economy. To recapitulate, the following factors led to this development:

---

l'administration et de la magistrature, Constantinople (Constantinople: The Annuaire Oriental & Printing, 1903), pp. 1649-50.

[56] Great Britain, Foreign Office Archives, FO 526/13, cited by Turgay, "Trade Merchants in Nineteenth-Century Trabzon," p. 295.

[57] Tsotsikian, *Arevmtahay ashkharh*, p. 776.

[58] Ibid., p. 623.

1. The Crimean War greatly impacted the emergence of a new middle class and merchants, leading to a large immigration of Armenians and Turks from the peripheries to the centers. This caused a significant demographic change in the area. At the end of the war, the Turks returned to the peripheries, while most Armenians remained in the urban centers.

2. Educational institutions played a central role in the economic advancement of the Armenian communities. The students in these schools had special courses in business and were trained in several European languages.

3. Great Britain and other trading partners of the Ottoman Empire often preferred to establish commercial bonds with non-Muslim Ottoman merchants, using them as intermediaries in trade with the Ottoman state. As a result of the associated privileges, many Armenian merchants improved their economic status. For example, the local British consul obtained a list of persons who had acquired Russian passports during eighteen months following the Crimean War. The roster included 89 Greeks, of whom 42 were merchants, and 116 Armenians, of whom 77 were merchants. According to Turgay, Russia, by extending its protection over these elements, was in fact providing the Greeks and Armenians with various capitulatory privileges and hence enhancing their domination of the city's economic life.[59]

Armenian Educational Institutions and Intellectual Life in Trebizond

The Armenian communities of the Black Sea experienced an entire century of national and educational enlightenment. This process was itself reflected in the increased number of educational institutions and societies, cultural organizations, and newspapers. The growth was part of the cultural nationalism that emerged during the nineteenth century in the Black Sea area and gradually transformed into political nationalism. In Trebizond, the first Armenian public school was established in 1803, after which the number of schools and students continued to grow, especially during the second half of the century.[60] In 1866, for example, the Azgayin Varzharan (National School) headed by principal Nerses Mezburian had 600 male and female students and seven teach-

---

[59] Turgay, "Trade Merchants in Nineteenth-Century Trabzon," p. 298.
[60] Hovakimian, *Patmutiun Haykakan Pontosi*, p. 20.

ers. The students were taught French, Armenian, and Ottoman, sciences, and religion. In addition to the national schools, there were also private ones, such as the Elmasian and the Farukhian schools. The Mekhitarist Catholic school established by Minas Nurikhanian in 1866 was another major educational institution in the life of the Pontic Armenian communities.[61]

According to the 1869 *Salname* of the vilayet, the Armenian community in the sanjak of Trebizond collectively had 34 schools, 3 of which were Catholic. In the sanjak of Samsun (Janik), there were 35 Armenian schools, 1 of which was Catholic; in the sanjak of Lazistan, there were 8 schools, of which 4 were Catholic; and in the sanjak of Gumushkhane, there were 5 Armenian schools.[62] Such findings suggest that already in 1869 the Armenians had 74 national or private schools with 1,753 students, and 8 Catholic schools with 584 students.[63]

Besides schools, the Pontic Armenian communities developed educational and cultural societies such as Enkerutiun Veratsnundian Tangarani (Society for Museum Revival), Surb Prkich (Holy Savior), Surb Gayanian (Saint Gayane), and branches of the Haykazian, Siuniats, Surb Stepanos, and Usumnasirats societies. The first newspaper, the short-lived *Hayastan* (Armenia), appeared in Trebizond in 1847. The Hayk printing press was set up there in the 1850s, publishing a series of periodicals such as *Khariskh* (Anchor), *Geghchuk* (Villager), *Motsak* (Mosquito), *Bzhishk* (Physician), and *Pontos*.[64] The historical journal *Dprots* (School), a monthly, was published for a time in Samsun.

Political Parties and the Hamidian Reaction

According to Karen Barkey, ethnic struggles emerge when groups perceive territories to have been assigned unjustly, when boundaries are decided by administrative fiat or manipulated by foreign powers, and when groups perceive that they have not been awarded what they should rightfully possess and enjoy.[65] These conditions all existed in

---

[61] Ibid., pp. 117-28.

[62] The *Salname* of 1869 of the Vilayet of Trebizond.

[63] While the numbers in the *Salname*s may seem a bit high, they are reasonable considering that in the villages alone there were nearly forty Armenian schools before 1915. See Hovakimian, *Patmutiun Haykakan Pontosi*, pp. 126-27.

[64] Tsotsikian, *Arevmetahay ashkharh*, p. 774.

[65] Karen Barkey, "Thinking about Consequences of Empire," in Karen Barkey

the case of the Armenians. The Armenians perceived, especially after the Congress of Berlin in 1878, that they had not been granted what was their due, namely reforms and broader autonomy. When diplomatic and peaceful efforts failed, resistance and revolutionary movements emerged.

The situation of the Armenians, not only along the Black Sea, but even more in the internal provinces was not satisfactory. Frequent Kurdish attacks, heavy taxation, friction with newly-immigrated Muslims from the Caucasus and the Balkans, corruption in the administration, as well as the failure of Armenian efforts to solve these problems diplomatically, all led to the emergence of Armenian revolutionary groups. The Treaty of San Stefano in March 1878, which offered so much to the Armenians at the conclusion of the Russo-Turkish war, was largely nullified by the European-imposed Treaty of Berlin in July of that year. Between 1878 and 1880, as the European powers limply reminded Sultan Abdul Hamid of his commitment to implement effective Armenian reforms, a major ideological shift was taking place within the Armenian communities of the empire. It was only after 1880 that self-defense movements emerged in the eastern provinces. Ideological and logistical tactics came from Europe and from Russian Armenia, which was experiencing a similar transformation. Initially, small groups emerged at Van and Erzerum "whose rudimentary programs called for defending the honor of the nation against those who violated the people, their religion and culture."[66] Their main aim was to fight against the oppression and the injustices of corrupt local officials and the encroaching Kurdish tribes.

The Armenians of Trebizond also began to organize politically. The first political group was formed there in the 1880s by several students whose goal was Armenian emancipation.[67] Then in 1889, a society called the Secret Educational Society (Krtasirats Gaghtni Enkerutiun) was organized by Ervand Zeytunjian.[68] The emerging revolutionary parties also established branches in Trebizond, although none of them chose Trebizond as their headquarters. It was only when the Hnchakian

---

and Mark Von Hagen Mark eds. *After Empire: Multiethnic Societies and Nation-Building* (Boulder, CO: Westview Press, 1997), p. 111.

[66] Richard G. Hovannisian, "The Armenian Question in the Ottoman Empire, 1876-1914," in Richard G. Hovannisian, ed., *The Armenian People from Ancient to Modern Times*, 2 vols. (New York: St. Martin's Press, 1997), vol. 2, p. 213.

[67] Hovakimian, *Patmutiun Haykakan Pontosi*, p. 133.

[68] Ibid.

Revolutionary Party first agreed to enter a proposed coalition with the Federation of Armenian Revolutionaries in 1890 that Trebizond briefly and only nominally became the center for the tenuous organization. The city was suggested by Hnchakian leader Khan-Azat as a compromise between Geneva, the center of his party, and Tiflis (in the Russian Caucasus), the organizational center of the party that soon assumed the name Armenian Revolutionary Federation (Hai Heghapokhakan Dashnaktsutiun). Although the union did not last, branches of both political parties were formed in many cities in Turkish Armenia, Cilicia, Constantinople, Trebizond and other Black Sea ports, Odessa, Russian Armenia and other parts of Transcaucasia, and Persia.[69]

An assassination attempt on Bahri Pasha, the governor of Trebizond, by an Armenian youth in 1895 held disastrous consequences for the Pontic Armenians. Rage against Armenian civilians filled the streets of Trebizond and resulted in a great loss of life, limb, and property in what has become known as the Hamidian massacres. According to Reverend Edwin Bliss, the assassination attempt was a purely personal matter, as the assailant seems to have been seeking vengeance for injustices done to his family and himself in Van while Bahri was the governor there.[70] The violent response revealed the general approach of the declining Ottoman center toward its subject populations. The Armenians of Trebizond were cruelly punished collectively for acts of individuals in the massacres and looting that spread over every eastern

---

[69] The Armenakan Party also had a branch in Trebizond. On the other hand, the Hnchak Party chose Constantinople as the center of its organizational activities in Turkey. Within seven months, the Hnchaks had enlisted 700 members in the capital. Most of them came from the educated class. The Hunchaks sent out leaders from Geneva and Constantinople to numerous towns and villages in Turkey. These places included Bafra, Marsovan, Amasia, Tokat, Yozgat, Agn, Arabkir, and Trebizond. See Louise Nalbandian, *The Armenian Revolutionary Movement: The Development of Armenian Political Parties through the Nineteenth Century* (Berkeley and Los Angeles: University of California Press, 1963), pp. 117, 154.

[70] Edwin Bliss, *Turkey and the Armenian Atrocities* (repr., Fresno, CA: Mshag Publishing, 1983), pp. 406-08. For more information about the Hamidian massacres in Trebizond, see Christopher Walker, *Armenia: The Survival of a Nation* (New York: St. Martin's Press, 1980), pp. 156-59; Robert Melson, *Revolution and Genocide: On the Origins of the Armenian Genocide and the Holocaust* (Chicago and London: University of Chicago Press, 1992), pp. 43-69. For more detailed information about the assassination attempt and its aftermath, see George H. Hughes, *Through Armenia on Horseback* (New York: E.P. Dutton, 1898); extracts in Vatche Ghazarian, ed., *Armenians in the Ottoman Empire: An Anthology of Transformation, 13th–19th Centuries* (Waltham, MA: Mayreni Publishing Co., 1997), pp. 732-85.

province of the empire during the winter of 1895-96. As a result, numerous Armenians emigrated from the Pontic region to the Caucasus and Russia and as far away as the United States of America.

Conclusion

The Armenian communities of the Black Sea area underwent major social, economic, and political transformations during the nineteenth century. They increased their access to education and their participation in local administration, and they prospered in the economic sphere. During the latter part of the century, the Armenian population declined, although those who remained continued to further their social, economic, and political endeavors. For a short period after the reforms of the 1860s, the government succeeded in maintaining the loyalty of the Armenians but in so doing perhaps also paved the way toward the emergence of new interest groups which would come to demand greater reforms to protect the interests of the Ottoman Armenian population. After the Treaty of Berlin in 1878, this issue became known as the Armenian Question. When all diplomatic and peaceful efforts failed, an Armenian self-defense and revolutionary movement emerged, provoking severe retaliatory measures by the sultan's regime. The Hamidian massacres had a direct impact on the decline of the Pontic Armenian communities. Yet, the Young Turk revolution in 1908 inspired new hopes and a brief period of revival. Such optimism was soon to be drowned, however, in the bloody events of 1915, leaving behind only a fading legacy of Armenian enlightenment, commerce, and civil service along the southern littoral of the Black Sea.

Appendix I

Armenians in the Province of Trebizond [by Kaza] According to Ottoman General Census of 1881/82-1893[71]

Trebizond Sanjak	Female	Male
Trebizond kaza	4,440	5,106
Ordu	3,586	3,966
Giresun (Kerasund)	610	629
Tireboli	232	281
Gorele	99	82
Vakfikebir	29	27
Akchaabad	1,367	1,591
Surmene	71	107
Of	---	---
Total	10,434	11,789

Janik/Canik (Samsun) Sanjak	Female	Male
Janik kaza	459	709
Charshamba	4,670	5,105
Unieh (Ünye)	1,662	1,973
Fatsa	354	448
Terme	763	878
Bafra	466	546
Total	8,369	9,659

Lazistan Sanjak	Female	Male
Rize kaza	---	---
Pazar (Atina)	20	22
Hopa (Khopa)	2	5
Total	22	27

[71] *Source:* BA(Y)/(P)/11s311, no. 215, in Kemal Karpat, *Ottoman Population, 1830-1914: Demographic and Social Characteristics* (Madison: University of Wisconsin Press, 1985).

Gumushkhane Sanjak	Female	Male	
Gumushkhane kaza	514	638	
Torul	---	---	
Kelkit	58	55	
Shiran	100	121	
Total	672	814	
Trebizond Province	**19,497**	**22,289**	
Grand Total			**41,786**
Catholics	629	644	**1,273**
Protestants	440	445	**885**

Appendix II

List of Trebizond Merchants Dealing in Foreign Trade
(December 1884)[72]

Exporters

NAME OF MERCHANT   EXPORTED ITEMS

NAME OF MERCHANT	EXPORTED ITEMS
Arnaoudoglou Brothers	Nuts, beans, tobacco, salt fish (anchovies)
Aznavourian Brothers	Nuts, beans, porpoise oil
Boyadjihis, P.	Bones, horn scrapings, rags
Caprielian Brothers	Skins, tobacco, nuts, beans, walnut loupes, wools
Captranian, M.	Cereals, beans, nuts, linseed, linen stuffs
Cacoulides, P.	Nuts, tobacco, maize
Caragheuzian Brothers	Boxwood, walnut loupes
Carvonides, Georges	Nuts, tobacco
Constantinoff, D.G.	Skins, beans, tobacco, cereals, nuts
Davidian, G.	Skins, tobacco, wax, linseed, beans, nuts
Dernersessian, M.	Beans, nuts
Diradourian Brothers	Cereals, nuts, beans, walnut loupes
Djermakian, G.	Guts, porpoise oil
Efremides, L.P.	Nuts, beans, tobacco, cereals, wax, porpoise oil
Ghiurekian, S.	Beans, nuts, cereals
Hadji Ali Halfouz Effendi	Wheat, nuts, tobacco
Hochstrasse and Co.	Nuts, tobacco, beans, etc.
Khedechi, Vartan	Linen stuff
Lemlioglu Brothers	Nuts, beans, tobacco, raisins, wax, cereals, etc.
Makhokhian, A.	Nuts, beans
Marmarian, S.	Tobacco, beans, maize, nuts, skins

---

[72] Source: FO 526/110, in Üner Turgay, "Trade Merchants in Nineteenth-Century Trabzon: Elements of Ethnic Conflict," pp. 308-10.

Melides, S.	Nuts, cereals, tobacco, linseed
Missir, O.	Skins, beans, nuts, maize, tobacco
Nourian Brothers	Beans, skins, nuts, maize, linen stuffs
Pareghentanian, S.J.	Beans, nuts, skins, maize, hair
Parigoris, Th.	Nuts, salt fish (anchovies)
Sahadjian, H. Boghos	Boxwood
Salihoglou, Ali Hafouz	Nuts, tobacco, beans
Sarafian, B.	Beans, nuts, guts
Sassi, A.	Porpoise oil, nuts
Saoulides, C.	Tobacco
Triandaphilides, A.	Maize, beans, nuts, tobacco, porpoise oil, etc.
Vartabedian Brothers	Nuts, maize, beans

Importers

NAME OF MERCHANT	IMPORTED ITEMS
Arabian, Maranian	Manchester goods, Aleppo goods, yarn bagging, metals, etc.
Arabian Brothers	Manchester goods, Aleppo goods, fezes
Arghiropolous, D.	Colonial wares, bags, shot, steel
Arnaoudoglou Brothers	Colonial wares, flour, metals, gold thread, jewelry
Boyadjidhis, P.	Fancy goods, perfumery, hosiery, cloth, etc.
Calpakdjides Brothers	Manchester goods (especially prints)
Capayanides, G.	Colonial wares, tea, soap, candles, metals, etc.
Caprielian Brothers	Colonial wares, bags
Captanian, M.	Flour, bags
Cariofili Brothers	Manchester goods, yarn
Casfkis, D.	Cloth, spirits wine, grocery

Condozi Constantinof	Grey goods, Aleppo goods, bags and bagging
Congalides Brothers	Colonial wares, metals, olives, oil, fruits, etc.
Constantinides, D.	Drugs, spices, haberdashery, hardware
Derhampartzoumian Brothers	Leather and shoemakers' articles
Djermakian, G.	Matches, scythes
Djoulfazoglou, Hadji Hussein	Grey goods, Aleppo goods, tea, metals
Efremides, P.L.	Flour, petroleum, indigo, hides
Elefteriadhi, Lefter	Gold thread and laces, haberdashery
Fetvadjian Brothers	Cloth, fezes, fancy goods, hardware, etc.
Goondoubzade, Vehib Effendi	Grey goods
Hamamdjizade, H. Ismael	Manchester goods
Hekimian, J.	Spirits, wine, beer, provisions, empty bottles
Israelian, Nigoghos	Sewing machines
Kazandjioglous Brothers	Manchester goods, Russian cotton manufactures
Khedechian, Caloust,and Cie	Manchester goods
Khederian, Artin	Fezes, tassels
Kytrides, Anesti	Grocery, looking glasses, lamps, bedsteads
Lemlioglou Brothers	General goods, colonial wares, metals, salt, etc.
Makhokhian, A.	General goods, colonial wares, metals, bags, candles, etc.
Marengo, J.B.	Apothecary
Marengo, J.N.	Apothecary
Meghavorian Brothers	Silken and woolen stuffs
Melides, S.	Sugar, spirits, matches
Metaxa Brothers	Manchester goods, bags, wax-cloth, fezes
Mikaelian, O.	Jewelry, watches
Missir, O.	Colonial wares, cochineal, bags, leather, etc.

Nourian Brothers	Aleppo goods, raw cotton
Pareghentanian, S.J.	Hides, cereals
Petropoulos, P.	Cereals
Sarafian, B.	Matches, steel
Serassi and Elefteriadi	Manchester goods (especially prints)
Serdarzade Salih Effendi	Yarns
Shoemakers' Society	Leathers and shoes, etc.
Sirinopoulos, Y.	Grey goods
Sofianopoulos, L.	Colonial wares, chemicals, dyes, paints, window glass
Taghmazian	Aleppo goods
Tailors' Society	Cloth, haberdashery, etc.
Tchairoglou, P.	Crockery and glassware, lamps, hardware, etc.
Tezopoulos, V.	Aleppo goods, yarn
Tigdaban, Vahid and Akif Effendi	Manchester goods
Tirakian, Garabed	Window glass, lemons and oranges
Triandaphilides, A.	General goods, colonial wares, rice, tea, metals
Tzouliadis G.	Flour, biscuits, and macaroni
Vafiadis, Mourad	Colonial wares, chemicals, dyes, paints, window glass
Vafiadis Brothers	Bags and bagging
Vartabedian Brothers	Grey goods, colonial wares
Velissaridhi Brothers	Cloth, fezes, fancy goods, haberdashery
Xifilino and Sofiano	Bookseller and binder, printer, stationer
Yanicapani, Panajoti	Silken and woolen stuffs, velvets
Yelkendjizade Brothers	Flour, maize
Zimplindes Brothers	Manchester goods

�֍ 11 ✱

REFORM, REVOLUTION, AND REPRESSION:
THE TREBIZOND ARMENIANS IN THE 1890S

Barbara J. Merguerian

The story of the Armenians of Trebizond (Trabzon) province during the 1890s is marked by sharp contrasts: economic growth in urban areas combined with extreme poverty in the villages, expanding educational and cultural opportunities hampered by restrictive measures instituted by the central and local governments, and aspirations for a just and egalitarian civil society destroyed with the utmost bloodshed and cruelty by reactionary authorities. A combination of circumstances gave Trebizond the distinction of becoming the site of the first outbreak of violence in the eastern provinces (*vilayet*s) during the 1895 massacres. Prominent among the eyewitnesses to the bloodshed in Trebizond was the American missionary stationed there (Moses P. Parmelee, M.D.) as well as two young American diplomats who happened to be passing through the city on their way to consular posts in the interior (Robert S. Chilton, Jr. and William Dulany Hunter). Following a series of shattering events, the Armenians of Trebizond emerged at the end of the decade scarred and damaged but with remarkable resilience, as they prepared to rebuild community and institutions.

Several features, many derived from its geographical location, distinguished the Trebizond Armenian community, but the events that took place there in the 1890s cannot be viewed in isolation. On the contrary, they can be understood only within the context of the larger forces at work in the Ottoman Empire as a whole and in the overall Armenian community of which Trebizond constituted one small part. The nineteenth century has been characterized by what is called the "Armenian awakening," a process marked by a rise in the educational level of the people, by a flowering of culture, especially in literature, and by a growing national self-consciousness that manifested itself in many ways. Politically, the crowning achievement of this period came with adoption in 1863 of the Armenian "National Constitution," an event that introduced more democratic elements into the governance of the community.[1] Historians may disagree as to whether the Armenian renaissance took place because of, in spite of, or independent of, the general reform effort known as the *Tanzimat* in the Ottoman Empire, a movement that reached its culmination with the promulgation of an Ottoman constitution in 1876. That movement was shattered in the late 1870s with the empire's crushing defeat in the war with Russia, preceded by the accession to the throne of the conservative, if not reactionary, Sultan Abdul Hamid II.

The Ottoman defeat in the Russo-Turkish war of 1877-78 provided ample opportunity for the European powers to intervene in the affairs of Turkey, but competition and mutual jealousies precluded strong action. The international agreements that most affected the Armenians included the Cyprus Convention of 1878, whereby Great Britain guaranteed Turkey's eastern borders in return for the sultan's promise to introduce administrative reforms and concrete measures "for the protection of the Christian and other subjects of the Porte in these territories," as well as the right to control of the island of Cyprus as a guarantee (and a strategic naval base in the eastern Mediterranean opposite the Suez Canal). That same year in July, the Treaty of Berlin (signed by Great Britain, France, Russia, Germany, Austria-Hungary, Italy, and the Ottoman Empire) specified in Article 61 that the Ottoman government "undertakes to carry out, without further delay, the improvements and reforms demanded by local requirements in the provinces inhabited by Armenians, and to guarantee their security against the Circassians and Kurds."

These provisions gave Armenians hope for an amelioration of their tribulations. The practical effect, however, was to provide the European powers, especially Great Britain, with excuses to meddle in Ottoman affairs, much to the annoyance of the sultan, who nonetheless cleverly managed to exploit Great Power rivalries to his own advantage.[2] More ominously, the sultan interpreted the military and eco-

---

[1] James Etmekjian, *The French Influence on the Western Armenian Renaissance, 1843-1915* (New York: Twayne Publishers, 1964); Vartan Artinian, *The Armenian Constitutional System in the Ottoman Empire, 1839-1863* (Istanbul: Isis Press, 1988).

[2] The standard literature on the Eastern Question and related Armenian Question in the nineteenth century includes Matthew S. Anderson, *The Eastern Question, 1774-1923* (London: St. Martin's Press, 1966); William L. Langer, *The Diplomacy of Imperialism* (New York: Alfred A. Knopf, 1951), chs. 5, 7, 10; A.O. Sarkissian, *His-*

nomic weakness of his empire as justification to reassert the despotism of earlier rulers and to seek unity by emphasizing the Islamic character of the country. Abdul Hamid turned his back on the reform movement, whose aim had been to place the government in the hands of an educated, rational, and professionally trained elite. Instead, he instituted a personal autocratic rule in which loyalty to the sovereign was defined as the greatest good. At the same time, the sultan took advantage of new technology, particularly the telegraph, to assert strict control over regional and local officials in his far-flung empire and enforced his authority through an elaborate network of spies and agents—a situation that provided ample opportunity for intrigue and corruption.[3] For the Armenians, perhaps the most disastrous initiative taken by Abdul Hamid was the establishment of the *Hamidiye* regiments, formed by arming the Kurdish tribesmen ostensibly to guard the eastern borders of the empire but in practice setting loose a military force that robbed and looted Armenian villages at will, creating a reign of terror for the unarmed inhabitants in the region. All of these problems were exacerbated by depressed economic conditions, especially in rural areas.

The Ottoman constitution promulgated in 1876 was quickly suppressed in 1878, and with it the promise of an effective and equitable judicial, administrative, and tax system. The Armenians were faced with the unpalatable choice of appealing for the redress of their grievances to an unresponsive government or else turning to foreign powers for support—the latter a course that did not endear them to the Ottoman rulers. As the social and economic situation of the Armenians deteriorated, a generation of young people (many of them coming from outside of the Ottoman Empire) developed radical programs to overthrow the Ottoman yoke and to introduce some measure of autonomy for their Armenian compatriots. The great tragedy of the Armenian community in the Ottoman Empire during this period was its inability under the existing situation to develop a moderate plan of action. The community had long been divided between the interests of a small, wealthy, but politically insecure upper class and a growing middle class in the large cites, on the one hand, and the vast majority of the impoverished population living in the rural areas, on the other. The

tory of the Armenian Question to 1885 (Urbana: University of Illinois Press, 1938).
    [3] Selim Deringil, *The Well-Protected Domains: Ideology and the Legitimation of Power in the Ottoman Empire, 1876-1909* (London: J.B. Tauris, 1998); Kemal H. Karpat, *The Politicization of Islam: Reconstructing Identity, State, Faith, and Community in the Late Ottoman State* (London: Oxford University Press, 2001).

Armenian Church, led by the Patriarch of Constantinople, attempted to play an enlightened leadership role, but it became trapped between an intractable government that only occasionally and begrudgingly responded to glaring abuses, and a Western-educated intelligentsia for whom the Church represented increasingly an obsequious and conservative force.

This situation provided an opportunity for Armenian radical and revolutionary groups, though small in numbers, to embark on bold and imaginative actions designed to attract maximum attention; their lofty idealism combined with flagrant pragmatism (they did not hesitate to use violence and intimidation to achieve their objectives) left many Armenians disconcerted and bewildered. The Ottoman government, for its part, responded with the utmost severity, making mass arrests with flimsy or no evidence of wrongdoing and leaving prisoners in unsanitary jails for long periods without filing formal charges, often inflicting torture to induce confessions. The government pretended and spread the word that Armenian activists represented a serious threat to the state; the effect being to stereotype the Armenians as seditious and to arouse the enmity of the Muslim population. One scholar has argued that the greatest single error of the Armenian revolutionary parties during the period of 1885 to 1908 was their mistaken assumption that the European powers would intervene in the Ottoman Empire in order to save the Armenian people from the clutches of Turkish misrule.[4] In fact, the two most interested powers, Great Britain and Russia, were too jealous of each other: Britain was satisfied with a weak Turkey that could nonetheless stand as a bulwark against Russian expansion, while Russia was content to stir up animosities but fearful that meaningful reforms in Turkey's eastern provinces would encourage Russia's Armenian subjects in the adjacent Caucasus region to seek greater rights and autonomy.[5]

---

[4] Christopher J. Walker, *Armenia: The Survival of a Nation* (London: Routledge, 1990), p. 127.

[5] See, for example, the comments of the Russian ambassador in Vienna, Prince A.B. Lobanov, to his British counterpart to the effect that any plan to grant autonomy to the Ottoman Armenians would place his government in a difficult position because the Russian Armenians, "who already give trouble enough, would take fire at once and formulate demands which it would be impossible to comply with." See Great Britain, Foreign Office Archives (cited hereafter as FO), FO 424 (Confidential Print, Turkey), vol. 178, "Further Correspondence Respecting Asiatic Turkey," no. 414, Sir E. Monson to the Earl of Kimberly, Vienna, Dec. 8, 1894.

Trebizond in the 1890s

The exposed geographic position of the city of Trebizond as a port on the Black Sea had a significant effect on the character and development of the local Armenians. This was a cosmopolitan community, with a number of minorities (in addition to Armenians, a large Greek population as well as Laz, Jews, Tatars, and others). Armenians made up a relatively small portion, numbering about 50,000 out of a total population estimated at more than one million in the vilayet.[6] Their relatively small numbers should not mask the importance of the Armenians, particularly in the city of Trebizond and to a lesser extent in Samsun, where their merchants and businessmen, along with the Greeks, dominated commerce. The trade passing through Trebizond had been growing rapidly since the middle of the century, and this trend continued well into the 1890s, until it was interrupted by the growing social and political unrest in the area. The fact that business, trade, and finance were concentrated in the hands of Greeks and Armenians, who nonetheless held little political power except within their own communities and who enjoyed only minimal representation in the courts and administration, presented a major element of instability.[7] The economic situation was very different in the countryside, where poverty was widespread and where conditions had steadily deteriorated since the Russo-Turkish war. Writing from the town of Ordu in 1894, American missionary Dr. M.P. Parmelee reported:

> The extreme prostration of business hinders every enterprise in which our people engage. In former years it has seemed as if the lowest depths had been reached. But lower depths have been found. To the

---

[6] Population figures are taken from FO 424, vol. 183, "Further Correspondence Respecting Asiatic Turkey, July-September, 1895," no. 30 (May 30, 1895), based on Vital Cuinet, *La Turquie d'Asie*. General information on the Armenians of Trebizond province in the late nineteenth century can be found in Raymond H. Kévorkian and Paul B. Paboudjian, *Les Arméniens dans l'Empire ottoman à la veille du génocide* (Paris: Editions d'Arts et d'Histoire, 1992), pp. 179-206; and Hovakim Hovakimian, *Patmutiun Haykakan Pontosi* [History of Armenian Pontus] (Beirut: Mshak Press, 1967), pp. 105-33.

[7] See A. Üner Turgay, "Trade and Merchants in Nineteenth Century Trabzon: Elements of Ethnic Conflict," in Benjamin Braude and Bernard Lewis, eds., *Christians and Jews in the Ottoman Empire*, 2 vols. (New York: Holmes & Meier, 1982), vol. 1, pp. 287-318. Turgay argues that the non-Muslim traders benefited from support by European powers, thus increasing social tensions.

steady pressure of increasing taxation, and the extortions of unfeeling tax-gatherers, has been added a short harvest, so that, instead of large exports of corn and beans, the people of Ordoo now get their flour from Odessa and Marseilles. The same is true of Trebizond. Certainly a country which has nothing but agriculture to depend on is in a sorry case if it cannot feed itself. This is exactly the state of large portions of Turkey. [8]

The inhabitants of Trebizond were especially well informed concerning contemporary political currents both within the Ottoman Empire and abroad. Trade and commerce brought in foreign businessmen as well as diplomats. News of the latest events in the capital or from abroad quickly spread; here it was relatively easy for foreigners to visit or for the locals to go abroad—to Constantinople or to Batum and then on to Russia or Europe. The same was true to a lesser extent of the city of Samsun, which served as a major gateway to the interior provinces. Foreign contact intensified the flowering of Armenian culture, and a wealthy commercial class made it possible for Armenians to develop a broad network of educational and cultural institutions. Given Trebizond's exposed geographical position, it was perhaps inevitable that the area should become a center of Armenian political activity as well, with young activists easily moving in from abroad or hastily departing when necessary.

Thus, the first Armenian revolutionary party, the Armenakan, established a branch in Trebizond soon after its formation at Van in 1885. Political activity in the province intensified with the arrival in January 1890 of Ruben Khan-Azat (Nshan Karapetian). One of the seven Russian-Armenian idealistic students who in 1887 had founded the Hnchakian Revolutionary Party in Geneva, Khan-Azat managed to obtain a teaching position in one of the Armenian girls' schools in Trebizond. He found fertile ground among the educated population to preach the Hnchak ideals of a democratic, socialist, and autonomous Armenia and soon established a local committee through which party literature was clandestinely distributed. The party took advantage of Trebizond's port; for example, one member whose name is known only as Ohannes managed to become a coffee server on one of the Turkish

---

[8] Archives of the American Board of Commissioners for Foreign Missions (cited hereafter as ABC Archives), Houghton Library, Harvard University, Unit 5, The Near East (1817-1919), Western Turkey Mission, 16.9.3, vol. 18, Documents & Reports, no. 68, "Annual Report of the Trebizond Mission, 1894-1895."

ships navigating in the Black Sea, thus enabling the group to communicate abroad without difficulty. Khan-Azat and a fellow Hnchak, Hakob (Hagop) Meghavorian, traveled to Constantinople to participate in the Kum Kapu demonstration on July 15, 1890, during which Armenian protestors demanded reforms from the Turkish government. Subsequently tracked down by the police, the two Hnchaks fled from the country, Khan-Azat to Batum and Meghavorian to Europe.

The groundwork prepared by Khan-Azat in Trebizond early in 1890 facilitated the organizational efforts of two Russian-Armenian political activists, members of the Armenian Revolutionary Federation, or Dashnaktsutiun, who arrived soon after. They were Simon Zavarian, one of the three intellectuals who had founded the Dashnaktsutiun in Tiflis in the summer of 1890, and Hovsep Arghutian, who as a member of the Young Armenia Society in Russia had been commissioned to investigate conditions in Turkish Armenia. The two Dashnakists were given a warm reception by segments of the local Armenian community, and most of the Hnchaks recruited by Khan-Azat entered into the new Dashnak organization. At the time, there was nothing unusual in this; the Dashnaktsutiun had been formed as a federation of Armenian revolutionaries, and the two parties became competitive and confrontational only after the Hnchaks withdrew from the Federation in 1891. Indeed Khan-Azat and Meghavorian had been the two Hnchak representatives present in Tiflis during the founding meeting of the Dashnaktsutiun, and they had helped to ensure that the Hnchaks would be part of the new organization. At that meeting in Tiflis, at the suggestion of Khan-Azat, Trebizond was designated as the headquarters for the Dashnaktsutiun (this was accepted as a compromise between the Hnchak center in Geneva and the Dashnak center in Tiflis). It soon proved impractical to have the headquarters in Trebizond or in any part of the Ottoman Empire and thus Tiflis remained the center. As the Turkish police clamped down on the Armenian revolutionaries, Zavarian was arrested and imprisoned. Since he was a subject of Russia, however, he was soon released and expelled, as was Arghutian.[9]

---

[9] A description of the formation of the Armenian political parties, including the participation of Khan-Azat, Meghavorian, Zavarian, and Arghutian, is in Louise Nalbandian, *The Armenian Revolutionary Movement: The Development of Armenian Political Parties through the Nineteenth Century* (Berkeley and Los Angeles: University of California Press, 1963), esp. pp. 146-58. Details about revolutionary activity in Trebizond in the 1890s are provided by Hovakimian, *Patmutiun Haykakan Pontosi*, pp. 134-38.

During this period, the Ottoman government reacted severely to what it considered sedition by the Armenian community. Throughout the empire police conducted wide-ranging interrogations; many Armenians were arrested and, without being informed of the charges against them, were thrown into prison. They languished there for weeks and months, not allowed to see friends and relatives and for all intents and purposes forgotten by the authorities. This situation was fraught with opportunities for abuse. In Trebizond, however, mistreatment was kept to a minimum, apparently because of the efficiency of the governor (*vali*) of the province, Kadri Bey (this according to the testimony of British Consul H.Z. Longworth). The competence of the Trebizond administration was corroborated by the American missionary Dr. Parmelee, who during an overland trip to attend a meeting in Constantinople in 1895 was appalled by conditions he encountered en route, particularly in the treatment of political prisoners. These unfortunate individuals, Parmelee reported, often were left incommunicado in their cells and in some cases died without anyone knowing of their condition until clergymen were notified of their death. "All this is in marked contrast with the treatment of prisoners in Trebizond, where I repeatedly visited them, knew their condition, and was able to aid them in many ways," Parmelee attributed the superior conditions in his region to the presence of a large number of foreign consuls posted there to encourage foreign trade.[10] Indeed, in order to carry out its responsibility under the Cyprus Convention and the Treaty of Berlin to oversee reforms in the empire, Britain had established several consulates in the eastern provinces, although (as one consul later admitted) this was not so much to oversee reforms as it was "on account of the importance of maintaining posts of observation on the Russian and Persian frontiers."[11] In any event, reports during this period by Consul Longworth are full of information about local conditions.

In early 1893, the British Ambassador in Constantinople, Sir Clare Ford, upon receiving reports of large numbers of Armenians unjustly arrested, directed the consuls to submit reports on the arrest and ill-treatment of Armenians within their districts. In response, Consul Longworth writing from Trebizond asserted that there were no Armenians political prisoners in the city of Trebizond, a circumstance he at-

---

[10] ABC Archives, 16.9.3, vol. 25, Letters, Parmelee, no. 60, May 1895.

[11] Robert Graves, *Storm Centres of the Near East: Personal Memories, 1879-1929* (London: Hutchinson, 1933), p. 110.

tributed to the administrative abilities of Kadri Bey. Longworth's report provides a revealing picture of the problems encountered by the local administration as the deteriorating political and economic conditions emboldened the Armenian revolutionaries. In one incident, a packet containing 320 copies of the newspaper *Hnchak*, published abroad by the party, was seized by the authorities in Trebizond. The packet, which also included some thirty letters enclosed in two envelopes for Armenians in Marsovan and Amasia, was in the care of the mate of the Pan-Hellenic steamer "Sparta" and was addressed to Arzoglou, the company's agent at Samsun, a young Greek whose mother was Armenian. Arzoglou denied any knowledge of the packet addressed to him. As an example of the moderation of Kadri Bey, Longworth reported that Arzoglou was not arrested but was placed under police surveillance pending his trial. (The incident was embarrassing to the United States, however, as Arzoglou was also serving as the U.S. consular agent in Samsun). "The consequence of the discovery has been the display of much greater vigilance on the part of the local authorities," Longworth wrote of the incident. "People are now more closely watched, and letters are intercepted." He again contrasted the moderation shown by Kadri Bey in this case with the aggressive actions of the officials in the neighboring province of Sivas, where 550 Armenians were imprisoned "on perhaps very frivolous political charges."[12]

In the face of the deteriorating political situation in the Turkish interior, Consul Longworth continued to praise Kadri Bey's governance in Trebizond. At the same time, he noted that local officials in the Ottoman Empire, in the age of the telegraph, were extremely limited in their powers. "Little or nothing," Longworth reported in early 1894, "can be attained of a durable nature without the sanction of the Porte [Ottoman government], or rather the Palace [Abdul Hamid]." He continued:

---

[12] FO 424/175, "Further Correspondence Respecting Asiatic Turkey," encl. 4 in no. 44, March 28, 1893. Longworth's assessment of the government's "moderation" in the Arzoglou case changed two years later, when he reported that Arzoglou and his father, prominent merchants, had been subsequently exiled to Smyrna and financially ruined for no reason other than the fact that literature deemed revolutionary had been addressed to them. See FO 424/181, no. 119, Jan. 23, 1895. Longworth's jurisdiction included Sivas as well as Trebizond, but in the absence of a British representative in Sivas he depended for his information largely on the U.S. consul there, Dr. M.A. Jewett.

The scope, in fact, of even an efficient Governor, is now-a-days in Turkey extremely limited, from a fear, it would seem, of his gaining undue popularity. Hampered in the initiative, he has been thus almost reduced to a mere automatic machine worked by wire from the capital, the manipulators of which are particularly remarkable for their dilatoriness, so much so that, as action is scarcely ever taken in the nick of time, the performance, as a rule, ends in failure.[13]

Not surprisingly, Longworth had little sympathy for the Hnchak party, because of what he described as the unrealistic nature of its goals and for its advocacy of "arson, robbery, and murder, as the only road to freedom," with a view of "enraging Moslems into such a massacre of the Christians as would . . . rouse the Powers to action in the interests of peace, humanity, and civilization." So outrageous were its tenants that "a firm and honest government would have no difficulty in suppressing such a movement." He concluded:

There would be no baneful effects were it not for the baneful conduct of a certain number of corrupt and tyrannical agents. It has indeed become now not seditious, but the cry of the oppressed against their oppressors. Moderate despotism may be tolerable enough, but the unwarrantable conduct of cruel and relentless spies and officials must render life in many instances quite unbearable, restrained as the Armenians are, indoors and out of doors, in talking, writing, walking, and travelling. The persecution is foolish in the extreme, and as wicked as it is dangerous, for it may drive the unhappy people to despair and thus engender complications of a serious nature.[14]

If relative peace prevailed in Trebizond, Longworth noted, it was because of the extremely restrictive measures adopted by the local administration, which banned most organizational activity, including evening meetings of any kind and allowed only cultural and benevolent organizations to function.[15]

---

[13] FO 424/178, no. 47, Jan. 31, 1894.

[14] Ibid. In the early 1890s the Hnchak leader Avetis Nazarbekian moved to London, where he and his family were under close surveillance by Scotland Yard, but he was not hampered in his activities in publishing the *Hnchak* newspaper. See, for example, the report in FO 424/181, no. 9, Jan. 5, 1895. Great Britain brushed aside appeals by the Turkish government to arrest the Hnchaks living in London. See FO 424/183, no. 159, Aug. 5, 1895.

[15] FO 424/178, no. 531, Dec. 17, 1894; Hovakimian, *Patmutiun Haykakan Pontosi*, pp. 139-40.

Beginning in 1895, however, a number of ominous incidents took place in Trebizond. In early January, after a three-month trial, five Armenian men were found guilty of revolutionary activity or of being accomplices, while another twelve were acquitted. The British consul sent a representative to the court, which was composed of a president, the public prosecutor, two Turkish members, one Greek member, and one Armenian member. The most serious case involved one Adom Aslanian, a native of Sivas arrested in Samsun, who confessed to being a revolutionary but used his court appearances to speak out vehemently about the absolute necessity for reforms and for the punishment of corrupt officials. At the end of the trial, Aslanian was sentenced to fifteen years imprisonment; two persons judged to be his accomplices were sentenced to ten years each, and two others from Charshamba were sentenced to five years each for distributing weapons. Longworth asserted that justice had been done in the trial, though aspects of it were troubling. The men had been arrested in early 1894 and had been held in jail in Samsun under appalling conditions for several months before being conveyed in the government cutter "Ineboli" for trial in Trebizond, where they were marched from the dock to prison heavily chained. There were many assertions of ill-treatment in the Samsun jail, as authorities sought to elicit false confessions.[16]

Another troubling incident centered around the Armenian primate of Trebizond, Very Reverend Eghishe Aivazian. In early 1895, Aivazian declined to sign a ceremonial letter expressing birthday congratulations to Sultan Abdul Hamid on the ground that it was up to the Patriarch of Constantinople, not to him, to perform this kind of function. His refusal aroused the suspicion of the governor, who in a complaint filed in Constantinople went on to criticize the allegedly inflammatory character of Aivazian's sermons. The governor held Aivazian responsible for the fact that a few months earlier two clergymen, Father Tatul Garmirian (Karmirian), pastor of the church in the village of Martil, in Charchamba, and Father Mikayel Tahmazian, pastor in the village of Chalgamlik, district of Unieh (Uniye; Unia), had been arrested on charges of belonging to a revolutionary committee and of keeping arms and munitions; several of their relatives and acquaintances had been detained in this connection.[17] The complaint by

---

[16] FO 424/181, no. 84, Jan. 11, 1895. Aslanian was subsequently shipped to Constantinople for further questioning. See FO 424/181, no. 198, Feb. 7, 1895.

[17] The Armenian Patriarch asserted, in a " Memorandum on the Situation of the

the governor was forwarded to the Armenian Patriarch in Constantinople, who asked Aivazian for an explanation. Under unclear circumstances, Reverend Aivazian resigned his position and planned to travel to Constantinople on May 25 but found himself faced with a group of about 500 Armenian demonstrators determined to prevent his departure—an event that further aroused the governor's suspicions. Receiving a message about the demonstration, Consul Longworth hurried to the prelacy and, according to his report, succeeded in dispersing the crowd and convincing Aivazian to remain in Trebizond. But the events had unnerved the primate, who two days later committed suicide by throwing himself from the top-storey window of the prelacy.[18]

These incidents in Trebizond represented local manifestation of the general lawlessness and unrest that were plaguing the empire during this period. The growing misery of the population, fueled by deteriorating economic conditions and broken promises of legal and administrative reform, encouraged the political activists to step up their activities in an effort to bolster their influence in the community. This in turn led the government to institute increasingly harsh measures against any indications of civic disobedience. The massacres of Armenians in the interior villages of Sasun in the fall of 1894 attracted the spotlight of the international press and shamed the European powers into diplomatic action. But the inability of the powers, particularly Great Britain and Russia, to agree on a policy confined most of their efforts to talk, not action, and again provided the sultan with the opportunity to play one power off against the other. Abdul Hamid was quick to label all petitions for the amelioration of conditions as machinations by foreign powers and as disloyalty on the part of the Armenians, rather than as efforts to reform and strengthen the empire. Local officials, eager to

---

Armenians in the Vilayet of Trabizond" submitted to British Ambassador Philip Currie on February 13, 1895, that the two clergymen (Tatul and Mikayel) had been arrested after they had refused to pay bribes to local officials and that no evidence of their guilt for any offense had been presented. The patriarch reported that more than fifty Armenians were in prison in Trebizond, none of whom had committed any crime other than receiving newspapers published abroad or protesting against abuses and injustices. See FO 424/181, encl. 2 in no. 188, Feb. 1, 1895.

[18] The incident is described in Hovakimian, *Patmutiun Haykakan Pontosi*, pp. 143-45; FO 424/182, nos. 331-332, May 25 and 27, 1895. According to a local priest (Father Vahan), at Aivazian's funeral, the Russian consul pointed out that the late primate had always run to the English consul for advice and assistance. By turning their faces away from Russia and toward England, the Armenians were making a mistake they would regret, the Russian consul declared. See Hovakimian, p. 145.

curry favor with the authorities, used every pretext to show their loyalty by arresting Armenians and charging them with sedition, usually on little or no evidence; the use of torture to extract confessions was endemic. Occasionally, on petition from foreign powers, the sultan would pardon or exile a group of Armenian political prisoners. But without basic reform in the administrative and judicial system, the problems persisted and multiplied.

The Turmoil of October 1895

Matters came to a head in the fall of 1895, both in Constantinople and in Trebizond. In the capital, negotiations intensified between the Ottoman government and the European powers (especially Britain and Russia, who cooperated for a brief period in the aftermath of the Sasun massacre of Armenians in 1894) to develop a plan for reform in the administration of the eastern provinces. On September 30, Armenians in Constantinople staged a protest known as the Bab Ali demonstration to demand the implementation of such reforms. This initially peaceful action quickly turned violent and led to ten days of terror instituted by the government and directed against Armenians living in the capital, hundreds of whom locked themselves up in the Armenian churches. Reports of these events, often exaggerated or inaccurate, quickly reached Trebizond, where General Bahri Pasha, the former governor of Van, happened to be spending a few days on his way back to the capital. A notoriously corrupt and inept administrator, Bahri was an unpopular figure with the Armenians and had been severely criticized by the British before being forced to resign. On Wednesday, October 2, accompanied by the commander of the local regiment (Hamdi Pasha), the Persian consul-general (Rezi Khan), and the telegraph inspector (Haji Omer Effendi), Bahri Pasha was walking along the street on his way to the dock to catch the steamer to Constantinople when two young men sprang out of a narrow passage and directed several shots at him before managing to escape. Bahri Pasha received a flesh wound in the hip, while Hamdi Pasha was shot in the ankle—neither man being seriously injured. The two assailants, Misak Kasparian and Khachig Aslanian, youths of sixteen and seventeen years of age respectively, managed to elude authorities and avoid arrest. News of the attack quickly spread throughout the province.[19]

In Trebizond, the situation became tense. Two days after the assassination attempt, on Friday evening, October 4, large bands of armed Muslims from neighboring villages took to the streets of the city, plundering Christian houses, breaking doors and windows, firing volleys in the streets, and terrifying inhabitants. According to the report of the French consul, a crowd of no fewer than 3,000 armed men gathered in the government square; the military force available to the authorities was completely inadequate to control such a mob, and it was only the firm stance taken by the governor that prevented the angry armed men from attacking the Christian quarters at that time.[20] Concerned about the ominous atmosphere, the next day (October 5) foreign consuls and vice consuls representing Russia, Persia, Austria, Italy, France, Greece, Belgium, and Spain, engaged five carriages and drove ostentatiously through the city to meet with the governor and local notables. "Though in plain clothes, some would like to think that our procession was as a spectacle imposing enough to calm the fears of the Christians and strike fear into the hearts of the Turks!" the British consul boasted. The governor assured his diplomatic visitors that he would take all necessary measures to insure public security, promising to have the troops reinforced, the gendarmerie increased, disreputable characters arrested, and the consulates, missions, and churches (where Armenians were taking refuge) effectively protected. Subsequently, however, as the local American missionary put it, the governor failed to keep a single one of his promises.[21] Either Longworth had been mistaken in his positive assessment of the Trebizond governor's competence, or the actions of Kadri Bey were being manipulated by outside forces.

On the following Monday, October 7, one of the Turkish men wounded during the Friday night's violence, a member of a prominent local family, died. The Muslim population widely assumed the death to be caused by Armenian violence, but some evidence suggests that the

---

[19] Hovakimian, *Patmutiun Haykakan Pontosi*, pp. 148-51; FO 424/184, no. 128, Oct. 5, 1895.

[20] France, Ministère des Affaires Etrangères, *Documents diplomatiques: Affaires arméniennes (supplément), 1895-1896* (Paris: Imp. Nationale, 1897), pt. 1, Events in Trebizond, no. 4, from Consul M. Cillière, Oct. 5, 1895.

[21] FO 424/184, no. 125, Oct. 5, 1895; ABC Archives, 16.9.3, 25/67, Parmelee, Letters, Oct. 14, 1895. The French consul also reported (*Documents diplomatiques*, no. 10, Oct. 15, 1895) that the governor had not kept his promises.

victim was caught inadvertently in the line of fire or, alternatively, that he was the losing party in a private, personal feud. Whatever the truth, tensions heightened, and that evening crowds of armed Muslims once again took to the streets but were prevented by the authorities from causing trouble. Thousands of Christians took refuge in foreign consulates and schools, hoping thereby to avoid any possible violence. At the same time, the governor, Kadri Bey, requested a meeting with representatives of the Armenian community during which he warned that he would be unable to continue to restrain the Muslim population unless the Armenians turned over the two young men who had attempted to assassinate Bahri Pasha. The governor brushed aside the protestations of the Armenian leaders that they did not know the whereabouts of the would-be assassins and that the entire community could not be held responsible for the actions of a couple of young hotheads.[22] The next day, Tuesday, October 8, an uneasy calm prevailed, and the businessmen opened their shops. Suddenly late in the morning violence broke out simultaneously in several parts of the city. The American missionary Parmelee, in a report widely quoted at the time, wrote:

> I ran to an upper window and saw men on every hand with guns and pistols and swords in their hands, and aiming and firing in different directions, one poor fellow falling just about our door. From every quarter came the sounds of the crash of arms. The attack had begun almost simultaneously in all parts of the town at about 11 o'clock a.m. and continued without interruption until 5 p.m. Every Armenian that was found on the streets was shot down—those fleeing were hunted up in their hiding places, and ruthlessly cut down.
>
> Houses were entered and the men cut down in the presence of their wives and children. The women and children were not hurt, except in a few instances, which seemed to be accidental. Harmless and quiet men were ruthlessly cut down though begging for mercy. . . . The frenzied rioters rushed through the market and carefully inquiring the shops of Armenians, attacked them with the greatest fury. If they were open they looted them, and carried off the booty. If they were shut, they had blacksmiths and locksmiths with them to open the shutters and doors and safes, from which they took bales of goods, handfuls of gold and other valuables. For hours that evening and the next morning the plunder was moving past my house. The anxiety and terror that prevailed may be conceived but cannot be described. . . . Not satisfied at killing and robbing, the maddened mob rented their spite on the

---

[22] Hovakimian, *Patmutiun Haykakan Pontosi*, pp. 151-52.

dead, stripping them of clothing, mutilating them, and dragging them like dogs along the ground. Wagonload after wagonload was carried off to be buried in trenches or cast in the sea.[23]

All the foreign eyewitness accounts report that the police and soldiers, far from trying to stop the violence, either stood by and allowed the rioting to continue or else directed and participated in the action and took their share of the spoils. These eyewitnesses concluded that the massacre had been centrally planned and was not a spontaneous outbreak by the fact that it began in several parts of the city at the same time and ended at the same time. As additional evidence, they noted that the attacks carefully targeted Armenian men, while women and children, as well as Greek inhabitants and even Catholic Armenians or Armenians who were Russian subjects, had been excluded. In some cases Armenians were told to "surrender," as if they had been engaged in some act of rebellion, but those who tried to save themselves in this way were arrested and thrown into prison. This was in line with the government's policy of labeling Armenians as criminals or traitors. Privately, in a memo marked "strictly confidential," Consul Longworth later speculated that a "secret agency" had been responsible for the violence, exciting the Muslim population and paralyzing the local authorities. In a conclusion admittedly based on conjecture but providing the most plausible explanation of events, the British diplomat suggested that the chief instigators of the massacres had been the spies of the palace, who had been infesting the country. [24]

Fear of another outbreak of violence was widespread, and every kind of wild rumor spread. On Wednesday, October 9, for example, it was reported that a large body of armed Armenians gathered from the neighboring villages was preparing an attack on the city in revenge for the recent events. "The idea was grotesquely preposterous," Dr. Parmelee pointed out, given the fact that the Armenian villagers were few in number and in any event "abjectly poor and ignorant." It was later discovered that "the poor Armenian villagers were being driven from their homes or murdered, their houses plundered and burned, and the only gathering was that of a crowd of helpless, trembling, half-naked refugees at the monastery two miles from the city."[25] On October 10, it was

---

[23] ABC Archives, 25/67, Parmelee, Letters, Oct. 14, 1895.

[24] FO 424/184, no. 275, Oct. 12, 1895; 424/184, no. 279, Oct. 26, 1895; 424/84, no. 538, Nov. 6, 1895.

[25] ABC Archives, 25/67, Parmelee, Letters, Oct. 14, 1895.

announced that the sultan had declared a state of siege in Trebizond and had assigned Major General Salib Pasha to take command of the city and conduct a court martial, which subsequently took place in great secrecy. News of the restoration of quiet in the capital, as well as the arrival in Trebizond harbor of the Russian gunboat "Teretz" on October 14, helped to bring about an uneasy calm.

From the city of Trebizond the massacre spread to other parts of the province. In the other large city, Samsun, armed Muslims threatened violence, but a firm and decisive governor was able to maintain order; prompt government action also prevented bloodshed in Ordu. These were the exceptions. In Gumushkhane, Armenians were massacred in the city and neighboring villages on October 25 and 26. In Charshamba (located in the sanjak of Samsun), troops sent in December to the village of Aghdja-Guney ostensibly to protect the people against brigands instead attacked the inhabitants, pillaged their homes, and desecrated the Armenian church. They profaned religious objects in the presence of the priest, whom they tied up, warning that all Armenians who did not convert to Islam would be treated in the same manner.[26] Of the devastation in rural areas, Parmelee reported:

> I have taken a list of sixteen villages, containing in all 1,330 Armenian houses, or not less than 8,000 souls, every one of which, with but one exception, was robbed and the greater part burned and the men, women, and children shot down and cut to pieces, or driven off or carried into captivity. One village, Varzahan, an interesting place with the ruins of three ancient churches, consisting of 100 Armenian houses, was completely wiped out of existence; a few escaped the flying bullets and got away, but the mass were butchered in cold blood. In Baiboort itself I was told by a widow just from there with her four small children, her husband being among the killed, that not more than twenty Armenian men were at large in the city. The rest were killed or in prison, or possibly a few in hiding.
>
> This terrible devastation was caused by Lazes from the coast and Kurds from the interior, assisted by neighboring Turks.[27]

Hundreds of Armenians had been arrested during and immediately after the bloodshed, but not a single Muslim was apprehended or even disarmed, causing Dr. Parmelee to note sarcastically: "Apparently all

---

[26] FO 424/185, no. 295, Oct. 16, 1895; 424/186, no. 146, Jan. 3, 1896.

[27] ABC Archives, 25/69, Parmelee, Letters, Dec. 6, 1895.

this murder of peaceable and law-abiding subjects of the Sultan is no crime worthy of notice."[28] British Consul Longworth reported that the local government persisted in the "make belief" that there was an insurrectionary movement in Trebizond even though unable "to name a single Turk as killed or wounded by Armenians on the occasion of the outbreak."[29] He stressed the imperative for the government to conduct an impartial investigation in order to identify and punish the "ring leaders" of the violence. Otherwise "lawless characters" would take advantage of the situation, and the cycle of death and destruction would continue. Acceptance of a reform plan by the sultan (which took place on October 17, 1895) was all very well and good, but Longworth doubted that this action would "meet the exigencies of the situation in these parts," which required "quick and decisive action." He continued:

> The country is, no doubt, passing through a severe political crisis. . . .
> There seems to me only one way out of the difficulty. It is the dispatch
> here, without unnecessary delay, of a strong Commission of Inquiry,
> and the replacement of the troops here by such as have taken no part
> whatever in the disturbances.[30]

No commission of inquiry took place, and the bloodshed spread throughout the Armenian provinces, as the British consul had feared.[31] It was as if Sultan Abdul Hamid had been determined to demonstrate to the European powers that, however much they might pressure his government for reform, he was in the final analysis master of his realm and could do as he pleased within it, without having to answer to anyone inside or outside of his domain. It was intended also, perhaps, as a warning to Armenian reform advocates within the empire of the terrible consequences that could follow appeals to foreign governments for assistance.

---

[28] Ibid., 25/67, Oct. 14, 1895.

[29] FO 424/184, no. 458, Nov. 2, 1895.

[30] Ibid., no. 370, Oct.21, 1895.

[31] On the 1895 massacres of the Armenians in the Ottoman Empire, see Vahakn Dadrian, *History of the Armenian Genocide: Ethnic Conflict from the Balkans to Anatolia to the Caucasus* (Providence, RI: Berghahn Books, 1995), pp. 113-71; Robert A. Melson, *Revolution and Genocide: On the Origins of the Armenian Genocide and the Holocaust* (Chicago: University of Chicago Press, 1992), pp. 43-69; Walker, *Armenia*, pp. 121-73.

Dr. Moses P. Parmalee

Estimates of Armenian losses vary. The official figures, which included only those Armenians who lived in Trebizond, totaled 298 killed in the city; Western observers doubled the figure to include Armenians who happened to be in the city at the time. That the loss of life was not greater can be explained by the fact that Armenians had flocked to the protection of foreign consulates and institutions. During the height of the violence, the local French convent alone sheltered an estimated 2,000 to 3,000 people. In February 1896, the British consulate submitted a summary report of the losses sustained by Armenians in the districts (sanjaks) of Trebizond and Gumushkhane alone during the previous October: 507 killed and 5,197 emigrated; 1,510 homes and shops looted and 320 burned.[32]

American Accounts

The mayhem in Trebizond (as well as in Constantinople) shattered the belief that the presence of foreign consuls could somehow prevent the outbreak of violence and protect the population. Indeed, Longworth, who found himself outside the British consulate when the massacre erupted, was fired on at close range, but fortunately for him the gun did not go off; his interpreter and guard were nearly hit.[33] Caught in the middle of the melee were two young American junior diplomats who happened by pure chance to be in the city during these dreadful days, Robert S. Chilton, Jr. and William Dulany Hunter. For many years the missionary interests in the United States had lobbied for a greater American diplomatic presence in the Turkish interior, where the missionaries had established a wide network of schools, churches, and other institutions. Thus far they had succeeded only in the opening of the first American consulate in the Turkish interior, at Sivas, but the events of 1894 prompted the United States to establish two additional consulates and to assign Chilton to Erzerum and Hunter to Kharpert (Harput). The two men arrived in Constantinople on July 26, 1895. When repeated efforts to secure their recognition from the Ottoman government were rebuffed, they were sent out to their posts without the required official papers. Arriving in Trebizond on October 5, the day after the initial outbreak of violence, the two Americans were taken under the wing of the British consul and registered at the local Belle-

---

[32] FO 424/186, no. 221, Feb. 7, 1896.
[33] Ibid., no. 194, Oct. 9, 1895.

vue Hotel. On October 8, Chilton had just finished writing a report to his superiors in Constantinople when he was caught up in the turmoil and quickly scribbled the following postscript:

> While I was finishing the above a great commotion began outside of the hotel and a few minutes later men began running wildly in all directions and shots began to ring out on all sides. There was no mistaking their meaning. For an hour or more a regular battle has been raging and as I write everything is in fearful confusion and we are in the thick of it. Half a dozen of us are waiting for a favorable chance to cross over to the Persian Consulate directly opposite as it is evident that we have not a fair show here for our lives. I am taking my official papers and leaving everything else. The Turks have stopped killing for the moment and gone to looting and as the Judge [Alexander W. Terrell, U.S. Minister in Constantinople] expressed it, "hell is let loose." Hunter went out with Longworth's cavass [guard] an hour or more before the trouble began and I hope to God has found refuge in the British Consulate and will be safe. It looks now as if we were doomed unless assistance comes from outside.[34]

Indeed, Chilton was ready to leave the city with the next steamer, exclaiming, "Heaven knows what is in store for us tonight," but he could not find Hunter and lacked the necessary travel documents.[35] Chilton later reported that Hunter had been walking on the outskirts of town when the violence erupted and "with difficulty and danger made his way to the British Consulate, having been several times threatened with guns and knives."[36] Only with the assistance of Longworth's cavass had he been able to reach the consulate safely. Chilton was escorted that same day from the hotel to the British consulate and viewed the destruction: "I had to pass through the square and one of the principal streets of the city, where bands of armed men were still assembled, though their work was nearly completed. Dead bodies were scat-

---

[34] US Archives, Record Group 59, General Records of the Department of State, Despatches from the U.S. Consulate in Constantinople, 1820-1906, vol. 20, no. 58 (Trebizond, Oct. 8, 1895). Chilton's subsequent reports from Trebizond (dated Oct. 9 to 24, 1895) are filed without numbers in the first section of Despatches from the U.S. Consuls in Erzerum.

[35] Ibid. Chilton despatch, Oct. 8, 1895.

[36] Ibid., Despatches from the U.S. Consuls in Erzerum, 1895-1904, vol. 1, Chilton to Secretary of State, Trebizond, Oct. 9, 1895.

tered over the streets all bearing fearful evidence of their cruel deaths."[37]

The British consulate had been threatened with an attack, and for the following several days a guard of ten to twelve Turkish soldiers was constantly maintained, while "Mr. Longworth and the rest of us are all armed and ready to make a good defense," Chilton reported. According to Longworth, the danger to the consulate resulted from rumors that the would-be assassins of Bahri Pasha had been harbored there and that Great Britain was "contemplating the formation of an independent Armenia." Chilton noted that he and Hunter had arrived in Trebizond without proper diplomatic papers but added that "even had I been fully qualified as a Consular officer I could not have done more than report the facts as I have done—the acts of all Consuls here being limited to that function during the disturbance."[38]

In subsequent reports, Chilton informed Washington that tension in the city remained high, with business generally suspended, guards maintained at the consulates, the streets patrolled by soldiers, and a renewed outbreak of violence feared at any time. Chilton expressed regret that except for the Russian gunboat "other vessels of war have not, or could not, be sent here at this time." Their presence, he believed, would be not only "a guarantee against further disturbances here" but would place the foreign representatives "in a position to insist upon the punishment of the guilty" and thus "avert trouble in other places."[39]

In regard to the arrest and trial by court martial of 300 to 400 Armenians, while not a single Turk had been arrested, Chilton wrote: "It will be a lasting disgrace to civilization if this travesty of justice is allowed to prevail. The only hope of fixing the responsibility for the affair and of punishing the guilty lies in a foreign commission backed by adequate force of arms."[40] After spending two weeks in the British consulate, Chilton and Hunter returned to their hotel. As the violence spread to nearby provinces and the Turkish government took no action to recognize the status of the two Americans, they were soon recalled.[41]

---

[37] Ibid.

[38] Ibid., Trebizond, Oct. 9, 11, 13, 1895; FO 424/184, no. 194, Oct. 9, 1895.

[39] U.S. Archives, RG 59, Despatches from the U.S. Consuls in Erzerum, vol. 1, Chilton despatch, Oct. 21, 1895.

[40] Ibid.

[41] U.S. Consulates were subsequently established in Erzerum in 1896 and Kharpert in 1900.

Dr. Moses Parmelee, along with most American missionaries in Turkey, was contemptuous of what he considered the weak diplomacy of the United States during this time. In December 1894, President Grover Cleveland had declined to take even the minor step of accepting the sultan's invitation to name an American representative to a commission assigned to investigate the Sasun massacres, on grounds that it might (in the words of Secretary of State Walter Q. Gresham) "lead the U.S. Government into complications which it was their policy to avoid."[42] Parmelee later wrote to Dr. James Barton at missionary headquarters in Boston in December 1897: "We are fortunate in having the English Consul to represent us here." Otherwise, he asserted, the missionaries would be "at the mercy of the limp style of American diplomacy," adding, "one's patriotism is sorely tried."[43] The missionary interests were especially critical of the Cleveland administration, which finally responded to pressure for a more active U.S. diplomacy by dispatching warships to the Mediterranean. The effort was poorly coordinated between the Department of State and Navy Department. The American naval officers assigned to this duty tended to accept the explanations provided to them by local Ottoman officials, and in any case there was little the ships could do to protect most of the American missionaries who were stationed in the interior provinces.[44]

In common with many American missionaries and their supporters, Parmelee was well connected politically. Home on furlough in early 1897, he managed to arrange a meeting with president-elect William McKinley. According to Parmelee's account, McKinley recognized the need for vigorous protection of American missionaries abroad and agreed to the elevation of the U.S. minister in Constantinople to the rank of ambassador.[45] The people of the United States in the 1890s were beginning to envision their nation as a world power, ready for overseas expansion, but their focus was set on strategic islands in the

---

[42] Barbara J. Merguerian, "American Response to the Armenian Massacres of 1895: A Foreign Policy Dilemma," *Journal of Armenian Studies* 4:1-2 (1992): 54.

[43] ABC Archives 16.9.3, 25/106, Letters, Parmelee, Dec. 27, 1897.

[44] Ralph Elliott Cook, "United States and the Armenian Question, 1894-1924," Ph.D. Thesis, Fletcher School of Law and Diplomacy, Tufts University, 1957, pp. 44-95; William N. Still, Jr., *American Sea Power in the Old World: The United States Navy in European and Near Eastern Waters, 1865-1917* (London: Greenwood Press, 1980), chs. 6 and 7; Merguerian, "American Response," pp. 53-83.

[45] ABC Archives 16.9.3, 25/74, Letters. Parmelee, Jan. 19, 1897; 25/75, Jan. 20, 1897; 25/76, Jan. 26, 1897.

Caribbean and the Pacific then belonging to Spain, and not on the Middle East.

The Consequences

In the wake of the Trebizond massacre, of the 400 or so Armenians imprisoned, all except thirty-five to forty were released. There is no indication that the government arrested or tried any Muslims. Many Armenians remained in prison until December 1896 when the sultan issued an amnesty for all political prisoners except those under sentence of death or notorious agitators.[46]

The Armenian losses precipitated a prompt and massive relief effort to save the survivors from hunger and exposure, with funds coming from the United States, Great Britain, Germany, France, and Switzerland. The greatest source of donations was the Duke of Westminster's Fund in London; accordingly, Consul H.Z. Longworth was placed in charge of the local committee directing the relief effort. Most of the distribution was carried out through Dr. Parmelee, assisted by the other American missionaries in the area; Parmelee continued to offer shelter in his home to approximately 200 refugees for several weeks; indeed, his home became a workshop for making quilts, thus providing employment for Armenian women and much needed protection from the cold. Longworth reported: "Through the good offices of the American missionaries, Dr. Parmelee and Mr. Crawford, the suffering of some 5,000 souls are being alleviated by the distribution of blankets, clothing and money."[47]

Under these circumstances, it is no wonder that many surviving Armenians who had the means emigrated to Russia, either permanently or until they considered it safe to return. Government regulations restricting the emigration of Armenians were inconsistent, and the exodus continued. Consul Longworth at the end of 1896 estimated that from the sanjak of Trebizond alone 7,600 Armenians had left the country. On the second anniversary of the massacres, Longworth reported the economy of the province to be in ruins, summarizing it as "a population reduced to penury, and an Administration encumbered by debts."

---

[46] FO 424/185, no. 851, Dec. 16, 1895; 424/189, no. 115, Sept. 17, 1896; 424/191, encl. 5 in no. 95, Jan. 3, 1897.

[47] Ibid., 424/186, no. 221, Feb. 7, 1896; ABC Archives, 16.9.3, 25/70, Letters, Parmelee, Jan. 24, 1896.

The harsh blow aimed at the Armenian community had left all of the inhabitants of the province in economic ruin, including Turks, Greeks, Jews, Laz, and all the people who made up this multi-ethnic society.[48]

The social and economic setback was reflected in the cultural life of the Armenians in the province. An estimated 1,200 households in the city of Trebizond were reduced to 450 in 1896, growing slowly to an estimated 600 households in 1897 as villagers who lacked the means to get abroad moved into the urban area. To cite one measure of the destruction, in 1896 all of the Armenian schools remained closed except for one girls' school with three classes. With the assistance of Western funds and involvement of the Patriarchate of Constantinople and the Armenian Catholic Mekhitarists of Vienna, the community was gradually able to rebuild and even expand its institutions. According to the figures of the Patriarchate, in 1902 there were 24,000 Armenians living in the sanjak of Trebizond, 41 churches and 47 schools with 3,000 students. The Armenian theater, which had been the special pride of the community, rebounded and continued its pioneering programs. Of course, such a cultural revival must have been based on an economic revival as well, and indeed by the turn of the century the Armenian merchants and traders were once again assuming their prominent role in the local economy. The Armenians in Trebizond had improved their financial situation sufficiently to be in a position to assist their poorer compatriots in the interior.[49]

* * *

What conclusions may be drawn about the eventful decade of the 1890s in Trebizond? Certainly, Armenians had exhibited their ability to survive, to rise from the lowest depths of misery and to rebuild family, community, and society. On the other hand, no definitive conclusion concerning the death and destruction was made available, no independent inquiry was made, and none of the instigators and perpetrators of the massacres identified or punished. The myth that Armenian agitators were responsible for the carnage hardly explains the massive, widespread, and brutal response on the part of the government. Moreover, none of the underlying social and political factors that were tearing society apart had been meaningfully addressed. Sultan Abdul

---

[48] FO 424/189, no. 267, Nov. 18, 1896; 424/192, no. 182, Oct. 7, 1997.

[49] Hovakimian, *Patmutiun Haykakan Pontosi*, pp. 166-73.

Hamid had agreed to a reform plan in late 1895, but the attention of the world soon shifted to other areas and different problems, while the corrupt and inefficient Ottoman system continued intact. Armenians remained without meaningful political rights, thus creating a climate in which radical revolutionary groups attracted a following. The cycle of reform, revolution, and repression continued. Nothing, it seems, had been learned by the events of the 1890s in Trebizond, thus leaving the way open for the greater tragedy that was to unfold in the coming years.

❊ 12 ❊

THE FATE OF THE ARMENIANS
IN TREBIZOND, 1915

Simon Payaslian

Trebizond *vilayet* or province was fairly integrated into international commercial networks, and the Armenians in the port towns of Trebizond and Samsun on the southern coast of the Black Sea greatly benefited from their cultural and commercial relations with Europe. Because of the geographical location of the vilayet, the Armenian communities in Trebizond were relatively more prosperous than those of their compatriots in the historically Armenian regions of Erzerum, Van, Bitlis-Mush, Diarbekir, Kharpert, and Sivas. By the second half of the nineteenth century, however, Armenians in the vilayet and across the Ottoman Empire experienced a heightened sense of physical and financial insecurity, as the economic and military decline of the empire, particularly during and after the general economic depression of the mid-1890s, undermined the political legitimacy of the sultanate and gave rise to movements of variegated hues of home-grown and imported ideologies.[1]

Most detrimental to the Armenians in the empire was the emergence of the fanatical nationalist faction within the Young Turk party,

---

[1] For a general survey of the Armenian communities in Trebizond vilayet, see Hovakim Hovakimian, *Patmutiun Haykakan Pontosi* [History of Armenian Pontus] (Beirut: Mshak Press, 1967). On manufacturing and trade in the region, see Suraiya Faroqhi, Bruce McGowan, Donald Quataert, Şevket Pamuk, *An Economic and Social History of the Ottoman Empire*, vol. 2: *1600-1914* (Cambridge: Cambridge University Press, 1994), pp. 739, 800-02, 817-20, 830-31, 911-12; Donald Quataert, *Ottoman Manufacturing in the Age of the Industrial Revolution* (Cambridge: Cambridge University Press, 1993), pp. 63-64, 75, 87-88, 94-95, 98-99, 100-01, 174-75. See also "Mineral Resources in the Trebizond Region," *Levant Trade Review* 1:2 (Nov. 1911): 131-32; Charles Issawi, "The Tabriz-Trabzon Trade, 1830-1900: The Rise and Decline of a Route," *International Journal of Middle East Studies* 1:1 (Jan. 1970): 18-27.

which sought cultural homogenization through Turkification to reverse the process of imperial decline. The economic advantages possessed by the Armenians in Trebizond could not alter the political and cultural reality that the Armenians belonged to the *Ermeni millet* or ethno-religious community and were considered second-class citizens. Although the *Tanzimat* (Reorganization) had granted equality before the law and civil, political, and administrative reforms, and although the Ottoman constitution of 1876 had introduced a parliamentary form of government, Sultan Abdul Hamid II (1876-1908/09) and the Young Turk leaders who overthrew him perceived Armenian demands for improvements in local administration and physical security as a threat to their authority and rule.[2] In fact, following the Russo-Turkish war of 1877-78, the sultan suspended the constitution in February 1878 and showed little interest in implementing the reforms stipulated by the Treaty of San Stefano (March 3, 1878) and the subsequent Treaty of Berlin (July 13, 1878), which concluded the war. Nor were the nationalists in the Young Turk movement willing to accommodate such a radical political liberalization as to permit fundamental systemic changes that could in turn facilitate the exercise of local authority by the Armenians.[3]

Massacres and a Revolution

The Armenian communities in the cities and villages across the vilayet of Trebizond had for centuries experienced sporadic bouts of political and economic oppression of various degrees as well as forced conversion to Islam, as in the area of Hamshen. The political repression and massacres in the late nineteenth century, however, proved qualitatively

---

[2] The Tanzimat reforms included the *Hatt-i Sherif of Gulhané* (Noble Rescript of the Rose Chamber), November 3, 1839, and the *Hatt-i Humayun* (Imperial Rescript), February 18, 1856. See Hagop Barsoumian, "The Eastern Question and the Tanzimat Era," in Richard G. Hovannisian, ed., *The Armenian People from Ancient to Modern Times*, vol. 2: *Foreign Dominion to Statehood: The Fifteenth Century to the Twentieth Century* (New York: St. Martin's Press, 1997), pp. 175-201; Şerif Mardin, *The Genesis of Young Ottoman Thought* (Princeton, NJ: Princeton University Press, 1962).

[3] M. Şükrü Hanioğlu, *The Young Turks in Opposition* (New York and Oxford: Oxford University Press, 1995); Feroz Ahmad, *The Young Turks: The Committee of Union and Progress in Turkish Politics, 1908-1914* (Oxford: Clarendon Press, 1969); Richard G. Hovannisian, *Armenia on the Road to Independence, 1918* (Berkeley and Los Angeles: University of California Press, 1967).

different in their magnitude of brutality exercised in the region. The massacres committed under Sultan Abdul Hamid against the Armenians between 1894 and 1896 resulted in the death of more than 100,000 and by some estimates as high as 300,000 Armenians, mostly in the six vilayets. The massacres in the vilayet of Trebizond occurred in October 1895 and claimed about 1,000 lives. Churches in thirteen villages were plundered and destroyed. The massacres and looting led to mass emigration and weakened Armenian community life.[4] Thus, the general economic depression experienced in the mid-1890s was further exacerbated by the massacres, placing additional burdens on local economies.[5]

Armenians hoped that the Young Turk revolution of 1908 and the new government would finally provide the long-awaited opportunity to improve conditions under a new regime by introducing the much promised but never implemented reforms under the sultan. The restoration of the 1876 constitution in 1908 could have instituted a representative government premised on such democratic, egalitarian principles as free elections, equality among Muslim and non-Muslim citizens, and freedom of religion and education. Yet, as the nationalist leadership within the Young Turk Ittihad ve Terakki (Committee of Union and Progress; CUP) consolidated power, it placed a greater emphasis on Turkism at home and pan-Turkism abroad.

While during the period from 1902 to 1908 Armenian political organizations had intensified their activities in the province so as to secure greater protection for the Armenian population, hopes for reforms and improvements in Turko-Armenian relations after the restoration of the constitution dissipated rapidly.[6] The Adana massacres in April 1909 heightened the concerns of Armenians about their protection. In fact, beginning in October of that year, the Armenians of Trebizond were

---

[4] Felix Charmetant, *Martyrologe arménien: Tableau officiel des massacres d'Arménie* (Paris: Bureau des Oeuvres d'Orient, [1896]), pp. 11-13, 46; Johannes Lepsius, *Armenia and Europe: An Indictment*, trans. and ed. J. Rendel Harris (London: Hodder and Stoughton, 1897), pp. 253, 280-85, 326; Armen Karo (Armen Garo), "Aprvats orer" [Days Lived], *Hairenik Amsagir* 1:9 (July 1923): 94; Richard G. Hovannisian, "The Armenian Question in the Ottoman Empire," in Hovannisian, *Armenian People*, vol. 2, pp. 222-26; Christopher J. Walker, *Armenia: The Survival of a Nation* (London: Croom Helm, 1980), pp. 156-64.

[5] Faroqhi et al., *Economic and Social History*, p. 871; Walker, *Armenia*, pp. 157-58.

[6] The Armenian community elected Harutiun Shahrikian (Shahrigian) as its provincial deputy to the Ottoman Parliament in Constantinople.

targeted for more repressive measures.[7] The local Turkish newspaper *Trabzonda meshveret* reported that an anonymous placard posted in the streets of Trebizond read:

> To give freedom to the Armenians and Greeks means the destruction of the state. The Ottoman state is already in decline. Therefore, the true friends of Islam will seriously think and take appropriate means to wipe out the Armenians and save the state from its fall.[8]

While the local Muslims were being urged to eliminate the Armenians, many Armenian intellectual and political leaders, encouraged by the reestablishment of the constitution, returned from abroad and resumed their political activities. The coastal towns on the Black Sea served as transport hubs for the Armenian activists. Through these towns, they maintained their connections with Europe and transferred into the Armenian vilayets returning political figures, publications, and weapons. Despite the shortcomings of the Young Turk government, well into October 1913 the Armenian communities in the province of Trebizond witnessed a reinvigoration of their political, educational, and cultural activities. Armenian educational and cultural institutions organized various social and cultural events, such as at the celebration of the 1500th anniversary of the creation of the Armenian alphabet, and local Turkish officials and foreigners often attended these functions.[9]

The Trebizond vilayet was home to nearly 100,000 Armenians in the 1880s, but the region witnessed emigration in large numbers as the political and economic situation deteriorated and physical security for the Armenians diminished.[10] Prior to World War I, there were an estimated 53,500 Armenians in the vilayet, nearly 13,000 of whom resided in the city of Trebizond and the nearby villages. In the *sanjak*s of Tre-

---

[7] Misak Torlakian, *Orerus het* [With My Days] (Los Angeles: Horizon, 1953), p. 111.

[8] Quoted in Kevork A. Suakjian, "Genocide in Trebizond: A Case Study of Armeno-Turkish Relations during the First World War," Ph.D. Diss., University of Nebraska, 1981, p. 57.

[9] Torlakian, *Orerus het*, pp. 22, 116-19; Suakjian, "Genocide in Trebizond," p. 58; Tigran Devoyants, "Kiankis drvagnerits" [Episodes from My Life], part 3, *Hairenik Amsagir* 22:2 (March/April 1944): 87-96.

[10] In the 1880s the *sanjak* (county) of Shabin-Karahisar was part of Trebizond vilayet. See Marcel Léart [Krikor Zohrab], *La Question Arménienne à la lumière des documents* (Paris: Librairie Maritime et Coloniale, 1913), p. 59.

bizond and Samsun, there were 35 and 39 churches, respectively, and 42 parishes in each.[11] The churches of Surb Stepanos (Saint Steven), Surb Hovhannes (Saint John), and Surb Astvatsatsin (Holy Mother of God) were located in Trebizond city. In the regions of Trebizond and Samsun, there were 74 schools with more than 144 teachers and 4,600 students. These communities were able to establish close relations with the outside world and attracted teachers from great distances. During the academic year 1913-14, some of the teachers in the Armenian schools were Russian Armenians or Persian Armenians, including Vahan Minakhorian at Samsun; Sargis Barseghian at Kerasund (Giresun); Artashes Hovhannisian and his wife, Anahit, at Trebizond; and Tigran Devoyants at Ordu. The schools maintained close ties with each other and together organized various cultural activities for the community.[12]

At the same time, however, the memory of previous massacres, revisited by the fear generated by the Adana massacres, convinced the leading Armenian organizations such as the Dashnaktsutiun (Armenian Revolutionary Federation) and the Social Democrat Hnchakian Party of the transitory nature of current improved relations between the Turkish leadership and the Armenians. Therefore, after the Adana massacres they began to prepare for self-defense. Indeed, during the Balkan wars (1912-13), although Armenian soldiers were loyally serving in the Ottoman army on that front, the government commenced repressive measures directed against the Armenian communities, including searches for weapons and arrests. Some forty Armenians were arrested

---

[11] Maghakia Ormanian, *The Church of Armenia*, trans. G. Marcar Gregory (3d rev. ed., New York: St. Vartan Press, 1988), Appendix II, p. 239; Suakjian, "Genocide in Trebizond," Table 4, p. 48; Germany, Politisches Archiv des Auswärtigen Amts (hereafter PA-AA), Embassy Constantinople, No. 35/J.No.Geh.(secr.) 316, Consul Bergfeld in Trebizond to Bethmann Hollweg, July 9, 1915, rev. ed. of Johannes Lepsius, *Deutschland und Armenien, 1914-1918: Sammlung Diplomatischer Aktenstücke* (Potsdam: Tempelverlag, 1919), doc. 109, pp. 99-101, complete text, English trans. Linda Struck, in "Documentation of the Armenian Genocide in World War I: The Armenian Genocide 1915/16 from the Files of the German Foreign Office," ed., Wolfgang and Sigrid Gust (www.armenocide.de), cited hereafter as Gust, "Documentation"; cf. Haikazn G. Ghazarian, *Tseghaspan Turke* [The Genocidal Turk] (Beirut: Hamazkayin Press, 1968), p. 82. U.S. Consul at Trebizond Oscar Heizer estimated that there were about 36,000 Armenians in the province, including 10,000 in Trebizond city and the vicinity. United States, National Archives, Record Group 59 (cited hereafter as US Archives, RG 59), 867.4016/114, Heizer to Secretary of State, July 12, 1915, encl., Heizer to Morgenthau, July 7, 1915.

[12] Léart, *La Question Arménienne*, p. 69; Devoyants, "Kiankis drvagnerits," p. 90.

in Trebizond city and other towns in the province.[13] In January 1913, the extremists of the Ittihad ve Terakki seized power in a coup against the government of the more liberal Hurriyet ve Itilaf (Freedom and Association) and established a military dictatorship.[14] During the next five years, the Ittihadist triumvirate of Minister of the Interior Mehmed Talaat, Minister of War Ismail Enver, and Minister of the Marine Ahmed Jemal ruled an empire mired in political turbulence, war, and genocide.

From Reforms to War and Genocide

Despite the various difficulties confronting the Armenians, one final effort at reforms gave hope for improvements. The compromise reform plan signed by the Ottoman Grand Vizier and Foreign Minister Said Halim and Russian Chargé d'Affaires Konstantin N. Gulkevich on February 8, 1914 (in the aftermath of the Balkan wars) provided for the consolidation of Trebizond, Sivas, and Erzerum into a single province, and the Van, Bitlis, Kharpert, and Diarbekir vilayets into another, with each province to be supervised by a European inspector-general. In mid-1914, Major Nicolai Hoff of Norway assumed his office as the inspector-general at Van, and Louis Westenenk of the Netherlands was expected to arrive at Erzerum soon thereafter.[15] The Young Turk leaders fiercely resented the plan and did everything in their power to sabotage its implementation,[16] but the Armenians of Trebizond, like their compatriots throughout the empire, took heart from the reform plan and hoped for further improvements in their condition. "The Armenian Question had . . . reached a new stage," commented Armenian Patriarch of Constantinople Zaven Der Yeghiayan in his memoirs. "New horizons were now opening up before the Nation, which had the right to expect a bright future" despite the knowledge that the Turkish government would "use all possible manipulations . . . to cause the reforms to fail."[17]

---

[13] Torlakian, *Orerus het*, p. 112; Suakjian, "Genocide in Trebizond," p. 58.

[14] Ahmad, *Young Turks*, pp. 116-20.

[15] Hovannisian, "Armenian Question," pp. 237-38; Simon Vratsian, *Hayastani Hanrapetutiun* [Republic of Armenia] (Paris: Navarre, 1928; repr., Erevan: Hayastan, 1993), pp. 5-6.

[16] See, for example, Djemal Pasha, *Memories of a Turkish Statesman, 1913-1919* (New York: George H. Doran, 1922), p. 276.

[17] Zaven Der Yeghiayan, *My Patriarchal Memoirs*, trans. Ared Misirliyan, anno-

Unlike the Armenian communities in neighboring provinces where internal friction had intensified, the Armenians in Trebizond for a brief period were enjoying relative calm, as indicated by reports presented by the regional delegates at the Dashnaktsutiun's Eighth General Congress held at Erzerum in the summer of 1914.[18] The outbreak of the war in Europe radically changed the situation. The military mobilization (*seferberlik*) decreed by the Young Turk government led also to the mobilization of Muslim sentiments against the perceived Christian enemies in Europe—that is, the Entente Powers (Great Britain, France, and Russia)—and at home.[19] In August 1914, some of the Armenian educational and cultural institutions came under attack by the local Muslims, most likely instigated by the government. These included search and seizure campaigns by the local authorities and the imprisonment of Armenian businessmen.[20] Armenian soldiers from Trebizond conscripted into military service were disarmed, sent to the region of Gumushkhane to work on road construction, and subsequently murdered.[21]

After the outbreak of the war, the Armenians in the coastal towns, whose location had enabled them to participate directly in international trade and finance, lost the advantages they had over their compatriots in most other provinces. The war stopped all commerce in the coastal towns, which instantly assumed strategic significance as arenas for military operations and transformed the advantages into disadvantages. The Russian naval activities in Turkish waters could only exacerbate the existing dangerous situation for the local Armenians since the mo-

tated by Vatche Ghazarian (Barrington, RI: Mayreni Publishing, 2002 [original Armenian, Cairo: Nor Astgh, 1947]), p. 27.

[18] Vahan Minakhorian, *1915 tvakane* [The Year 1915] (Venice: Mekhitarist Press, 1949), p. 66.

[19] Der Yeghiayan, *My Patriarchal Memoirs*, pp. 41-42; Ghazarian, *Tseghaspan turke*, pp. 23-24; W.E.D. Allen and Paul Muratoff, *Caucasian Battlefields: A History of the Wars on the Turco-Caucasian Border, 1828-1921* (Cambridge: Cambridge University Press, 1953), p. 234; Vahakn N. Dadrian, *The History of the Armenian Genocide: Ethnic Conflict from the Balkans to Anatolia to the Caucasus* (Providence: Berghahn Books, 1995), pp. 220-21.

[20] Suakjian, "Genocide in Trebizond," pp. 109-11; Jean Naslian, *Les mémoires de Mgr. Jean Naslian, Évêque de Trébizonde, sur les événements politico-réligieux en Proche-Orient de 1914 à 1918*, 2 vols. (Vienna: Mekhitarist Press, 1951), vol. 1, p. 170.

[21] Jon S. Kirakosyan, *Arajin hamashkharhayin paterazme ev arevmtahayutyune 1914-1916 tt.* [The First World War and the Western Armenians, 1914-1916] (Erevan: Hayastan, 1967), p. 299.

bilization and especially after the declaration of *jihad* or holy war in November 1914.[22] As the war on the Western front escalated, the Turks and Russians carried on their historic hostilities for land and sea, and in particular for control over the Caucasus. From early to mid-December, as the Russian army retreated from the eastern border districts of Erzerum after a brief advance, the Turkish army destroyed entire villages, leaving behind a population scattered throughout the region. Then, Enver's disastrous winter campaign at Sarikamish (December 1914-January 1915), which caused the loss of more than 75,000 Turkish soldiers, turned the tide decidedly toward policies of mass arrests and violence.[23] During February and March 1915, the Armenian soldiers in the Ottoman army were disarmed and placed in labor battalions (*amele taburi*) on road construction between Erzerum, Erzinjan, Trebizond, and Sivas.[24]

The unfolding crisis in the Armenian communities was amplified by Russian naval activities along the coast of the Trebizond vilayet. On February 8, 1915, Russian destroyers attacked Trebizond, and Russian cruisers bombarded Kerasund on April 20.[25] Between these two dates, hostilities toward the Armenians intensified and paralyzed their community. In the city of Samsun between April 11 and 15, Suleyman Nejmi Bey, the *mutasarif* (county governor) of the Janik (Samsun) sanjak from 1914 to 1916, ordered the arrest of more than thirty prominent Armenians.[26] In Trebizond city and the neighboring towns, on April 19 and for several days thereafter, the government conducted extensive house-to-house searches for weapons and deserters. Unable to unearth a significant number of weapons and deserters, the gendarmes arrested those suspected of revolutionary activities and collaboration with the Russians. Subsequently, several Armenian houses were torched. In response to the escalating Turkish hostilities, the local Dashnaktsutiun and Hnchakian parties began to prepare for self-defense.[27] The Arme-

---

[22] Naslian, *Les mémoires*, vol. 1, pp. 11-12.

[23] Allen and Muratoff, *Caucasian Battlefields*, pp. 253, 261-62, 284; *Current History* 2 (Sept. 1915): 1042.

[24] Henry Barby, *Au pays de l'épouvante: L'Arménie martyre* (Beirut: Hamazkayin Press, 1972; first published, 1917), pp. 20, 45-46.

[25] *Current History* 2 (Aug. 1915): 870-72.

[26] *British Foreign Office Dossiers on Turkish War Criminals*, ed. and comp. Vartkes Yeghiayan (La Verne, CA: American Armenian International College, 1991), p. 400.

[27] Torlakian, *Orerus het*, pp. 189-91, 195-97; Vahan Mazmanian, "Husher heghapokhakan antsialen" [Memories from the Revolutionary Past], *Hairenik Amsagir* 15:1

nian prelate of Trebizond, Kevork Turian (Gevorg Durian), protested the imprisonment of the Armenian leaders, but to no avail. Instead, Turian was declared *mou'zir* (dangerous) by the *vali* (governor) of the province, Jemal Azmi.[28] By April 24, when the authorities in Constantinople arrested and sent into exile more than 200 Armenian intellectuals and community and business leaders, mass arrests, forced conversions to Islam, and tortures had already begun in Trebizond, Samsun, Kerasund, and smaller Pontic towns and villages.[29]

On May 24, the Entente Powers jointly issued a public condemnation of the deportations and massacres committed by the Turkish government against the Armenians and declared that they would hold the Ottoman government and its agents "personally responsible" for the massacres.[30] The declaration rather than deter further bloodshed seems to have emboldened the Young Turks to intensify their campaign for the destruction of the Armenian communities. On May 29, the Young Turk government adopted the Temporary Law of Deportation, granting the military full authority to supervise the wholesale deportation of the Armenians across the vilayets.[31] The law accorded legitimacy to a pol-

---

(Nov. 1936): 119-30; M. Gushakchian, "Trapizoni ev Samsoni teghahanutiunn u jardere" [The Deportation and Massacres of Trebizond and Samson], in *Hushamatian Mets Egherni, 1915-1965* [Memorial Volume of the Great Crime, 1915-1965], ed. and comp. Gersam Aharonian (Beirut: Atlas, 1965), p. 468.

[28] Suakjian, "Genocide in Trebizond," p. 110.

[29] Ervand Fntkian [Fundukian], "Hishoghutiunner 1915-i Trabizoni jardi ev teghahanutian sev orerits" [Memories from the Black Days of the 1915 Massacres and Deportations of Trebizond], *Hairenik Amsagir* 19:10 (Aug. 1941): 55-71. For a chronology of events in 1915, see Naslian, *Les mémoires*, vol. 1, pp. 183-88.

[30] US Archives, RG 59, 867.4016/67, Secretary of State Bryan to American Embassy, Constantinople, May 29, 1915, and Sharp to Secretary of State, May 28, 1915; France, Archives du Ministère des Affaires Etrangères (A.M.A.E.), Guerre 1914-1918, *Turquie*, "Communication de l'Ambassade de Russie au Département," May 11, 1915, "Communication de l'Ambassade de Grande-Bretagne au Département," May 19 and 21, 1915, "Note du Département à l'Agence Havas," May 24, 1915, and M. William Sharp, Ambassadeur des Etats-Unis à Paris, à M. Declassé, Ministère des Affaires Etrangères, May 28, 1915, in *Les Grandes Puissances, l'empire Ottoman et les arméniens dans les archives françaises (1914-1918)*, ed. and comp. Arthur Beylerian (Paris: Panthéon-Sorbonne, 1983), pp. 23, 25-29, 31.

[31] Great Britain, Parliament, *The Treatment of Armenians in the Ottoman Empire, 1915-16: Documents Presented to Viscount Grey of Fallodon, Secretary of State for Foreign Affairs*, Miscellaneous no. 31, 1916, comp. and ed. Arnold Toynbee. (London: H.M.S.O., 1916 [3d ed, Beirut: G. Doniguian and Sons, 1988]), docs. 12, 22, 23, 33, 34, 35, 77, 126, cited hereafter as *Treatment of Armenians*. The postwar Ottoman Parliament repealed the Temporary Law of Deportation on November 4, 1918.

icy already implemented since November 1914.[32] The government subsequently formed the Commission on Abandoned Property for the purpose of confiscating properties left behind by the deported Armenians.[33]

Deportations and Massacres

In early June 1915, Eyub Zade, a provincial representative, reportedly asked Nail Bey, the principal CUP agent (responsible secretary) in Trebizond: "What will our response be to the European nations asking for an account one day or another?" Nail Bey responded: "If we win the war, there will be no accounting. If we lose, the end result is simple. The extermination will be added to our responsibility. In the process, however, we would have finished the Armenian question."[34] In the meantime, the government made further arrests in Trebizond and on June 25, 1915, issued a proclamation ordering the Armenians of the city to deliver, within five days, their properties to the government and prepare for their journey to the interior on July 1.[35] Aware of the conditions suffered by their compatriots in the neighboring provinces, the Armenians of Trebizond fearfully expected similar treatment at the hands of the gendarmes.[36] In fact, on orders of Vali Jemal Azmi to the Erzerum War Council, Prelate Kevork Turian, along with his personal guards, was strangled by the escorting gendarmes on the road to Erzerum on June 10/23.[37] The following evening, on June 11/24, 1915,

---

See Dadrian, *History*, pp. 221-22.

[32] Christopher J. Walker, "World War I and the Armenian Genocide," in Hovannisian, *Armenian People*, vol. 2, pp. 252-53.

[33] Henry H. Riggs, *Days of Tragedy in Armenia: Personal Experiences in Harpoot, 1915-1917* (Ann Arbor: Gomidas Institute, 1997), p. 92.

[34] Ghazar Makunts, *Trabizoni Hayots teghahanutiune* [The Deportation of the Trebizond Armenians] (Tehran: Alik, 1963), pp. 61-62, as quoted in Suakjian, "Genocide in Trebizond," p. 114.

[35] On June 26, 1915, the local Turkish newspaper, *Trabizonda Meshveret*, published the official proclamation for the deportation of the Armenians of Trebizond. See US Archives, RG 59, 867.4016/85, Heizer to Morgenthau, June 28, 1915; Naslian, *Les mémoires*, vol. 1, pp. 170-71.

[36] US Archives, RG 59, 867.4016/93, Morgenthau to Secretary of State, July 13, 1915, encl. Heizer to Morgenthau, June 30, 1915.

[37] Germany, PA-AA, Embassy Constantinople, DuA doc. 149 (abbr.), J. No. 3841, Colonel Stange, Erzerum, to the German Military Mission, Constantinople, "Report on the Deportation of the Armenians," Aug. 23, 1915, rev. ed. Lepsius, *Deutschland*, doc. 149, pp. 138-42, complete text, English trans. Linda Struck, in

about twenty-five leading members of the Dashnaktsutiun and Russian Armenians were arrested and taken to the government building in Trebizond on the pretext that they were to testify before the War Council at Samsun. They were then put in chains and taken to Platana, about 7 miles west of Trebizond city, and immediately thereafter taken to the open sea, escorted by a ship full of Turkish soldiers who shot them.[38]

In a telegram dated June 27, 1915, German Consul Heinrich Bergfeld at Trebizond expressed concerns to the embassy in Constantinople regarding the humanitarian calamities awaiting the Armenians:

> About 30000 persons are affected by the deportations just in the Vilayet of Trapezunt. A mass transport of this kind for hundreds of kilometres along routes that are lacking in accommodation and supplies, and where 300 kilometres must count as being completely infested with typhus fever, would claim enormous numbers of victims, particularly among the women and children.[39]

On June 28, U.S. Consul at Trebizond Oscar Heizer sent a copy of the government proclamation of June 25 to U.S. Ambassador Henry Morgenthau, informing him that "within five days from [the date of the proclamation], the entire Armenian population of Trebizond and vicinity including men, women and children will be obliged to turn over to the government such property as they cannot take with them and start for the interior, probably for Eldjezireh [Jezire] or Mosul where they will remain until the end of the war. Upon their return after the war their goods will be returned to them." He continued:

> It is impossible to convey an idea of the consternation and despair the publication of this proclamation has produced upon the people. I have seen strong, proud, wealthy men weep like children while they told me that they had given their boys and girls to Persian and Turkish

---

Gust, "Documentation"; Suakjian, "Genocide in Trebizond," pp. 114-15n20; Barby, *Au pays de l'épouvante*, p. 51.

[38] Germany, PA-AA, Embassy Constantinople, No. 35/J.No.Geh.(secr.) 316, Consul Bergfeld, Trebizond, to the Reichskanzler (Theobald von Bethmann Hollweg), July 9, 1915, doc. 109, pp. 99-101, English trans. Linda Struck; Yeghiayan, *British Foreign Office Dossiers*, p. 432; Suakjian, "Genocide in Trebizond," pp. 115-16; Naslian, *Les mémoires*, vol. 1, pp. 172-73.

[39] Germany, PA-AA, Embassy Constantinople, BoKon/169, Consul Bergfeld to German Embassy, Constantinople, Telegraphic Report, June 27, 1915, rev. ed. of Lepsius, *Deutschland*, doc. 100, pp. 91-92, English trans. Linda Struck, in Gust, "Documentation."

neighbors. . . . Even a strong man without the necessary outfit and food would be likely to perish on such a trip. . . . The people are helpless but are making preparations to start on the perilous journey.

The Armenians were not permitted to sell or to take any of their belongings with them, but the proclamation promised that they could reclaim their goods upon their return after the war.[40] Carl Schlimme, a German consular employee at Erzerum, witnessed during an assignment in Trebizond that "police officers in front of the police station took pitiful bundles away from the passing deportees."[41]

The Armenians of Trebizond were thus condemned to march on foot for hundreds of miles. Armenians and foreigners petitioned the authorities to stay the deportations. A group of Armenian community leaders, including the assistant primate Shegha Zulalian, Reverend Zakarian of the Protestant community, and businessman Gaydzag Arabian (Kaitsak Arapian) petitioned Jemal Azmi and Nail Bey to stop the deportations, but to no avail. Also petitioning were Consul Heizer, Greek primate Archbishop Chrysanthos, and German Consul Heinrich Bergfeld.[42]

On June 30, 1915, Heizer dispatched additional information regarding the situation in Trebizond and the deplorable conditions of the Armenian refugees. He reported that in Erzerum, hundreds of Armenian women and children were in wretched conditions, "wandering about in the forests and the mountains, some of them naked, having been robbed of their honor and their clothing." The Armenians of Trebizond, preparing for their journey, were aware of these conditions and expected a similar treatment at the hands of Turkish gendarmes. Although an effort was made to change their destination from Mosul to Gumushkhane to keep them in the Trebizond vilayet, most were nonetheless being deported to Mosul, where the Ittihadist Ibrahim Fezi was assigned the task of organizing a branch of the *Teshkilat-i Mahsusa* (Special Organization) for the purpose of murdering the Armenians within his jurisdiction and those arriving from other deportation routes.

---

[40] US Archives, RG 59, 867.4016/85/105/114, Heizer to Morgenthau, June 28, 1915; Morgenthau to Secretary of State, July 26, 1915; Heizer to Secretary of State, July 12, 1915, encl., Heizer to Morgenthau, June 28, 1915; Ghazarian, *Tseghaspan Turke*, pp. 74-77.

[41] Germany, PA-AA, Embassy Constantinople, DuA doc. 149 (abbr.), J. No. 3841, Colonel Stange, "Report."

[42] Suakjian, "Genocide in Trebizond," pp. 119-20.

Governor Jemal Azmi informed Heizer that the authorities had decided to make an exception for Catholic Armenians, old men and women, widows, pregnant women, and government employees, but that all others had to leave.[43]

On the morning of July 1, 1915, the first caravan consisting of about 600 Armenians accompanied by gendarmes with fixed bayonets marched out of Trebizond city. A second caravan followed two days later on July 3. Consul Heizer reported that within the first three days of the month nearly all the "clergymen, merchants, bankers, lawyers, mechanics, tailors and men from every walk of life" were deported. On July 5, another caravan, comprising nearly 2,000 Armenians, left Trebizond city.[44] A caravan totaling 700, which left Trebizond on July 7, reached as far as the Kemakh gorge south of Erzinjan where most were massacred. The last major group, composed of about 1,000, left the city on July 18.[45] Although at first, as claimed by Jemal Azmi, the government exempted some Armenians, soon they, too, were exiled. Armenians holding Russian, Persian, or Bulgarian citizenship were also sent away despite petitions on their behalf.[46]

Consul Heizer recommended that "some measures be taken at Constantinople to secure a withdrawal of this order if possible or at least a modification so as to spare the old men, women, and children from such a journey which would mean certain destruction." Heizer also met with the governor to request some exceptions to the deportation orders. The vali refused to make any promises but noted that he had telegraphed Constantinople "asking that an exception be made for Armenians in official positions," perhaps including Heizer's two Armenian consular *kavases* (guards/attendants) and the clerk. Heizer advised other Americans in the empire to be cautious in communications with the embassy concerning the Armenians so as not to "appear to the local authorities here that the consulate was taking too active a part in an af-

---

[43] US Archives, RG 59, 867.4016/93/114, Morgenthau to Secretary of State, July 13, 1915, encl., Heizer to Morgenthau, June 30, 1915; Heizer to Secretary of State, July 12, 1915, encl., Heizer to Morgenthau, June 30, 1915.

[44] Hovakimian, *Patmutiun Haykakan Pontosi*, pp. 128-29; Torlakian, *Orerus het*, pp. 96-98; Suakjian, "Genocide in Trebizond," pp. 132-36.

[45] Hovakimian, *Patmutiun Haykakan Pontosi*, pp. 128-29; Torlakian, *Orerus het*, pp. 96-98; Suakjian, "Genocide in Trebizond," pp. 132-36.

[46] US Archives, RG 59, 867.4016/126, Morgenthau to Secretary of State, Aug. 18, 1915, encl., Heizer to Morgenthau, July 28, 1915.

fair between the Turkish government and its own subjects."[47] After the deportations began, Consul Heizer reported:

> On Thursday, July 1st, all the streets were guarded by gendarmes with fixed bayonets, and the work of driving the Armenians from their homes began. Groups of men, women and children with loads and bundles on their backs were collected in a short cross street near the Consulate and when a hundred or so had been gathered they were driven past the Consulate on the road toward Gumushkhané and Erzingan. . . .[48]

Within weeks about 6,000 Armenians had been deported from the city and its environs; most of them were deported south toward Gumushkhane, about 90 miles (195 kilometers) from Trebizond.[49] As the Armenians were evacuated from their houses, the authorities posted public notices warning all against protecting Armenians under the penalty of death. The CUP officials rejected a plan by the Greek metropolitan, Archbishop Chrysanthos, to provide safe haven for the children in schools and orphanages. Instead, boys were handed over to Turkish farmers, while girls were "kept in houses for the pleasure of members of the gang which seems to rule affairs here." The German consul at Trebizond did not expect that the Armenians would return home after the war.[50] Nearly 3,000 children had been placed in so-called "Turkish orphanages" under Turkish *mudirs* (directors) and guarded by the gendarmes. Heizer commented: "Very disquieting reports concerning the treatment of these people who have been sent

---

[47] US Archives, RG 59, 867.4016/93/114, Morgenthau to Secretary of State, July 13, 1915, encl., Heizer to Morgenthau, June 30, 1915; Heizer to Secretary of State, July 12, 1915, encl., Heizer to Morgenthau, June 30, 1915.

[48] US Archives, RG 59, 867.4016/126, Morgenthau to Secretary of State, Aug. 18, 1915, encl., Heizer to Morgenthau, July 28, 1915.

[49] US Archives, RG 59, 867.4016/114/126, Heizer to Secretary of State, July 12, 1915, encl., Heizer to Morgenthau, July 3, 1915; RG 59, 867.4016/114, Heizer to Secretary of State, July 12, 1915, encl., Heizer to Morgenthau, July 7, 1915; Morgenthau to Secretary of State, Aug. 18, 1915, encl., Heizer to Morgenthau, July 28, 1915; *Treatment of Armenians*, docs. 72, 73, 76; Sebuh Akuni, *Milion me hayeru jardi patmutiune* [The Story of the Massacre of a Million Armenians] (Constantinople: Hayastan, 1921), p. 177.

[50] US Archives, RG 59, 867.4016/114/126, Heizer to Morgenthau, July 3, 1915; Heizer to Morgenthau, July 7, 1915; and Heizer to Morgenthau, July 10, 1915, encl., Heizer to Secretary of State, July 12, 1915; Morgenthau to Secretary of State, Aug. 18, 1915, encl., Heizer to Morgenthau, July 28, 1915.

away are current and if one half turn out to be true it will be shocking."[51]

The deportations in the cities of Kerasund, Ordu, and Samsun commenced on July 10. Mutasarif Nejmi Bey at first offered exemption from the deportations to Armenians who converted to Islam. It is an exaggeration, however, that in Kerasund 200 out of 400 Armenian families and in Ordu 160 out of 250 families converted to Islam to avoid deportation.[52] Still, even most of those who did convert did not escape deportation. Many were moved westward to Bafra, only to be ordered south to Kavak and thence to Sivas. There, the vali, Ahmed Muammer Bey, whose anti-Armenian campaigns had gained him much notoriety but also the confidence of the Ittihadist regime, organized death squads to murder both the local Armenians and the refugees marching through his province.[53] The first caravan, consisting of 1,200 people, nearly half of the Armenian population of Kerasund, marched to Dari-Koy, where the elderly were separated from the group and murdered in the nearby hills. On the next day, the men, nearly 500 in all, were separated from the caravan and forced to the mountains of today's Eğribel in Giresun Dağları and killed. The caravan continued southward to Shabin-Karahisar and Tamzara. The Kurds of a village near Shabin-Karahisar abducted the young women. The rest were ordered to march on to the village of Adzbder (Aydzbder), where the remaining men were massacred. After days of torment, the caravan marched to Demir Maghara, an area that became the cemetery for the deportees from Kerasund. A small number of the survivors reached Agn in Kharpert vilayet.[54]

In Samsun, where the arrest of leading Armenian figures began in April 1915, the authorities permitted, prior to the deportations, those accepting Islam to remain, thus saving approximately fifty Armenians. As the caravans began to march out of Samsun, the men were separated from their families and killed about a mile from the city. German Consul M. Kuckhoff at Samsun maintained that the Turkish govern-

---

[51] US Archives, RG 59, 867.4016/93/103/114, Morgenthau to Secretary of State, July 13, 1915; Morgenthau to Secretary of State, July 20, 1915, encl., letter by Heizer to Morgenthau, July 7, 1915; Heizer to Secretary of State, July 12, 1915.

[52] US Archives, RG 59, 876.4016/122, Morgenthau to Secretary of State, Aug. 10, 1915, encl., doc. 3, report of Dashnaktsutiun Committee, Balkan Section.

[53] Yeghiayan, *British Foreign Office Dossiers*, p. 399.

[54] By the end of the deportations, no more than 2,000 Armenians of Trebizond had survived. Akuni, *Milion me hayeru jardi patmutiune*, pp. 183-84.

ment, claiming to react to revolutionary activities by Armenians, particularly in Van, engaged in the wholesale destruction of the Armenian nation. While some Armenians were in fact involved in such affairs, Kuckhoff wrote, most did not participate but became the innocent victims of a concerted policy of Islamization and destruction. He added:

> In the area around Samsun, all Armenian villages have been converted to Islam, in Uniah likewise. Privileges were not granted to anyone except the renegades. All Armenians without exception: men, women, the old, children, even babies, the Orthodox, Protestants and Catholics—the latter never took part in any national revolutionary movement and were also spared by Hamid—had to leave. No Christian Armenian is allowed to stay here; not even those of foreign nationality; the latter are to be expelled from the country. The destination of those exiled from Samsun is said to be Urfa, according to a statement by the Mutessarif.
>
> For sure no Christian Armenian will reach this destination. According to news from the interior, there are already reports of the disappearance of the deported population of whole towns.[55]

At Trebizond, after the deportees left the city, the men were taken into the mountains and massacred. The women were forced to march in deplorable condition toward Erzinjan, but their exact whereabouts could not be confirmed. Most did not survive far beyond Gumushkhane, as they were murdered a little distance from the town. Some of the refugees trudged on to Enderes, Amasia, Tokat, Sivas, and Malatia, being robbed, raped, and murdered all along the way. After three months on the road, a small number of survivors reached Suruj.[56] Drowning and disposal in the sea paralleled the deportations and massacres on land.[57] An unknown number of Armenians were promised to

---

[55] Germany, PA-AA, Embassy Constantinople, Ambassador (Hans von) Wangenheim, Constantinople to the Reichskanzler, No.449, July 16, 1915, encl., Kuckhoff, Samsun, No. 349, July 4, 1915, rev. ed. of Lepsius, *Deutschland*, doc. 116, pp. 104-06, English trans. Linda Struck, in Gust, "Documentation."

[56] Akuni, *Milion me hayeru jardi patmutiune*, pp. 180-82; Germany, PA-AA/ R14088, Scheubner-Richter, Erzerum, to Hohenlohe-Langenburg, Constantinople, J. No. 580/Secret Report No. 23, Aug. 5, 1915, encl., German consular employee at Erzerum, Karl Schlimme, "Report on My Journey to Trebizond," in rev. ed. of Lepsius, *Deutschland*, docs. 129 and 130, pp. 116-22, English trans. Vera Draack, in Gust, "Documentation"; Naslian, *Les mémoires*, vol. 1, pp. 172-73.

[57] Yeghiayan, *British Foreign Office Dossiers*, pp. 435-36; A.H. Papazian, *Hayeri tseghaspanutiune est Eritturkeri datavarutian pastatghteri* [The Armenian Genocide

be taken from Trebizond city to Samsun by sea but were thrown into the sea as their boats were steered away from the shore. Heizer wrote that this form of disposal became a common practice, as boats loaded with people left Trebizond but soon returned empty.[58]

In an urgent appeal to Bishop Ghevond Turian, Prelate of Bulgaria, for outside assistance, Patriarch Zaven wrote in mid-July 1915:

> Not a single house has been exempted from these searches: no Prelacies, no churches, and no schools. Hundreds of women, girls, and even children are languishing in jails today; churches and monasteries have been robbed, destroyed, and desecrated. Even Prelates have not been spared: Prelate of Brusa, Barkev Vartabed Tanielian; Prelate of Trebizond, Kevork Vartabed Turian; Prelate of Gesaria, Khosrov Vartabed Behrigian; Vaghinag Vartabed Torigian of S[habin] K[ara] Hisar; Kevork Vartabed Nalbandian of Charsanjak etc. have been jailed and taken to the court-martial. . . . The entire Armenian community in Turkey is now under detention, and mail and telegraphic communication have entirely ceased.[59]

On July 28, 1915, Consul Heizer sent a lengthy report to Ambassador Morgenthau, complaining that the proclamation for deportations contained no provisions for the protection of Armenian lives:

> If a person was an Armenian that was sufficient reason for being treated as a criminal and deported. . . . There is no attempt at classification [of goods] and the idea of keeping the property in "bales under the protection of the government to be returned to the owners on their return" is simply ridiculous.[60]

According to the Documents of the Trials of the Young Turks] (Erevan: Armenian Academy of Sciences, 1988), pp. 44, 168.

[58] US Archives, RG 59, 867.4016/93/103/114/126, Morgenthau to Secretary of State, July 13, 1915; Morgenthau to Secretary of State, July 20, 1915, encl., Heizer to Morgenthau, July 7, 1915; Heizer to Secretary of State, July 12, 1915, encls., Heizer to Morgenthau, July 3, 7, 10, 1915; Morgenthau to Secretary of State, Aug. 18, 1915, encl., Heizer to Morgenthau, July 28, 1915. See also Germany, PA-AA, Embassy Constantinople, DuA doc. 149 (abbr.), J. No. 3841, Colonel Stange, "Report," Aug. 23, 1915; Akuni, *Milion me hayeru jardi patmutiune*, pp. 177-78; Barby, *Au pays de l'épouvante*, p. 46.

[59] See the text of the letter, Zaven Der Yeghiayan to Bishop Ghevond Turian, Prelate of Bulgaria, June 30/July 13, 1915, in Der Yeghiayan, *My Patriarchal Memoirs*, pp. 85-87.

[60] US Archives, RG 59 867/4016/126, Morgenthau to Secretary of State, Aug. 18,

Italian Consul Gorrini observed that for some Armenians, especially women, the traumatic experience was too horrendous to bear, and they physically dropped in the streets in total emotional paralysis. An unknown number of women jumped off nearby bridges or committed suicide in other ways; some went insane; and others rushed to the Greek and American institutions to secure protection for their newly-born children.[61]

Approximately 300 children attending the American school were left behind under the care of the American missionaries Dr. and Mrs. Lyndon S. Crawford. The authorities soon notified Crawford that he was required to place the children and their money and articles left with them under government supervision.[62] In fact, while the Armenian population was being removed from their homes and neighborhoods, the authorities confiscated their houses, schools, shops, bank accounts. One local official, Mehmed Ali Bey, who held the post of assistant director of customs at Trebizond, robbed hundreds of Armenian girls and women of their jewels and other possessions, kept some of the girls at a branch of the Red Crescent Hospital for his personal pleasure, and distributed others among the Ittihadist leaders in Trebizond. Other women and children kept in temporary orphanages under Mehmed Ali's control were after two or three months forced to the outskirts of Trebizond and massacred near the river Deyermen-Dere. Mehmed Ali's close associates who were engaged in the planning and execution of the deportations and massacres in the region included, in addition to the governor Jemal Azmi, Ali Sahib (Saib), the principal medical officer of Trebizond vilayet; Avni Bey, the medical officer in charge of the hospital; Nail Bey, CUP responsible secretary in Trebizond; Nuri Bey, police chief; Mustafa Effendi, chief of intelligence operations in Trebizond; and Talaat Bey, deputy chief of gendarmes.[63] The German and Austro-Hungarian consuls at Trebizond were said to have petitioned the central government and local authorities for some modification in

---

1915, encl., Heizer to Morgenthau, July 28, 1915.

[61] See the Italian consul's report in *Treatment of Armenians*, p. 292. See also Naslian, *Les mémoires*, vol. 1, p. 47.

[62] US Archives, RG 59, 867.4016/114, Heizer to Secretary of State, July 12, 1915, encl., Heizer to Morgenthau, July 7, 1915; Yeghiayan, *British Foreign Office Dossiers*, p. 432.

[63] Kirakosyan, *Arajin hamashkharhayin paterazme*, p. 300; Yeghiayan, *British Foreign Office Dossiers*, pp. 431-36. See also Papazian, *Hayeri tseghaspanutiune*, p. 167.

the brutal treatment of women and children, but such appeals were to no avail.[64]

A small group of Armenians sent from Samsun to Amasia in Sivas vilayet in late June 1915 journeyed within the jurisdiction of a compassionate official who threatened the escorting gendarmerie with severe punishment if they mistreated the refugees. When the latter reached Amasia, however, the men were separated from the group and bound in groups of five and forced away at night to an unknown location, most probably murdered on the road to Turchul (Turhal), Chiftlik (Tashli-chiftlik), and Tokat.[65]

Writing from Erzerum, the German vice consul at Erzerum, Max Erwin von Scheubner-Richter, reported to Ambassador Prince Ernst Hohenlohe-Langenburg in Constantinople:

> Large massacres of Armenians have been carried out on the Khänus plain and almost all of the men in Vilayet Trapezunt have supposedly been killed. In fact, while in Ersindjan I did not notice any men among those Armenians from Vilayet Trapezunt passing through. The method of expulsion was also much more brusque; for example, the Armenians in Trapezunt were only given a few hours and they were forbidden to sell their things. They were not given any means of transportation by the government, so that most of them had to walk. The Armenians in Siwas were treated in a similarly brusque manner.[66]

Groups of refugees from Ordu, Trebizond, and other towns on the coast of the Black Sea were merged with other caravans of refugees, mostly women and children, coming from Erzerum and Erzinjan; when combined this large caravan consisted of 8,000 deportees by the time it reached the outskirts of Kharpert en route to more distant destinations.[67] "If it were simply a matter of being obliged to leave here to go

---

[64] US Archives, RG 59, 867.4016/93, Morgenthau to Secretary of State, July 13, 1915, encl., Heizer to Morgenthau, June 30, 1915.

[65] US Archives, RG 59, 867.4016/220, Morgenthau to Secretary of State, Oct. 26, 1915, encl., report by W. Peter, Aug. 26, 1915; Yeghiayan, *British Foreign Office Dossiers*, pp. 401-02.

[66] Germany, PA-AA/R14088, Scheubner-Richter, "Secret Report."

[67] "Statement of Dr. Tacy W. Atkinson," dated April 11, 1918, in James L. Barton, comp., *"Turkish Atrocities": Statements of American Missionaries on the Destruction of Christian Communities in Ottoman Turkey, 1915-1917* (Ann Arbor, MI: Gomidas Institute, 1998), pp. 42, 44; Leslie A. Davis, *The Slaughterhouse Province: An American Diplomat's Report on the Armenian Genocide, 1915-1917,* ed. and intro. Susan K. Blair (New Rochelle, NY: Aristide D. Caratzas Publisher, 1989), pp.

somewhere else," U.S. Consul Leslie A. Davis at Kharpert observed, "it would not be so bad, but everyone knows it is a case of going to one's death."[68] Some of the refugees from Trebizond vilayet remained near Kharpert until November, when another round of deportations from that city and its environs forced them out, although some were offered the option of conversion to Islam to secure survival.[69] During a meeting with German Ambassador Count Paul von Wolff-Metternich some months later, Ottoman Minister of Foreign Affairs Halil Bey "categorically denied" that the government ever attempted forcibly to convert the Armenians. Wolff-Metternich commented in a memorandum to Berlin that Halil Bey contradicted reports the German embassy had received from different regions.

> From the detailed statements of Vice-Consul Kuckhoff in Samsun, which have been confirmed from other sources, it can be concluded that in particular in the districts around the Black Sea the attempts to Islamize the Armenians, partly through persuasion and partly through threats, has been carried out on a very large scale.
>
> Elsewhere, moreover, where numerous Armenians on their own initiative have decided to turn to Islam in order to avoid exile and the confiscation of their property, the authorities have not given any privileges for this gesture and have deported them despite their conversion.
>
> Apparently it is feared that the real purpose of the Armenian deportations, that is the total extermination of the Armenian race, could be thwarted by further mass conversions.[70]

In late August, a small number of Armenians—including personnel

---

59-60; Henry H. Riggs, *Days of Tragedy in Armenia: Personal Experiences in Harpoot, 1915-1917* (Ann Arbor, MI: Gomidas Institute, 1997), p. 120.

[68] US Archives, RG 59, 876.4016/122, Morgenthau to Secretary of State, Aug. 10, 1915, encl., Davis to Morgenthau, July 11, 1915.

[69] Maria Jacobsen, *Oragrutiun 1907-1919: Kharpert* [Diary 1907-1919: Kharpert], trans. from Danish by Bishop Nerses Bakhtikian and Mihran Simonian (Antelias: Catholicosate of Cilicia, 1979), p. 139; "Statement by Isabelle Harley," dated April 15, 1918, in Barton, *"Turkish Atrocities,"* p. 70. For a brief historical background on Armenian Muslims in Trebizond vilayet, especially Hamshen, see Hakovbos Tashian [Hagop Dashian], *Hai bnakchutiune Sev tsoven minchev Karin* [The Armenian Population from the Black Sea to Karin] (Vienna: Mekhitarist Press, 1921).

[70] Germany, PA-AA/R14089, Embassy Constantinople, Wolff-Metternich, Ambassador in Extraordinary Mission in Constantinople, to the Reichskanzler, Jan. 24, 1916, rev. ed. of Lepsius, *Deutschland*, doc. 230, pp. 229-30, English trans. Robert Berridge, in Gust, "Documentation."

of the Ottoman Bank and the French tobacco concession Régie de Ta-
bac—who had been spared until then were deported from Trebizond at
night and were believed to have been killed immediately on the outskirts of the city.[71] By late September 1915 when the Turkish government published the text of the provisional law regarding the confisca-
tion of Armenian goods across the vilayets,[72] nearly all Armenians in
Trebizond vilayet had been removed from their lands and forced to
march in various directions—Kemakh, Amasia, Malatia, Kharpert,
Urfa, and as far as Deir el-Zor in the Syrian desert. Thousands of exiles
from the Trebizond vilayet had been killed on the mountain roads and
passes.[73]

Failed Responses to the Genocidal Policies

The Armenian responses to the deportation orders and the massacres
ranged from silent compliance to suicide as a form of resistance. Most
Armenians, acceding to the superior power of the Turkish military, followed orders and were marched to their death. In a handful of places,
as in Van, Shabin-Karahisar, Urfa, Zeitun, and Musa Dagh, the Armenians resorted to armed resistance. In Trebizond, the Dashnaktsutiun
and Hnchakian parties had organized self-defense units in response to
the Adana massacres in 1909, and when the government issued mobilization orders in the summer of 1914 some Armenian men in several
towns and villages fled to the hills nearby. There they held out for several months. In September 1915, the Russian navy traversing by the
shores reportedly attempted to reach them but without success. It was
not until April 1916 that the Russian army entered Trebizond and rescued the remnants of the survivors.[74] Misak Torlakian, an active mem-

---

[71] Germany, PA-AA/R14087, Embassy Constantinople, Hohenlohe-Langenburg,
Ambassador in Extraordinary Mission in Constantinople, to the Reichskanzler, No.
549, Sept. 4, 1915, rev. ed. of Lepsius, *Deutschland*, doc. 160, pp. 147-48, English
trans. Vera Draack, in Gust, "Documentation."

[72] Germany, PA-AA/R14088, Arthur Gwinner, Chairman, Board of Directors,
Anatolian Railway Company, to Foreign Office, Oct. 7, 1915, rev. ed. Lepsius,
Deutschland, doc. 222, pp. 214-16, English trans. Vera Draack, in Gust, "Docu-
mentation."

[73] Ghazarian, *Tseghaspan Turke*, p. 79. According to Ghazarian, p. 82, there were
90,000 Armenians in the vilayet of Trebizond before the massacres and by August 16,
about 60,000 Armenians from Trebizond had been massacred.

[74] Allen and Muratoff, *Caucasian Battlefields*, pp. 390, 396, 404; Kirakosyan,
Arajin hamashkharhayin paterazme, pp. 301-02.

ber of the Dashnaktsutiun in the region, gives a detailed account of the resistance movement that spared the lives of some Armenians.[75] According to Vahan Minakhorian, a number of Armenian community leaders proposed razing the Armenian homes to the ground to deny their attackers the material gains of genocide, while others recommended first to seek refuge in the Greek quarter and in so doing to buy time to organize a resistance, despite being fully aware of the government's military superior capabilities.[76] Such schemes did not materialize.

Nevertheless, the Russian occupation of Trebizond in 1916 had allowed a small number of Armenian survivors to return to their communities. They hoped to revive Armenian life after the war, and their expectations ran high in 1920 when President Woodrow Wilson, in fulfilling his charge according to the Treaty of Sèvres, awarded Trebizond to the Republic of Armenia in his arbitration decision. By then, however, the Kemalist movement had gained momentum, and the Armenian communities of the Black Sea coast were to fall victim yet again to further Turkish atrocities.

---

[75] Torlakian, *Orerus het.* See also Hovakimian, *Patmutiun Haykakan Pontosi*, pp. 124-25.

[76] Minakhorian, *1915 tvakane*, p. 145.

Kevork Vardapet Turian, Primate
of Trebizond, Strangled, 1915

Hamazasp Vardapet
Yeghiseyan, Primate of
Samsun, Killed near Tokat,
1915

Hagopos Der Kalustian,
Protestant Minister of
Ordu, Perished in Deportation,
1915

Archbishop Chrysanthos, Greek
Metropolitan of Trebizond

294

Deported Jamgochian and Balakian Women of Trebizond

Deported Payladzu Captanian
of Bafra

Armenian Partisans in the Pontic Mountains

Village of Totz, Requiem, 1916

Trebizond: Surb Stepanos Church, 1919

❋ 13 ❋

ORDU ON THE BLACK SEA

Vartiter Kotcholosian Hovannisian

This photographic essay is based on my first exploration of the Armenian homeland, combined with archival materials and eyewitness accounts of survivors of the Armenian Genocide.* The *Aghet/Mets Eghern* (Calamity/Great Crime) erased an entire people from its native soil. The next targeted victim became the historical record and memory itself. Nonetheless, the salvaged remnants of the nation, internalizing their deep wounds, labored to revive their intrinsic way of life in far-flung lands. It was up to subsequent generations, the inheritors of the trauma continuously renewed by denial, to solidify the revitalization of national culture.

Unfortunately, even after the dislocations caused by the genocide, new Armenian migrations were triggered by destabilizing crises such as the Stalin Terror and internal mass deportations of Soviet nationalities; Hitler's inferno and *Deutschland über Alles*; the perennial turmoil and superpower rivalries in the Middle East; the devastating Armenian earthquake in December 1988; the massive flight of more than 200,000 Armenian inhabitants of Azerbaijan and other parts of the Caucasus between 1988 and 1991; the disintegration of the USSR; and the social and economic collapse that enervated most of the post-Soviet states. These constant migrations beyond the bounds of historic Armenia have modulated into a formidable contemporary "Diaspora without Frontiers" and a politically blockaded, geographically truncated Republic of Armenia as the successor of the Armenian Soviet Socialist Republic.

---

* I am grateful to those who contributed to this chapter by sharing their personal experiences and revealing their inner worlds and to those who provided photographs and bibliographic materials. Mark Gulezian kindly reproduced several of the photographs of Ordu. The incessant quest for justice of my sister, Nazik Kotcholosian Messerlian, reinforced my own effort to engage and preserve memory. The invaluable Armenian oral history collection at UCLA has provided the basis for presenting the personal accounts of the four survivors included in this essay.

The immediate link in this writer's transgenerational/trans-territorial lineage is a bright-eyed six-year old girl by the name of Khngeni (Incense Tree), born in Ordu on the Black Sea. She somehow survived the bloodbath of 1915 and thereby unknowingly contributed to the transmission of the legacy of her ancient people.

Homeland-Bound (Tebi Ergir)

In the summer of 1995, a group of Californians—professionals and educators— set out with skilled tour organizer Armen Aroyan to find their parents' or grandparents' ancestral homes. Heirs, turned tourists, with reverence and pain, viewed the centuries-old architectural marvels, majestic even in their present desecrated state—yearning all the way for living connections. In towns and villages, they asked the elders, who knew all too well, and the younger ones, who were taught otherwise. They searched in the familiar innocence of children's eyes and voices. The sixteen-day journey took them from Istanbul (Constantinople) across central Anatolia to the capital, Ankara, through Cappadocia, and then into historic Greater Armenia (Mets Hayk). In the process they did find their hearths, whether intact or in ruin, occupied or neglected, or even vanished.

Before proceeding to the Black Sea-Pontus region, the group had come face to face with the places where Armenians had lived for centuries: Ismid, now Izmit; the barely identifiable vestiges of the famed Armash Monastery; Kesaria/Kayseri with its former Armenian settlements; Zeitun; Gurun; Malatia; Kharpert with its numerous villages of the "Golden Plain"; Lake Tsovk/Geoljuk; Mush; Van—Akhtamar, Varagavank, Bergri/Muradiye Falls; the River Arax; Mount Ararat of the twin peaks; Kars, and Ani; then backtracking to Sarikamish and Erzerum with its highland plain fanning out toward the north; Terjan/Mamakhatun; Erznka (Erznga)/Erzinjan; Baberd (Papert)/Baiburt. The hinterland was rugged and primitive, with ruins dotting the landscape.

On the way north from the historic Armenian Highland to the Pontus, the city of Gumushkhane turned out to be a post-1915 settlement. The original town, perched high in the hills, was virtually obliterated. The bus driver skillfully navigated the neglected dirt road into the panoramic hills where ruins of large churches stood in silence. A professor from Istanbul, hiking with his young son, identified the sullen shells as Greek and Armenian monasteries. Being matter of fact about 1915, he felt it was time to acknowledge the truth.

Toward the Sea

The oppressive cloak of reigning injustice notwithstanding, an unexplainable sense of exaltation and anticipation seized my sister Nazik and me as we set out in search of our mother's shattered childhood. Traversing the Pontic Mountain range, we slowly made our way up a winding road that passed through nature's picturesque green wonderland. There, we admired nestled high on misty cliffs the now-abandoned but recently renovated twelfth-century Greek Monastery of Sumela, carved out of the face of the mountain and now a popular and lucrative tourist attraction.

Descending to the Black Sea littoral, we viewed a picture postcard come alive, the impressive port and city of Trabzon (Trebizond; Armenian: Trapizon or Trabizon). The city's center, where older structures were giving way to modern facades, boasted an abundance of mosques that periodically emitted loudspeaker calls to prayers—a reverberating dissonance on the backdrop of the erased cosmopolitan history and silenced churches. The official tourist literature and maps occasionally make mention of a Greek relic but nothing Armenian.

As if to comfort our unspoken exasperation, the bus driver negotiated a narrow winding mountainous passage in the eastern suburbs to the remnants of the Amenaprkich (All Savior) Monastery known locally as Kaymakli. Perched high above the city, this Armenian monastic complex is now scarcely a shadow of what it had been, the bare weathered church having survived as a storage space for hay. A sapling green tree stood upright on the flattened roof in the place of the long-gone cross.

Descending toward the city through the bountiful garden suburbs once inhabited by Armenians all conjured up deep emotions. So did the dark foreboding waters of the Black Sea, clearly visible from the terrace of the Trabzon Museum, housed in the majestic erstwhile Greek Cathedral of Saint Sophia. Another sadly redeeming experience was the unexpected discovery of fragments of Armenian-engraved tombstones, captioned as "Kaymakli"—randomly placed in the museum's garden.

Leaving behind Trabzon with its bountiful filbert (hazelnut) groves, the source of livelihood of many Pontic Greeks and Armenians, we

traveled west on a paved scenic coastal highway near fields of corn en-
twined in a symbiotic relationship with the embracing green stems of
the interspersed string-bean stalks, about which Khngeni often spoke.
Impatient and anxious, we reached Ordu, the place of our proud maternal ancestral lineage, before resuming our odyssey to Samsun then
southward into historic Armenia Minor—Amasia, Marsovan, Gu-
mushhajikoy—and on to Bolu, Adabazar, and Istanbul.

Ordu was the birthplace of Khngeni in 1909 and her lively younger
brother Hovannes in 1911. In 1915, when they were just six and four
years old, they were to be torn away from their family. Their staying
alive came at an immeasurable price of extreme dehumanization and a
precarious shifting existence in the years to come. They sometimes
asked if it would have been more merciful or moral to have been
drowned along with the countless other children in the angry waters of
the Black Sea or to have perished with loved ones on the death
marches into the interior.

Ordu—Before 1915

Ordu, a panoramic seaside town situated almost midway between Samsun in the west and Trebizond in the east, had been the seat of one of
the districts of the Trebizond *vilayet*. The Armenians of the town originally lived in the lofty heights of Boz Tepe, which later served as a rec-
reation/picnic area for the townspeople. The well-established Armenian
sector was situated high up on the westerly slopes, running into the
Greek quarter below, while the Turkish quarters extended easterly
down to the seaside flats and government buildings and market place,
where during business hours the menfolk of all ethno-religious groups
intermingled.

Armenians played a significant role in the economy. They made up
the majority of the artisans and craftsmen—shoemakers, carpenters,
blacksmiths, coppersmiths, goldsmiths, textile workers, bakers—and
they competed with the Greeks in commerce. In the latter part of the
eighteenth century, filbert saplings were introduced from Trebizond
and Girason (Giresun). The filbert industry quickly flourished, the
product becoming the region's chief export, augmenting Ordu's prosperity. Moreover, construction of the Ordu-Sebastia (Sivas) overland
road in the 1880s led to an economic boom and the influx of many
Armenians from the Sebastia region.

In contrast with the geographically isolated regions of the Armenian Highland, the Black Sea Armenians had an advanced lifestyle, without compromising their ancient traditions. Yet state regulations and customary practices imposed strict limitations on the infidel *giavur*s. Periods of relative calm were interrupted by times of repression, unequal taxation, and even usurpation of goods and properties.

As in all Armenian communities, school and church were the focus of cultural life in Ordu. In the center of the Armenian quarter called Zeitun was the Surb Astvatsatsin (Holy Mother of God) church. Adjacent to the church was a large three-storey stone edifice housing a kindergarten through eighth-grade co-educational school, having earned the reputation of being one of the most efficient and progressive schools of the Armenian Pontus. A dedicated board of trustees and teaching staff oversaw the education of some 350 students. They could not have known, of course, that this cradle of enlightenment would soon be converted into an orphanage for some of the parentless children who survived the calamity of 1915. At present, the building is still being used as a school, even if for Turkish children alone.

Ordu, 1995

The moment of touching the reality had arrived. Suspended in a state of surreal trepidation at the gateway to the sanctuary—the altar of embracing one's wholeness—the bus rolled effortlessly into a typical seaside resort town, busy with its daily routines. Our driver, Jemal, quickly located the Toroman pharmacy, from where a physician brother and pharmacist sister had for years served the health needs of the area. That day the vivacious pharmacist guided us into the town's past. The last Armenian master coppersmith's door was locked. No sign of Armenian or Greek life. Uncounted young infidels had been absorbed without a trace into the local Islamic tapestry.

Our local guide pointed out identifiable Armenian structures. On the western slopes, surrounded by old houses, stood the silenced, now cross-less Greek church. Climbing steep passages we entered the former Armenian neighborhood, in the center of which stand trophies of a way of life prior to 1915. First is the three-storey school. Having housed an American-supervised orphanage after World War I, it later reverted to a school building. The friendly young Turkish principal took us on a tour— everything was so familiar. The second trophy, the Armenian church, has been replaced by a mosque. On the contiguous stone wall, now crumbling, prayer rugs were draped, harmonizing with nature's green and the sun. We were unable to find the location of the Armenian Protestant church (*zhoghovaran*), which reportedly ministered to nearly a thousand *parishioners.*

We walked the Armenian neighborhood streets. Forlorn, benumbed, our eyes penetrating the neglected and the stately homes, striving to detect a viable connection. Eureka! We found it—Khngeni's early childhood castle.

This narrative also touches on some of the dynamics of dealing with the unsettled effects of the Armenian Genocide as they continue to impact diasporan descendants decades after the crime. The fortuitous, seemingly miraculous, preservation of some family photographs empowers the progeny to realize the quintessence of their proud, productive, yet mercilessly violated forebears.

The Human Factor in Perpetuity

Individual, variously motivated acts of intervention and rescue in the face of significant risk paradoxically represent the altruistic component in the atrocious record of genocide. Placed in historical context, the intercession by non-Armenians living under the watchful eyes of officials and agents of the Young Turk regime became a critical link in the chain of survivability of a condemned people. While nothing could save most of the Armenian leaders and menfolk, there were both Greeks and Muslims who harbored Armenian women and children. The heart-wrenching, ever-haunting experiences of the survivors were in a sense tempered by having been rescued, even for a brief time, by forthcoming individuals—be they Turk or Greek, and, during the death marches, by Kurd, Arab, or Bedouin. Survival is the springboard of revival. And so it was that the bewildered Khngeni and her brother Hovannes survived apart from one another in a series of Greek and Muslim households until the end of World War I when a now unfamiliar (and for Hovannes even an unwanted) hand of a relative came to fetch them. But the war's end did not bring peace for long as partisans of Mustafa Kemal, such as Topal Osman, wreaked havoc among the surviving Christian population, ultimately scattering even the dispossessed orphans into a global "Diaspora sans frontières."

Family life, now transnational, was eventually reassembled as the orphans came of age and found their mates in many different countries, even as picture brides in trans-Atlantic arrangements. For the most part, traditional unspoken affection, emotional restraint, and persistent labor became the benchmarks of the survivor generation. During extensive travels in the United States and abroad, I interacted with many of these survivors and their families. The aged men and women had stoically internalized their unhealed wounds, and most of them had fastidiously spared their offspring the details and scope of their torment, yet in their sunset years the wounds seemed to resurface accompanied by agonizing frustration.[*] The inhuman wall of institutionalized denial deprived them of the opportunity to learn what happened to lost children or siblings or to express gratitude to their rescuers.

Several of 800 recorded interviews with survivors in the UCLA Armenian Oral History program have been utilized in this essay. They are presented below in condensed form in order to capture their essence. Obviously, summarizing in English translation very personal, emotion-filled narratives strips the original spoken word of much of its quality—dialect, diction, intonation, and even quivering hesitation. The interviewees were advanced in years when they were asked to share their indelible memories of their tender youthful years. They are the children of Ordu on the Black Sea:

Khngeni Kalenjian - born 1909
and Hovannes Kalenjian - born 1911
Shnorhig Teknejian (Chitjian/Kalenjian) - born 1909
Suzanne Tzerounyan - born 1909
Evnige Kabadayan - born between 1897 and 1899

---

[*] In essence, it seems I must have been in search of my own identity. My early childhood was derailed by Stalin's purges, followed by the inferno of World War II, with freight trains and labor camps as a way of life for the uprooted masses. Yet even amid this chaos, poetry and music were a must in war-torn Europe. In the occasional improvised piano recitals, my favorite piece was Mozart's "Turkish March" (Sonata No. 11 in A major), which I played enthusiastically, unimpeded by the word "Turkish" in the title. Apropos, the Hippocratic oath, administered to those embarking on a medical career, was taken as unquestionably and naturally binding during my own practice regardless of the patient's background. Ironically, however, among the master planners of twentieth-century genocides, especially under the cover of World War I and II, were men of medicine—doctors who willfully discarded and dishonored the Hippocratic oath.

Fast Forward

This "fast forward" element, that is, the worldwide progeny of genocide survivors, has emerged to reclaim its usurped legacy, striving to redress the unbearable consequences of 1915. As not so uncommon an example, Khngeni's American-born grandchildren are instinctive participants in the transnational Armenian renaissance. The sequenced photographs in this essay represent the transgenerational evolution generated by the geopolitically imposed migrations of an extended family and of the human strivings to find a place in the sun.

This abridged pictorial narrative is followed by four condensed oral histories of survivors from Ordu. Three of them are of then very young girls who were spared from the death marches but suffered the pains of separation and alienation in and around their native town. The fourth is of a teenage girl, who was among the deportees driven over the mountains all the way to Agn and Kharpert and who eventually ended up in the Crimea and Abkhazia and then Soviet Armenia before enjoying her final years in California.

Khngeni and Hovannes

Khngeni Kalenjian was born in Ordu in the spring of 1909, being one of six children granted to a progressive young couple, Garabed Kalenjian and Hranush Chitjian. But nature, in concert with malevolent humans, erased four of the six. And the two who survived did so at the price of an irreversibly violated childhood. Khngeni, age 6, and brother Hovannes, age 4, would forevermore bear that burden wherever they went, together in Abkhazia, Ukraine, and Germany, and finally one in California and the other in Soviet Armenia.

The Kalenjians and Chitjians, a prominent extended family, lived in the Chitjian neighborhood (*Chitjents tagh*) on the upper slopes of Ordu's Armenian quarter called Zeitun. While the clan was close-knit, the constituent families lived in separate homes. Grandparents commanded unspoken traditional authority and, living with the eldest son, were regarded as the head of household. So it was with Garabed, who doted over his young family. The bubbly vigor of Khngeni earned her horseback rides to the marketplace with her father. He had his hands full at home dealing with the pranks of his precious, mischievous ball of fire—little Hovannes "*agha*." In childhood innocence, the youngsters played outdoors and visited friends and relatives freely under the protective eye of the community. She vividly remembers the cobble-stone street in front of her home, very near the Armenian church.

Garabed worked as a blacksmith and saddle-maker and managed the jointly-owned Kalenjian filbert groves. In the marketplace, there seemed to be a congenial relationship between the Muslims and the Armenians, despite their religious differences. All this was before 1915, when a radicalized lethal ideology interrupted that relationship and implemented a master plan of annihilation of an entire people and its material and spiritual culture. With deep trembling emotion, Khngeni still relives the moment when her world was shattered. The following excerpts are from her oral history interview in Fresno, California, in May of 1977.

***

I remember, as if in a vague dream, being awakened at night. There is a strange commotion. My brother Hovannes and I are hurriedly entrusted to our widowed aunt, who also takes her own four children and our grandmother to the Greek quarter for safety. Father, mother, and the twin infants remain behind. There are kerosene barrels placed everywhere around the Armenian quarter, ready to be set ablaze if all the men fail to come outdoors as ordered. To avoid the worst, my mother Hranush urges Garabed to comply . . . she will manage with the twins. When Garabed emerges from the house, the gendarmes march him off with the other men to the central prison.

Some time after the men are taken away, my gentle mother gives me a handwritten note and money wrapped in a lace handkerchief, instructing me how to take it to the prison, saying that surely I remember the horseback rides through the lower part of the town. I slip through the crowds and guards, get to the barred windows. . . . I see him—Father, pale, moist eyes. Like him, I stand silent and speechless. He reads and then quickly writes a few lines and hands the paper back to me. That is the last time I see him.

When I make my way home from the prison, everything is in turmoil. Strange people are hurrying inside, while others are leaving with the family's bedding, utensils, clothing, everything. . . . Another intruder grabs my six-month old brother, but Mother wrests the infant back. But there is no reprieve. Deprived of the menfolk, our helpless families are ordered to gather only their essentials and to be ready to move out. No one knows why, where, how. My mother Hranush tries to save her children by leaving one of the twins, along with the family's milking cow, with a Turkish business acquaintance, and the other twin, along with the family's valuables, with a Greek family living near the Armenian church. I, together with a cousin, am sent to yet another Greek home. Suddenly my mother appears in our hiding place to give a parting embrace and a small bundle. She says: "Only Hovannes is coming with me; there are two of you here, take care of each other." Breathlessly, she utters, "Remember me," and quickly disappears. The Greek woman shuts the window. There is a ruckus. We do not understand Greek. The woman presses our lips shut. I still feel the pain of that separation. I am renamed Frosia and start to learn Greek.

Then the *aksor* (exile) begins, with three consecutive caravans leaving the town accompanied by gendarmes. Some exemptions are made, as the very frail and the small children are allowed to stay. Initially, many of these youngsters like me find a place in Greek and Turkish homes, while the less fortunate ones are fed to the waves of the Black Sea. Thereafter another decree orders the Greeks to evict all Armenians in their care or else suffer the consequences. The Greek woman has to put my cousin and me out. I am taken in by a Turkish family and given a new name, Hurriye. My poor cousin dies of typhus. In the summer, my new family moves to a nearby village where various kinds of preserves are made for the coming winter months. Then, one day, I suddenly see two cousins; with tight embraces and uncontrollable sobs, I cry out, "*Mairig . . . Hairig*" (Mother . . . Father), but all is in vain. I am mocked by the village children who gather round and taunt me. So, I have no choice but to submit to my fate and, although only six or seven years old, I become the caretaker for my new mama's and papa's baby, who is strapped to my back all day. I am given many household chores and have no time for play. With the toddler on my back, I sit on a large boulder with my back to the slope, looking and watching. Where is my little brother, Hovannes?

Later, I learn what happened to my family. My mother Hranush and the extended family depart with the first caravan. My father's mother insists that Hovannes, "the light of her eye," remain with them. Just outside of town, a large group of men, stripped to their undergarments, march by the caravan. Broken, half-crazed men and more stoic ones are tied together in twos and threes. My father is among them. In desperation, he implores Hranush to give the gendarmes her valuables and to let a willing Muslim take Hovannes from the caravan. All along the road, local villagers and Muslim refugees, the *muhajir*s, are watching gleefully and in anticipation. Soon the sounds of gunfire and cries come from the nearby woods. Garabed and the rest of the men are killed under the heavy blows of axes, daggers, and bullets. When Hranush tries to give Hovannes to a Muslim woman, as the caravan is being pressed forward toward Melet, the terrified child runs away and back to town where he sees other Armenian youngsters being rounded up, so he climbs the hill to the doorstep of his deserted house. An aunt who is preparing to leave with the last caravan hears the boy's heartbroken sobs and does what she can to console him. She takes him to the marketplace and persuades a sympathetic Turk to take care of the child. The man's teenage son befriends Hovannes, who quickly accepts his new identity as Yusuf. One day, he climbs a tree to pick fresh leaves for the goat he is tending—he falls, bloodied, an unattended leg injury. Unfortunately his guardian dies of the typhus, and many unknown other things happen before Yusuf ends up in the home of an old woman, where he is given various chores.

The seasons come and go. Some of the women, enduring abduction, rape, and extreme deprivation, begin to trickle back to Ordu, there to search for their abandoned children and sometimes to be rewarded with painful yet joyous reunions. I am ecstatic when my mother finds me. We take shelter in a Greek home until we are forced out again by another governmental decree. A Swiss couple who has come to Ordu on business wants to adopt a girl. Somehow, they choose me, shower me with gifts, and offer a lifetime of love and comfort. My mother consents for my sake and leaves the hotel after a final embrace. But I weep incessantly, crying "*Mairig, Mairig.*" Finally, angered and frustrated, they throw me out of their room. I go to the Greek house where we had found shelter earlier, but the woman will not take me in. I sit and cry until one of the daughters hides me and then her father arranges for me to go to a village where my aunt Armenouhi is a servant in a Turkish household. There, I become a part of the family and am put in charge of a Turkish orphan girl. Later, the family moves to Ordu and settles in one of the many vacant homes.

When the war ends in 1918, the survivors emerge from their hiding places; search for their loved ones; look for any kind of work to subsist. My adoptive mother releases me to my mother, but Hovannes–Yusuf, my brother, has forgotten his Armenian origins and runs away from his relatives. The Turkish woman finally hands him over once she is paid off. Yusuf, deeply browned by the sun and in rags, resumes his shattered Armenian childhood. But troubled times follow us—hunger, destitution, political unrest. With little choice, my aunts Imasdouhi and Haigouhi (who had to abandon her two small children born from a Turkish captor) arrange for Hovannes and me to be placed in the newly-organized Armenian orphanage in the former schoolhouse. But this was only a brief respite from the whirlpool of events that would cast us on the eastern shores of the Black Sea, first Batum, then Sukhum. The unforeseen turn of events was to take me to Kharkov in the Ukraine and then during World War II to Belorussia, Poland, and Germany (a Stuttgart Displaced Persons camp after the war), and ultimately to the sweltering heat of the vineyards of the San Joaquin Valley of California, and finally to a bustling houseful of a new generation of eight grandchildren (Raffi, Armen, Ani, Garo, and Hrair, Arpi, Vahe, Aram) in our modest, welcoming abode in Fresno's old Armenian Hazelwood district.

***

The pictorial section that follows spans the twentieth century and combines images of a personal journey of rediscovery at the end of the century with the faces and places existing at the time of the great calamity of 1915.

Ordu as It Was

Ordu as It Is

The Familiar Corn and Bean Stalks

On the Threshold

Surb Astvatsatsin Church
Converted to a Mosque

The Armenian School and
Then Orphanage

Discovery of
Khngeni's Home

Doorway, Old Armenian
Quarter

Grandmother Srpouhi Kalenjian

Hranush and Garabed Kalenjian

Hranush, Cousin, and Sister in Traditional Dress

Baby Khngeni, 1909

Teachers, National Coeducational School, Principal Tigran
Devoyants, Seated Center

Graduating Class, 1913, Principal Tigran Devoyants, Seated, Aram Manukian, Center, Siranoush Hekimian and Evnige Kabadayan to His Right

318

Boz Tepe, School Picnic, Aram Manukian Standing Center

Sukhum: Relocated Pontic Armenian Schoolchildren, 1922-23

Kharkov: Rescued Sisters, Imasdouhi, Hranush, Armenouhi, 1926

320

Kharkov: Hovakim Kotcholosian and
Khngeni, 1927

Kharkov: Khngeni and Hovannes,
1926

Kharkov: Khngeni and Hovannes, with New Generation of Cousins and Vartiter on Lap

Fresno: Hazelwood District, 1972

New York: United Nations, March 2, 1992, Grandson Raffi K.
Hovannisian as Armenia's Foreign Minister

Shnorhig Kalenjian (Teknejian)

Shnorhig, born 1909 in Ordu, remembers her violated childhood in 1915—orphaned, expelled from her hometown, struggling for survival, and then trekking halfway around the world via Constantinople, Greece, Romania, Soviet Armenia, and finally Los Angeles, where her interview was recorded in May of 1996. She is collected, with subdued dignified demeanor, alert and articulate, as she describes her dreamlike family world—an older and two younger brothers, parents, grandparents—in a traditional three-storey stone house on the hilltop overlooking the Black Sea, with the laundry area downstairs, kitchen and living-room above, and sleeping area on the upper level. Her maternal grandfather's six brothers and their families resided nearby in similar homes so that the neighborhood was known as *Chitjents tagh*. Her memory of the church is hazy, but she remembers the school clearly, especially as that three-storey stone building was to become a decisive link in her precarious survival. Her summarized semi-paraphrased interview follows.

***

Fifteen days before the *aksor*, they started rounding up the men. A neighbor's house is set afire; no one emerges. As my father does not go out, they start pouring kerosene around our house. My father then dashes out and is taken away, never to be seen again. He was a respected church trustee. A gendarme slaps my mother as they leave. That day, they apprehend seventeen others who are killed a short distance from town and dumped into a well. I remember that later we stood frozen over the well that had been filled with rocks. At the time of the deportation, my grandfather's Turkish business acquaintance pleads for the children to be left behind, for certain death awaits everyone who has to leave. So, my brother and I are adopted by him and given the names of Nuriye and Jemal. Father, together with many other relatives, perishes; my grandfather, his six brothers with their wives, do not return. Only some of the children sheltered by Turks and Greeks remain alive and later are able to regain their identity.

Mother gives her one-and-half year old son to a Greek family, and taking her eldest son departs with the deportation caravan. Timeless time goes by. A gendarme on horseback is searching for sheltered Armenian children. Our adoptive Turk mother hates us and turns us in.

We are taken to the government house, which is crowded with Armenian children. I recognize cousins and my sick uncle but never see them again. Cries, tears, confusion. My adoptive father who was near the mosque rescues us, but our stepmother becomes even more abusive, always keeping us hungry and frightened.

My real mother who becomes very ill during the deportation is saved by a Greek woman and manages to Ordu with her son. Much time has gone by. She finds us and takes us to another Greek family where her toddler is. There, we learn about the children who were turned out of the Greek and Turkish homes and taken to the government house. We hear that they were loaded on boats and drowned in the open sea. A twelve-year old cousin, a beautiful girl, was spared and taken home by one of the perpetrators. Horrified, shaken, she becomes ill. A Greek woman takes care of the terrified, jaundiced child, but she suffers an agonizing death.

Once more the government orders all Armenians to be expelled. What are we to do? We return to the adoptive Turkish father, who cannot help; he is a government official. He advises us to go to Fatsa, where the authorities are not as severe. We go back to the Greek family. The poor Greeks, though not massacred like the Armenians, will later be exiled from their ancestral homes. The Greek family finds a horse for us. So, here we are, a mother and son who have escaped a two-year deportation, together with her other rescued children, now all "illegals" in their own native town. When we get to Fatsa, we find the home of Ardem, my mother's childhood friend who is married into the Yorganiants family.

We share a small, narrow hiding space with other survivors. My brother goes begging at night with the three Yorganiants brothers and rests during the daytime. They behave, dress, and speak Turkish and have Turkish names. With the small scraps of bread they manage to beg and scrounge, we subsist for a while longer. My mother hears that my grandfather may be alive in Melet, so we set out on the road, barefoot, hungry. I don't remember how many days, but, in vain, because we find that grandfather has been killed. We are again rounded up and put on the road of exile toward Hoylasar. On the way we have to pass through the Idirdagh woods—piles of corpses are being assaulted by flocks of noisy vultures. I remember this all vividly. My mother learns that these were men from Tamzara who were recently killed. We are in a dwindling caravan of only about 60 women and children, who, when lying down for the night, take note of who isn't there any longer. One day, my elder brother is counted among the lost.

In Tamzara, which is now a ghost town, rumors are heard that the Russians are approaching Lazistan and Trebizond. The gendarmes suddenly disappear. We turn around and begin to walk toward Lazistan. Barefooted, no food, eating only grass and greens that Mother recognizes as being edible, but even so our bellies swell up. We finally reach Surmene on the sea and remain there—Turkified, with Turkish names, several families in one house, and we children can no longer speak Armenian.

One day, a Turkish doctor announces: "Armenians are free to return to their homes." Maybe the war is over. Still disguised as Turks, we find space in a boat. Not having money, Mother offers the Laz boatman some yardage that she has gotten from a Greek shopkeeper. We finally reach Ordu—sadness, desolation, loneliness—seven brothers' semi-ruined, deserted houses. The doors, windows, and woodwork of our home have been carried away and the upper storey is demolished.

***

Shnorhig goes on to tell about her life after the war. The Ordu orphanage in the Armenian school becomes a beacon amid the ruins, a modicum of security, basic care, and education giving hope. Within a year, however, because of renewed unrest, the orphans are moved to the Ortakiugh orphanage in Constantinople. Then, in 1922, the Kemalist victory and occupation of Constantinople necessitate the swift transfer of the children to Greece. During her three years in an orphanage there, Shnorhig takes vocational education classes, remembering fondly Dr. and Mrs. George White, Armenian-speaking American missionary educators with years of service at Anatolia College in Marsovan. In 1926, Shnorhig's mother, who has ended up in Romania, is finally able to reclaim her now seventeen-year old daughter.

In Bucharest, with an active Armenian community that has a school, church, scouts, and other organizations, Shnorhig meets and marries a young Ordu survivor, Hampartzum Teknejian, in 1927, but he dies six years later. A young widow, Shnorhig works hard to raise her two young sons. In 1946, she repatriates with her family to Soviet Armenia, where great disillusion awaits them, as thousands of repatriates are sent to Siberia while others live in constant fear. In 1986, the now-enlarged family succeeds in immigrating to the United States.

In Erevan, on every April 24, Shnorhig's family, with tens of thousands of others, walked up to the Tsitsernakaberd Genocide Memorial to place flowers around the eternal flame. In California, only once was she able to climb to the Armenian Martyrs' Memorial in Bicknell Park in Montebello. As she declined physically, her mind remained ever alert; she was an avid reader. Each April, she would telephone the Turkish consul general in Los Angeles with an important message. Not once permitted to reach beyond the receptionist, she nonetheless delivered her somber monologue in excellent Turkish. The office personnel promised to relay the recorded heart-to-heart message to the "occupied" or "absent" consul general. If he ever listened, this is what she said: "The unrequited pain in the hearts of the brutally violated victims notwithstanding, I must tell you that your government's immoral and shameful denial of the genocide leaves no room for me and others like me to acknowledge and express gratitude to the rescuers, the good Turks, who, whatever their motives, made our survival possible."

Los Angeles: Shnorhig Teknejian Testifying at UCLA Conference, 2002

Suzanne Tzerunyan

In 1994, 85-year old Suzanne Tzerunyan was interviewed in Pasadena, California. Ironically, it was to be her last *dun* (home) in a long chain in her oft-changing life that extended over four continents. This sequence of *dun*s beginning in her birthplace of Ordu reflects the disruption of her life but not of her lucid memory. Her condensed testimony follows.

* * *

In 1915, we were five sisters: Haigouhi, 10; Hasmig, 8; Suzanne, 6; Zvart, 4; Sirvart, 1½. I remember Father would line us up for exercise. Sirvart, who had just started walking, would be bundled up and tied to Haigouhi's back. So, I was six years old when the massacres began.

They came at night and took my father. Father was sleeping with his brother. The gendarmes shouted: "If you don't come out now, we will hang your entire family on your threshold." Mother was terribly frightened. "Janig," she cried, "get up, get up and go, get dressed, the children—*meghk en* [they are helpless; to be pitied], and so forth. My father got up and went outside, but not his brother. They took my father. So, he was among the first to be taken and, of course, we did not hear from him again. My father was the first in our family to be killed. We were scattered to different *dun*s—Greek, Turkish—because I have to say that the Turks of our Ordu were very decent. They would say to the Armenians: "This can't be, this can't be; you cannot take the children with you; it is a shame; leave them, and when you return, we will return them to you." I was placed in a Greek *dun*, Sirvart and Hasmig in another Greek *dun*, and Haigouhi in one Turkish *dun,* and Zvart in another.

Soon after, however, the Greeks were ordered to turn out all the sheltered Armenian children. The Greek priest with whom I was staying had to announce this in the church service, yet he did not want me to leave. But he was chastised by those who asked why he was telling them to give up their Armenian children while he was still keeping me. I knew I had to go, and so I left and became a waif. I remember waking up one night with a very dark stranger looking down at me. He lifted me . . . I was screaming and thrashing, but the stranger took me to the home of his relatives and then to another house where he had a Greek servant look after me. She took care of me, combed my hair, and so forth. The strange man showered me with toys, sweets, and fancy gifts like lace stockings. Apparently, I was intended as the bride-to-be for his son.

I recall being taken to the seashore . . . on a boat headed to Surmene, the stranger's home. The voyage was interrupted by Russian bombardment of the coast, so we had to stop in Trebizond in a hotel. An Armenian teenager from Ordu was there, and she begged to go with us to be saved. I was extremely seasick all the way to Surmene, where I learned that the stranger was a *bey* in a nearby village. He had three children, including a teenage son, my intended future husband. The girl who had joined us in Trebizond was to take care of me, but we could speak no Armenian. The man even threatened to kill us and dump us into the sea if he heard us speaking Armenian. Soon, he no longer allowed her to be with me and instead made her a household servant. I was sent to a Turkish school. My sense of time was marked by changes of the seasons. Heavy snow fell in the winter. I remember that on the way to school through deep snowdrifts, I slipped and was hurt. Children from a nearby house, whom I later found out to be Armenian, had been watching me and rushed out to help. The season changed again. It was spring. The snow was melting. At the same time, the Russian bombardments intensified, and the Turkish army began to retreat. So, after about six months, we went back to Ordu.

Meanwhile my sister Zvart was in the *dun* of a kind Turk. Because she cried day and night, he wanted to find members of her family and, by asking here and there, found out where the other sisters were. So, when he heard that we had returned to Ordu, he came and asked me, "Do you know Suzanne?" I answered, "I don't know any Suzanne," but then he told me that he had come to take me to my sister. I trembled with such excitement that I spilled the glass of water in my hand. The next day came the emotional reunion with my sister. By then, my mother had escaped from the deportation caravan and, with the help of a Turkish lady, a *khanum,* and dressed in Muslim garb, she had managed to get back to Ordu and find my eldest sister, Haigouhi. Thus, we became reunited. I was in terrible shape, in tattered clothes and covered with lice. My sisters removed my infested clothes and took me to a special place where Turkish women were able to cleanse me and turn me into a pretty doll. I was saved in this way. Then our family was placed in the large home of Ali Bey in a nearby village. He was such a kind man. I recall being taught by him to read the Quran. That large family had helped and harbored many Armenians. Some Armenian young men who had escaped the massacres had gone up into the hills with their arms. I remember their passing by Ali Bey's home, where from my hiding place behind a tree I saw them riding armed on horseback. They were given food and drink at Ali Bey's home.

It must have been the end of the war, because one day the leader of the armed band, whose name was Garabed, came and placed me on his knee, asking: "Do you want to go to school?" By that time, I was speaking only Turkish. Yes, I wanted to go to an Armenian school. Ali Bey was so concerned about us that he loaded us down with food and supplies as my family set out for Ordu. Were we to find our *dun*? No, it had been ransacked and we were destitute. There were so many of us, five girls, that we were placed in the orphanage. My mother became a cook there, and my eldest sister taught the alphabet to kindergarteners in the Armenian church, while the upper classes met in the school building.

This may have lasted a year. Then, news that the terrifying Topal Osman was coming forced the orphanage to prepare to flee overnight. We had heard that in Marsovan he had slaughtered all the orphans and children who had been rescued and had even burned some of them in ovens. We were soon on a ship to Bolis [Constantinople], where we were received well in the Ortakiugh and Beshiktash orphanages. Excellent care, cleanliness, orderliness, instruction, crafts. But the victory of Mustafa Kemal's forces triggered a new exodus, perhaps it was the autumn of 1922, to Corfu. I remember that there, on New Year's Eve, it snowed for the first time in forty years.

* * *

Suzanne goes on to tell of orphanage life; relocation to Egypt and going to an American school there; the solicitousness of an American missionary couple, the Atchesons; later repatriation to Soviet Armenia, where, like so many others, her family experienced bitter disappointments until managing to immigrate to the United States. With no calendar record or ability to rely on her seasonal perception any longer, Suzanne gave the following approximate chronology of *dun*s since the disruption of 1915:

1915-16: Ordu, Greek home; homeless; Trebizond; Surmene
1916-18: Ordu, Turkish home and Ali Bey's village

1918-19: Ali Bey's village; Ordu, ruined family home and
    Armenian orphanage
1919-22: Constantinople orphanages
1923-25: Corfu, Greece, orphanage
1925-27: Syros, Greece, orphanage
1927-48: Egypt, school and work
1948-90: Soviet Armenia
1990 onward: California and "Diaspora sans Frontières"

***

Evnige Kabadayan

Evnige, a teenage graduate of Ordu's only coeducational school in 1913, was taking sewing lessons when deportation orders reached her hometown. In 1980, at the age of over 80, she was interviewed in a small Hollywood apartment with a family of five, her final residence on her tortuous and torturous trek of life. She reminisced longingly about her beloved Ordu. Some of the questions of the interviewer are omitted from the excerpts of that interview which follow (the questions are in italics and brackets).

***

Our city was on the coast. It was a beautiful city. When we looked out of our window, we could see the sunrise. It was beautiful. There were three separate quarters—Armenian, Turkish, and Greek. Of course, the government buildings were located in the Turkish quarter. The market-place was also a large place on the border between the Greek and Turkish quarters. The Armenian quarter was on a high hill. The Greek quarter was in a vale, and the Turkish one was on another, much lower easterly hill. The Armenian quarter was way up and had two parts. They were close to each other but were separated by a ravine. One side was called Zeitun, but the other side didn't have a name, I don't know why.

The Armenian quarter was the nicest with good roads and streets. I have never been in the Turkish quarter, but the Greek one was just spread out along the seashore. . . . We had a school and a church. We had a kindergarten and an eight-year normal school. I graduated from that school and they took our photograph. Aram Pasha [Manukian] was in that picture, too—Dashnaktsakan Aram Pasha. . . . He was a highly respected head teacher.

[*Did Aram Pasha do anything else in your village besides being a teacher-administrator?*]

He could have had a connection wherever the Dashnaktsakan party was active. . . . Both the Dashnaktsakan party and the Hnchakian party existed in our city. . . . I do not know what they did, but I know that, for example, my mother's brother was a member of the Dashnaktsakan party. But we didn't make any inquiries about the work they did, so I don't know.

[*O.K. What did your father do?*]

My father owned a small grocery store. It was his occupation. We could barely make a living. We had a very humble house. It was a small house of two rooms. Later my father built a kitchen, too. My grandmother had bought that house. She had worked weaving cloth for many years and had saved enough money to buy the house when my father was fifteen years old.

[*Generally, what did the Armenians do?*]

What did they do? All the trades belonged to the Armenians: copper work, pharmacy, and so on. In short, the Armenians applied their abilities well everywhere. All of the handymen, barbers, and bakers were Armenian. There were some Greeks, too, but very few. They occupied themselves with commerce more often.

[*Did you have any relations with the Turks?*]

We, the women, did not socialize with them. But the men did because, for example, my father traded with them. He bought goods from villagers. If we met a Turk on the street, we just went our own ways. No one said a word to us. If we passed by the marketplace, there were some Turkish houses. Nobody said anything to us. There have been cases when I had to walk through an entire street in order to go home, and no one said anything. There were two baths, one in the Turkish quarter and the other in the Greek quarter on the shore. We tried to go to the bath in the Greek quarter. Of course, there were separate days for the Armenians and the Turks. Well, I don't know about men. I don't remember that. I don't remember when they went there.

[*All right. How did you get the news about World War I? Were you informed in your home that the war had started?*]

How could I not be informed? As the saying goes, "News passes very quickly by word of mouth," especially when we had an Armenian who had some connections with important Russian people. I think he was following their ships or something like that. They used to say he was a Russian ambassador. He wasn't an ambassador, but they used to say that. I remember it that way. We could find out everything. The steamers came and left constantly. So, there was information. . . . The Turks conscripted Armenians for the war, too. For example my older *keri* [mother's brother] was drafted and was sent to the Bulgarian front. . . . He wrote that a bullet hit his gun, and his gun broke: "If it had hit a bit left or right, I would have been killed." When the war ended, he left for America, and didn't return to Ordu.

[*Did the Turks announce that everyone had to give up their weapons? Do you remember anything like that in your city?*]

There was no one in our city who owned weapons. I know that no one in our neighborhood had a weapon. . . . Now I can say that in 1915 the Russian ships came close to the shore and fired at the Turkish quarters, at the buildings, at the houses, yes, and the Turks from those parts came to our side, to our quarter, for safety. I remember that. That happened, because I remember they passed by in large groups.

[*Did deportations take place in your city? I mean, did they deport the Armenians from Ordu?*]

Oh, yes, they did. It was in June of 1915 if I am not mistaken. It was in June, but our Armenians appealed to the government asking for intervention so that they wouldn't have to go. The Turkish government said: "Become Turks. Convert to Islam, and you won't leave. You won't be deported." And some people converted. Certainly not everyone. Several families went there and converted: "God is one. There is no other God, and Mohammed is His Prophet." They were relieved that they would no longer be exiled. But the central government decided that nevertheless they were the same Christians even though they had converted to Islam, and so they should be deported, too.

Then they started deporting us in groups. Before that, they had imprisoned some of the men. They sent away those tied up prisoners in advance. For example, my mother's brother and my grandfather were imprisoned. An Armenian soldier who had deserted and was in hiding passed by their house while the men were outside. Just for that, they were all arrested and taken to prison. . . .

My uncle was in a very bad mental condition in prison. My father went and signed for him and brought him home. I remember that very well. I made coffee when my uncle came. I said: "Uncle, this one is for you and this one is for father." There were two separate cups because my father liked his coffee with little sugar. Then my uncle attacked me: "So you are trying to get me to drink poison?" He was already mentally disturbed. Then I went away crying, and my mother said, "Hush, Hush . . . calm down." Then my uncle slowly recovered, and they took him back to prison because my father had got him released temporarily. My father was a very resourceful man; he could find a common tongue with anyone. When they took my uncle back, we decided to leave the city but it was too late, because they were already deporting my uncle and my grandfather, so we followed them. For some time, they were with us. They were in our group. We were together.

We didn't sell the house, but I remember that we took the stuff out. They probably sold those. For instance, my uncle and my grandfather took out the things they had; they probably sold those. We had nothing to do with these things. The adults took care of that.

[*You left with your entire family?*]

No, not with the entire family. They issued an edict that children under ten were allowed to stay in the city. The next-door neighbor to my father's store was Greek. My father asked him to take care of my younger brother. He agreed. We took my brother's clothing, bed, and so forth to the man's house. My brother came to see us off when we were leaving. He bade farewell to us crying. . . .

My father bought two horses. They loaded the bedding, the clothing, and whatever we needed, for instance, two-three small pots so that we could cook something to eat on the way. We took only the very necessary items. But we loaded a lot of bedding on the horses. We went by foot and put those on the horses. On the way, we were with my mother's sister and my grandmother. Our family was in that group. My other grandmother was a very old woman—my father's mother. She stayed behind. They supposedly gathered up people like that. . . . Later we learned that they were thrown into the sea. . . . Yes, my grandmother, too. Marine's sister had just delivered a baby, and she had been left there, too. She survived. They took away the baby, but she managed to survive. She later told us that they had thrown everyone into the sea.

[*What reasons did they give you when they deported you? Did they say why you had to leave?*]

Why? It was just an order, and we had to obey it. Why would they care to give us explanations about their actions? They assigned several gendarmes to our group. We walked during the day and rested at night. We lay down and continued our way again the next morning. . . . So we went on like that. One night, a woman gave birth to a child next to a Greek house. Whether it was a girl or a boy, I cannot recall. They gave the baby to the Greeks, and the next day, the baby's mother had to continue on the road. We reached the town of Melet. There I got sick, and they called a doctor. The doctor was a Turk, of course. He gave me some medicine, and then he said: "It is a pity to take this girl with you and ruin her. Give her to me." My uncle lied: "That is my wife. How can I leave her?" The doctor didn't say anything else, and we went on. Oh, I shouldn't forget to say that when we became [converted] Turks, we started covering ourselves like the Turks. You could see only our eyes so that you couldn't tell whether we were girls or women, ugly or beautiful. After Melet, there was a building. I don't know what kind of building it was, but it was abandoned. It might have been a rich Armenian's house. I am not sure. As it was vacant, we occupied it. Several Armenians came. They wanted to give away their daughter to a Turk so that they could stay there. I don't know if they were able to do that or not.

We continued on toward Agn. We hadn't reached Arabkir yet. It was Agn. We were very poorly fed there for a long time. They were selling cheap cows there. My father bought one and killed it. He said: "Our shoes are worn out. We can make shoes from its skin to wear." But it certainly didn't work out. Whether it was because of that beef or something else, people got sick with diarrhea. We went on like that and got to Arabkir. We met a few women who were staying there. They later joined us. We found out that they were from Tripoli [Tireboli], which is also on the shore of the Black Sea. . . . We walked and walked. My father was very ill. I told you already what happened after we ate the beef. But I, on the contrary, became more energetic.

[*Were you constantly accompanied by gendarmes?*]

Yes. Oh, I forgot to say that when evening came the gendarmes demanded money, gold. The people gathered money among themselves and gave it to them. One morning we were in that building that I mentioned when the gendarmes demanded the horse of a rich Armenian who was with us. He refused to give it. They cursed: "You will never walk again." They took him away, and we heard how they shot him. The gunshots were heard. Then they took his horse.

Later on, we were resting again. We hadn't spread out the bedding. We were lying directly on the tied-up bedding, and my brother was lying on my father's coat. The gendarme shouted at him: "Get up! I want to rest, too. You have been on it long enough." My brother refused. He was a kid. The gendarme told him, "You will not be alive tomorrow." My mother heard that. My father wasn't there at that time, and when he came back, she told him about that. My father asked which one it was, and my mother explained. He then went to the gendarme, who turned out to be an acquaintance. My father said: "Oh, you are an acquaintance of mine. Let me give you a gift." And he gave his coat to him so that he wouldn't kill my brother the next day.

Then there was a woman from our city. One day, she saw a necklace on one of the gendarme's neck and started to cry. My mother asked, "Why are you crying?" She answered: "That is my husband's necklace. They have taken it from him, and this means that they have killed him." Things of that sort happened very often.

At first, the Armenians were able to collect money and give it to the gendarmes, but later on, they no longer had any money. So, at nights the gendarmes searched them and took away whatever they could find. They got everyone naked from head to foot. They searched thoroughly. They even stuck their fingers into the women's you-know-what because they had noticed that women were hiding money and gold there. And they seized it all. After that, they hit them shouting, "Why were you hiding it?"

One night, they were searching like that again, and I was afraid. I didn't want to come forth. I saw that they had already stuck their fingers into a girl, and she could no longer take it. She was crying and turning from one side to another. I got extremely scared. There was almost no one else left to be searched. My father said, "She is my daughter," and my grandfather said, "she's my daughter-in-law." They hit everyone, and my grandmother pulled me by my arm and took me to the other side because the gendarmes were on this side, and the ones who had already been checked were on the other side. Thus, I was saved. But I suffered so much, so much. . . .

Oh, I have forgotten to tell about something else, too. Once, in broad daylight . . . they usually searched at night, but this time they were doing it during the day. There was something like a cave on a small hill. They told us to go there. . . . They drove us all into the cave, and they started searching and letting us out one by one. My father's two cousins, two sisters, one of them pretended that the other one was sick so that she could go first. The thing is that the other one was hiding money inside herself, and they wanted to save the money. The gendarmes searched her, found the gold and took it out of there. They started to beat her with a whip. Then they continued searching and searching. . . . Fortunately, some other people were passing by, and the gendarmes were afraid that they would see what was happening, so they let everyone out and told us not to say anything. We were saved that way from it all.

Another time, the gendarmes saw a girl and wanted to take her. They told her father: "Give this girl to us." He answered: "How can I give you my daughter? Wherever I go, my daughter comes with me." That same night, when we settled somewhere, in a house, the *chetes* [brigands] came and searched everywhere. I was lying there and was not feeling well. They looked at the faces of every girl to see if there were any young and beautiful ones, and I was lying there. They told my mother to lift the cover so that they could see my face. I am not sure if it was by chance or I was pretending, but I was shaking. Was it for real or not, I don't know. They said: "Go back to bed, go back! We don't need her." My mother gave some gifts to them. . . . We learned the next morning that they had taken away several girls. My father's cousin came and saw that I was there and that they hadn't taken me away. They had taken her daughter. She started walking around in an angry manner because they had not taken me, but they had taken her daughter. They had taken away several girls. I remember that. The next day, we started walking. That girl's father, the one whom the gendarmes wanted to take, he was sitting right in front of my eyes and rolling a cigarette when a gendarme came up from behind and shot him. He fell.

[*Without saying anything?*]

Yes, without a word. I don't know if they buried him or not. They wouldn't allow it. They took his clothes off and kept them. So, we went on our way like that. We walked and walked and got to a Kurdish village. My mother said: "The Kurds are looking for a girl. If someone likes you, just go with him." That really hurt me. She explained: "Your father says that they will eventually take you away along the way. So, what difference does it make whether it's here or there?" I cried, "I won't go."

[*Why did your mother say that?*]

To save me. If I could have saved them all, I would have agreed. But why would I want to be away from them just to save myself? Lusanoush's two sisters stayed there. Their father was a barber. They needed him, so he stayed, too. But they didn't survive. Only one of Lusanoush's sisters and her brother survived. I don't know what happened to them.

[*Did they marry Kurds and stay there?*]

Yes, they stayed. Their parents stayed, too. We continued our way. We were passing by the river Murad, the Euphrates, and I was extremely thirsty. There wasn't any water anywhere. I wanted to go and drink some water, but my mother wouldn't let me. I found an opportunity and ran to the river. It was full of corpses. I tried not to look anywhere. I just went there, drank the water, and came back. My mother got very angry. But I was very thirsty. . . . There were bodies on the ground, too. The sick ones fell down and stayed like that. There was a woman's body. It looked like a horse. It had swollen badly under the sun. I can still see it in front of my eyes. There were bodies everywhere. After that, it all started. Bodies, bodies, bodies . . . both on the ground and in the river. Once, there was a dead woman next to the road, and her baby was moving weakly in her lap with its eyes open. I felt so bad, so bad. I didn't have any strength left in me, but if that child had been a bit healthier, I would have carried it with me. That's what has been imprinted in my memory. It's a very bad thing.

The Turks took away everything we had. The Turkish villagers attacked us and took everything away. They probably had bribed the gendarmes. They gathered and took away everything, and we were left with nothing. We reached the bridge of that River Murad. Before we crossed the bridge, my father died. He had been very gravely ill. I told my mother: "I don't care what they will do to me. Even if they kill me, I will bury my father." My mother answered: "You think I don't want that? I want to bury him, too. I will bury your father. We will stay here with your uncle, and we will bury him together. Your grandfather is weak. You should help him cross the bridge. You should go ahead and slowly cross it, and we will catch up with you." They persuaded me that way, and I went with my grandfather. We went forward for quite a while, and then they caught up with us. . . . They put my grandmother on a donkey, and we went ahead. My grandmother died on the way. We put her in a hole, and the Turks were waiting above it so that when we move away, they could take off her clothes. My uncle was sitting there with tears in his eyes. Anyway, my mother could no longer walk, and when the donkey became available, she got on it. She had already become sick, and she could hardly walk. She had no strength left in her. Even when she was sitting on the donkey, she had to lean on me with one arm. I was walking by the donkey. She said: "Ah, it's so good that you are with me." She remembered that I refused to leave. We went to an Armenian village, which was in ruins.

[*Do you remember the name of that village?*]

No, I don't. It was a short way from Kharpert. Not actually Kharpert, but Mezre. Kharpert was an old city. Mezre was a new one. The Turks, those scoundrels, had built it. I lay down next to my mother. We used to spread something thin on the ground. It was rough. Then, I felt that my mother was cold. I started crying. My aunt took me away, and in the morning, we buried my mother. The next day, we stayed there the whole day. We had walked a long distance. Then, my grandfather died, and we buried him. Everyone helped us. We couldn't have done that by ourselves.

A Turk saw me there and started asking around about me. When my mother died, my aunt became my mother. He came to my aunt and asked her to give me to him. My aunt came to me and told me about it, and I said that if he agreed to take my family with him, too, I would sacrifice myself and would marry that Turk. If not, I wouldn't. My aunt goes to him and tells him that if he agreed to take my mother (actually my aunt), father (my uncle) and brother with him, then he could marry me. The Turk went to the authorities and was told that he could take my aunt, my brother, and me, but not my uncle. When I learned that, I said no. My aunt tried to persuade me: "You are a woman. My brother is gravely ill; he will most likely die soon anyway." I said I wouldn't marry the Turk. So, I hid away from my aunt, and started walking separately from her. We were passing by Mezre, at a distance, of course. . . .

We had left Mezre far behind when some Turkish women with three kids asked: "Are there any young people among you?" I replied, "What for?" I approached them. I wasn't afraid because they were women. That woman got a strong hold of my arm and said, "Come with me!" Both my uncle and my aunt caught up with us. The Turkish woman said: "Let her become our servant." I asked my uncle: "What should I do. Do you think I should stay with them or come with you?" He said: "I cannot tell you anything. In this short amount of time, you have amassed so much life experience that you should be the one to decide." The gendarmes were approaching us, and I was quickly covered so that they wouldn't see me. The caravan moved on toward Mosul, and I stayed. . . . I was in such bad condition but they made me carry their child, who was a boy of about 6-7 or maybe 5 years old. They made me carry him even though I was in bad shape. I went with them. We went to a Turk's house and they brought some food. We ate and then returned to their home. Again, they made me carry the child.

Then somehow my aunt joined us. Oh yes, there was an Armenian woman sitting there. She was about thirty years old. They have brought her, too. . . . We were foolish, but that woman was smart. She had been brought there as a servant but was pretending to be sick and just sitting there. She secretly told us that there were Protestant missionaries in Kharpert. Mezre was in a valley, but Kharpert was an old city on the highlands.

A local Armenian woman explained that this house had belonged to a doctor, an Armenian doctor. They had killed him and had thrown his pregnant wife out. Then they had moved in. The Turkish pasha's secretary had moved in there. He was from Trebizond. He had two or three daughters and a little son. His oldest daughter was married to a man from Ordu who knew my father. After he learned that, his attitude toward us changed. After my aunt joined us, we were allowed to go to the public bath. We were crying and crying; there were plenty of lice on our heads. We took a bath crying all the time and came out and went home.

So, our days passed like that, and one day my aunt learned that a Turk from Ordu was going back. My aunt asked him to take us with him because she had four children left behind there. She had seen a dream with four shaky pillars under the house, so she thought that meant we were going to be freed. It was on her mind all the time, and one day she asked, "Where are they [the Turkish family]?" I answered, "In the garden." She slipped away to the garden of a Greek neighbor. I was supposed to meet her at night and get away to Kharpert. But at night I went out several times and couldn't find her, and for the next several days I cried myself to sleep.

[Evnige describes in detail her life in the Turkish home, her eventual escape with the assistance of two Assyrian women, and her reunion with her aunt in the American missionary compound of Kharpert, where the two remained until the second half of 1916. They then joined a small band of Armenian women trying to get back to their Black Sea towns to seek out their children. They paid Kurdish intermediaries to get them safely across the Dersim district to Erznka (Erzinjan), which had been occupied by the Russian army and Murad's Armenian volunteers. From Erznka they made their way to Trebizond, where they waited anxiously for the Russians to occupy Ordu so that they could return home, but such hopes were dashed by the Russian revolutions in 1917 and the retreat of the Russian armies from the occupied Ottoman territories. The narrative then continues].

We went to Trebizond in the fall of 1916. In 1917, there was a man from a village of Trebizond whose name was Puzant Fundukian. He asked to marry me. He had two brothers, Nerses and Haig or perhaps it was Aram. My husband was taking supplies to the soldiers or something like that. His younger brother was a wagon driver, and the other one was a store manager or something like that. My aunt was with me. I gave birth to a baby at the end of 1917. Then we had to move again. The men had a meeting and decided to defend the country and go to Erznka and beyond to Agn and Arabkir. They wanted to defend the areas from which the Russian army was retreating. My aunt refused to come and left for Abkhazia. . . . But the Turks attacked us and we had to fall back. By the way, I have to say that there were Armenians who had come from other countries, too. There were Armenians from America, France, and so forth. When we were retreating toward Erznka, we met them there. All of them were Turkish Armenians who had come from Europe and other places.

My brother-in-law rented a carriage for me and the baby while the men were to stay behind and defend us. But the coachman abandoned us. When I woke up, I saw that the baby had frozen to death. . . . Then I am not sure what happened, but I started walking, and there were some women with me. I certainly wasn't all alone. It got dark. I don't know how it happened, but I had already come a long way and I was tired when I met a soldier, an Armenian soldier. I cried: "Sir, let me sit behind you." He was probably retreating, too. So, we went and reached Erznka. We hadn't had any sleep and felt numb. He left me in a house. I stayed there and woke up in the morning. Some women had gathered and were talking. They were preparing to leave, too. The Russians had retreated from Erznka. The Armenians were left alone. The men were defending the front to give us a chance to get away without being massacred. . . . So, we lost each other.

In Erzerum, some Dashnaktsakans told us to go in the direction of Kars. At one place, we were in a carriage. I don't remember who put us there and how it happened. There was a very sick child in the mother's lap. They probably helped us on the way. I don't remember it very well. Exhausted, we stayed near Kars for a few days and then we started looking for one another. I found my father-in-law. They were gathering together in Leninakan [then Alexandropol; now Gumri].

From there, I went to Batum with my father-in-law. My husband's cousin lived in a village in the Crimea. They were living there before the war. My father-in-law knew those places. We went there together. Later, my brother-in-law came back, but my husband didn't. My husband had been killed during the battle of Erzerum. . . . I wanted to come to America. We went to Simferopol. The ambassador of the Dashnaktsakans [the Armenian government in Erevan] was there. I went there and asked, but the man's wife explained: "Now, you cannot just go abroad so easily. We cannot help you." She was a very nice woman, but we came back disappointed.

Once I saw a dream that I had gone back to Ordu. Our house was in ruins on all sides with only one pillar standing. They told me: "This means that one person from your household is alive." And just about then I received a letter from an aunt saying that my brother was alive and in an orphanage in Constantinople. I was overjoyed.

***

Evnige concludes her life's story by telling of her move to Abkhazia where she taught in the schools of the Hamshentsi Armenian inhabitants; her failed attempts to join relatives in the United States; her relocating to Soviet Armenia, where she worked as a nurse and midwife; her marrying there but soon losing her husband in World War II. She immigrated with her daughter's family to the United States in 1980 and took great pride in the achievements of her physician grandsons, Hakob and David. "I am very glad that we came. I like it here a lot. When I go outside, my heart opens up. Trees, flowers. . . . It's very nice." Yet, though comforted, Evnige confesses that she can never forget the image of that emaciated child lying on the flattened breast of a dead mother and wondering, although it was probably hopeless, whether she should have or could have intervened to save the doomed child. That tormenting question went with Evnige to the grave.

A Compelling Legacy

These glimpses into the lives and tribulations of four girls born in Ordu are simply examples of the poignant personal narratives of survivors from throughout the Pontus and all of the Ottoman Empire. The name Khngeni—Incense Tree or Bush—was common among the Pontic Armenians. In time, little Khngeni came to be known also by the variant Khngouhi, which may be rendered as "source of incense." Hence, let this essay be taken as a censer of *khung* being swung in memory and reverence of a generation that bore such great pain and sorrow with such great strength and dignity. It is a compelling legacy.

❧ 14 ❧

THE POSTWAR TREBIZOND COURT-MARTIAL

Richard G. Hovannisian

The Turkish surrender to the Allied Powers by the Mudros Armistice on October 30, 1918, was followed by the flight of the chief architects of the Armenian Genocide. The triumvirate of Talaat, Enver, and Jemal pashas, Dr. Ahmed Nazim, Dr. Behaeddin Shakir, and other Young Turk leaders went into hiding in Germany, and several ended up in Russia where they used and were used by the nascent Soviet government for their respective goals and objectives.[1]

As early as May 24, 1915, the British, French, and Russian governments (Entente Powers) had condemned the Turkish treatment of the Armenian population as a crime against humanity and gave notice that they would hold the Turkish government responsible both individually and collectively. After the fall of the Young Turk regime and flight of its leaders at the end of 1918, there was a clamor to punish the

---

[1] This survey of the postwar court-martial proceedings involving organizers of the deportations, massacres, and drowning of Armenians in the Trebizond area is based on the following sources: Vahakn N. Dadrian, "The Turkish Military Tribunal's Prosecution of the Authors of the Armenian Genocide: Four Major Court-Martial Series," *Holocaust and Genocide Studies* 7:1 (1997): 28-59; idem, "The Documentation of the World War I Armenian Massacres in the Proceedings of the Turkish Military Tribunal," *International Journal of Middle East Studies* 23:4 (1991): 549-76; Taner Akçam, "The Founding and Operation of the Ottoman Military Tribunals *(Divan-i Harbi Örfi)*," and "The Sixty-Five Trials Conducted during the Armistice Period: A Collection of Available Cases before the Military Tribunal *(Divan-i Harbi Örfi)*," papers presented at the Fourth Turkish-Armenian Workshop on "Ideologies of Revolution, Nation, and Empire: Political Ideas, Parties, and Practices at the End of the Ottoman Empire, 1878-1922," Salzburg, Austria, April 15-17, 2005; idem, *A Shameful Act: The Armenian Genocide and the Question of Turkish Responsibility* (New York: Metropolitan Books, 2006), pp. 205-302, 349-76; Avetis Papazyan, *Hayeri tseghaspanutyune est Eritturkeri datavarutyan pastatghteri* [The Genocide of the Armenians According to the Documents of the Trial of the Young Turks](Erevan: Armenian Academy of Sciences, 1989; reprinted in classical Armenian orthography, Los Angeles: Nor Hayastan, 2005).

culprits who had secretly plunged the Ottoman Empire into the world war as an ally of Germany and who had perpetrated unspeakable crimes against the Ottoman Armenian citizenry.

The urgency of bringing the Young Turk dictatorial clique to justice was motivated in part by the rancor of the political foes of the Ittihad ve Terakki party and the hope that punishment of the Young Turk leaders would demonstrate that the new government of the Ottoman Empire repudiated the vile acts of the preceding regime and that a remorseful distancing from the criminal atrocities would moderate the territorial and other losses that the Allied victors certainly intended to impose. From December of 1918 until the spring of 1919, numerous decrees were issued to establish commissions of investigation and tribunals, initially with both civilian and military members but subsequently solely as military courts-martial. There were many restructurings of the tribunals during the next two years, sometimes influenced by political developments in the country and the relationship between the then-current grand vizier (prime minister) and Mustafa Kemal's Nationalist movement, which emerged and strengthened in the interior provinces throughout 1919. There were many complaints about the slow pace and ineffectiveness of the trials and of the increasing leniency that was shown toward known primary figures in the massacres and plunder of the Armenian population. This fact notwithstanding, several very important trials were completed and the relevant verdicts were published as supplements in the semi-official journal *Takvimi Vekayi*.

The first decree to establish a commission to gather evidence regarding the Armenian deportations and massacres was issued on November 23, 1918. Known as the Mazhar commission after the name of its chairman, the former governor (*vali*) of Bitlis, the body sent teams into the interior to gather evidence, including ciphered and regular telegrams, instructions and commands, other kinds of documents, and eyewitness testimony. A significant corpus of evidence was collected in several but not all locations as there was strong pressure for the trials to begin as soon as possible. It was decided to try by court-martial former cabinet ministers, Ittihadist central committee members and provincial "responsible secretaries," and local officials who were complicit in the crimes against the civilian population and in the expropriation of and profiteering from the confiscated goods and properties. Numerous local tribunals were established in the interior. Some of these functioned for a period of time, but most were of short duration and were closed or suspended as the Kemalist movement grew in strength. Only fragmentary records, primarily newspaper accounts, remain from these provincial trials that extended from Bursa and Izmir to Samsun and Aintab.

The trials of the former cabinet ministers and Ittihadist leaders as well as several of the provincial trials, primarily Yozgat (Yozghat), Harput (Kharpert), Erzinjan (Erznga), Baiburt (Papert: Baberd), and Trabzon (Trapizon; Trebizond), were conducted in Istanbul (Constantinople) itself. Despite all the obstacles and drawbacks related to these trials, they demonstrated conclusively the premeditated nature of the Armenian Genocide and the role of the Special Organization (*Teshkilat-i Mahsusa*) under the direction of Dr. Behaeddin Shakir in implementing the secret lethal decisions of the party leaders. In July 1919, the main trial concluded with the sentence of death imposed on Enver, Talaat, Jemal, and Nazim. Behaeddin Shakir was condemned to death in relation to the Harput trial, but none of the sentences could be carried out because all of the condemned had already escaped. It remained for Armenian vengeance seekers to track down several of the leading fugitives and impose the sentence in bold acts of assassination. Enver may have escaped an Armenian bullet, although it is rumored that the Soviet soldier who shot and killed him as he led the anti-Soviet Basmachi revolt in Central Asia was himself an Armenian. Dr. Nazim survived until 1926 when he was among those hanged by Mustafa Kemal for involvement in an alleged plot against the Turkish president.

The Trabzon/Trebizond Court-Martial

Paralleling the proceedings against the Ittihadist leaders were the local trials in the provinces. Although the records of those proceedings are not available, if they still exist, the provincial trials that were transferred to the Ottoman capital provide important insights into the organization and execution of the Armenian Genocide. The Trebizond trial took place between March 26 and May 20 in twenty sessions. The chief defendants were the former vali/governor Jemal Azmi Bey, who had also been commandant of the Trebizond garrison, chief of military supplies and port facilities, and president of the provincial court-martial, and the Ittihadist Responsible Secretary Nail Bey (Yenbahcheli), who supervised the annihilation process. Both men were fugitives and were therefore tried in absentia. Others on trial were Mehmed Ali, director of customs and trustee of the Red Crescent Hospital;

Adjente (Agent) Ahmed Mustafa, representative of a maritime company; police chief Nuri Effendi; deputy commander of the gendarmerie and military requisitions committee member Talaat Bey; hotel manager and merchant Niyazi; director of health services Dr. Ali Saib (Sahib); and head of the Trebizond Special Organization Major Yusuf Riza.

The prosecutor Feridun demanded the death sentence for Jemal Azmi and Nail Bey, and long prison terms for the others, although he found mitigating circumstances for Dr. Saib in that the charge of his having poisoned Armenian children could not be proved without recovering their bodies from the sea and conducting autopsies. The doctor may have given the children overdoses of medications and could therefore be charged with being an accessory to their drowning. Subsequently, the cases of Ali Saib and Yusuf Riza were detached from the main trial for individual prosecution. Among those who testified during the court-martial proceedings were Colonel Mukhtar, chief of staff of the Trebizond and Lazistan armed forces; Avni Pasha, Trebizond military commandant; Colonel Vasfi, Trebizond chief of staff; Colonel Arif, Giresun commandant; Nazim Bey, former vali of Van; Tahsin Bey, former vali of Erzerum; Kenan, judicial inspector of Trebizond; Nejmeddin, head of the recruitment office; and Lieutenant Fadil Harun of the Special Organization, who bore witness to the poisoning of Armenian children in the Red Crescent Hospital and the drowning operations in the Black Sea.

The main verdict in the Trebizond trial was rendered on May 22, 1919. It reaffirmed that under the guise of deportation, the authorities had issued secret instructions and orders for massacre. Hardened criminals were recruited for the purpose. Once the Armenian men were eliminated, the remaining population was victimized as the women were stripped of their money and jewelry, and many were raped. Infants and children were loaded on barges and in boats to be drowned at sea. In a unanimous verdict, Jemal Azmi Bey and Nail Bey were condemned to death in absentia. Azmi was singled out as the prime organizer of the annihilation of the Armenian population. The verdict also took note of cases of mass drowning. Customs inspector Mehmed Ali was sentenced to ten years of hard labor. Police chief Nuri and Adjente Ahmed Mustafa received light sentences of one year imprisonment, while the hotel manager Niyazi and gendarme commander Talaat were acquitted for lack of sufficient evidence. Manastirli Tevfik, commander of a gendarmerie regiment, whose trial was attached to the Trebizond series after it had begun, was found guilty of being an accomplice of

Jemal Azmi.[2] Although the Turkish justice system failed to impose the prescribed punishment on Jemal Azmi, he, along with Behaeddin Shakir, was felled on the streets of Berlin on April 17, 1922, by Arshavir Shiragian and Aram Yerganian. Nail Bey, like Dr. Nazim, was hanged by Mustafa Kemal in 1926.

When Dr. Ali Saib's trial resumed in July 1919, health services inspector Dr. Ziya Fuad testified that according to information given by Dr. Ragib and Dr. Vehib, who had worked with Saib in the Red Crescent Hospital, the latter had administered strong doses of morphine to the children before they were dumped into the sea. But Vehib later denied such testimony. Subsequently, when the anti-Ittihadist and anti-Kemalist cabinet of Damad Ferid Pasha fell and was replaced by a grand vizier sympathetic to Mustafa Kemal, a new presiding judge was appointed to the Trebizond court-martial. This culminated in the acquittal of Dr. Saib for lack of sufficient evidence, allowing the doctor so deeply implicated in the murder of countless Armenian children and infants, like many other criminals, to escape any and all punishment.[3]

The Trebizond Trial Verdict

The verdict of the Trebizond trial as published in *Takvimi Vekayi* has been translated into Armenian and this, in turn, into an English version.[4] A new, more literal, translation has been prepared but is not yet published.[5] Thus, rather than a definitive verbatim text of the entire verdict, a paraphrased semi-literal version of the document is given below:

VERDICT

The charges, explanations, and defense of both sides were heard and all documents were studied and examined. Although the defendants denied the

---

[2] Dadrian, "The Turkish Military Tribunals' Prosecution," pp. 39-42.

[3] Ibid., pp. 40-41.

[4] The Armenian translation of the Turkish court-martial proceedings was done by Avetis Papazyan in *Hayeri tseghaspanutyune est Eritturkeri datavarutyan pastatghteri* (see note 1 above), with the Trebizond verdict on pp. 236-45. The English translation is edited by Vartkes Yeghiayan, *The Armenian Genocide and the Trial of the Young Turks* (La Verne: American Armenian International College Press, 1990), with the Trebizond verdict on pp. 159-65.

[5] The new translation is part of a larger work co-authored by V.N. Dadrian and Taner Akçam.

accusations, the evidence demonstrates the opposite to be true, and the panel of judges therefore is unanimous in the following opinion:

The sublime commands of Islam and the customs of Ottoman law dictate that the preservation of the honor, life, and property of all Ottoman subjects without distinction is among the primary obligations of all officials. Despite this, Ittihadist Responsible Secretary Nail Bey gained power by utilizing secret orders from the governor Jemal Azmi Bey. In conformity with the secret orders received, the pair planned the massacre and elimination of the Armenians under the guise of deportation.

The defenseless Armenians were deported by guards bereft of morals, hardened criminals, and gendarmes who were willing to cooperate. Some distance from the city in an out-of-the-way place, the men and women were separated and their goods were plundered. After the men had been killed in the most atrocious of ways, the women were taken to another place where they were stripped of their valuables and clothing and where many were raped. The massacre and looting of the Armenians did not occur within but rather outside the city in an organized fashion.

Although the women were sent away on foot for months in a forced march, they were then ordered to yet another location by way of Erzinjan. They were so exhausted that many of them died of hunger and thirst and the hardships of the march. Some of the women who were left behind in Trebizond, along with boys and girls who had been sent to the houses of religious sheikhs and to hospitals supposedly for protection, were placed on barges and in boats to be sent to another location. But after being lost from sight, they were drowned and murdered by being thrown overboard.

The director of customs Mehmed Ali Effendi had on orders from Jemal Azmi Bey been engaged in the commission on abandoned property, jewelry, and military materials and in the customs bureau for checking passports of those arriving and leaving, as well as the agency dealing with women's issues at the Red Crescent Hospital, so that he was an accessory to the abuses of the governor. In addition, Armenian women and girls were gathered at the hospital and the homes of the religious sheikhs for protection as a patriotic duty, but in fact Mehmed Ali violated their honor by giving the women to men who wanted to marry them or to reduce them to misery and ruin through abusive servitude. The fact that the women were quickly taken away and those in the hospital violated was confirmed by eyewitness testimony. Ignoring warnings of his superior that involvement in illegal matters beyond the scope of his official duties would have serious consequences, Mehmed Ali willingly assisted in nearly all of these reprehensible actions.[6]

---

[6] It is of interest that Mehmed Ali was on the first list of criminals compiled by

Although the police chief Nuri Effendi was responsible for maintaining order and was appointed to the commission to manage the acquired jewelry and property, he did not adopt effective disciplinary or administrative measures and made no effort to protect, record, and transport to secure depots the property gathered from the homes of the deportees. Rather, he allowed the

---

the Armenian Patriarchate of Constantinople in January 1919. He was described as "a notorious criminal" who "threw into the Black Sea little children stuffed in sacks," and who forced some of the girls whom he had robbed to live in the Red Crescent Hospital "while he distributed the rest among important persons of the Ittihad in Trebizond."

In testimony given to the British High Commission in Constantinople, Sophie Tahmazian, daughter of a prominent merchant, Onnik Mahokian, stated that on June 23, 1915, about twenty-five Armenian subjects of Russia were taken out to sea and shot. Only one got back to shore wounded to tell what had happened. The woman then described the deportation process, including the actions of Vali Jemal Azmi, Dr. Ali Sahib, Nail Bey, Agent Mustafa, and Mehmed Ali Bey as they took away batches of women and children from the Red Crescent Hospital and then filled their places with others, most of whom met the same fate. "With the others mentioned above, Mehmed Ali is responsible, actually responsible, for all the cruelties, deportations and murders that I have described. It was he who first stripped the women entering the hospital of all that they possessed. . . . It was Ali Sahib's duty to order which of the children were to be sent away. I have constantly seen him packing large baskets full of infants' corpses that the *hamals* [porters] took away and threw into the sea."

Siranouche (Siranush) Moutafian, daughter of Trebizond carpet merchant Nazareth Moutafian, was taken to an orphanage when the deportations began. "Adjente [Agent] Mustafa, Ali Sahib, Mehmed Ali, Nuri, and other Turks whose names I do not know came to the Orphanage and proceeded to separate out various groups of women and children, some were for deportation, some to be 'married' to Turks, etc. I clung to my mother and cried. My mother cried and begged Mehmed Ali. Mehmed Ali got angry with my mother, laid hands on her, gave her over to a Gendarme with the order to kill her along with the other women. I understand Turkish and heard all that was said. Two or three days later the same Gendarmes told us all in the Orphanage that my mother and the other women had been massacred by them near the Deyermen Déré [River], just outside Trebizond. This was not an exceptional incident; the Gendarmes continuously fetched away women from the Orphanage. On the same day some hundred children from 5 to 9 years old were taken away and have not since been heard of. They were drowned at sea. This again was not exceptional. Babies were constantly dying; there was no food or any sort of care. Ali Sahib seemed to be in charge of the babies." Siranouche then went on to describe in detail the drowning of an Armenian woman and her two children and two other Armenian women.

Mehmed Ali was among the convicts and prominent suspects whom the British interned in Malta. He arrived there in September 1920 but is reported to have escaped in December of that year.

For the British file on Mehmed Ali, see Vartkes Yeghiayan, ed., *British Foreign Office Dossiers on Turkish War Criminals* (La Verne: Armenian American International College, 1991), pp. 430-36.

properties to be stolen and subject to loss. Nuri did have some gendarmerie officials sent before a military tribunal for stealing abandoned property, but he did nothing to prevent such acts. He knew that Jemal Azmi Bey and those in his service had smuggled out such goods, just as he knew that women and children were transported by the police and gendarmes on to boats to be drowned at sea. He claimed that he was so terribly distressed by all this that he even locked himself in his office, but he did nothing to halt the misdeeds of the governor and did not even have the courage to resign so that a successor might have the chance to prevent further perpetration of these shameful acts.

Adjente Mustafa Bey, although having only the rank of private, was able because of his association with Jemal Azmi to gain important military positions, including responsibility for the harbor and for shipping. He abused his powers, however, by using military naval vessels to transport the abandoned and personal goods seized by Jemal Azmi and those the governor entrusted for this purpose. Mustafa Bey did save some Armenians from deportation through his influence with the governor and his own personal standing. He had a personal fortune and, according to testimony in his favor, there was no reasonable cause for him to sacrifice his honor for the sake of further enrichment. Based on the accounts of witnesses and his own confessions, he nonetheless allowed jewelry and money which were found in a dresser delivered to him to pass into the greedy hands of Jemal Azmi without any accounting.

The defense arguments for Nuri Effendi, Mehmed Ali Effendi, and Adjente Mustafa Bey, based on the evidence, are not valid and the unanimous decision is to convict the former governor Jemal Azmi, party secretary Nail Bey, and Mehmed Ali in accordance with article 45 of the Ottoman penal code and to convict police chief Nuri and Adjente Mustafa for having misused their official positions.

Jemal Azmi and Nail Bey have been determined to be the principal co-perpetrators and as such, according to article 45, are to be punished as if each is the sole perpetrator. That article states that those who use bribery, threats, or fraud or who take advantage of their influence or office to incite others to commit a crime, or who knowingly procure arms or other means to help with the crime, or who assist a principal perpetrator in the commission of a crime are deemed to be accessories to the crime. Those who are aware of the deeds and acts of criminals who engage in brigandage or who use violence against the safety of the government or public tranquility and the security of life and property are deemed to be accessories. Mehmed Ali therefore is judged to be an accessory.

Because the actions of Jemal Azmi Bey and Nail Bey correspond to article 171 of the penal code for the military, which states that looting or damaging of collectives stores, provisions, or possessions by armed or unarmed attack or damaging a building or applying pressure on persons to do so shall be punishable by death, and because these actions also correspond to article 170 of the penal code for officials, which states that premeditated murder is punishable by death, Jemal Azmi and Nail Bey are sentenced to death and their property is seized.

In accordance with article 45 of the penal code on being an accessory to the commission of a crime, Mehmed Ali Effendi is sentenced to hard labor for a period of ten years commencing from the day of his arrest.

Because the actions of Adjente Mustafa Effendi and Nazif Effendi, based on article 172 of the penal code for officials which states that officials who misuse their positions are to be sentenced to prison for a period of three months to three years (or no less than 15 days or a fine if there are mitigating circumstances) and shall be permanently or temporarily stripped of their title, the two convicted men are sentenced to prison for one year and stripped of their titles of office for two years.

As regards Niyazi Effendi, it is understood that he was traveling back and forth to Istanbul by motorboat to transport mines that were gathered from the sea and that his return to Trebizond did not correspond to the period of the deportations. There is no evidence that he participated in the massacres or engaged in looting. Although he did receive abandoned goods at a very advantageous price through the favorable disposition of Jemal Azmi Bey, he did not become corrupted or take personal advantage of the situation. Rather, using the influence he earned by courageously transporting mines to the capital, he was able to stop the auctions of the seized properties and instead to purchase some of these through a public offer. Since only a small part of the properties he acquired was purchased during the most dangerous period of the war, his actions cannot be deemed a legal offence, and Niyazi Effendi is acquitted of the charge of massacre, plundering, and looting and is not held responsible for the other matters.

Talaat Bey, although he did not participate in the crimes being considered and as the testimony of certain witnesses against him have not sufficiently demonstrated whether or not he carried out honorably his responsibilities in the commission on war taxes and because these actions are outside the scope of the current proceedings, he is acquitted and the issue will be taken up by the appropriate department. If Talaat Bey and Niyazi Effendi are not being held on other charges, they are to be released.

As for chief health official Ali Saib Bey, a separate trial will be held for him to allow for further investigation of certain matters that appear to require elucidation.

This decision is given unanimously in the presence of all defendants except for Jemal Azmi and Nail in absentia.

Signed: Lieutenant General Mustafa Nazim Pasha; Major General Zeki Pasha; Major General Mustafa Pasha; Major General Ali Nazim Pasha; Colonel Rejeb Ferdi Bey.

Chief Recorder of the Courts-Martial, Abidin Taver, 22 May 1335.[7]

---

[7] *Takvimi Vekayi*, 22 Mayis 1335 (May 22, 1919).

Jemal Azmi

Behaeddin Shakir

Arshavir Shiragian

Aram Yerganian

❃ 15 ❃

PONTUS AND ARMENIA, 1914-1922

Richard G. Hovannisian

The period from 1914 to 1922 was a critical turning point in the history of the Pontus region, which extended from the Chorokh River Valley and Lazistan in the east to beyond Samsun in the west. When in October 1918 the Ottoman Empire surrendered to the Allied Powers in World War I, critical questions loomed about the future of the region and its diverse ethno-religious populations. For the decimated Armenians, Trebizond (Trapizon; Trabzon) and other nearby ports were regarded as essential in the creation of a new nation state with unhindered access to the outside world. With neither firm historic nor ethnographic claims to the coastline and its rugged backing terrain, Armenian spokesmen were to pose strategic and economic arguments in their quest to establish lifelines to the sea. Such aspirations, however, did not sit well with the large indigenous Greek population, the various Muslim elements, and the organizers of the postwar Turkish Nationalist movement.

World War I

The outbreak of World War I in the summer of 1914 and Turkey's entry into that war as an ally of the German Empire a few months later dashed the last hopes for legal reforms as a way to safeguard Armenian life and property in the Ottoman Empire. The Young Turk government led by Enver, Talaat, and Jemal quickly nullified the internationally-brokered reform project that it had been forced to accept in February of that year and resolved to settle the Armenian Question once and for all by eliminating the Armenian population.

In the city of Trebizond in April 1915, a number of prominent community figures were arrested on the trumped up charge of concealing weapons. Then on June 24 (June 11, Old Style), more than forty

Armenian leaders were sent toward Samsun, supposedly for legal proceedings, but they were ambushed and killed en route. On June 26
(June 13, Old Style), the government issued the official proclamation
of deportation of the Trebizond Armenians.[1] Pleas and petitions to re-
scind the decree or at least to delay its implementation were of no
avail. The agony of Pontus had begun. Italian Consul Giacomo Gorrini
wrote that the orders came from the central government, a fact that was
repeatedly confirmed: "The consular body intervened, and attempted to
save at least the women and children. We did, in fact, secure numerous
exemptions, but these were not subsequently respected, owing to the
interference of the local branch of the 'Union and Progress Committee'
and to fresh orders from Constantinople."[2] On July 1, the first caravan
was marched out of the city, followed by the second and third on July 3
and 5. By the end of July, the number of Armenians deported from
Trebizond alone reached 10,000. Some of the unfortunate people were
loaded on boats and dumped overboard into the sea, while most were
marched inland over the mountains toward Gumushkhane. The same
occurred in all the Armenian towns and villages throughout the Trebizond *vilayet* and Janik *sanjak*, with only a small number of men escaping to hideouts in the mountains.[3]

The wartime secret agreements of the Entente Powers (Russia,
Great Britain, France) regarding the future partition of the Ottoman
Empire reserved for Russia the eastern half of the Armenian Plateau
and most of the province of Trebizond. The Russian offensive into
these regions in the spring of 1916 led to the occupation of Van, Mush,
Erzerum, and Erzinjan (Erznka), while in April of that year General V.
Liakhov's divisions advanced into Rize, Surmene, Of, and Trebizond.[4]

---

[1] See Hovakim Hovakimian (Arshakuni), *Patmutiun Haykakan Pontosi* [History
of Armenian Pontus] (Beirut: Mshak Press, 1967), pp. 221-24. This detailed study
includes sections on geography, history, urban and rural economy, church and religion, cultural and educational structures, civic and political societies, interethnic relations, and the anti-Armenian persecutions prior to, during, and after World War I, as
well as sketches of the main Pontic coastal towns and the Hamshen villages of the
interior.

[2] Great Britain, Foreign Office, *The Treatment of Armenians in the Ottoman Empire*, Miscellaneous no. 31 (1916), ed. Arnold Toynbee (London: H.M.S.O., 1916), p.
291; also in Walker, *Armenia*, p. 216.

[3] See the chapter by Simon Payaslian in this volume.

[4] W.E.D. Allen and Paul Muratoff, *Caucasian Battlefields: A History of the Wars
on the Turco-Caucasian Border, 1828-1921* (Cambridge: Cambridge University
Press, 1953), pp. 378-83; E.V. Maslovskii, *Mirovaia voina na Kavkazskom fronte,*

Armenian partisans were then able to descend from the mountains, and many women and children were rescued from Muslim households. This work was supported by Armenian benevolent societies from Russia and the Caucasus.[5] Eventually many of the survivors made their way to the port cities between Batum and Sochi or on the Crimean peninsula.

Conditions changed rapidly as the result of the Russian revolutions in 1917 and the abandonment of the Caucasus front by the Russian armed forces. Desperate attempts by the caretaker Transcaucasian executive and legislative bodies in Tiflis, the Commissariat and the Seim, to hold on to Trebizond and Lazistan as well as the occupied portions of the Erzerum, Bitlis, and Van vilayets failed. The small Georgian and Armenian contingents that tried to fill the void left by the retreat of the Russian armies were no match for the Turkish armies. At the end of February 1918, while Soviet Russia negotiated for peace with Germany and its allies, Turkish forces reoccupied Trebizond and, after the Soviet government ceded all of Western Armenia, along with Kars, Ardahan, and Batum, to the Ottoman Empire in the Treaty of Brest-Litovsk (March 3, 1918), the Turkish army advanced as far as Batum, while other divisions regained all of the Western Armenian provinces and marched into the province of Kars and all the way into parts of the provinces of Tiflis and Erevan.[6]

It was only at the price of Armenian acquiescence in these losses that the Turkish government assented to recognize the tiny Armenian republic that was formed around Erevan and Lake Sevan in May 1918. That fragile state survived under extremely precarious conditions until the Allied victory over the Ottoman and German empires several months later gave it a little breathing room. As the Turkish armies withdrew from Transcaucasia by terms of the Ottoman surrender, the Republic of Armenia was able to incorporate most of the provinces of Erevan and Kars, thereby approaching the prewar 1914 Russo-Turkish border.[7]

1914-1917 g. [The World War on the Caucasus Front, 1914-1917] (Paris: Vozrozhdenie-La Renaissance 1933), pp. 326-30.

[5] Hovakimian, *Patmutiun Haykakan Pontosi*, pp. 270-83.

[6] Hovannisian, *Armenia on the Road to Independence, 1918* (Bekreley and Los Angeles: University of California Press, 1967), pp. 101-05, 121-24, 131-37, 157-66, 174-76.

[7] Ibid., pp. 190-202, 207-15, 238-42.

The Armenian Republic and the Pontus

The Allied victory in World War I opened new vistas for the Armenian people. The Allied leaders had made numerous pledges about the rehabilitation of the Armenian people and the determination never again to allow the Armenians to be subjected to Turkish tyranny.[8] Armenians around the world believed that the Allied declarations meant that Armenia would be given protection as an independent or autonomous state and allowed to incorporate the six Western Armenian provinces of Van, Bitlis, Diarbekir, Erzerum, Kharpert, and Sebastia and perhaps even Cilicia and its ports on the Mediterranean Sea.

As the Armenian government at Erevan prepared to send Avetis Aharonian to the Paris Peace Conference to present the Armenian claims, the legislature (*Khorhurd*) defined those claims as the unification of Eastern (Russian) Armenia and Western (Turkish) Armenia with outlets on the Black Sea. Although the Armenians were a minority in the Pontus region, it was argued that economic considerations justified its inclusion in the new Armenian state.[9] The Armenian claims were contested by the Georgian republic, which had also been created in May 1918 and now declared that the eastern half of Trebizond vilayet—Lazistan—was inhabited by Georgians who had been forcibly converted to Islam and should now be restored to home country.[10] A more serious consideration was that most Pontic Greeks, who heavily outnumbered the Armenians, did not want to live under Armenian rule and sought to restore Greek dominion over the region. Their distinguished leader, Archbishop Chrysanthos, petitioned the Paris Peace Conference for a separate state of Euxine Pontus.[11] Of course, the majority of the population there was neither Armenian nor Greek, but

---

[8] For examples of British, French, Italian, and American declarations, see Richard G. Hovannisian, "The Allies and Armenia, 1915-18," *Journal of Contemporary History*, 3:1 (1968): 45-55.

[9] Al. Khatisian, *Hayastani Hanrapetutian tsagumn u zargatsume* [Creation and Development of the Republic of Armenia] (Athens: Nor Or, 1930), pp. 97-98; Richard G. Hovannisian, *The Republic of Armenia*, 4 vols. (Los Angeles, Berkeley, London: University of California Press, 1971-1996), vol. 1, pp. 250-52.

[10] Great Britain, Foreign Office Archives, FO 608/88, 356/2/2/4366; Délégation Géorgienne à la Conference de la Paix, *Mémoire presénté à la Conférence de la Paix* (Paris, 1919).

[11] FO 371/3659, 110915/512/58; FO 608/82, File 342/8/1; United States National Archives, Record Group 256 (RG 256), Records of the American Commission to Negotiate Peace, 876B.00/42.

Muslim, albeit the Muslim population was divided into Turkish, Kurdish, formerly Christian Laz and Hemshin (Hamshen), and other ethnolinguistic groups.

When the Armenian delegates, Avetis Aharonian and Boghos Nubar Pasha (the latter representing the Western Armenians), appeared before the Supreme Council of the Paris Peace Conference in February 1919, they argued for the award of Trebizond to Armenia for the same reasons that the Danzig corridor to the Baltic Sea was being created for the new Polish state. They were encouraged that Greek Prime Minister Eleutherios Venizelos had made it known that Greece would stake no claim to Trebizond, which he conceded should be included in Armenia to ensure its economic viability. Venizelos was pleased, in turn, with Armenian assurances that the Pontus region would be accorded the broadest possible autonomy.[12]

Although the Armenian pretensions may in retrospect seem highly unrealistic, especially after Aharonian, at the insistence of Boghos Nubar, agreed to expand the Armenian desiderata to include Cilicia, these claims in fact corresponded with the confidential British and American preliminary plans for peace. The British government's Eastern Committee, chaired by Foreign Secretary Lord George N. Curzon, was responsible for making recommendations relating to the forthcoming peace treaty with the Ottoman Empire. The committee called for retention of a Turkish state in Asia Minor but advised that it should extend no farther east than a line from Samsun on the Black Sea to Selefke on the Mediterranean Sea, whereas the areas of mixed population east of the Kerasund-Sivas-Mersina line should be detached and given the "historic name of Armenia." The western border of Armenian state, it was foreseen, would touch the Black Sea somewhere between the ports of Trebizond and Tireboli (Tripoli). An attached map showed Armenia extending from the Black Sea at a point just to the west of Ordu, along the Anti-Taurus Mountains to the Mediterranean coastline of Cilicia. The Eastern Committee later also recommended that Trebizond, Batum, and Poti on the Black Sea, and even Baku on the Caspian Sea be made into free ports.[13]

---

[12] Archives of the Delegation of Republic of Armenia to the Peace Conference (Rep. of Arm. Del. Archives), File 104ª/3ª; *The Armenian Question before the Peace Conference* (London, 1919).

[13] Great Britain, Cabinet Office Archives, Cab 27/37, E.C. 2525, and 27/24, Eastern Committee, 40th Minutes (Annex), Dec. 2, 1918. See also FO 608/83, 342/8/4/7142.

The Western Asia Division of the American delegation to the Paris Peace Conference also advocated the separation of Armenia from a residue Turkish state, which should reach no farther east than the Anti-Taurus Mountains. This Division, headed by Professor William L. Westermann, went on to specify that the Armenian regions of Trans-caucasia should be combined with the Armenian provinces of the Ottoman Empire. The western and southern boundaries of the new state (which should be placed under the protection of a mandatory power serving on behalf of the League of Nations) were "fixed by nature"— the Anti-Taurus and Taurus mountain ranges. Thus, Armenia should extend from Cilicia to the Black Sea harbors in and around Trebizond and eastward to Kars, Akhaltsikh, Akhalkalak, and Erevan. It was argued that, in view of the horrific deportations and massacres and the historic injustices done to the Armenian people, a liberal interpretation of the principle of self-determination should be applied in this case.[14]

Later, in the summer of 1919, an American field investigation to Constantinople, Cilicia, and Syria-Lebanon-Palestine (King-Crane Commission) expressed concern that the Armenian claims were excessive and violated the principle of majority rule. The commission recommended that, for the sake of the Armenians themselves, their state should be limited to Russian Armenia and those parts of the eastern vilayets that had been occupied by the Russian armies in 1916. This implied that even such a smaller Armenian state should include the eastern Ottoman provinces as far west as Erzinjan and Mush and the Black Sea coastline as far as the city and port of Trebizond.[15]

Retreat of the Allied Powers

The realization of plans regarding the future of Armenia and outlets on the sea was dependent on the ability and determination of the Allied Powers to remove the Turkish armed forces that continued to control the interior provinces of the Ottoman Empire. What was more, after a deep sense of pessimism and fatalism had descended over the Turkish leadership at the end of World War I, new life was blown into the

---

[14] David Hunter Miller, *My Diary of the Peace Conference of Paris, with Documents*, 21 vols. (New York: Appeal Printing Co., 1924), vol. 4, pp. 254-60.

[15] United States, Department of State, *Papers Relating to the Foreign Relations of the United States: The Paris Peace Conference, 1919*, 12 vols. (Washington, DC: Government Printing Office, 1942-1947), vol. 12, pp. 819-28.

Turkish nation by a military champion, Mustafa Kemal Pasha. Through amazing feats of courage and cunning, he was able to organize a resistance movement whose fundamental purpose was rejection of any territorial concessions to Armenians or Greeks. At gatherings of Muslim notables in Erzerum and Sivas in the summer of 1919, Kemal insisted that the natural frontiers of the Turkish state included all the eastern provinces and the entire vilayet of Trebizond. The Turkish Nationalists would defy all attempts of the Allied Powers to partition the Turkish homeland.[16]

Intense rivalries among the Allied Powers and their unwillingness to commit the requisite troops to crush the Kemalist movement led by the end of 1919 to a retreat on the Armenian Question. All the Armenian appeals for the Allies to disarm the Turkish armies in the eastern provinces and repatriate the survivors of the genocide had achieved no positive results. Moreover, it had become clear that the United States would not accept the role of the protective mandatory power for the new Armenian state and would not even participate in drafting the treaty of peace with Turkey. The Americans were turning away from Europe and moving into the era of "splendid isolation." President Woodrow Wilson was unable to persuade the U.S. Congress to grant authorization to assume the Armenian mandate or even to ratify the Treaty of Versailles with Germany, which had been signed in June 1919 and which included the Covenant of the League of Nations with provisions for the assignment of mandates to advanced countries for the supervision and assistance to developing states while they progressed toward the goal of ultimate self-sufficiency and independence.[17]

With the United States no longer in the picture, the British, French, and Italian leaders adopted a policy of trying to appease both the official Turkish government in Constantinople and the Kemalist counter-government at Ankara (Angora). They reversed their initial intent to expel the Turks from Constantinople and the last remaining European territories and also conceded that the region of Cilicia should remain under Turkish sovereignty. Armenia, it was decided, had to be cut back in size to take in the existing Armenian republic in Transcaucasia and

---

[16] See Hovannisian, *Republic of Armenia*, vol. 1, pp. 429-38, and vol. 2, pp. 342-44.

[17] See James B. Gidney, *A Mandate for Armenia* (Kent, OH: Kent State University Press, 1967); Ralph Stone, *The Irreconcilables: The Fight against the League of Nations* (Lexington: University of Kentucky Press, 1970).

only a part of the former Turkish Armenian provinces.[18] By the beginning of 1920, the question, in the words of Foreign Secretary Curzon, was whether there should be a "larger" or a "smaller" compact Armenian state.[19]

During Allied consultations in London in February 1920, Curzon conceded that the concept of a Greater Armenia with a Mediterranean outlet was no longer feasible.[20] The issue now at hand was whether Armenia should have the fortress city of Erzerum and the seaport of Trebizond. He was in favor of giving Armenia an outlet in Lazistan even though most inhabitants there were Muslims of Georgian stock. Furthermore, Batum should be made into a free port. French Foreign Minister Philippe Berthelot suggested that Armenia should follow the example of Switzerland by having guaranteed railway access to and commercial privileges at some port on the Black Sea.[21]

From internal correspondence of the British government, it becomes clear that the British Foreign Office favored the inclusion of Trebizond in Armenia. The reasons were explained in a memorandum by W.S. Childs:

> Trebizond in possession of Armenia would make the Armenian state a compact, self-contained, independent economic unit which in self-interest and sympathies would look to us. It would provide a growing source of revenue to the State. It would encourage the growth of a national consciousness in Armenia in a way that no treaty rights of access to Batum or any other foreign port could do. . . . Armenia has neither ethnographical nor historical claims to the Trebizond seaboard, and the inclusion of this district can only be justified on grounds of expediency. But I am confident that the expediency is great, and that the possession of such an historic city of Trebizond—which geographically is the natural Armenian port—would do more for the stability and unity and prosperity of the State than the addition of any other territory whatever.[22]

---

[18] Hovannisian, *Republic of Armenia*, vol. 2, ch. 13.

[19] *Documents on British Foreign Policy*, lst series, ed. W.L. Woodward, Rohan Butler, J.P.T. Bury et al. 27 vols. (London: HMSO, 1947-1986), vol. 7, pp. 81-82 (cited hereafter as *British Documents*).

[20] For minutes of the London conference, see Great Britain, Foreign Office, Secret/General/102/1, International Conference of Prime Ministers, nos. 24-92. These records have been published in *British Documents*, vol. 7, pp. 1-462.

[21] *British Documents*, vol. 7, pp. 42-43, 81-82.

[22] FO 371/4952. E646/58/1.

To study and make recommendations on this and related questions, the London conference formed a committee known as the Armenia Commission. After several consultations and interviews with Aharonian, Nubar, and other interested parties, the commission submitted its recommendations at the end of February 1920. However desirable it was to award Trebizond to Armenia, the commission considered that such a solution was not realistic, because the Armenians had been so badly decimated that they could not possibly populate the area. Strategically, the inclusion of Trebizond in Armenia would have helped to safeguard the approaches to the Armenian Plateau and to make it easier to defend, but for political and ethnographic reasons, this could not be done. The territory assigned to Armenia should be sufficiently compact so that within a short period of time the Armenians would become the majority element. As a safeguard, the land to be left to the Turks should be demilitarized between Trebizond and Tireboli, and all the fortifications at Trebizond itself should be dismantled. Thus, the Armenian boundary would run from the Pontic Mountains at the juncture of the Trebizond and Erzerum vilayets southward to Baiburt, Mush, Sasun, Bitlis, and Van. Armenia's need for access to the sea could be satisfied by granting it the right to build a railway or highway to Batum through the Chorokh River Valley via the Kars-Ardahan-Artvin route and by making Batum itself into an international free state. It was also possible that Lazistan could be placed under nominal Armenian suzerainty as an autonomous district. The Laz, it was stated, had no Georgian sympathies and would prefer to live as independently as possible. This solution would allow Armenia to utilize the carriage roads from Baiburt to the small ports of Rize and Of. In addition, Armenia should also enjoy special transit privileges from Erzerum and Baiburt to Trebizond with guaranteed import-export facilities at the port.[23]

The American Connection

Although the United States had withdrawn from the peace process, it nonetheless continued to react to pressure from the pro-Armenia lobby by urging the European Allies to be as generous as possible toward the new Armenian state. On March 24, 1920, after the Senate had refused

---

[23] *British Documents*, vol. 7, pp. 268-69, 280-82; Rep. of Arm. Del. Archives, Files 116/15, 132/31, 234/133, 241/140; Hovannisian, *Republic of Armenia*, vol. 3, pp. 20-35, 53-57.

for a second time to ratify the Treaty of Versailles, Secretary of State Bainbridge Colby called for recognition of the legitimate claims of the Armenian people "and particularly to give them easy and unencumbered access to the sea." He argued that special rights over Lazistan alone would not assure Armenia that essential access. Taking into consideration that Trebizond had always been the terminus of the trade route across Armenia and that Prime Minister Venizelos had expressed on behalf of the Pontic Greeks the preference for a connection with Armenia rather than with Turkey, the United States now urged the European Allies to grant Trebizond to Armenia.[24]

When the Allied leaders continued their deliberations at the Italian coastal resort of San Remo in April 1920, they replied to Washington that they shared the strong sentiments about creating an independent Armenian state and wished to give it as much territory as might be reasonably claimed for its current needs and future expansion. But because the United States was unable to help in removing the Turkish armies and safeguarding Armenia, it would not be in Armenia's best interest to award the new state too much territory. The maximum would be access to the sea through Batum, the inclusion of Lazistan (east of Trebizond) in Armenia, and transit rights and privileges at the port of Trebizond.[25]

During the Allied deliberations at San Remo, strong differences between the British Foreign Office and War Office were revealed. Lord Curzon favored the award of Erzerum to Armenia, while the War Office under Winston Churchill was firmly opposed.[26] In a clever maneuver to shift responsibility for the consequences of granting either Erzerum or Trebizond to Armenia, Prime Minister David Lloyd George on April 24, 1920 came up with the idea of turning to President Wilson once more and asking him to arbitrate the Armenian boundaries within the four eastern vilayets of Trebizond, Erzerum, Bitlis, and Van. In the forthcoming peace treaty with the Ottoman Empire, the Turkish government would be required to consent in advance to whatever boundary the president of the United States drew within the limits of those

---

[24] United States, Department of State, *Papers Relating to the Foreign Relations of the United States, 1920*, 3 vols. (Washington, DC: Government Printing Office, 1936), vol. 3, p. 751.

[25] *British Documents*, vol. 8, p. 33.

[26] For the deliberations of the San Remo conference relative to Armenia, see Hovannisian, *Republic of Armenia*, vol. 3, pp. 71-112.

four provinces. Two days later the Allied leaders approved the text of the invitation to be sent to Wilson.[27]

Surprisingly, even after it was clear that the United States would do nothing to enforce the terms of the forthcoming peace treaty with Turkey, on May 17 Woodrow Wilson accepted the Allied invitation.[28] It then took the State Department several weeks to assemble a team of experts to study the issue and make recommendations.[29] Hence, when the Turkish delegates of the sultan's government were summoned to Paris to sign the Treaty of Sèvres on August 10, 1920, the wording of Article 89 read:

> Turkey and Armenia as well as the other High Contracting Parties agree to submit to the arbitration of the President of the United States of America the question of the frontier to be fixed between Turkey and Armenia in the Vilayets of Erzerum, Trebizond, Van and Bitlis, and to accept his decision thereupon, as well as any stipulations he may prescribe as to access for Armenia to the sea, and as to the demilitarisation of any portion of Turkish territory adjacent to the said frontier.[30]

By that time, the United States team of specialists, headed by William Westermann, were at work to fulfill the president's assignment.[31] In its report submitted to the State Department on September 28, 1920 (six weeks after the Treaty of Sèvres was signed), the commission explained that it had used geographic, economic, and ethnographic considerations in formulating its recommendations. The territory being assigned to the Armenians was less than half of what they had originally requested, but developments during the past months had made this adjustment necessary. Regarding Armenia's access to the sea, the com-

---

[27] *British Documents*, vol. 8, pp. 145, 156-58, 177-78; *Foreign Relations, 1920*, vol. 3, p. 780.

[28] *Foreign Relations, 1920*, vol. 3, p. 783; FO 3761/5107, E527/58, 44, enclosure.

[29] *British Documents*, vol. 8, pp. 217-19; *Foreign Relations, 1920*, vol. 3, pp. 779-83.

[30] "TREATY OF PEACE between the British Empire and Allied Powers (France, Italy, Japan, Armenia, Belgium, Czecho-Slovakia, Greece, the Hedjaz, Poland, Portugal, Roumania and the Serb-Croat-Slovene State) and Turkey—Sèvres, August 10, 1920)," in *British and Foreign State Papers*, vol. 113: 1920 (London: H.M.S.O., 1923), pp. 672-73.

[31] For materials on the boundary commission, see US Archives, RG 59, file.760J. 6715.

mission wrote that various possibilities had been considered. The route through the Chorokh River Valley to Batum provided a commercial outlet only for those districts formerly within the Russian Empire and was problematic because of the unstable political conditions there. To the west along the coast of Lazistan were the small harbors of Rize and Of, but they afforded poor anchorage and were so exposed to rough weather that in certain months cargoes could not be landed; they also lacked suitable roads to the hinterland. In keeping with President Wilson's sentiments, therefore, the commission had come to the conclusion that free access to the sea necessitated the inclusion of Trebizond in Armenia, even though the Armenians had no ethnic claims to the city or vilayet. The economic requirement was "absolute and decisive." Because there would be insurmountable difficulties in attempting to build a railway along the old caravan route from the port of Trebizond directly up to Baiburt and Erzerum, the Kharshut River Valley, ending near Tireboli, should be placed in Armenia as the obvious course of the railway from the sea to the Armenian Plateau. The Turkish and Pontic Greek claims to the region "must be regarded as secondary to the economic welfare of the Kurdish, Turkish and Armenian population of the three vilayets of Van, Bitlis and Erzerum." Therefore, Trebizond and Tireboli should be awarded to Armenia and safeguarded through the establishment of a demilitarized zone on the Turkish side of the new boundary.[32]

The final boundaries, as drawn by the commission, assigned to Armenia most of the Trebizond and Erzerum vilayets (including the city of Erzerum) as well as two-thirds of the vilayets of Van and Bitlis. The borders of Armenia would begin on the Black Sea between Tireboli and Kerasund (Girason; Giresun) and rise up over the Pontic Mountains to the headwaters of the Kelkit River at a point west of Gumushkhane and east of Shabin-Karahisar. The Kharshut River Valley to the west of Trebizond would therefore fall within the Armenian state, and there would be no further need to consider special transit and port privileges for Armenia, since it would now take in Trebizond and other outlets in Lazistan.[33]

---

[32] US Archives, RG 59, 760J.6715/65, "Full Report of the Committee upon the Arbitration of the Boundary between Turkey and Armenia," pp. 1-23. See also Hovannisian, Republic of Armenia, vol. 4, pp. 28-40.

[33] US Archives, RG 59, 760J.6715/65, pp. 50-64.

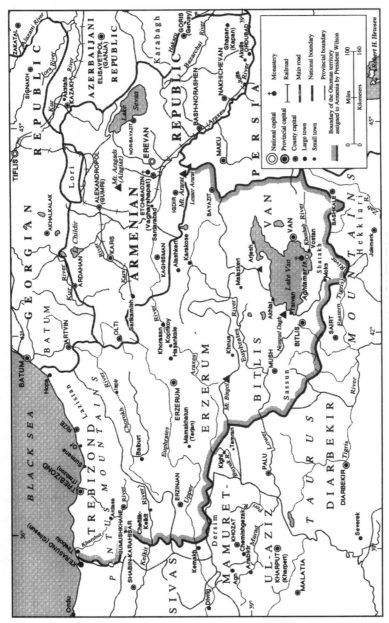

Pontus by the Treaty of Sèvres, 1920

The Outcome

Although the Department of State received the report at the end of September 1920, it took two more months for President Wilson to relay the recommendations to the Allied Powers. By that time, it had become clear that the Allies would enforce neither these provisions nor many other sections of the Treaty of Sèvres. It was to be a bitter irony for the Armenians that it was over Trebizond and the small harbors of Lazistan that Mustafa Kemal would receive words of encouragement from Soviet Russia, followed by shipments of Soviet arms and gold to be used against the common imperialist enemies.

In the summer of 1920, a Turkish delegation headed by Bekir Sami Bey arrived in Moscow to seek support from and enter into treaty arrangements with Soviet leaders. Taking advantage of the preliminary work already done by Young Turk fugitives such as Enver and Jemal pashas, Bekir Sami successfully negotiated a preliminary Soviet-Turkish treaty of friendship, which was initialed on August 24, 1920. The first article of the treaty committed each contracting party to refuse to recognize any treaty or obligation forcibly imposed on the other. Russia specifically recognized the Nationalist government at Ankara as the sole representative of Turkey and pledged to reject any international instrument (such as the Treaty of Sèvres) which had not been ratified by that body. The draft treaty, along with secret protocols relating to Soviet military and financial assistance, were carried over the Black Sea from Tuapse to Lazistan by delegation member Ali Kemali Bey, who in mid-September telegraphed the terms to Mustafa Kemal in Ankara and gave assurances that Russia would not intervene in case of Turkish military operations against the existing Armenian republic in Transcaucasia.[34]

It was only after receiving this welcome news that Kemal ordered General Kiazim Karabekir's 15th Army Corps to advance into the province of Kars and crush the Armenian army as an effective response to the Treaty of Sèvres and everything it represented. During the brief Armeno-Turkish war from late September to November 1920, pro-Armenian groups in Europe called for a naval descent of Allied or Greek forces at Trebizond to halt the Turkish offensive. Although such appeals were heard in the chambers of the League of Nations and ap-

---

[34] See Hovannisian, *Republic of Armenia*, vol. 4, pp. 128-66.

peared in certain Western newspapers, no effective action was taken, and the prostrate Armenian government had no choice but to save whatever possible by transferring power to the Soviet order on December 2, 1920, and submitting a few hours later (albeit now illegally because of the change of regime in Erevan) to the Treaty of Alexandropol by which all Armenian claims to Ottoman territories were relinquished and half of Russian Armenia was also given up.

In the agreement to establish Soviet rule in Armenia, the envoys of Soviet Russia pledged to restore the boundary as it had existed prior to the Turkish invasion, meaning that Russia would influence its Turkish friends to relinquish Kars, Ardahan, and Mount Ararat to the new Soviet Armenian republic. All such hopes were dashed a few days later, however, as the Soviet Military Revolutionary Committee that established itself in Erevan repudiated the accord. Mustafa Kemal continued on his triumphant path by playing the Allied Powers and Soviet Russia against each other as a means of gaining the maximum concessions from each side. The Turkish Nationalist successes on the Soviet side were crowned in the Treaty of Moscow (March 1921) and Treaty of Kars (October 1921), and in the West with France relinquishing claims to Cilicia in October 1921 and withdrawing from the region shortly thereafter and with the Treaty of Lausanne in July 1923, which superseded the Treaty of Sèvres and recognized Turkey's new expanded boundaries in the east. The Armenian Question was neatly shelved at Lausanne, as neither the word "Armenia" nor "Armenian" could be found anywhere in that treaty.[35]

* * *

Thus, Armenian aspirations to a revived, united homeland combining the former Russian and Ottoman provinces of historic Armenia with lifelines to the outside world through Trebizond and other seaports ended in utter disappointment. The pledges, assurances, and commitments of the Allied Powers since the reform plan of 1914 and the onset of the Armenian Genocide in 1915 gave way to considerations of *realpolitik* by 1921. What was more, the compulsory population exchanges between Greece and Turkey in 1922, after three years of conflict and

---

[35] For a discussion of the Turkish invasion, the futile deliberations in the League of Nations, and the partition and Sovietization of the Caucasian Armenian republic, see Hovannisian, *Republic*, vol. 4, chs. 6-9.

the burning of Smyrna/Izmir, ended all dreams and schemes of Christian recovery in the Pontus. The Pontic Greek population was forcibly removed from its cities, towns, villages, and monasteries and shipped to mainland Greece. Most of the surviving Armenian population, on the other hand, made their way to Abkhazia and the Kuban along the eastern and northern shores of the Black Sea where they would try to recover themselves and find the means to perpetuate their identity and way of life within the ideological and socioeconomic parameters of the Soviet system.

❋ 16 ❋

HISTORY AND IDENTITY AMONG THE HEMSHIN

Hovann H. Simonian

In the summer of 1962, the renowned French linguist Georges Dumézil was introduced in Istanbul to a young man said to speak a "strange
idiom" as his first language. This "strange idiom" was in fact a dialect
of Armenian called Homshetsma spoken in some two dozen villages in
northeastern Turkey by the Hemshin or Hemshinli, the descendants of
Islamicized Armenians of the Hamshen district.[1] For one month,
Dumézil would meet every evening with this young man, İsmet Akbıyık, to study his dialect. The results of Dumézil's research appeared in
four articles published between 1964 and 1986. The most fascinating
part of the story, however, is that the young Hemshinli did not know
that he spoke an Armenian dialect and was most surprised when
Dumézil informed him of this fact. İsmet Akbıyık, who came from the
village of Ardala near Hopa, had been living in Istanbul for ten
months. He had noticed while at the beach that he could understand
parts of conversations held in a non-Turkish language by people (Is-

---

[1] In this article, the two forms, "Hemshin" and "Hemshinli," are used interchangeably to describe the Islamicized Armenians of Hemshin. Some scholars prefer
the first variant, arguing that Hemshin describes more properly members of the ethnic
group, while Hemshinli is more a geographic description. Others opt for Hemshinli,
as they maintain that the term is used exclusively to describe members of the group
and would not be used to designate outsiders—even if the outsiders were to settle in
one of the many settlements with a name containing the word Hemshin. The form
Rize, Bash, or Western Hemshin or Hemshinli is used to describe members of the
group living in the traditional Hemshin region, in the province of Rize. Hopa or Eastern Hemshin or Hemshinli is used for the members of the group settled principally in
the Hopa county of Artvin province. "Hamshen Armenians" or "Hamshentsi Armenians" refers to the Christian ancestors of the Hemshin and the descendants of those
who refused to convert to Islam, now settled primarily in Abkhazia and southern Russia. Generally, "Hamshen" is used to designate the district prior to the Ottoman conquest, while "Hemshin" is used for the period after the conquest.

tanbul Armenians) who obviously did not hail from his region, but he had not pursued the matter further.[2]

Anecdotes that tell of accidental meetings between Istanbul Armenians and Hemshin and describe the surprise of the latter to learn that they speak Armenian are not uncommon.[3] They add to the mystery surrounding the Hemshin as former Christians who converted to Islam centuries ago yet did not assimilate into the culture of the surrounding Muslim populations, as Turks who speak Armenian yet are not aware of it, as Muslims who continue to celebrate feasts that are part of the calendar of the Armenian Church, and as descendants of Armenians who, for the most part, have chosen to deny their Armenian origins in favor of recently invented myths of Turkic ancestry.

The Hemshin have been the focus of increased interest in recent years by scholars and laymen alike. Armenians, both in the Diaspora and in Armenia, have rediscovered the existence of this group of people speaking Armenian yet professing Islam and are curious to learn more about them. With the gradual softening of restrictions on political freedom in Turkey during the 1990s, Turks have felt freer to discuss Muslim ethnic groups, a subject taboo until then in a country that only recognized non-Muslim Greeks, Armenians, and Jews as official minorities. A large number of publications on ethnic groups ranging from Cretan Muslims to Circassians have appeared in recent years.[4] It is rare today to find bookstores in Istanbul that do not display an *"etnik"* section. This has allowed a certain awareness of the Hemshinli to take

---

[2] Georges Dumézil, "Notes sur le parler d'un Arménien musulman de Hemşin," *Académie Royale de Belgique: Mémoires, classe des lettres et des sciences morales et politiques*, 57:4 (1964): 6. The three other articles were published in *Revue des études arméniennes:* "Notes sur le parler d'un Arménien musulman d'Ardala (Vilayet de Rize)," n.s., 2 (1965): 135-42; "Trois récits dans le parler des Arméniens musulmans de Hemşin," n.s., 4 (1967): 19-35; and "Un roman policier en arménien d'Ardala," n.s., 20 (1986): 7-27.

[3] Verzhin S. Svazlian, *Polsahayots banahyusutyune* [The Folklore of the Armenians of Constantinople] (Erevan: Armenian Academy of Sciences, 2000), p. 370; "Hemshintsinere bavakan ush andradardzan, vor irenk haykakan tsagum unin" [The Hemshin Realized Quite Late That They Have Armenian Origins], *Marmara* (Istanbul), Nov. 25, 1996, as reprinted in *Abaka* (Montreal), Dec. 30, 1996, p. 3.

[4] For a review of developments in the 1990s in Turkey on the subject of ethnic minorities, see Peter Alford Andrews, "A Reappraisal," in Peter Alford Andrews with the assistance of Rüdiger Benninghaus, eds., *Ethnic Groups in the Republic of Turkey: Supplement and Index* (Wiesbaden: Dr. Ludwig Reichert Verlag, 2002), pp. 9-25. The first volume was published in 1989.

hold in Turkey, even though they are much less known or discussed than larger groups such as their Laz or Georgian Muslims neighbors.

Increased interest in the Hemshin is certainly not limited to Armenians and Turks and has taken on an authentic international character. The collapse of the Soviet Union in 1991 has contributed to the opening up of the entire eastern Black Sea region and to an increase in the flow of visitors to the area. In the particular case of Hemshin, opportunities to go trekking and mountain-climbing in the Kachkar (Kaçkar) Mountains have attracted an increasing flow of Turks and foreigners since the early 1990s. The mystery of Hemshin origins and identity, the linguistic peculiarities of the Hemshin, their fair complexion and light-colored eyes, the bright, traditional headgear worn exclusively by Hemshin women,[5] and the striking beauty and lushness of their mountains and valleys, have all combined to make the Hemshin and their home region a favorite topic of authors of guidebooks about Turkey and of journalists writing articles on travel in that country.[6] An August

---

[5] The headgear, known as *pushi* (*puşi*), is made of a scarf placed on the head around which is tied a synthetic or silk cloth with a leopard-skin type pattern combining bright-colored—generally either yellow, orange or red—spots on a black background. The bright colors of the pushi made two British alpinists say that local "women dress like peacocks in splendid costumes." See Robin Fedden and Basil Goodfellow, "Kaçkar (North Eastern Turkey)," *Alpine Journal* 69:308 (May 1964): 131.

[6] Newspaper and magazine articles include Hugh Pope, "Bullfights and a Secret Quest for Gold," *The Independent*, July 21, 1990, p. 41; "Market Scene: Cashing in on Glasnost in a Remote Corner of Turkey," *Los Angeles Times*, Aug. 7, 1990, sect. H, p. 4; Jonathan Futrell, "Hidden Turkey," *Sunday Times*, May 9, 1999; John Kellie, "Summit Else," *Scottish Daily Record*, Jan. 5, 2002, pp. 1, 11; Jeremy Seal, "On the Road in the Land of Noah," *Sunday Times*, April 7, 2002; Erla Zwingle, "Crucible of the Gods," *National Geographic Magazine* 202:3 (Sept. 2002): 74-101; Johnny Morris, "Grail Trail: Mad Honey," *The Daily Telegraph*, June 21, 2003, p. 18; and Jill Crawshaw, "Floral Delight," *The Times*, Jan. 29, 2005, p. 19.

In addition to the excellent travel guides published in Turkey by Sevan and Müjde Nişanyan, guidebooks mentioning the Hemshin include the following: Marc Dubin and Enver Lucas, *Trekking in Turkey* (Victoria, Australia: Lonely Planet Publications, 1989), pp. 125-26; Karl Smith, *The Mountains of Turkey* (Milnthorpe, Cumbria, England: Cicerone Press, 1994), p. 44; Rosie Ayliffe, Marc Dubin, and John Gawthrop, *Turkey: The Rough Guide*, 3d ed. (London: The Rough Guide, 1997), pp. 655-59; Tom Brosnahan and Pat Yale, *Turkey: A Lonely Planet Travel Survival Kit*, 5th ed. (Victoria, Australia: Lonely Planet Publications, 1997), pp. 641-43; Astrid Lorber, *Turquie de l'ouest et mer Noire* (Paris: Guide Bleu Evasion/Hachette Tourisme, 1998), p. 286; Semra Mesulam et al., eds., *Let's Go Turkey 1999* (Cambridge, MA: Let's Go Publications/New York: St. Martin's Press, 1999),

2005 article with the evocative title "How Green Is Their Valley," which the renowned British weekly *The Economist* devoted to the development of tourism in Hemshin and its sometimes attending negative consequences on the environment, is an example of the world's growing awareness of the region.[7]

If there is increasing curiosity among outsiders to learn more about Hemshin history and the Hemshin's perception of their own identity, this curiosity is not always welcomed by the Hemshinli themselves, many of whom would prefer that the spotlights be pointed away from them. There can be little doubt that many Hemshin miss the period when, isolated in their valleys, they could simply exist without having to answer questions about their identity. No Hemshin intellectuals have come forward to "invent" or establish the credentials of a Hemshin nation.[8] Yet, the question as to who are the Hemshin is increasingly asked not only by outsiders but by the younger generation of Hemshinli, many of whom were born or raised in the large cities of western Turkey. Moreover, the tenacious survival of the Hemshin as a distinct group under circumstances that threaten the survival of a minority's identity warrants a discussion on how the Hemshin conceive of their history and manage identity issues. This discussion is not only relevant to the Hemshin themselves but also to studies on the Turkish state and on Armenians at large. The continued existence of the Hemshinli impels an examination of the policies of the Turkish state and its nationalist elites vis-à-vis minority groups such as the Hemshin and affects, even if marginally, long-held assumptions on Armenian identity.

Hemshin Territories and Demographics

Peoples and communities are the product of their geography, and the Hemshin do not constitute an exception to this rule. The protection offered by the formidable mountains of the Pontus or Pontos has created from times immemorial a milieu particularly favorable to the survival of numerous tribes and communal groups. The Pontic Mountains, which run parallel to the Black Sea, separate the coastline of Asia Mi-

---

pp. 66, 347-48, 350-53; Frédérique Sarfati et al., eds., *Turquie* (Paris: Guides Bleus/Hachette Tourisme, 2001), pp. 714-16, 730-31.

[7] "How Green Is Their Valley," *The Economist*, Aug. 27, 2005, p. 43.

[8] On the role of intellectuals in "creating nations" or awakening "dormant" ones, see Ernest Gellner, *Nations and Nationalism* (Ithaca, NY: Cornell University Press, 1983).

nor from the interior Armenian Plateau, resulting in a geographical setting similar to that of Lebanon and the Caspian provinces of Iran,
which through the centuries have been known to provide a refuge to
minority groups. The eastern Black Sea region of Turkey, composed of
a succession of parallel valleys running south to north, from the mountains to the sea, has thus been a repository of cultural, ethnic, and linguistic diversity. In addition to the Hemshin, the region is home to
Islamicized communities speaking Greek, Lazi, and Georgian.

The valleys of the two branches of the Firtina (Fırtına; Furtuna)
River form a highland district that corresponds to the southern part of
the present-day Chamlihemshin (Çamlıhemşin) county (ilçe) of the
Rize province (il). It is in these highlands that the first Armenians to
migrate north of the Pontic Mountains in the late eighth century established their initial settlement. The Firtina valley (dere) later constituted
the heartland of the historical Hamshen canton, which became known
in Ottoman times as Hemshin.[9] It is in the section where the sources of
the Firtina River rise, a place today referred to as the Kachkar range
and known in the past as the Paryadres (Barhal or Parhal) chain, that
the Pontic Alps reach their highest altitude and are closest to the coast.
The mountains of the Kachkar range reach an average height of more
than 3,000 meters/11,800 feet and are in some areas less than 50 kilo-
meters/30 miles from the coastline. On sunny days one can see, from
the place where the Firtina flows into the sea, the Kachkar at 3,932
meters/15,480 feet, the Tatos at 3,560 meters/14,016 feet, and the
peaks of Verchenik (Verçenik; Armenian: Varshamak/Varshambek) at
3,711 meters/14,610 feet. According to the authors of a travel guide to
the region, "those are some of the highest spots that can be seen at sea
level anywhere on earth, rivaled only by a few points on the Andes and
in New Guinea."[10] Clear days, however, are rare, for the mountains
hem in the clouds coming from the sea, provoking abundant rainfall.
Travelers to the region, such as the German botanist Karl Koch, have
depicted the contrast between the mist-covered valleys and the sun-
bathed mountain summits and pastures (yayla) above the layer of
clouds.[11] With an annual average of 114 days of rain—a figure that

---

[9] The Firtina River is the Prytanis and Pordanis (Portanis) of earlier times. Its two
branches are the smaller Hala (Khala) Dere and the main Büyük Dere.

[10] Sevan Nişanyan, Landon Thomas, and Gabriele Ohl, Zoom in Black Sea: A
Traveler's Guide to Turkey's Black Sea Region (Istanbul: Boyut Yayın Grubu/Boyut
Publishing Group, 1990), p. 117.

[11] Karl Koch, Wanderungen im Oriente während der Jahre 1843 und 1844, vol.

does not include foggy days with drizzle, one of the most frequent weather patterns in the region—the Firtina valley is the most humid area in the Black Sea region and throughout Turkey.[12] The consequence of such abundant rain is "a natural flora of astonishing wealth and diversity: a quasi-tropical luxuriance that surpasses any other part of the Black Sea coast."[13]

The other notable physical characteristic of Hamshen or Hemshin is its difficulty of access, if not outright inaccessibility. In addition to difficult access from the south due to the Paryadres/Kachkar Mountains, entrance to the region from the coast is restricted by steep, rugged relief and dense forests, which also hinder travel and transport within Hemshin itself. Some of the paths are too narrow to be taken by horses and mules, leaving to humans the charge of sumpter beasts.[14] The quasi-permanent fog that covers Hemshin, as well as the impediment to access caused by its forests, mountains, and ravines, have left a strong impression on the rare visitors and writers who have heard of the district. In *La Fleur des histoires de la terre d'Orient*, Hetum of Korykos, of the royal Armenian house of Cilicia, the Frère Hayton of French sources, observed:

> In the realme of Georgi appered a gret meruayle, which I darred nat tell nor reherse yf I hadde nat sene it. But for bycause I was there and se, I dare say that in Georgi is a prouynce which is called Haynsen,

---

2: *Reise im pontischen Gebirge und türkischen Armenien* (Weimar: Druck und Verlag Landes Industrie Comptoirs, 1846), pp. 32-33.

[12] This figure has been calculated as the average between 1980 and 1985, the year the meteorological observatory in Chamlihemshin (Çamlıhemşin) was closed. Erhan Gürsel Ersoy has provided this data.

[13] Sevan Nişanyan and Müjde Nişanyan, *Karadeniz: Meraklısı için gezi rehberi— Black Sea: A Traveller's Handbook for Northern Turkey* (Istanbul: Boyut Yayın Grubu, 2000), p. 140.

[14] Ibid.; Ruy González de Clavijo, *Embajada a Tamorlán*, ed., intro., and annotated by Francisco López Estrada (Madrid: Editorial Castalia, 1999), pp. 352-53; P. Tumayian, "Pontosi Hayere: Ashkharhagrakan ev kaghakakan vichak Trapizoni" [The Armenians of the Pontos: Geographic and Political Situation of Trebizond], *Luma: Grakan handes* [Luma: Literary Journal] 4:2 (1899): 164; for a physical description of the Pontus, see Anthony Bryer, "Greeks and Türkmens: The Pontic Exception," *Dumbarton Oaks Papers* 29 (Washington, DC: Dumbarton Oaks, 1975): 118-20; reprinted in *The Empire of Trebizond and the Pontos* (London: Variorum Reprints, 1980); Anthony Bryer and David Winfield, *The Byzantine Monuments and Topography of the Pontos* (Washington, DC: Dumbarton Oaks, 1985), pp. 1-7, 54-57; Xavier de Planhol, *Minorités en Islam: Géographie politique et sociale* (Paris: Flammarion, 1997), pp. 53-54, 132-33.

the which is well of iii dayes iourney of length or there about; and as long as this sayd prouynce lasteth, in euery place is so great obscurite that no man is so hardi to come into the sayd lande, for they can nat cum out agayn. And the dwellers within the same lande sayde that of-ten tymes there cometh noyse of men, cockes crowyng, and horses neynge; and by a fludde that cometh out of that place come tokens ap-pering that there is resorting of people. Verily they fynde in thistores of Armeny redyng, and Georgi, that there was a cruell emperour in Persy name Sauorelx. This emperour worshypped the ydols, and cru-elly persecuted the Cristen men. . . And than the sayd Cristen men made a gret cry to Our Lorde God, and sone after came this great darknes that blinded themperour and all his men; and so the Cristen men scaped, and the sayd Emperour with his men taryd in the sayd darknes. And there thei shall abyde, as they beleue, to the worldes ende.[15]

From their heartland in the Firtina valley, Hamshen Armenians spread over the centuries to the highland sections of neighboring val-leys, such as those of the Zugha (Zuğa or Susa), Senes (Senoz) and Jimil (Cimil) rivers, which were included in the medieval principality of Hamshen and later in the Ottoman *kaza* of Hemshin.[16] In a subse-quent, undetermined period, with estimates ranging from the mid-seventeenth century to the early nineteenth, and in unknown circum-stances, some of the by-then Islamicized Hamshen Armenians, or Hemshinli, migrated eastward to the Hopa area. This migration led to the separation of the Hemshin into two communities almost oblivious to one another's existence and separated not only by territory but also

---

[15] Hetoum, *A Lytell Cronycle: Richard Pynson's Translation (c 1520) of La Fleur des histoires de la terre d'Orient (c 1307)*, ed. Glenn Burger, Toronto Medieval Texts and Translations, no. 6 (Toronto, Buffalo, and London: University of Toronto Press, 1988), pp. 14-15.

[16] The Zugha or Susa River is now called Hemshin (Hemşin) in its upstream sec-tion and Pazar when it approaches the coast; it was known in classical times as the Zagatis, from which was derived the name Zugha or Susa in the Ottoman period. The valley formed by this river now constitutes the county of Hemshin (Hemşin) and part of the county of Pazar. The Senes or Senoz River, the valley of which corresponds to the Kaptanpasha (Kaptanpaşa) *bucak* (district) of the Chayeli (Çayeli) county, was known in classical times as the Adienos. The Jimil River is an affluent of the Kalopo-tamos River. From their base in the valley of the Jimil River, the princes of Hamshen periodically brought under their control the highland section of the entire basin con-stituted by the Kalopotamos and its other affluents, that is, the modern-day İkizdere county of the Rize province. The Kalopotamos or Kalos River is now called İkizdere in its upstream section and becomes the İyidere when it nears the sea.

by language and culture. The Hemshin who remained in their original homeland—known as Western, Rize, or Bash Hemshin—have been Turkish-speaking since around the second half of the nineteenth century. The exclusively Laz county of Arhavi separates them from the Hopa, or Eastern Hemshinli. The latter, whose villages are now located administratively in the Hopa and Borchka (Borçka) counties of the Artvin province, have maintained the usage of the Hamshen Armenian dialect—Homshetsma. Furthermore, the two Muslim Hemshin groups remain for the most part unaware of the existence of yet a third related community speaking a close if not identical dialect. These are the Christian Hamshentsi Armenians of Abkhazia and the Krasnodar region in Russia, whose ancestors fled Hamshen from the seventeenth century onward to escape forced Islamization.

In the late Ottoman period and in republican Turkey, Hemshin settlement and migration have been characterized by four main trends. The first trend, in the aftermath of the 1877-78 Russo-Turkish war, was migration toward the western Black Sea region, where some fifteen or so Hemshin villages were established by both Bash and Hopa Hemshin groups in what are now the Düzce and Sakarya provinces. The Hemshinli had been preceded in the region by Hamshen Armenians who had migrated to the western Black Sea region from their villages around Ordu in 1873. According to Minas Gasapian (Kasabian), there appears to have been some solidarity between the two groups originally from Hamshen, with the Christian Hamshentsi Armenians helping the Muslim Hemshinli to settle in the region.[17]

The second trend was a northward expansion of the Hemshin into coastal areas. In the province of Rize, this migration started in the late Ottoman period when swamps around the coastal town of Ardeshen (Ardeşen) were drained and made suitable for cultivation. Inroads into coastal areas continued during the first half of the twentieth century, changing the age-old pattern whereby the Hemshin lived only in highland areas while the coastal areas were the preserve of the Laz. The Hemshin who moved toward the coast, however, did not mix with the Laz but tended instead to establish their own separate neighborhoods (*mahalle*) within Laz villages. Expansion into coastal areas has allowed the Hemshin to participate in the cultivation of tea, a highly profitable cash crop introduced on a large scale in Rize by the Turkish

---

[17] Minas G. Gasapian [Farhat], *Hayere Nikomidioy gavari mej* [The Armenians of the County of Nicomedia] (Bardizag: Azatamart, 1913), pp. 85-86, 106-11.

government after 1950. However, the Hemshin have generally not been able to benefit from the rise of the tea industry in Rize as much as the Laz, as tea could not be grown in traditional Hemshin villages located at higher altitudes or at least yielded a poorer return there than in coastal areas.[18]

A third, rather contemporary trend, shared by both Rize and Hopa Hemshin, is the acquisition of an apartment in coastal towns such as Pazar, Ardeshen, and Hopa, where families spend the winter months. This modern-day transhumance allows people not only to spend the harshest winter months in the milder climate of the coast but also to take advantage of the better schooling, shopping, and recreational opportunities of the coastal towns.[19]

A fourth and perhaps more important migratory trend that started in the 1950s and continues to this day is the large-scale exodus of the Hemshin toward the large metropolitan centers of western Turkey, as a result of which many Hemshin-populated areas have declined in their number of inhabitants. The original Hemshin heartland in the Firtina valley (the Chamlihemshin county) has been particularly affected by this out-migration, with its Hemshin population standing at less than 3,000 people in 1997 compared with a figure of 6,500 some thirty years earlier in the 1965 census.[20] Moreover, this remaining population is mostly composed of elderly, the young having left their villages for Istanbul, Ankara, and Izmir. The latter typically return to their birthplace only during their summer vacation. In contrast, the Hopa Hemshin region has been relatively less affected by migration toward large cities and has thus been able to maintain its population levels.

---

[18] Nikolai Iakovlevich Marr, "Iz poezdki v Turetskii Lazistan: Vpechatleniia i nabliudeniia" [Travels to Turkish Lazistan: Impressions and Observations], *Izviestiia Imperatorskoi Akademii Nauk—Bulletin de l'Académie Impériale des Sciences de St-Pétersbourg*, 6th ser., 4:8 (May 1, 1910): 609-12; Chris Hann, "Ethnicity, Language and Politics in North-East Turkey," in Cora Govers and Hans Vermeulen, eds., *The Politics of Ethnic Consciousness* (London: Macmillan, 1997), p. 129; Ildikó Bellér-Hann and Chris Hann, *Turkish Region: State, Market and Social Identities on the East Black Sea Coast* (Santa Fe, NM: School of American Research Press, 2001), pp. 48-56, 200-01, and note 8.

[19] Chris Hann, "Ethnicity, Language and Politics in North-East Turkey," pp. 137-38.

[20] The title of a 1972 article in a Hemshin magazine was "Let This Flow Stop." See Günhan Tarakçı, "Dursun artık bu akın," *Seyran (Pokut): Makrevis mahallesi yardımlaşma ve kalkındırma derneği* [Seyran (Pokut): The Makrevis Mahalle Association of Mutual Help and Development] (Ankara) 4:4 (March 19, 1972): 8.

Determining the figures of Hemshin population is difficult, as official statistics in Turkey do not include data on ethnicity. Exact figures can be obtained from Turkish censuses for the villages exclusively populated by the Hemshinli, but one has to rely on estimates for all mixed settlements in the Rize and Artvin provinces and of course for the Hemshin living in the large cities of western Turkey. The Bash Hemshin are estimated to number around 29,000 individuals in the Rize province, while the Hopa Hemshin are estimated at around 26,000. To these figures must be added the fifteen or so villages in the northwestern Black Sea provinces of Düzce and Sakarya, settled by both Bash and Hopa Hemshin groups during the last decades of the nineteenth century, with a population of around 10,000. Large communities of Hemshin are also to be found in regional centers, such as Trabzon/Trebizond and Erzerum, and in the large cities of western Turkey. Hemshin living in Ankara, Izmir, and Istanbul probably now outnumber those who have remained in their home villages. Also, an estimated 3,000 Hemshin live in the former Soviet Union. Consequently, a total figure of approximately 150,000 individuals can be given as a realistic estimate.[21]

A Synopsis of Hemshin History

The history of Hamshen is covered elsewhere in this volume.[22] Only the main points of Hemshin history will be provided here as a reminder before the introduction of the alternative, revisionist historical materials that have come to light during the twentieth century. Hamshen was founded in the late eighth century by Armenian migrants fleeing Arab domination. The migrants were led by two members of the Amatuni princely family, Shapuh and his son Hamam. A principality of Hamshen survived until the late fifteenth century, when it was conquered by the Ottomans. Known to the Turks as Hemshin, the district maintained its almost exclusively Armenian population until the mid-seventeenth century, when a wave of conversion to Islam started. The segment of the population refusing to convert left the area, as a result of which Hemshin became a predominantly Muslim region by the early nine-

---

[21] Hagop Hachikian, "Notes on the Historical Geography and Present Territorial Distribution of the Hemshinli," in Hovann H. Simonian, ed., *The Hemshin* (London: Routledge, 2006), pp. 168-76.

[22] See in this volume the chapter by Anne Elizabeth Redgate on the foundation of Hamshen and that by Claire Mouradian on the Islamization of Hamshen Armenians.

teenth century. The decline of central power in the Pontus from the mid-seventeenth century on and the ensuing instauration of a period marked by disorders and insecurity played a significant role in the conversion of the population of Hamshen to Islam. Until the reassertion of central power in the 1830s, regional power would be in the hands of competing local chieftains known as valley lords (*derebey*). The often tyrannical rule of these valley lords and the anarchy caused by their wars would bring much misery to the local population. The situation was most unbearable for local Christians, many of whom were forced to seek protection in conversion. The converted population, however, did not, at least initially, adhere sincerely to Islam and often remained secretly Christian at heart. As in other Armenian-populated areas where forced conversions occurred, the crypto-Christians of Hemshin became known as *kes-kes* (half-half in Armenian). Most of the Hemshin population in the eighteenth century was constituted of kes-kes and of those few remaining openly Christian.

In a process that probably took the entire nineteenth century, the number of kes-kes gradually diminished as the number of sincere adherents to Islam conversely increased. Christian rituals perpetuated by the Hemshin, such as the celebration of the feast of *Vardavar*, would gradually lose their inherent religious meaning, the significance of which would be completely forgotten by the twentieth century. Indeed, many Hemshinli would accomplish prestigious careers as Muslim clerics (*ulema*) in the last decades of the Ottoman Empire, while others would successfully climb the social ladder to become members of the Ottoman and later republican Turkey political elite. These developments demonstrate not only the extent of the Islamization of the Hemshinli, but also their complete integration within Ottoman Muslim society from the 1830s onward, following the weakening of the derebeys and the reassertion of central power.[23]

A development parallel to Islamization would be the loss of the use of the Armenian language in Hemshin at some point in the second half of the nineteenth century, along with its replacement by a Turkish dialect peculiar to Hemshin and containing numerous Armenian loanwords. The process of Turkification would be completed when Armenian surnames such as Amedanch, Andun, Apeloghlu, Arakeloghlu,

---

[23] On the integration of the eastern Black Sea region or Pontus in the Ottoman Empire, see Michael E. Meeker, *A Nation of Empire: The Ottoman Legacy of Turkish Modernity* (Berkeley, Los Angeles, London: University of California Press, 2002).

Avedikoghlu, Kirkoroghlu, and Matoslar, which some Hemshin families had continued to carry, had to be abandoned after the adoption of a
law reforming names in 1934.[24] It is not known when the Armenian
first names still reported to be in use among Hemshinli women during
the 1890s fell out of use.[25]

Yet, with astonishing resilience, the Armenian dialect of Hamshen,
or Homshetsma, continued to be spoken by one Islamicized community, namely the Hemshinli who had settled in the region of Hopa, to
the east of Hemshin proper. The factors accounting for this survival are
in all likelihood related to the Hopa Hemshinli not having participated
in the social ascent enjoyed by the Bash Hemshin beginning in the
1850s and their lesser degree of integration when compared with the
latter in Ottoman society as it developed in nineteenth-century Pontus.
Consequently, the Hopa Hemshinli were under less pressure and had
fewer incentives to abandon their mother tongue.

Turkish Nationalist Representations
of Hemshin History

Few Hemshinli in Turkey are acquainted nowadays with the historical
account that has been presented above. Most, however, are familiar
with a version of the Hemshin past that is more in keeping with the
historical theories promoted actively by the Turkish state. In its broad
strokes, this version of Hemshin history argues that the Hemshin people are of pure Turkish stock and that they are the descendants of an
authentic Turkish tribe. Historical and cultural links with Armenians
are downplayed or simply denied, and the use of the Armenian language by the Hopa Hemshin is attributed to their coexistence with Armenians in a distant past. This narrative is basically an extension to the
Hemshin of historical and linguistic theories, the Turkish history thesis
(*Türk tarih tezi*) and the extravagant "sun language theory" (*güneş-dil
teorisi*), which were created and supported by the Turkish republic

---

[24] Rüdiger Benninghaus, "Zur Herkunft und Identität der Hemşinli," in Andrews
and Benninghaus, *Ethnic Groups in the Republic of Turkey*, p. 479 and note 17;
Hamdi Alemdar, *Rize İli 100. yıl örnek köyü: Cimil rehberi* [On the Occasion of the
100th Anniversary [of Atatürk's Birth], A Model Village of the Rize Province: The
Guide to Cimil] (Samsun?, n.d.), p. 190.
[25] Piro, "Tachkatsats hayer" [Turkified Armenians], *Nor-Dar* [New Age] (Tiflis)
10, no. 227 (Dec. 21, 1893), p. 3.

since the early 1930s as an integral part of the nation-and state-building process.[26]

Theses claiming that Turks had been an established presence in Anatolia since at least two or three millennia before the Christian era and that the Hittites were a Turkic people had actually been advanced even before the official birth of the Turkish history thesis in 1932.[27] In the case of the Hemshin, one of the first recorded attempts to provide them with Turkish roots may also precede the early 1930s, as a Turkish author, Hüseyin Avni Bey (Tirebolulu Alparslan), spoke of "Hemşin Türk" villages when referring to the Hemshin villages in the region of Hopa in 1921.[28] Since it is not clear, however, whether he meant that the Hemshin were of Turkish origin or whether he used "Turk" to describe a population that was Muslim and not Laz, the first certain attribution of Turkish origins to the Hemshin will have to be dated to the period immediately following the establishment of the Turkish history thesis. In a book first published in 1933, M. Rıza, the author of this first attribution, and an army officer like Tirebolulu Alparslan, made the following claim about the Hemshinli:

> Customs, lifestyle and ethnographic similarities show that this people derives from the Hati-Hittite Turks. As stated at the beginning of this book, Armenian was once spoken by the pre-Islamic Turks due to the influence of the faith they had adopted, but as Muslims they returned to their Turkishness and acquired their national identity. Today, this people speaks Turkish; it does not know any other language.[29]

---

[26] For more details on the birth and development of the official Turkish historiography, see the brilliant study of Étienne Copeaux, *Espaces et temps de la nation turque: Analyse d'une historiographie nationaliste, 1931-1993* (Paris: CNRS Editions, 1997).

[27] As an example, see the introductory pages in *La question du Pont-Euxin* (Constantinople: Imp. Ahmed Ihsan et Cie, 1923), a book published to counter Greek claims on the Pontus; Copeaux, *Espaces et temps de la nation turque*, pp. 33-49.

[28] Hüseyin Avni Bey (Tirebolulu Alparslan), "Trabzon İli Lâz mı Türk mü?" [Is the Trabzon Province Laz or Turkish?], in İsmail Hacıfettahoğlu, ed., *Sakarya Şehidi Binbaşı Hüseyin Avni Bey—Tirebolulu Alparslan—Hayatı-eserleri—Trabzon İli Lâz mı Türk mü? Tirebolulu H. Alp Arslan* [The Sakarya Martyr Commander Hüseyin Avni Bey—Tirebolulu Alparslan—His Life-Works—Is the Trabzon Province Laz or Turkish?] (Kocatepe/Ankara: Atlas Yayınları, 1999), p. 136. The original work was published in 1921.

[29] M. Rıza, *Benlik ve dilbirliğimiz* [Identity and the Unity of Our Language], 2d ed. (Ankara: Türk Kültürünü Araştırma Enstitüsü, 1982), pp. 35-36. The main objec-

The chief and most influential proponent of the thesis affirming Turkish origins for the Hemshin has been the historian M. Fahrettin Kırzıoğlu. In a 1966 article published in *Türk Folklor Araştırmaları*, Kırzıoğlu relates how he was infuriated by scholars such as Nikolai Marr and Vladimir Minorsky who had dared to claim that the Hemshin were Islamicized Armenians. Also, having met some Hemshinli, he was told by them that the Hemshin were the descendants of two Armenian Christian brothers, Ham/Hem and Shen/Shin, who had arrived in the current Hemshin region from the area between Kars and Erzerum or from Ani. Later, the descendants of these two brothers converted to the "beautiful and true" Muslim religion. Kırzıoğlu consequently set out to correct these mistakes and to inform the Hemshin of their authentic Turkishness.[30]

According to Kırzıoğlu, the Hemshinli were a Turkish tribe which, originating in Khorasan, settled in the region of Hamadan in the mid-third century B.C. From Hamadan, the ancestors of the Hemshinli moved with the Arsacids to the area of Oshakan and Aparan in Armenia during the rule of an Ardashes II (85-123 A.D. [*sic*]), who is also presented as an Arsacid. The name of the ruling family of this Turkish tribe, "Amad-Uni"—why he splits the name Amaduni into two is not really clear—is said to have been derived from their long stay in Hamadan. Since Kırzıoğlu equates the Amadunis (Amatunis) with the Arsacids, who were Parthians and hence, according to the Turkish history thesis, Turks, the Hemshinli are presented by him as "an ancient Oghuz" (*Eski-Oğuz*) tribe. The Amadunis migrated to the valley of the Chorokh (Çoruh) River in 604 and to the region of Hemshin in 620. The leader of the migrants, the "İlbeği Hamam Beg," rebuilt the destroyed city of Dampur/Tambur and renamed it after himself, Hamamashen. The suffix "shen," however, should not be understood as the Armenian "built by," but derives from the Turkish word *şenlendirmek* (to populate). Hence Kırzıoğlu's preference for "Hemşenli"; it fits his theory on the etymology of Hemshin better than the conventional Turk-

---

tive of the book was to prove the Turkishness of the Kurds; the Hemshinli were only mentioned marginally.

[30] M. Fahrettin Kırzıoğlu, "Eski-Oğuz (Arsaklı-Part) kalıntısı Hemşenliler" [The Remnants of the Old Oghuz (Arsacid-Parthian): The Hemshenli], *Türk Folklor Araştırmaları* (Istanbul) 17:10 (June 1966): 4099-4104. This article is considered Kırzıoğlu's seminal work on Hemshin history. In it, he mentions having written an article on the subject for a Hemshin magazine published in Ankara in 1950. He later disseminated his ideas in many other publications.

ish spelling "Hemşinli." Adorned with such Turkish credentials, it should come as no surprise that the "Hemshenli" are said to be "solid Muslims, pure Turks" (*sağlam Müslüman, temiz Türk*) and to have a physical appearance of "the most beautiful Oghuz/Türkmen type" (*en güzel Oğuz/Türkman tipinde*). Since he is forced to acknowledge that some Hemshin speak "ancient Armenian," he tries to diminish the number of those speaking this dialect and insists it is mixed with "ancient Oghuz."[31]

Throughout his writings, Kırzıoğlu "finds" a Turkish connection with every personal name or toponym that comes across his path. Thus Aparan is linked with the Avars, the Balkhar (the modern name of the Paryadres) Mountains with the Bulgars, or Sysperitis (Sper) with the Scythians.[32] Two German scholars, Wolfgang Feurstein and Tucha Berdsena, have aptly summarized this technique:

> At first Kırzıoğlu assaults the reader with a flow of names of historical peoples; he then searches for some kind of phonetic correspondence or similarity with an old Turkish tribe, flavors this alleged historical outpouring with a pinch of "Islam," and presents himself as a competent researcher of Turkishness. Probably never before has a single person in Turkey falsified history so massively![33]

Indeed, factual mistakes or outright fabrications do not seem to have bothered Kırzıoğlu, and they abound in his texts. There was no Arsacid king of Armenia named Ardashes. The Parthians and their ruling family were of Iranian, not Turkic, origin, while the Amadu-

---

[31] Kırzıoğlu, "Eski-Oğuz," pp. 4100-04; Idem, *Karadeniz bolgesindeki Türk boylarından Lazlar ve Hemşinliler'ın tarihçesi* [From the Turkish Tribes of the Black Sea Region: The History of the Laz and the Hemshinli] (Ankara: Rizeliler Kültür ve Dayanışma Derniği Yayınıdır, 1994), pp. 12-16.

[32] Along with the Amatunis and the Arsacids, most Armenian dynasties and historical figures are presented by Kırzıoğlu as Turkic. This extends to Saint Gregory the Illuminator ("Aziz Greguvar" or "Aziz Grigor"), who as a Parthian is consequently also a Turk; to the Mamikonians who, according to Kırzıoğlu, came not from China but from Kashgar (in eastern Turkestan); and to the Bagratunis, who are presented as "Sakas" (Scythians), and therefore as Turks. Also, to avoid classifying someone as Armenian, Kırzıoğlu tends to replace that identification with "Grigoryen."

[33] Wolfgang Feurstein and Tucha Berdsena, "Die Lasen: Eine südkaukasische Minderheit in der Türkei," *Pogrom: Zeitschrift für bedrohte Völker* (Hamburg), no. 129 (1987): 38. The translation of this passage into English is taken from Rüdiger Benninghaus, "Turk and Hemshinli: Manipulating Ethnic Origin and Ethnic Identity," in Simonian, *The Hemshin*, p. 359.

ni/Amatuni name antedated Hamadan by several centuries, as the Ec-tabana of classical times became Hamadan only after the Muslim con-quest.[34] Moreover, Kırzıoğlu's style is often confused and his writings are marred with contradictions. Thus, after claiming that the Hemshinli are Oghuz Turks, he states in another of his publications that they are Balkar Turks. The latter actually do not belong to the Oghuz but to the Kipchak branch of the Turks.[35]

Further examples are not necessary, as it is not the aim of this dis-cussion to demonstrate the fallacy of Kırzıoğlu's theories but rather to study how they have influenced Hemshin identity. And indeed Kırzıoğlu's theories have influenced the Hemshinli. No scholar has en-joyed more influence than Kırzıoğlu among the population of the east-ern Black Sea region in general and the Hemshinli in particular. A Kırzıoğlu school of Black Sea and Hemshin history can be said to have come into existence, with an overwhelming majority of local historians finding their inspiration in his theories. Like their mentor, these writers produce spurious scholarship from a mixture of ignorance and nation-alism. Many acknowledge their intellectual debt to Kırzıoğlu and ex-press admiration for him. Thus, one of these historians, Ali Gündüz, praises him as "our great historian M. Fahrettin KIRZIOĞLU, the au-thority on the history of north-east Anatolia."[36] Another amateur histo-rian, possibly himself a Hemshinli, Ibrahim Dilmaç, after similarly praising Kırzıoğlu—and complaining that the latter's "fruitful work" was "a bit underestimated"—writes that Kırzıoğlu has "completely crushed" claims about an Armenian origin of the Hemshin.[37]

---

[34] The Amatunis are first mentioned in the fourth century A.D.

[35] For a critical analysis of Kırzıoğlu's theories, see Rüdiger Benninghaus, "Zur Herkunft und Identität der Hemşinli," pp. 479-82; Ildikó Bellér-Hann, "Myth and His-tory on the Eastern Black Sea Coast," *Central Asian Survey* 14:4 (1995): 491-95, as well as Erhan Gürsel Ersoy, "'Herkesin Türklüğü'ne dair yerel yansımalara örnekler: Lazlar ve Hemşinliler" [Examples of Local Reflections Regarding 'Everybody's Turkishness': The Case of the Laz and the Hemshinli], *Toplum ve Bilim* (Istanbul), no. 96 (Spring 2003): 75-92. I am indebted for this section to Rüdiger Benninghaus' last work on Turk-ish historiography and the Hemshinli, "Turk and Hemshinli," pp. 353-88.

[36] Ali Gündüz, *Hemşinliler: Dil—Tarih—Kültür* [The Hemshinli: Language—History—Culture] (Ankara: Ardanuçlular Kültür ve Yardımlaşma Derneği, 2002), pp. 49-50.

[37] Ibrahim Dilmaç was born in the county of Ardeshen (Ardeşen), which includes both Laz and Hemshinli. He is a functionary and a member of the ultra-nationalist *Milliyetçi Hareket Partisi (MHP)* (The Nationalist Movement Party). See Benning-haus, "Turk and Hemshinli," pp. 375n39 and 377n61. A thorough discussion of these

Kırzıoğlu's works and the ones produced by his pupils are ubiquitous and constitute the dominant, if not exclusive, paradigm presented in the histories of the region. With the exception of a small book prepared by an Armenian from Istanbul,[38] none of the books published during the past fifteen years in Turkey on the Hemshinli and their history contests the Kırzıoğlu line or present the Hemshinli as descendants of Islamicized Armenians. These studies are often the only ones available in local libraries and bookstores. Moreover, they have now spread on the internet, where almost every website dedicated to a particular Hemshin district or village includes as its history page a verbatim replica or slightly modified variant of an article promoting the Turkishness of the Hemshinli.[39] Kırzıoğlu's works or those inspired by him have also appeared over the past thirty years in official publications such as the yearbooks of the provinces of Rize and Artvin.[40] This is not surprising, as "his work not only strengthens the official ideology of the Turkish state; it also provides the basis upon which such ideologies may be built."[41]

Hemshin Perceptions of History

When asked about their origins, the great majority of Hemshin will now answer that they have Turkish roots stretching back to Central

---

local histories as they have appeared in print or on the internet is included in Benninghaus' article.

[38] That small book was a translation into Turkish of Levon Khachikyan's article on the history of Hamshen Armenians that had originally appeared in 1969 in the journal *Banber Erevani Hamalsarani* [Bulletin of Erevan University]. See Levon Haçikyan, *Hemşin gizemi: Hamşen Ermenileri tarihinden sayfalar* [The Mystery of Hemshin: Pages from the History of Hamshen Armenians], trans. and ed. Bağdik Avedisyan (Istanbul: Belge Yayınları, 1996; 2d rev. ed., 1997). Hâle Soysü, *Kavimler kapısı* [The Door of Peoples], vol. 1 (Istanbul: Kaynak Yayınları/Güney Yayıncılık ve Sanayi, 1992), also discusses the Armenian origin of the Hemshinli. The book is not devoted exclusively to the Hemshin but includes several other minority groups as well.

[39] Benninghaus, "Turk and Hemshinli," pp. 358ff. See also Ersoy, "'Herkesin Türklüğü'ne dair yerel yansımalara örnekler," p. 85n19.

[40] For examples, see the history sections of *Artvin 1967 İl yıllığı* [The 1967 Yearbook of the Artvin Province] (Ankara: Güneş Matbaası, 1968); *Artvin 1973 İl yıllığı* [The 1973 Yearbook of the Artvin Province] (Ankara: Mars Matbaası, 1973); *Cumhuriyetimizin 75. yılında Rize* [Rize in the 75th Year of Our Republic] (Rize: Rize Valiliği/Akademi Yayıncılık, 1998).

[41] Bellér-Hann, "Myth and History on the Eastern Black Sea Coast," p. 491.

Asia. There may be wide variations among the answers that are offered—with some very extravagant ones indeed—but most narratives
will have in common a claim of Turkish ancestry and a denial of an
Armenian one.[42] These views are a clear confirmation that the historical accounts elaborated by Kırzıoğlu and his pupils, with which the
Hemshinli have been relentlessly propagandized, have left their marks
on the Hemshin, who appear to have internalized Kırzıoğlu's version
of history to a large extent.

These views are also not surprising considering the hostile feelings
harbored by a large majority of Turks toward Armenians. Given the
pronounced Turkish-Armenian antagonism, why would anyone expect
the Hemshinli to present themselves as being of Armenian origin or as
Islamicized Armenians? Moreover, why would anyone expect them to
identify themselves with Armenians, who constitute the most hated
ethnic group in Turkey? Both Rüdiger Benninghaus and Erhan Ersoy
have reported how the Hemshinli feared being associated with Armenians in the eyes of Turkish public opinion at a time, in the 1970s and
1980s, when Armenian militant groups were mounting armed attacks
against Turkish targets in various countries.[43] The Hemshin who have
migrated to the large cities of western Turkey, where they have established lucrative businesses or are pursuing successful careers in the
government bureaucracy, clearly prefer a historical narrative that does
not jeopardize their relations with the Turkish state. If Kırzıoğlu's version of Hemshin history has become so popular, it might well be that it
is because there was a demand among the Hemshinli for such a narrative. Pursuing this line of thought, one could argue that had Kırzıoğlu
not existed, the Hemshin may have invented him.[44]

The Western or Rize Hemshin are more determined than the Eastern or Hopa Hemshin to assert Turkish origins and deny Armenian
ones. The Rize Hemshin are helped in their endeavors to deny Armenian origins by the fact that they have spoken Turkish since the mid-
nineteenth century. The perpetuation of Armenian traditions, such as

---

[42] Perhaps the one exception to the claim of Turkish ancestry was the version this
author was told during a trip to the region in 1998, namely that the Hemshin were
"Arabs from Central Asia." Yet the mention of Central Asia still maintains the connection with Turkishness.

[43] Benninghaus, "Zur Herkunft und Identität der Hemşinli," p. 486; Erhan Gürsel
Ersoy, "The Hemshin People: Ethnic Identity, Beliefs and Yayla Festivals in Çamlıhemşin," in Simonian, *The Hemshin*, p. 323.

[44] Benninghaus, "Turk and Hemshinli," p. 358.

the holding of a festival to celebrate Vardavar (called *Vartevor* by the Hemshin) along with the presence of numerous Armenian loanwords in the Turkish dialect spoken by the Western Hemshin are explained by the latter as a natural consequence of their long cohabitation with Armenians in former times. This author was told several times by Hemshin informants: "The Armenians transmitted to us some of their culture; they left, we remained." In order to cut all links with Armenians, some Rize Hemshin also tend to dissociate themselves from the Hopa Hemshin, who still happen to speak Armenian. This dissociation is made all the easier by the virtual absence of contacts and solidarity between the two Hemshin groups.[45] Thus, in a letter sent to a newspaper published in the Black Sea region, a Rize Hemshin stated that his group, unlike the Hopa one, was of Turkish origin, and that it had always spoken Turkish. To prove his argument, he pointed out that all the ethnic groups in the region had maintained their separate languages and that consequently, had the Rize Hemshin ever spoken Armenian, there would have been no reason for them to have lost its usage. The author of the letter, Ali İhsan Arol, a member of the board of the Çamlıhemşin and Hemşin Foundation, wrote:

> It is not true that all Hemshinli have Armenian roots. Yes, there are Hemshinli living in the interior of Hopa speaking the Armenian dialect. However, it is known that the Hemshinli in Fındıklı, Ardeshen, Pazar, Chamlıhemshin, Hemshin and Chayeli [counties of the province of Rize] are of Turkish descent. Despite the fact that all other ethnic groups in the area have their own mother tongues, the mother tongue [of the Hemshinli] in the above-mentioned places is Turkish. Imagine a place where Islamicized Armenians speak their tongue, Islamicized Greeks, the Laz, Georgians, Circassians, Abkhaz speak theirs, but the "Western Hemshinli forget Armenian."[46]

The Hopa Hemshin have certainly not been at the forefront of the battle for denying Armenian origins to the extent that the Rize Hem-

---

[45] On the cultural, social, and economic differences between the two Hemshin groups and the lack of a common consciousness uniting them, see Benninghaus, "Zur Herkunft und Identität der Hemşinli," p 487-90; and Hagop Hachikian, "Some Particulars of Hemshin Identity" in Simonian, *The Hemshin*, pp. 305-06.

[46] Ali İhsan Arol, 'Her Hemşinli Ermeni değil' [Not Every Hemshin is Armenian], *Yeni Yüzyıl* (Istanbul), Nov. 30, 1996, reprinted in Levon Haçikyan, *Hemşin gizemi*, pp. 91-92. The translation of this passage into English is taken from Hagop Hachikian, "Some Particulars of Hemshin Identity," p. 309.

shin have, because it is more difficult for them to do so since they speak Armenian. This continued use of an Armenian dialect by the Hopa Hemshin appears to be a pebble in the eye of Turkish nationalists, including some Hopa Hemshin themselves. Thus, a local Turkish historian from the neighboring province of Trabzon relates how, during his visit to Hopa in the 1940s, he was surprised to hear that Armenian was spoken in some villages of the region. Having asked why the Armenian language had not yet been abandoned, he was told by one of the Hemshinli: "We would like to abandon [Armenian], but for some reason can not manage to do so" (*Bırakmak istiyoruz, fakat bir türlü muvaffak olamıyoruz*).[47] Decades later, some Turkish nationalist Hopa Hemshin appear to have found a way to get rid of their cumbersome language. One of them claimed on an internet posting that Hopa Hemshin families are not teaching Homshetsma to their children any longer; the intention here is clearly to hasten the disappearance of the dialect.[48]

However, it is possible that the Hopa Hemshin's lesser virulence in claiming Turkish origins and denying Armenian ones is perhaps more perception than fact, a perception deriving from the difference in the education levels of the two groups. Enjoying a higher degree of education than the Hopa Hemshin, the Rize Western Hemshin have consequently been more active in both printed outlets and on the internet in discussing their origins, and hence more visible. This hypothesis finds confirmation in two recent publications prepared by Hopa Hemshin in which the latter are presented as Turks hailing from Khorasan. The author of one of these works, Remzi Yılmaz, claims that the Hopa Hemshin do not speak Armenian, but a "Kipchak/Oghuz" dialect containing some Armenian loanwords. Moreover, Yılmaz does not hide his hostility toward Armenians, who, he says, only desire to create problems for Turkey.[49] While not going as far as Yılmaz in denying that Homshe-

---

[47] Hasan Umur, *Of ve Of muharebeleri* [Of and the Battles of Of] (Istanbul: Güven Basımevi, 1949), p. 11. Of is one of the counties of the province of Trabzon. Some of its inhabitants, the *Oflu*, are Muslims speaking a Pontic Greek dialect.

[48] Benninghaus, "Turk and Hemshinli," p. 366.

[49] Cihan Topaloğlu, "Merhaba Topaloğulları" [Hello the Topaloğulları], *Topaloğulları: Topaloğulları derneği yayın organıdır* [The Topaloğulları: The Publication of the Association of the Topaloğulları] (Akçaabat/Trabzon) 1:1, January-February-March, n.d. (probably published between 1998 and 2000): 15-16. This article was published in the magazine of the Topaloğlu (Turkish plural Topaloğulları), a Hopa Hemshin family whose members claim to be the largest family in Turkey. The politician Köksal Toptan, who was at various times during the 1990s a member of the

tsma is an Armenian dialect, several Hopa Hemshin whom this author met attribute their use of Armenian to coexistence with Armenians in past times.

Of course, one might wonder whether the Hemshin really do believe in their Turkish origins as strongly as they are claiming and whether they have so fully internalized the historical narratives offered to them by nationalist Turkish historians that they have completely eliminated from their memory any knowledge of Armenian ancestry. This question would only be natural in view of the political context in Turkey, which is not really conducive to an acknowledgement of Armenian origins. Are the Hemshin practicing a form of *taqiyya*, the art of dissimulation elaborated centuries ago by Middle Eastern minorities fearing persecution, and have they preserved, even as "an uncomfortable private secret," some knowledge of their Armenian ancestry?[50] It is difficult to find an answer to this question, especially as outsiders to the group are not likely to receive an answer if they ask the question and also because answers might vary according to individuals. Some perhaps have heard about Armenian ancestry but prefer not to discuss it or to deny it, while others might be sincerely unaware of such ancestry, as in the case of İsmet Akbıyık, the informant of Dumézil on the Hemshin dialect.

However, an Armenian origin of the Hemshin, denied by most and conceivably kept as a dark secret by others, is admitted openly by a few, as one still comes across Hemshin individuals among both Rize and Hopa groups who admit to a certain Armenian connection. In some cases, this Armenian connection is mixed with a Turkish one. Thus, the anthropologist Paul Magnarella was told in 1986 by several Hemshinli of "their combined Armenian and Turkish ancestry."[51] Others who admit to some sort of Armenian ancestry will mention that their family founder was a migrant to the area, usually from Central Asia, who married within the Hemshinli community and gradually assimilated. This

---

Turkish government, belongs to this family. Remzi Yılmaz was born in Hopa and is in all likelihood a Hopa Hemshinli himself, even if he does not acknowledge this explicitly. Remzi Yılmaz, *Hemşin'in tarihi köklerine doğru: Yöresel tarih araştırması* [Towards the Historical Roots of Hemshin: A Research in Local History] (Istanbul: Kum Saati Yayıncılık, 2003), pp. 14-27.

[50] Taqiyya was invented and used by Shia Muslims who feared persecution at the hands of the Sunni Muslim majority. Benninghaus, "Turk and Hemshinli," p. 367; Bellér-Hann and Hann, *Turkish Region*, p. 11.

[51] Paul J. Magnarella, "The Hemshin of Turkey: Yayla, a Pasture above the Clouds," *The World and I* 4:5 (May 1989): 658.

claim could be true in a few individual cases, as it is possible that a few immigrants, if not Turks from Central Asia, but more probably Turks or other Muslims from various parts of the Ottoman Empire, settled in Hemshin and became "Hemshinized" over time.[52] Yet it is first and foremost a way of "saving" one's family past while admitting the "painful truth" for the rest of the group.

In other cases, Armenian origins are openly acknowledged without reference to mixture with Turkish elements. Most of those recognizing such ancestry tend to be elderly people who have lived all their lives in the rural Hemshin areas of the provinces of Rize and Hopa. Indeed, there appears to be a reverse correlation between wealth and influence on the one hand and acknowledgement of Armenian origins on the other. Unlike the Hemshin established as business owners or government officials in Istanbul or Ankara, elderly farmers who have remained in their villages do not feel the same need to maintain positive relations with the state system. Less constrained to tell a version of history that tows the official state line, they do not see a problem in admitting Armenian origins. As elderly, they are also less worried about the future.[53]

Thus, an elderly Hemshin woman this author met in one of the yaylas of Chamlihemshin, while very proud of her father's service in the Kemalist army, said when asked about her origins, "We are converts from the Armenians." After a pause of a few seconds, she added: "I am not afraid, what can they do to me?" Then, her daughter added, "all the yayla names you see in this region are Armenian. This used to be an Armenian area." Elderly women, less indoctrinated than men as a result of not having attended school for very long and not having had to perform military service, are generally more forthcoming than men in admitting to Armenian ancestry. In contrast, one is likely to get a very hostile reaction from men in their fifties or sixties at the mention of any Armenian connection of the Hemshin. Members of the younger generation, especially those raised in the large cities of western Turkey, appear to be confused on the question of Hemshin origins yet are quite curious to learn more about them.

---

[52] Given the poverty and rugged terrain of Hemshin, it is very unlikely that there was any significant inflow of population in the region. Some government officials may have chosen to stay after having served in the region. On this possible immigration in Ottoman times, see Hovann H. Simonian, "Hemshin from Islamization to the End of the Nineteenth Century," in Simonian, *The Hemshin* pp. 82-83.

[53] Erhan Gürsel Ersoy, "The Hemshin People," pp. 323-24.

Even as most Hemshin try to forget any connections with Armenians, they are reminded of these links by their Laz neighbors, some of whom refer to the Hemshin as *Sumekhi*, and to the land of Hemshin itself as *Sumekhiti*, the equivalent in the Lazi language (*Lazuri*) of the word used in the related Georgian language to describe Armenians, *Somekhi*, and Armenia, *Somkheti*.[54] More derogatorily, the Laz also often refer to the Hemshin as "Armenian converts" (*ermeni dönmesi*), or as "thick-ribbed Armenians" (*kalın kaburgalı ermeni*). The Hemshin, in turn, retaliate by calling the Laz "Mingrelian converts" (*megrel dönmesi*).[55] Both groups thus appear to be calling into question the authenticity of the other's Turkish descent, as well as the sincerity of its devotion to Islam, while maintaining no doubt about their own Turkish descent and the strength of their Islamic faith.[56]

The consciousness of Armenian origins is also felt in folktales with allusions to an Armenian element in the foundation of the Hemshin community. It was the story of the two Armenian brothers Ham and Shen who settled in Hamshen and whose descendants later converted to Islam which sparked the ire of Kırzıoğlu and led him to embark on his project of rewriting Hemshin history.[57] In some of these narratives, the Armenian element is mixed with a Turkish one, thus reflecting the mixed Armenian and Turkish influences in the formation of Hemshin identity. In one such tale, two Hemshin youths named Azakli and Bozaji were wandering in the lower sections of the Firtina valley some 300 to 400 years ago when they spotted wood shavings indicating the presence of settlements higher up the valley. They went upstream to the yaylas, where they were taken prisoner by an Armenian lord. In the end, the lord gives his daughters in marriage to the two youths and bequeaths them his lands.[58]

Another tale traces the foundation of the village of Tepan (now Bilen, in the Hemshin (Hemşin) county of Rize) to an Armenian valley lord named Osker who was later joined by a Turk nicknamed Kelesh/Keleş (handsome) in one version and Koroghlu/Köroğlu (son of a

---

[54] Wolfgang Feurstein, "Bemerkungen zur Ethnologie der Hemschinen" (unpublished manuscript).

[55] Benninghaus, "Zur Herkunft und Identität der Hemşinli," p. 491.

[56] On relations between the Hemshin and their Laz neighbors, see Ildikó Bellér-Hann, "Hemshinli-Laz Relations in Northeast Turkey," in Simonian, *The Hemshin*, pp. 338-52.

[57] Kırzıoğlu, "Eski-Oğuz," p. 4100. See section on Kırzıoğlu above.

[58] Erhan Gürsel Ersoy, "The Hemshin People," p. 324.

blind man) in another. All the inhabitants of the village are said to be descendants of the Armenian Osker and the Turk Kelesh.[59] The mixed Armenian and Turkish components of Hemshin identity are similarly mirrored in a third folktale, narrated this time by a Hopa Hemshinli. According to this story, the Hemshin are the descendants of a Turkish pasha and his Armenian bride. The pasha is said to have abandoned his wife when he was appointed to another position outside the region.[60] In addition to folktales, some folksongs show that the knowledge of Armenian origins is still being preserved in the Hemshin's collective memory, even at a subconscious level. Thus, a song that is performed at Rize Hemshin weddings contains the following lines:

> Uncle cook are you here
> *Aşçı dayı burda misen*
> Are you still of the old religion
> *Gene eski dinden misen*
> Are you an Armenian convert
> *Ermeniden dönme misen*[61]

Ottoman Era Roots of Hemshin Identity

The acceptance by most Hemshinli of historical theories giving them a Turkish lineage and their rejection of Armenian origins is obviously linked to Armenian-Turkish antagonism. It is better to claim Turkic ancestors from Central Asia than Armenian ones in the Republic of Turkey. Yet, the preference of the Hemshinli for this thesis also has deeper roots that go back to Ottoman times. In order to understand fully how modern-day Hemshin identity was shaped, a historical perspective must be considered along with more recent factors.

In the pre-national context of the Ottoman Empire, people identified themselves in terms of their membership in a particular religious community, or *millet*. Thus, being "Armenian" prior to the penetration of the European idea of nation meant belonging to the Armenian Apostolic Church and the millet it composed. Leaving the Armenian Church

---

[59] Orkun Yaman, "Etniklik ve Hemşin üzerine (bulutların ülkesi Hemşin 4)" [Ethnicity and Hemshin (The Land of Clouds Hemshin 4)], *Halkbilimi: Orta Doğu Teknik Üniversitesi Türk Halk Bilimi Topluluğu* (Ankara), no. 7 (Autumn 1998): 57 and notes 13-14.

[60] Hachikian, "Some Particulars of Hemshin Identity," p. 309.

[61] Yaman, "Etniklik ve Hemşin Üzerine," p. 57n11.

to join another Christian denomination or Islam also meant that one stopped being part of the Armenian "nation." During his visit to the region in the 1840s, German botanist Karl Koch was told by his guides in the Kiskim district that he would be taken to a village inhabited by "Franks." Along the way, he wondered how a European colony had settled in such a remote place.[62] Once he arrived in the village of Karmirk, he was surprised to find a total absence of Europeans; the local population was composed exclusively of Armenians, called Franks (*Firengi*) because of their Catholic creed (Catholic villages in Armenia are still designated as Firengi).

Reflecting on the variances in the understanding of the idea of nation, Koch—who came from a Germany where the concept of nation was fermenting—stated that "in Asia, peoples [*Völker*] are more frequently differentiated by religion than by descent."[63] "Armenian" was used interchangeably with "Christian," and "Turk" with "Muslim"—a practice that continues to this day among most of Turkey's rural population. That one could possibly be "Turk" and "Christian" or "Armenian" and "Muslim" was—and still is—a concept simply beyond the grasp of most of the Ottoman Empire's inhabitants. The amalgamation of nation and religion in the Ottoman Empire was sometimes extended to language. Anthony Bryer, British historian of the Pontus, was told in the 1960s by a local Turkish peasant that Greek people who spoke "Christian" once used to live in the region of Trabzon.[64] Amalgamation between nation, religion, and language could explain, in combination with social and economic factors affecting Ottoman society in the Pontus from the 1840s on, in addition to government persecution, the disappearance of the Armenian language from Hemshin proper, or Bash Hemshin.

This analysis is important as it could help to compensate for the lack of sources or documents on the exact circumstances of the disappearance of Armenian in Hemshin, which are largely unknown. Nineteenth-century Armenian authors are silent on the loss of language in

---

[62] The immediate neighbor of Hemshin to the south, the former Ottoman *kaza* of Kiskim, was also known in the earlier Ottoman period as Pertakrag or Peterek. In ancient times, it was the Arseatspor canton of the Armenian Tayk/Georgian Tao province and is now the modern-day Yusufeli county of Artvin province.

[63] Koch, *Wanderungen im Oriente,* vol. 2, pp. 55-58. The trip to Karmirk was not all lost, given the excellent brandy prepared in the village, which to Koch's surprise was also highly appreciated by his Turkish guides.

[64] Anthony Bryer, "The Tourkokratia in the Pontos: Some Problems and Preliminary Conclusions," *Neo-Hellenika* 1 (1970): 45n45.

Hemshin. They do, however, mention large-scale persecution by government officials from the mid-nineteenth century on that led to the disappearance of Armenian speech in the region of Sev Get, or Karadere, where there was an Islamicized Armenian community of Hamshentsi origin.[65] According to Sargis Haykuni and P. Tumayian, government officials launched a campaign to eradicate the Armenian language in Karadere after part of the Islamicized population of that district attempted to revert to Christianity in the wake of Sultan Abdul Mejid's promulgation in 1856 of the *Hatt-i Humayun* decree, which granted religious equality between Muslims and non-Muslims. Measures were also taken to increase Islamic religious teaching in order to stem the flow of reversion to Christianity among both Islamicized Greek and Armenian populations of the Pontus. It is possible, and even highly likely, that similar measures aiming to forbid the use of Armenian were taken in Hemshin during the same period.

Even though certain languages were thus associated with particular religions, there was in theory no legal or religious obstacle in the Ottoman Empire that would prevent members of any millet from speaking any language. There were frequent cases all over Asia Minor of Armenians speaking Turkish—or Kurdish for that matter—as their first or even as their only language. Since Turkish was the medium of communication among the peoples of the empire, it was a logical development that Armenians or members of other minority communities chose to adopt it.

The reverse case, in which members of the dominant Muslim millet spoke a language identified with the *gâvur* (giavur or infidels) was a much rarer occurrence and constituted a paradox, if not a transgression. Thus, Muslims of the Artvin region who spoke "Georgian-Christian" confessed to Koch that they were aware of committing a sin by using in the homes of true believers "a language of giaours which, however, they had received from God with their mother's milk." Yet, their hopes of going to Paradise were not lost, since they knew "the holy Turkish language"; hence, "God and the angels would be understanding."[66] Similarly, the *agha* of Atina (now Pazar) told the German

---

[65] The valley of the Karadere/Sev Get River (Hyssos in classical times), located to the east of Trebizond, was one of the major routes of passage connecting the Armenian Plateau through Baiburt with the Pontic coast. This valley constituted the western part of the Sourmaina/Surmene district of Trebizond and now roughly corresponds with the Araklı county of Trabzon province.

[66] Koch, *Wanderungen im Oriente,* vol. 2, p. 167.

linguist Georg Rosen that speaking Lazi was tantamount to committing a sin.[67]

By dropping Armenian for Turkish at some point during the second half of the nineteenth century, the Islamicized Armenians of Hemshin put an end to what amounted at the very least to a paradoxical situation and was often held as a sin. They also completed, in the words of Bryer, religious conversion with "social conversion" and achieved their transition from the Armenian millet to the Muslim one.[68] The connection between loss of language and religious conversion to Islam is echoed in the words of a Hemshin woman, Aynur Altaş (Altash) who, in an article titled "Hemşinoloji" wrote that "a language was born, a religion was born . . . a language was changed, a religion was changed" (*Dil doğdu, din doğdu . . . dil değişti, din değişti*).[69]

Furthermore, the Pontus had entered a new era during the 1840s, marked by the defeat of the derebeys and the reassertion of central power. This new era offered opportunities for social and economic mobility that may have contributed to the abandonment of the Armenian language. The careers of Mehmed Ali Pasha—who became grand-admiral and grand-vizier and married a daughter of the sultan—and of numerous members of the ulema epitomize the advancement of Hemshinli in Muslim Ottoman society, or as Michael Meeker calls it, "the imperial system."[70] The correlation between social status and loss of language was also visible among the Laz during the second half of the nineteenth century, as it was often men of influence and wealth who expressed to European travelers contempt for their native language.[71]

---

[67] Georg Rosen, *Über die Sprache der Lazen* (Berlin: Lemgo and Detmold, Meyersche Hofbuchhandlung, 1844), p. 2.

[68] Anthony Bryer, "The Crypto-Christians of the Pontos and Consul William Gifford Palgrave of Trebizond," *Deltio Kentrou Mikrasiatikon Spoudon* (Athens), no. 4 (1983): 24-25.

[69] Aynur Altaş, "Hemşinoloji," *Seyran* (Pokut) (Feb. 28, 1969): 14. This article lists words of the Turkish dialect of the Rize Hemshin, including many Armenian loanwords.

[70] Meeker, *A Nation of Empire*. Mehmed Ali Pasha (1813-68) occupied the position of grand admiral six times and that of grand vizier once. He was married to a daughter of Sultan Mahmud II, giving him the title of *damad* (son-in-law). His progeny were known as Damad Mehmed Ali Pasha Zâdeler, as well as Hemshinlizâdeler. On Mehmed Ali Pasha and other Hemshinli who achieved prestigious careers see Alexandre Toumarkine, "Ottoman Political and Religious Elites among the Hemshin, Mid-Nineteenth Century to 1926," in Simonian, *The Hemshin*, pp. 100-23.

[71] Alexandre Toumarkine, *Les Lazes en Turquie (XIXe-XXe siècles)* (Istanbul: Isis, 1995), p. 46.

Even the Hemshinli who did not attain prestigious careers may have felt it necessary to adopt Turkish as a first language in lieu of Armenian. Migrations—as well as military conscription—are likely to have played a central role in the language switch. Driven by economic necessity to larger coastal towns or to Istanbul where they primarily spoke Turkish, Hemshinli men may have continued to do so after returning to their villages. The fate of Armenian in Hemshin—and in Sev Get/Karadere—may have been similar to that of another regional language, Breton. The loss of the latter is believed to have been caused to a greater extent by soldiers who continued to speak the French they had grown accustomed to in the trenches of World War I after returning home to Brittany than by the mandatory education of children in French, introduced a few decades earlier.[72]

The weakness of the rationale linked to economic and social mobility, however, is its failure to explain why, placed in similar circumstances, various Georgian, Lazi, and Greek-speaking Muslim communities managed to cling to their ancestral languages, while the Hemshinli and others abandoned them.[73] Moreover, language is primarily transmitted by mothers, not by fathers, and the migration factor does not explain how Hemshinli women, who did not attend school and who remained in their home villages, came to stop speaking Armenian. A possible answer might be that the Armenian language in Hemshin went underground rather than having disappeared. Writing on the Islamicized Armenians of the Chorokh (now Çoruh) Basin, in Olti (Oltu) and elsewhere, the Armenian author Atrpet complained that they had lost their language, while the Islamicized Georgians of Ajaria had managed to preserve theirs. Yet, he noticed that while these villagers had lost Armenian for Turkish, "their tone, pronunciation, declamation and phrase structure were those of Armenian, and even in their spoken dialect many Armenian words continued to be used."[74] The same happened in Hemshin, as the local Turkish dialect replacing Armenian contained numerous Armenian loanwords. The importance of these

---

[72] Gaëlle Dupont, "Le parler breton s'est perdu dans les tranchées," *Le Monde*, Nov. 6, 1998, p. 12.

[73] This question was first asked in 1904 by A.P. Megavorian [Meghavorian], "K voprosu ob etnograficheskikh usloviiakh razvitiia narodnostei Chorokhskago basseina" [On the Question of Ethnographic Circumstances in the Development of the Nationalities of the Chorokh Basin], *Izvestiia Kavkazskago otdela Imperatorskago russkago geograficheskago obshchestva* (Tiflis) 17:5 (1904): 367.

[74] Atrpet [Sargis Mubayajian], *Chorokhi avazane* [*The Chorokh Basin*] (Vienna: Mekhitarist Press, 1929), pp. 197-98.

loanwords, often used in emotionally attached activities, has led Wolfgang Feurstein to write that the linguistic context in Hemshin would be
more correctly described as a transfer of essentially Armenian elements
into a new medium, the Turkish language, rather than as a displace-
ment of Armenian.[75]

It is in all likelihood their marginal existence as pastoralists that allowed for the survival of the Armenian language among the Hopa
Hemshin. The latter were too unimportant to be a cause of worry for
the state, and they were certainly not worth the same type of government pressure that contributed to the abandonment of Armenian in
Karadere. Also, provincial secular and religious authorities, as Russian
officials in later times, may simply not have been aware of or even
have suspected that this small Muslim community, which some believed to be Kurdish, was actually Armenian-speaking. A second possible reason for the preservation of the Armenian language lies in the
absence of economically induced migrations among the Hopa Hemshinli, who did not share the economic mobility of their compatriots in
Bash Hemshin. The Hopa Hemshinli, furthermore, did not participate
in the sometimes spectacular social ascent enjoyed by the Bash Hemshinli beginning in the 1850s or even earlier. Not so integrated into Ottoman society as it developed in nineteenth century Pontus, the Hopa
Hemshinli consequently were under less pressure and had fewer incentives to abandon their mother tongue.[76]

Conclusion

An overwhelming majority of Hemshin have adopted a version of history that describes them as having Turkish ancestry and emphatically
denies an Armenian one. This thesis has the advantage of bringing
Hemshin history in line with the official Turkish history thesis that has
been promoted by Turkish authorities since the early 1930s. It also
provides the Hemshin with historical credentials acceptable within the
current socio-political context of Turkey, in which Armenians constitute one of the most despised ethnic groups. Furthermore, the Hemshin's adoption of a Turkish nationalist version of their own history has

---

[75] Feurstein, "Bemerkungen zur Ethnologie der Hemschinen" (Unpublished manuscript). On Armenian loanwords in the Turkish dialect spoken in Bash Hemshin,
see Altaş, "Hemşinoloji," p. 14; Uwe Blaesing, "Armenian in the Vocabulary and
Culture of the Turkish Hemshinli," in Simonian, *The Hemshin*, pp. 279-302.

[76] Benninghaus, "Zur Herkunft und Identität der Hemşinli," p. 485.

deeper roots, as Islamic community and Turkish ethnicity have been considered one and the same by most inhabitants of Turkey since Ottoman times.

However, knowledge of Armenian origins has not been entirely displaced among the Hemshin. It has survived in the open admission of Armenian ancestry by elderly people encountered in their villages or pasturelands. Knowledge of a link with Armenians has also survived at a subconscious level in the collective memory of the Hemshin, occasionally resurfacing in expressions of local folklore, such as the celebration of Vardavar, in folktales, or in popular songs. In addition to the preservation of Armenian by the Hopa Hemshin and of Armenian loanwords by the Bash Hemshin, it is this knowledge, even if residual, that has allowed the Hemshin to maintain their distinct group identity to this day.

That a few Hemshin acknowledge Armenian ancestry or some sort of links with Armenians should not, however, be confused with a desire to return to the fold of Armenianness. For more than three centuries now, the Hemshin have been part, along with the other ethnic groups of the region, such as the Laz, Muslim Georgians, or the Greek-speaking Muslims, of a common Black Sea Muslim society that has successfully managed to transcend ethnicity and impose itself over ethnic differences.

Hemshinli Women and Children

Hemshinli Home

Hopa Hemshin Child in Summer *Yayla*

✽ 17 ✽

ARMENIAN PONTIC COMMUNITIES
IN THE KUBAN AND ABKHAZIA

Igor Kuznetsov

According to the historians Ghevond and Hovhan Mamikonian, 12,000 Armenian warriors and their families migrated to Pontus (Πόντος; Byzantine *thema* Chaldia) in the period of Arab dominion over Armenia. They were settled by Prince (*Ishkhan*) Hamam, a son of Shapuh Amatuni, in Tambur or Hamamashen, located between present-day Trebizond/Trabzon and Hopa. From Armenian *Hamamashen* = *Hamam* and *shen* "settlement" or "town" came *Hamshen* and hence *Hamshenahayer*/Hamshen Armenians); in Ottoman times—*Hemshin*; and at present *Chamli Hemshin* (*Çamlı Hemşin*), *Bash Hemshin (Baş Hemşin),* and *Hemshinli (Hemşinli)*. Hovhan Mamikonian's version is more detailed, as he explains that as a result of a quarrel between King Hamam and his uncle, the Georgian king Vashdean, the latter ordered that Tambur should be burned and that Hamam should be quartered. After Hamam's ultimate victory over his kinsman, he built a new town on the site of Tambur and called it by his own name, Hamamashen.[1]

Most scholars now think of contemporary Hamshen Armenians (Hamshentsi) as having descended from these Amatuni's warriors while the Hemshins (Hemshinli) are the Islamicized element of Hamshen Armenians.[2] Actually, the process of formation of both segments

---

[1] Ghevond, *Patmutiun Ghevondeay Metsi Vardapeti Hayots* [The Great Armenian Vardapet Ghevond's History] (St. Petersburg, 1887), pp. 167-69; Hovhan Mamikonian, *Patmutyun Taronoy* [The History of Taron] (Erevan: Matenadaran, 1941), p. 284; Levon Khachikyan, "Ejer Hamshenahay patmutyunits" [Pages from the History of Hamshen Armenians], *Banber Erevani Hamalsarani* [Herald of Erevan University] 2 (1969), p. 115; idem, "Patmakan hamarot aknark" [A Short Historical Outline], *Hay azgagrutyun ev banahyusutyun: Nyuter ev usumnasirutyunner* [Armenian Ethnography and Folklore. Sources and Materials], vol. 13 (Erevan: Armenian Academy of Sciences, 1981), p. 7.

[2] See, for example, Khachikyan, "Ejer Hamshinahay patmutyunits," pp. 115-44;

is probably far more complicated. Anthony Bryer concurs that the term Hemshin relating to a geographic area derives from the name of the ruling dynastic family. This pattern also existed much later at the time of the travels of the diplomat Ruy González de Clavijo, when the district was known by name of its ruler, Arakel.[3]

Two conclusions follow. First, the ancestors of today's Muslim Hemshinli might be both Armenians and other elements who under the influence of the Amatuni and the Armenian Church eventually adopted the dominant Armenian language. The materials gathered by Laz researcher Tsate Batsashi and Nikolai Marr's hypothesis of a Laz substratum for the Hamshen dialect might support this suggestion.[4] Second, there is a possibility that Amatuni's descendants were not to be found among the Armenian peasantry, which had lost their noble class in the Pontus and elsewhere by the Ottoman period. There could have been subsequent waves of immigrants until the eighteenth century. For example, refugees from Ani (Shirak) escaping from the Seljuk invader Alp Arslan settled in and around Trebizond in 1064.[5] After the *theme* of Chaldia with Trebizond separated from the Byzantine Empire with the support of Georgian Queen Tamar to become the Empire of Trebizond at the beginning of the thirteenth century, a new wave of Armenian immigrants fleeing from the Mongols arrived in around 1240. Migrations from Ani to the Pontus, mostly to Trebizond, are known to have occurred also in the 1320s.

L.M. Melikset-Bekov was among the few scholars who had some doubt about the existence of Hamam Amatuni, the founder of Ham-

---

Barunak G. Torlakyan, ed., *Hamshenahayeri azgagrutyune* [The Ethnography of Hamshen Armenians], as vol. 13 of *Hay azgagrutyun ev banahyusutyun* [Armenian Ethnography and Folklore] (Erevan: Armenian Academy of Sciences, 1981).

[3] Anthony Bryer and David Winfield, *The Byzantine Monuments and Topography of the Pontos,* 2 vols. (Washington, D.C.: Dumbarton Oaks, 1985), vol. 1, p. 337.

[4] Tsate Batsashi, "Etnoreligioznyi sostav naseleniia severo-vostochnoi Anatolii v XIX-nachale XX veka" [Ethno-Religious Composition of the Population of Northeastern Anatolia, 19th-Early 20th Centuries] (Ph.D. Thesis Abstract) (Tbilisi, 1988); Nikolai Marr, "Materialy po khemshinskomu narechiiu armianskogo iazyka" [Data for Hemshin Subdialect of Armenian], in *Zapiski kollegii vostokovedov pri Aziatskom muzee Rossiiskoi akademii nauk* [Proceedings of a Colloquium of Orientalists at the Asian Museum of the Russian Academy of Sciences], vol. 1 (Leningrad: Izd-vo Akademii nauk SSSR, 1925), pp. 73-80.

[5] Hakobos Dashian, *Hay bnakchutiune Sev tsoven minchev Karin: Patma-azgagrakan harevantsi aknark me* [Armenian Population from the Black Sea to Karin: Cursory Historic-Ethnographic Survey] (Vienna: Mekhitarist Press, 1921), p. 24.

shen.[6] In general, the information given by the Armenian medieval chroniclers is accepted as fact by most scholars in Armenia. Thus, Academician Levon Khachikyan has written that in the eighth century the Amatuni magnates had possession of the counties (*gavars*) of Aragatsotn and Kotayk of Ararat province (*nahang*) and that the migration of Armenians to the Pontus began precisely from this region.[7] On the other hand, there are no original sources except for Ghevond and Mamikonian which attest to these events of the eighth century. V.H. Bdoyan has tried to compare the types of agricultural implements found in the Pontus and various districts in Armenia.[8] Then, this author did a comparison based on the dialectological data.[9] Both attempts had to rely on materials from the late nineteenth and early twentieth centuries and dealt with very mobile elements of culture, so it is not feasible to say with any certainty that there was a clear and firm connection.

Unfortunately, under the existing circumstances, it is not possible to conduct related archaeological research in Turkey, although as far back as the beginning of the nineteenth century Minas Bzhshkian saw ruins of buildings and buried caches of ancient weapons as well as candles in various places in the Pontus, including the suburbs of Trebizond and at Bash Hemshin (ancient Hamshen), which he sometimes linked with Tambur and sometimes with refugees who had fled from Ani in medieval times.[10] Bryer has noted that many of these artifacts still remain.[11] Fifteenth-century sources (de Clavijo; Matenadaran manuscripts; Jerusalem Mss 1617, 3701) bring us back to the Armenian principality (land of Arakel) in Pontus after more than six centuries of silence. But with the fall of the Empire of Trebizond in the fifteenth century and the

---

[6] L.M. Melikset-Bekov, "Pontica Transcaucasica Ethnica (po dannym Minaia Medichi ot 1815-19)" [Pontica Transcaucasica Ethnica, According to Data of Mina Medichi from 1815-19], *Sovetskaia etnografiia* [Soviet Ethnography] 2 (1950): 165.

[7] Khachikyan, "Ejer Hamshinahay patmutyunits," p. 118; idem, "Patmakan hamarot aknark," p. 9. Igor Kuznetsov, *Odezhda armian Ponta: Semiotika material'noi kul'tury* [Pontic Armenian Clothing: Semiotics of Material Culture] (Moscow: Nauka, 1995), pp. 13-19.

[8] V.H. Bdoyan, "Pontosi hayeri varogh gortsiknere" [Agricultural Implements of the Pontic Armenians], *Patma-banasirakan handes* [Historical-Philological Journal] 4 (1971): 199-202.

[9] Kuznetsov, *Odezhda armian Ponta,* pp. 13-19.

[10] Minas Bzhshkian, *Patmutiun Pontosi or e Sev Tsov* [The History of Pontus on the Black Sea] (Vienna: Mekhitarist Press, 1819), p. 97; Melikset-Bekov, "Pontica Transcaucasica Ethnica," p. 166.

[11] Bryer and Winfield, *Byzantine* Monuments, vol. 1, pp. 335-43, and vol. 2, plates.

flight of the last Armenian prince of Hamshen in the late fifteenth century, the entire Pontus region was incorporated into Ottoman Empire.

During the next several centuries, the process of Islamization took place in historic Hamshen (Muslims are first mentioned here by de Clavijo) as well as areas inhabited by the Greeks and Laz. The general view is that this process led to the appearance of Muslim Hemshin near the historic Hamshen territories in the seventeenth and beginning of the eighteenth century. During this time, a part of the Hamshentsi population moved westward to the Karadere (Surmene) area, but they, too, were eventually Islamicized. Although as late as the early nineteenth century and even later in some areas such as Rize, vestiges of Christianity (perhaps, crypto-Christianity) were noted among the Hemshinli, the truly Christian population, that is, the Hamshentsi Armenians, survived only farther to the west.[12] Traditionally, according to nineteenth-century scholars Sargis Haykuni and Minas Bzhshkian, the rural Armenians in the Trebizond, Ordu, and Samsun (Janik) districts were believed to be descendants of the refugees from Hamshen who moved to avoid forced Islamization.[13] But it is also possible that these immigrants from Hamshen were not the first Armenians in these districts and formed only an upper stratum.

The first Hamshentsis from the Pontic Black Sea coast arrived on Russian shores (Kuban, Abkhazia, Crimea) in the 1860s. The migration continued thereafter, and following the Russian annexation of Kars, Ardahan, and Batum in 1878, a number of Hemshin villages fell within the Batum district (*okrug*) of Ajaria (Adjaria; Adjarstan). The transfer of Hamshentsis to the Russian coastal regions escalated during the Armenian Genocide (*Mets Eghern*) and after World War I.

In the years from 1926 to 1953, most of the Hamshentsis in the Krasnodar Region (*krai*) or Kuban lived within the bounds of the Armenian National Region (*Armianskii natsional'nyi raion*), which consisted of 7 settlement councils (*sel'sovety*) and 63 Armenian villages with a total of 7,000 inhabitants.[14] Nowadays, Hamshen Armenians are

---

[12] Bzhshkian, *Patmutiun Pontosi*, pp. 92-93, 96-97; V.A. Gordlevskii, *Izbrannye sochineniia* [Selected Works], vols. 1-4 (Moscow, 1962-1968), vol. 3, p. 329.

[13] Sargis Haykuni, "Nshkharner, korats u moratsvats hayer: Trapizoni hay mahmetakan giughern ev nrants avandutiunnere" [Relics, Lost and Forgotten Armenians: The Trebizond Armenian Muslim Villages and Their Traditions], *Ararat* (Etchmiadzin, July-Aug. 1895): 239-43, 293-95; Bzhshkian, *Patmutiun Pontosi*, pp. 96-97.

[14] Vladimir Adobashyan, "Obrazovanie v sostave Krasnodarskogo kraia Armianskogo raiona" [The Formation of the Armenian District in the Krasnodar Krai], *Banber Hayastani arkhivneri* [Herald of Armenian Archives] 3 (1970): 167-74; Viktor

spread over a wide area in more than 230 settlements from the Anapa *raion* or *rayon* (administrative district/region) in the north to Ocham-chira in the south. Except for a small group from the Crimea and recent refugees from Abkhazia during the Abkhaz-Georgian war (1991-93), all of the inhabitants of these settlements are the direct descendants of the refugees from Turkey.

During World War II, Stalin deported the Muslim Hemshinli from the Ajarian Autonomous SSR to Kazakhstan and Kyrgyzstan. Since the 1980s and especially in the wake of the Uzbek-Kyrgyz conflict in 1989, some Hemshinli have moved to the Apsheron (Apsheronsk) raion of the Krasnodar krai. This migration ceased in the early 1990s because of rising interethnic tensions in Krasnodar. But those Hem-shinli who did move to Krasnodar suddenly found themselves face to face with their Christian Hamshentsi counterparts, both with common origins in the Pontus.

History of Research

Study of the Pontic (Hamshen) Armenians has its own long history. The first mention of them is found in Ghevond's manuscript. During the last two hundred years, there have been many publications in Rus-sia, the Caucasus, and the West which describe this community and various aspects of its history and culture.[15] There are, however, very

---

Hakopian, "Natsional'nye raiony i ikh offitsial'nyi iazyk (Armianskie raiony Sever-nogo Kavkaza v 20-e gody)" [National Districts and Their Official Language: Arme-nian Districts of the North Caucasus in the 1920s], in *Studia Pontocaucasica*, vol. 2: *Armiane Severnogo Kavkaza* [Armenians of the Northern Caucasus] (Krasnodar, 1995), p. 153.

[15] Among these publications are the following: P.P. Korolenko, "Turetskie emi-granty v Kubanskoi oblasti" [Emigrants from Turkey in the Kuban Region], in *Ku-banskii sbornik* [Kuban Anthology], vol. 9 (Ekaterinodar, 1904); V.M. Sysoev, "Po goram Kubanskoi oblasti. 4. Sredi armian i grekov; ot st. Elizavetpol'skoi do Kurinki" [In the Mountains of Kuban Region. 4. Among the Armenians and Greeks; from the Settlement of Elizavetpol to Kurinka], in *Kubanskie oblastnye vedomosti* [Registers of Kuban Region] 28 (1901): 33, 35-37; Sargis Haykuni, "Trapizoni Ze-fanoz, Kromilahay giughoreits sovorutiunner u barbare" [Customs and Dialect of the Armenians of the Trebizond Village Zefanoz of Kromila], *Ararat* (May 1892): 428-47; idem, "Aratsner Trapizoni giughatsots barbarov" [Proverbs in the Dialect of Tre-bizond Peasants], *Ararat* (Aug 1895): 293; idem, "Hay Gaspare" [Armenian Gaspar], *Ararat* (Oct. 1895): 397-400; idem, "Korats u moratsvats hayer," *Ararat* (July-Aug. 1895): 239-43, 293-97; idem, Trapizoni hay giughatsu kianke [The Life of the Tre-bizond Armenian Peasants], *Ararat* (1905): 37-46, 934-42, 1034-41, and (1906):

few studies of the Hamshen Armenians of the Kuban (Krasnodar krai) and Abkhazia. It was during the 1960s and 1970s that Hamshen Armenian ethnographers living in the Kuban and in Erevan began to work on this subject. A new publication, *Dzayn Hamshenakan* (Voice of Hamshen), featured literary pieces, folklore, and lists of dialectical terms gathered by members of the Hamshen compatriotic associations.[16] Barunak Torlakyan, a native of the village of Kushana near Trebizond, was a pioneer in this endeavor.[17] What may be termed ama-

---

180-89; Nshan Khshtian, "Aratsner i Trapizon" [Proverbs of Trebizond], *Masis* (1886); idem, "Azgayin zhoghovrdakan aratsner Trapizoni" [National Popular Proverbs of Trebizond], *Handes Amsorya* [Monthly Journal], series, 1890-1895; idem, "Pontakan gavarabarbarneren nshkhark" [Relics of thr Pontic Dialects], *Handes Amsorya* (1895): 183-86; Babgen Kiuleserian, "Chaniki vichakin mej gtnvogh hamshentsineru gavarabarbare" [The Dialect of the Hamshens Found in the Janik Sanjak], *Biurak* (1899) and (1900); idem, "Hamshentsineru hayerene" [The Armenian of the Hamshens], *Loys* (1906); P. Tumaiants, "Pontosi hayere" [The Armenians of Pontus], *Luma,* vol. 2 (1899); H.D. Muradian, *Hamshentsi hayer* [Hamshen Armenians] (Tiflis, 1901); Hovakim Hovakimian, *Patmutiun Haykakan Pontosi* [History of Armenian Pontus] (Beirut: Mshak, 1967); George Dumézil, "Notes sur le parler d'un Armenien musulman d'Ardala (Vilayet de Rize)," *Revue des études arméniens,* n.s., 2 (1965): 135-42; idem, "Notes sur le parler d'un arménien musulman de Hemsin," in *Mémoires de l'Academie Royale de Belgique, Cl. des Lettres,* 2 ser., t. 57, fasc. 4 (1964): 5-52; idem, "Trois recits dans le parler de arméniens musulmans de Hemsin," *Revue des études arméniens,* n.s., 4 (1967): 19-35; Paul Magnarella, "Yayla: A Pasture above the Clouds," in *The World & I (*May 1989); Bert Vaux, Sergio La Porta, and Emily Tucker, "Ethnographic Materials from the Muslim Hemshinli with Linguistic Notes," *Annual of Armenian Linguistics* 17 (1996): 25-45.

[16] Sero Khanzadyan, ed., *Dzayn Hamshenakan* [The Voice of Hamshen] (Erevan: Hayastan, 1971), and Andranik Zeytunyan, ed. (Erevan: Hayastan, 1979).

[17] See especially the following contributions by Barunak G. Torlakyan: "Hamshenahayeri masin" [On the Hamshen Armenians], *Banber Hayastani arkhivneri* 2 (1970): 197-202; "Hamshenahayeri ev Pontahayeri bnakavayrer u tvakanake 1914 tvakanin" [Settlements and Number of Hamshen and Pontic Armenians in 1914], *Patmabanasirakan handes* 2 (1970): 202-15; "Drvagner Hamshenahayeri patmutyunits" [Episodes from the History of the Hamshen Armenians], *Banber Erevani Hamalsarani* 2 (1971): 198-203; "Ejer Hamshenahayeri XVII-XVIII dareri patmutyunits" [Pages from the History of Hamshen Armenians in the 17-18th Centuries], *Patma-banasirakan handes* 4 (1972): 133-36; "Hamshenahayeri taraze XIX dari verjerin" [The Clothing of Hamshen Armenians in the Late 19th Century], *Patma-banasirakan handes* 3 (1976): 143-56; "Trapizoni nahangi haykakan krtakan ev kronakan hastatutyunnere arajin hamashkharhayin paterazmi nakhoryakin" [Armenian Religious and Educational Institutions of Trebizond Province on the Eve of World War I], *Banber Hayastani arkhivneri* 3 (1977): 73-87; "Hamshenahayeri bnakaranayin hamalire" [The Household Complex of Hamshen Armenians], *Patma-banasirakan handes* 2 (1984): 93-104; *Nshkharner Hamsheni ev Trapizoni banahyusutian* [Relics of Hamshen and Trebizond Folklore] (Erevan: Erevan State University, 1986).

teur Hamshen ethnography served to stimulate interest among academics. Field research was initiated by Zhenia Khachatryan and since 1977 has been conducted by members of the Institute of Ethnology and Anthropology in Moscow, namely Natalia Volkova, Tatiana Aristova, Alla Ter-Sargisyants, and Mikhail Chumalov.[18] Erevan journalist Sergei Vardanyan has since 1984 steadily interacted with the Hamshentsis in the Kuban and Abkhazia.[19]

I began my own research on Hamshen Armenians in 1983. Later, some of my students at Kuban State University in Krasnodar joined me. During the expeditions of the following years, much material was gathered on the history, demography, ethnography, and dialectology of the Hamshen Armenians and other Pontic peoples such as Greeks and Laz. The data included field diaries, interviews, audio and video recordings, and photographs.[20]

The first time I visited two Muslim Hemshin families was in 1988 to gather information for a dissertation project with the assistance of Gaspar Gasparyan, a graduate of Kuban State University who worked

---

[18] Tatiana F. Aristova, "Transformatsiia lichnykh imen armianskogo naseleniia pos. Esheri Sukhumskogo r-na Abkhazskoi ASSR" [Transformation of the Personal Names among the Armenian Population of Esheri Settlement in the Sukhum District of the Abkhazian ASSR], in *Etnicheskaia onomastika* [Ethnic Onomastics], ed. R.Sh. Dzharylgasinova and V.A. Nikonov (Moscow: Izd-vo Nauka, 1984), pp. 96-99; Natalia Volkova, "Armiane Abkhazii (voprosy etnokul'turnykh kontaktov)" [The Armenians of Abkhazia: Questions of Ethnocultural Contacts], in *Polevye issledovaniia Instituta Etnografii, 1979* [Fieldwork of Institute of Ethnography, 1979] (Moscow: Izd-vo Nauka, 1983), pp. 104-14; Alla Ter-Sargisyants, "Sovremennyi byt armian Abkhazii" [The Contemporary Lifestyle of the Armenians in Abkhazia], in *Kavkazskii etnograficheskii sbornik* [Caucasian Ethnographic Anthology], vol. 8 (Moscow: Izd-vo Nauka, 1984), pp. 3-21; Mikhail Chumalov, "Armiane Abkhazii (k probleme stabil'nosti etnodispersnoi gruppy)" [The Armenians of Abkhazia: On the Problem of Ethnodispersed Group Stability], in *Malye i dispersnye etnicheskie gruppy v evropeiskoi chasti SSSR* [Small and Dispersed Ethnic Groups in the European Part of the USSR] (Moscow: Moskovskii filial Geogragraficheskogo obshchestva SSSR, 1985), pp. 107-19.

[19] Sergei Vardanyan, "Hamshentsi musulman hayeri usumnasirutyan patmutyunits" [From the History of Study of Hamshen Muslim Armenians], *Iran-Name,* 1-3 (1998): 2-11.

[20] Igor Kuznetsov, Ivan Gololobov, Anthon Popov, Alexander Siver, "K issledovaniiu Pontiiskoi istoriko-kul'turnoi oblasti (Pontica Caucasica Ethnica. III-IX)" [On Research of the Pontic Historical-Cultural Area], in *Arkheologiia i etnografiia Severnogo Kavkaza* [Archaeology and Ethnography of the Northern Caucasus] (Krasnodar: Kuban State University Press, 1998), pp. 333-80; *Studia Pontocaucasica*, vol. 2: *Armiane Severnogo Kavkaza* [The Armenians of the North Caucasus] (Krasnodar, 1995); *Studia Pontocaucasica*, vol. 3: *Pontiiskie greki* [The Pontic Greeks] (1997).

in the Neftegorsk settlement council at the time.[21] Before that, only Sergei Vardanyan, then the correspondent of the *Garun* (Spring) magazine in Erevan, had visited the Hemshinli in Krasnodar in 1984.[22] In October 1994 and June-July 1995, Aleksandr Ossipov of the Institute of Ethnology and Anthropology in Moscow studied this population.[23] Then in 1997-98, a group of my students from Kuban State University took several field trips to meet with Hemshinli of the Apsheron raion. Thereafter, in 2000-01, Arkady Leibovsky, Ardavast Tulumjyan, and I received a grant from the Soros Foundation to study the social and cultural changes, especially identity in transition, among the Hemshin Muslims and Hamshen Armenians in the Krasnodar krai.[24]

Population

The Armenian inhabitants of the Pontus formed between 3.4 and 5 percent of the total population (primarily Turks, Greeks, and Laz). Since the 1920s and 1930s, after the resettlement on the Russian eastern shores of the Black Sea, their relative percentage compared with Russians, Adygheans, Abkhazians, and others has been approximately the same, 3.4 to 3.7. In the Krasnodar krai (including Adyghea—the largely Cherkess-populated autonomous republic around Maikop which was part of the Krasnodar krai until 1991), they form 2.1 to 2.5 percent, while in Abkhazia, 13.9 to 15.9 percent.[25]

It is difficult to determine the exact number of Hamshen Armenians in various periods, because in Turkish sources they were subsumed under the general category of Christian, while in Russian sources they were never differentiated from other Armenians. According to Barunak

---

[21] Igor Kuznetsov, "Hemshily Krasnodarskogo Kraia v 1980-1990-ie gg." [The Hemshins of Krasnodar Region, 1980-90s], in *Staryi Svet: arkheologiia, istoriia, etnografiia* [The Old World: Archaeology, History, Ethnography] (Krasnodar: Kuban State University, 2000), pp. 110-39; idem, "Turki-hemshily ili islamizirovannye armiane?: sluchai neiasnoi etnicheskoi identichnosti" [Turks-Hemshins or Islamicized Armenians?: A Case of Indefinite Ethnic Identity], *Diaspora* 1-2 (2000): 2-11.

[22] Sergei Vardanyan, "Hamshentsi musulman hayeri usumnasirutyan patmutyunits" [From the History of Study of Hamshen Muslim Armenians], *Iran-Name*, 1-3 (1998): 2-11.

[23] Alexander Ossipov, "Hemshiny, hemshily, hemshinli" [Hemshins, Hemshils, Hemshinli] (Moscow, manuscript), p. 8.

[24] The title of the project is "Transnational Groups and Natives of the Caucasian Black Sea Coast in Transition" (Open Society Institute, RSS#1179/2000).

[25] Kuznetsov, *Odezhda armian Ponta*, pp. 24-25.

Torlakyan, the Hamshentsis prior to the 1915 Genocide inhabited some 320 villages and numbered 81,500. About 54 percent of this population lived in the *sanjak* (county) of Janik, 30 percent around Ordu, and 15 percent around Trebizond.[26] Regarding Trebizond and Giresun (Girason; Kerasund), there are the following Turkish statistics by year: 1869–1,254 and 325 Armenians respectively; 1872–1,349 and 225; 1895–3,138 (Trebizond only); 1903–6,028 and 828; 1906–3,530 and 633.[27] The decrease between 1903 and 1906 was the result of migration to the Caucasus and the Crimea.

The flight of Hamshentsis to the Kuban, Abkhazia, and the Crimea became massive after the beginning of World War I and the Armenian Genocide, which also engulfed the Trebizond *vilayet*. According to a statistical report after the Russian occupation of Trebizond in 1916, in the districts of Trebizond and Platana there were only 165 Armenians left in seven villages.[28] The tragedy was repeated in 1918 during the Turkish reoccupation of the Pontus. Almost all the remaining Hamshen Armenians fled to Russian territory. Their numbers in the Kuban and Abkhazia continued to grow until the 1930s. By the 1980s, in the Krasnodar krai (including Adyghea) and Abkhazia, they and their descendants had reached more than 150,000 (a figure derived from the 1989 census of the Armenian population in the raions corresponding to the Hamshentsi areas). According to Mikhail Minasyan, chairman of the Hamshen Association in Erevan, there were about 10,000 in Armenia. Some Hamshentsis also figured among the 16,000 Armenians of Ajaria.[29]

During the 1970s and 1980s, there was a decrease in the number of Hamshen Armenians in Abkhazia and a growing concentration in the Krasnodar krai: 1959–64,425; 1970–74,850; 1979–73,350; 1989–76,541.[30] This process accelerated during the Georgian-Abkhaz conflict, but it is impossible to separate the Hamshentsis from the general

---

[26] Torlakyan, "Hamshenahayeri masin," p. 214; Kuznetsov, *Odezhda armian Ponta,* p. 20.

[27] Mesut Çapa, *Pontos Meselesi: Trabzon ve Geresun'da Milli Mucadele* [The Pontus Question: Trabzon and Giresun in the National Struggle] (Ankara: Türk Kültürünü Arastirma Enstiüsu, 1993), p. 102.

[28] S.R. Mintslov, *Statisticheskii ocherk Trapezondskogo okruga. Noiabr' 1916* [Statistical Account of the District of Trebizond, November 1916] (Trebizond, 1916), pp. iii, 1-13.

[29] Kuznetsov, *Odezhda armian Ponta,* p. 24.

[30] Alexandre Bennigsen and S. Enders Wimbush, *Muslims of the Soviet Empire: A Guide* (Bloomington and Indianapolis: Indiana University Press, 1986), p. 215.

Armenian refugee population from the South Caucasus which settled in Krasnodar. It may nonetheless be estimated that the total number of Hamshen Armenians is presently around 170,000 to 180,000.[31]

According to the 1926 census, the total number of Muslim Hemshinli in Russia was 627, all but two of whom lived in the Ajarian region of Georgia.[32] Their number had grown to 1,400 at the time of their deportation in 1944.[33] Subsequent censuses did not identify them as a separate ethnicity (*natsional'nost'*). In their domestic passports, most Hemshinli are identified as "Hemshil" or "Turk." Nevertheless, the instructions for the last census recommended that Hemshils be categorized as Armenians, perhaps because of their language and the usual inattention of officials to religion. Nonetheless, most Hemshinli continue to be identified as Turks.

In the early 1980s, several Hemshinli families, together with a few Turkish and Kurdish families, moved to Belorechensk raion of Krasnodar from Central Asia, and between 1982 and 1984 an additional 22 families moved from Kyrgyzstan to the Apsheron raion. Several dozen refugee families from Osh and other districts of Kyrgyzstan (about 200 families according to Aleksandr Ossipov's data) also moved there because of the Uzbek-Kyrgyz conflict in 1989.[34] Now, this group forms the majority of Hemshinli of the Krasnodar region. The data from my 1997-98 fieldwork show that there were 58 Hemshin families in the region, aside from the settlement (*stanitsa*) of Pshekhskaia, where there were 172 Hemshinli in 1993.

Aleksandr Ossipov gives a higher number of Hemshinli—150 families in the Krasnodar krai and a total number of more than 200 families in Russia as a whole. About 30 families live in the Kamensk raion of the Rostov *oblast'* (province) and 30 others live in the Gribanovsk raion of the Voronezh oblast'. There are at least 280 to 300 families in Kyrgyzstan as follows: Jelalabad oblast'–130-140; Osh oblast'–100-140; Bishkek–50. In Kazakhstan, there are about 100 Hemshinli families in the Sairamsk raion of Chimkent oblast', and an equal number

---

[31] See also Kuznetsov, *Odezhda armian Ponta*, pp. 20-25.

[32] *Vsesoiuznaia perepis' naseleniia 1926 goda* [The All Union Census of Population, 1926], vol. 14. *Zakavkazskaia SFSR* [Transcaucasian SFSR] (Moscow, 1929), pp. 16, 25.

[33] Nikolai Bugai, "K voprosu o deportatsii narodov SSSR v 30-40 gody" [On the Question of the Deportation of Peoples of the USSR in the 1930s-40s], *Istoriia SSSR* [History of the USSR], vol. 6 (Moscow, 1989), p. 141.

[34] Ossipov, "Hemshiny, hemshily, hemshinli," p. 6.

live in the Jambul raion of the Jambul oblast'. Thus, there are close to 700 Hemshinli families or 3,500 to 4,000 Hemshinli in the former Soviet Union.[35] More recent data collected in January 2001 about the number of Hemshinli in the Apsheron district show 840 people: Yerik– 197; Kalinin–203; Kim–288; Kubanskaia–96; Vperiod–53. This figure is also broken down into unregistered–602; registered–238; citizens– 217.

Subgroups and Settlements

Bert Vaux divides all the Hamshen dialect speakers and their heirs into three groups: Western Homshentsik, who live in the Turkish provinces (now called *il*s) of Samsun, Ordu, Giresun, Trabzon, and Rize, speak Turkish, and are Sunni Muslim; Eastern Homshentsik, who live in the province of Artvin, speak a language called Homshetsma, and are also Muslim; and Northern Homshentsik, who live in Georgia and Russia, speak Homshetsma, and are Christian.[36] This classification is mainly geographic and does not account for the peculiarities of identity for each subgroup. Vaux's Eastern Homshentsik prefer to call their Western Homshentsik neighbors as Bash Hemshinli. Northern Homshentsik, that is, Hamshen Armenians, until recently were not aware of their connection with Hamshen and had no special name for their language. There are, moreover, several well-defined subgroups among both the Muslim Hemshinli and the Hamshen Armenians.

In the Pontus, as in the Caucasus and Near East, internal divisions are based on two major types of cultures. The first type is the territorial subgroups that identify with present or past administrative divisions. Both Hamshen Armenians and Pontic Greeks had such territorial subdivisions. The Greeks still fall into derivative groups corresponding to the *sanjak, kaza,* and *nahiye* (village cluster) in which they once lived: Trebizond, Kerasund, Ordu, Samsun, Bafra, Matsouka, and so forth. Thus, the first type consisted mainly of Christian cultures of the Pontus. These territorial subgroups take their self-given names according to the toponymic or oikonymic principle. Hamshentsis of Krasnodar krai and Abkhazia divide into three subgroups: *Janiktsik* (people from the sanjak of Janik), *Ordutsik* (people from the kaza of Ordu),

---

[35] Ibid.

[36] Bert Vaux, "The Forgotten Black Sea Armenians" (text of lecture, Columbia University, March 1996), pp. 1-2.

and *Trabizontsik* (people from the sanjak of Trebizond). The significance is that these names come straight from administrative subdivisions. During the first years after the migration from Turkey to the
Russian Empire, it was common for Hamshentsis to identify themselves as *Charshambatsik* (people from the kaza of Charshamba, in
Samsun sanjak), *Uniyatsik* (people from the kaza of Unieh), and so
forth, correlating with the smaller administrative units in Turkey. In his
studies, Hrachia Acharyan (Ajarian) noted the same phenomenon.[37]
Nowadays, only the elders who remember Turkey and some of the
Trabizontsik cling to these identities. It is significant, however, that the
others have started to accept identities based on a larger geographic region but still according to the administrative principle.

The second type of inner division for cultures is based not on the
territorial principle but rather on the extraterritorial tribal structure
(*kabila* in Muslim tradition). This type of inner organization is common for the Pontic Laz and Ajar Muslims. The inner division of the
Hemshinli after their acceptance of Islam apparently followed a similar
form. While having a territorial dimension, the Hemshin divisions are
based primarily on kinship relationships. There are two territorial subgroups of Hemshinli. First, there are the so-called Bash Hemshinli of
the rural areas of Rize. Second, there are Hemshinli who live near
Hopa and in the neighboring Ajarian territory. In 1878, twelve settlements of Lazistan up to Makrial settlement (contemporary Kemalpaşa)
were placed in the Batum okrug of the Russian Empire. Eight of these
villages were inhabited exclusively by Hemshinli, three primarily by
Laz with some Hemshinli, and one by Kurds and Hemshinli.[38] The Batum okrug existed in those bounds until 1921, when this sector was
taken back by Turkey. But six settlements that were inhabited by Hemshinli remained in the Ajarian ASSR: Carnal (Charnali), Koriat, Avka,
Gonio, Kızıl Toprak, and Sarpi (Sarp). Now, all of them are part of the
Ajarian Khelvachauri raion. Later, some Hemshin families settled in
Feria, another village in Khelvachauri which is inhabited by Ajars and
descendants of Cherkess (Circassian) refugees.

The Hemshinli of the Krasnodar krai know that the Bash Hemshinli
stayed on their historic territory and that their own ancestors moved
farther east. They also realize that the Bash Hemshinli are completely

---

[37] Hrachia Acharyan, *Knnutyun Hamsheni barbari* [Study of the Hamshen Dia-
lect] (Erevan: Armenian Academy of Sciences, 1947).

[38] Torlakyan, *Hamshenahayeri azgagrutyune*, pp. 27-31.

Turkish-speaking and more numerous. Several families of Turkish-speaking Hemshinli from Rize lived in Ajaria. Nowadays, their descendants live mostly in Central Asia: the Djordan or Jordan-oghli, Zuluf-oghli, Kavaz-oghli, Karamahmed-oghli, Sarimahmed-oghli, and Haji Dursun-oghli families.[39] Except for two families of unclear origin, none of them moved to the Krasnodar krai. Hemshin informants speak about these families (Jordan-oghli and Kavaz-oghli) as just Turks.

Hopa Hemshinli also distinguish two subgroups among themselves: *Ardeletsik* and *Turtsevantsik*. My informants tried to interpret the term *Ardeletsi*, using different kinds of folk etymologies (Armenian: *ard*, field). They tried to prove that one part of their ancestors were real farmers, while others were herdsmen, lived in mountains, and so on. In fact, this name comes from the village of Ardala, whose subdialect was studied by George Dumézil. But neither Torlakyan nor my Hemshin informant from Turkey, who is Ardeletsi himself, ever mentioned such a settlement.[40] The origin of the term Turtsevantsik is unclear. Thus, divisions of the Hopa Hemshinli are based on the territorial principle like that of the Hamshen Armenians, though not so rigidly. Ardeletsik live in Turkey, mainly in six settlements, and only in Carnal in Ajaria. The number of Turtsevantsik settlements is as many as five in Turkey and three in Ajaria. There is insufficient data to place others in either subgroup. Informants state that the settlement of Hendak is inhabited by Hemshinli of Topal-oghli, who belong to neither group, while Carnal is inhabited by members of both subgroups. These examples therefore do not follow the principle of territorial division.

There were several other groups connected with the Hemshinli but with unclear status. One of them is the Kurdo-Hemshinli. In Ajaria, there were two such families, Beshli-oghli and Shakir-oghli. They now live in Central Asia, but there are also members living in Pshekhskaia stanitsa in the Krasnodar krai. We have had no contact with them. Probably, the Kurdo-Hemshinli came from Rize and are completely Turkish-speaking. Two other groups are the Islamicized Armenian descendants of Karadere (Surmene) and the Gungormush Turks. The first

---

[39] Ossipov, *Hemshiny, hemshily, hemshinli*, p. 4; V.P. Kurylev, "Nekotorye malye etnicheskie gruppy iuzhnogo Kazakhstana (greki, kurdy, turki, hemshily)" [Some Small Ethnic Groups of Southern Kazakhstan: Greeks, Kurds, Turks, Hemshils], in *Materialy polevykh etnograficheskikh issledovanii, 1988-1989 gody* [Data of the Ethnographic Fieldwork in 1988-1989] (St. Petersburg, 1992), pp. 29-30.

[40] Torlakyan, *Hamshenahayeri azgagrutyune*, pp. 27-31; also personal information of Heluk Köse (an Ardeletsi).

group lived on the territory of the contemporary *ilche* (districts) of
Surmene, Araklı, Arsin, and Yomra in Trabzon province, to the west of
Bash Hemshin. A part of the population of these villages may be descended from the refugees from Hamshen. Sargis Haykuni knew of this
group. In his time, residents of villages such as Zimla, Mironos, and
Mandra still spoke Armenian, a fact that distinguishes the Muslims of
Karadere from the Bash Hemshinli. Torlakyan even lists some of their
surnames: Aved-oghli (Avedyan), Kirkor-oghli (Krikorian), and so
forth.[41] The Turks of nine no-longer-existent villages in Esiroghlu
(formerly Gungormush) in the district of Machka were situated to the
west of Surmene and Trebizond. According to Torlakyan, this population also had Armenian origins, and in his time some of its representatives had Armenian nicknames.[42] The fate of this group is unknown.

The Linguistic Situation

Both Hamshen Armenians and Hemshin Muslims speak the Hamshen
dialect, which belongs to the so-called *ke-* or *ge-* branch of Armenian
dialects. From a sociolinguistic point of view, it would be better to call
the speech of the Hamshentsis an Armenian dialect, whereas the Hemshinli speak a distinct language known as Homshetsma. Although
modern Western Armenian (*ashkharhabar*) is based on one of the *ke*
dialects, comparative data point to the Hamshen dialect (language) as
being one of the most deviated from standard Armenian. Correlations
between this and other Armenian dialects are rare and the closest to the
Hamshen are the dialects of Cilicia (Zeitun, Hajin, Svedia), Armenia
Minor/Sebastia (especially the village of Brgnik), and Agn (especially
the village of Aslanbeg). Among the most specific morphological and
phonetic features of the Hamshen dialect are the formation of verbal
infinitive with single *-ush* instead of *-il, -el, -ul, -al* as in ancient Armenian (*grabar*) and in the other dialects, the existence of progressive
tenses, and sound changes $r > y$ (or $r > sh$, $r > \emptyset$) and $a > o$ (or *an* >
on). The picture is completed with a number of endemic glosses, such
as *mashmurk* (chestnut) and so on.[43]

---

[41] Ibid., pp. 32-33.

[42] Ibid., p. 51.

[43] Hrachia Acharyan, *Hay barbaragitutiun: Urvagits ev dasavorutiun hay bar-
barneri (barbaragitakan kartesov)* [Armenian Dialectology: Outline and Classification of Armenian Dialects (with a Dialectical Map)] (Moscow: Lazarian Academy,

Today, we have no firm position on the classification of local variants in Hamshen speech. On the one hand, there is Acharyan's skeptical statement that while there are differences they should not be considered as being separate subdialects. On the other hand, there is Ararat Gharibyan's categorical viewpoint that Hamshen speech has two subdialects: Mala and Janik.[44] I have offered a scheme mainly based on the phonetic principle which divides the Hamshen subdialects into three groups: Western (Janik-Ordu), Central (Trebizond-Mala), and Eastern (Hemshin).[45]

Because of the lack of data, it is impossible to say with certainty how many subdialects the Eastern group has. There are five Hemshin subdialects at least, but in reality certainly many more. The differences between them are felt less than in the center of the Hamshen dialectological area, but more than between the subdialects of the Western (Janik-Ordu) group. In the subdialects of the Central group, there are isoglosses and sound changes combined with the Trebizond urban dialect, which is distinct and far closer to Standard Western Armenian. Many features of the Hamshen dialect seem to be preserved in the Eastern (Hemshin), but in the Western (Janik-Ordu) the greatest homogeneity combines with an apogee of development of the same features. Sound change $a > o$ in a number of Hemshin subdialects shows great irregularity: compare the Hemshin Zaluna *manch* (boy; son) with the consistent Janik-Ordu *monch*; at the same time, Hemshin Gonio-Koriat *okhpar* (brother) with the Janik-Ordu *akhpar*. Nikolai Marr pointed out that in Hemshin this sound change (*okan'ie*) does not depend on whether or not there is a nasal *n* after a.[46] In the Janik-Ordu subdialects, however, the same change is always connected with a postposition of *n (m)* and is always consistent.

1911); idem, *Knnutyun Hamsheni barbari*; idem, *Hayeren armatakan bararan* [Armenian Etymological Dictionary], 2d ed., ed. M.G. Nersisyan et al., vol. 1 (Erevan: Erevan State University, 1971), pp. 20-25; Ararat Gharibyan, *Hay barbaragitutyun: Hnchyunabanutyun ev dzevabanutyun* [Armenian Dialectology: Phonetics and Morphology] (Erevan: Haypethrat, 1953), pp. 397-407; *Hayereni barbaragitakan atlas (usumnasirutyunner ev nyuter)* [Dialectological Atlas of Armenian (Studies and Materials), ed. H.D. Muradyan, 2 vols. (Erevan: Armenian Academy of Sciences, 1982-1985; Vaux, Columbia lecture, "The Forgotten Black Sea Armenians."

[44] Acharyan, *Knnutyun Hamsheni barbari*, p. 15; Gharibyan, *Hay Barbaragitutyun*, pp. 397-404.

[45] Kuznetsov, *Odezhda armian Ponta*, pp. 13-15.

[46] Marr, "Materialy po khemshinskomu narechiiu armianskogo iazyka," pp. 73-79.

The Armenian speech of the Hemshinli frequently preserved some original Armenian forms in the place of Turkisms, which is typical for subdialects of the Western and Central groups; for example: Zaluna *aklar* (Armenian: *aklor,* rooster) and Janik-Ordu *khoroz* (Turkish: *horoz*). Also, the Hemshin language has no labial *ä, ö, ü,* and syntactic constructions like Janik *nä... nä...* (Turkish: neither...nor) are absent here. Sometimes the speech of Janiktsik seems more like jargon in contrast with the Homshetsma language of the Hemshinli, which is closer to the Standard dialect. This could be the result of a strong Turkish substratum and may be evidence of the late Armenianizing of the Armenians of this subgroup. The Greeks, another Christian people in the sanjak of Samsun, are known to have adopted the Greek language only after migrating to the Russian Empire, whereas before they spoke only Turkish. Until the present, both in Greece and in the Caucasus, Greeks from Bafra, not far from Samsun, have remained Turkish-speaking. There is a possibility that refugees from ancient Hamshen were assimilated by Turks who influenced the Western Pontus and that these people reclaimed their Armenianness only at the beginning of the nineteenth century when Armenian schools and churches were established by Armenian enlighteners.

The study of the separate glosses can give an interesting picture. Unlike the Mala-Trebizond subdialects, the Janik-Ordu one has no Armenian *andzrev* (rain). For that word, Janik and Ordu use the local gloss *vraik/vraiek,* which has no Armenian etymology and is unknown in other Armenian dialects. It is feasible that Pontic Greek *vreshin* (compare New Greek βροχη "rain," βρεχω "to water, to make wet," influenced the Hamshen Armenian gloss "rain": Greek, βρεϛ–/βρεχ– >; Armenian, *vra-,* where sound change *e > a* may be the result of folk etymology (Armenian *vra,* on); *-ik* is the typical Armenian name suffix, but the disappearing Greek sh/χ. is unclear. According to Artavazd Tulumjyan, previously Hamshen Armenians used to interpret the word "rain" with particular euphemisms without using the word itself. Hemshin informants confirm this (Tatar-oghli, Gonio-Koriat): *chugh kuka* (literary "water is coming," meaning "it is raining"). In general, it seems to be an example of the widespread taboo on the use of certain words.[47]

---

[47] Kuznetsov, Gololobov, Popov, Siver, "K issledovaniiu Pontiiskoi istoriko-kul'turnoi oblasti," pp. 333ff.; Tamaz Gamkrelidze and Viacheslav Ivanov, *Indoievropeiskii iazyk i indoievropeitsy* [Indo-European Language and Indo-

The use of *azhdaha/izhdaha* as the designation of a mythological creature of Iranian origin has many parallels in ancient Armenian and is another interesting case. The Armenian king of demons *Azhdahak* (Zoroastrian: Azhi Dahaka) appears in early Christian Armenian manuscripts, but it is unknown in Armenian peasant culture of the last two centuries. In Pontus, *Azhdaha*, heard more often as *Izhdaha,* is the hero's name from Turkish, Greek, and Laz myths and sometimes acts as antipode to Saint George the Dragon-Slayer. His appearance here is probably the result of a late Turkish tradition borrowed from Iran and spread over a vast territory from Afghanistan to Asia Minor and the Balkans (Tajik, Tatar, Turkish: *Azhdaha*; Slavic Bulgarian: *Azhder*). Reflection of the name *Azhdaha* is known to Hamshentsis and Hemshinli as Trebizond *azhdahar* (giant) and as Hemshin *izhdaha* (crocodile; water beast). But I am not sure if there is a proper phonetic fixation in the last Hemshin form. After comparing these two words, it becomes obvious that their meanings are opposing poles that fit into the general context of the serpent-fighting myth: giant (horseman)/serpent (chthonic beast). It is a Hamshen Armenian, not a Muslim Hemshin form of inversion. I believe that both examples show the complicated historical relations of the Hamshen dialect of Armenian and the Hemshin language. On the one hand, in the first case there is evidence of a common origin or at least deep-lying corresponding features. On the other hand, the second case points to the Christian Hamshen Armenian subdialects having signs that reveal their secondary origin or late formation, unlike the Hemshin language.

After the migration of Hamshentsis to Russia, there were mixed conditions for the retention of their subdialects. The early wave of migration from Unieh (Uniye) and Charshamba arrived in the Krasnodar krai in the 1860s to the 1880s. Here in a difficult mountain region the compact Janiktsik area known as the Armenian raion was formed. Armenian schools did not appear for a long time, and Standard Armenian did not replace the dialectal speech. It created a perfect atmosphere for an isolated existence and conservation of the Unieh-Erinjugh subdialect. On the other hand, there was a strong influence of the Russian language throughout the Krasnodar krai.

Hamshen Armenians appeared in Abkhazia in the 1880s and 1890s, and now all three subgroups live along side each other. This has caused the mixing and loss of specific features of numerous subdialects. Ham-

Europeans], vol. 2 (Tbilisi: Metsniereba, 1984), p. 680.

shentsi children go to dozens of Armenian schools. Many dialectal forms are replaced by common Armenian words. The classification of subdialects must be reviewed for the Muslim Hemshinli as well. Their rather small community almost disintegrated after the deportation to Central Asia and flight to the Krasnodar krai.

Hemshinli and Hamshentsis are multilingual and use Armenian, Turkish, Russian, and other languages, but they also have their own specific languages: Homshetsma and Turkish. Homshetsma is almost the only language of household discourse for the Hemshinli, except for the small completely Turkish-speaking Kurdo-Hemshinli group. This language continues to exist only in its oral form, although there were a few unsuccessful attempts to adapt it to Cyrillic or, according to Sergei Vardanyan, to create a special Hemshin system of writing in Kyrgyzstan. There are many persons, except for the elders, who speak also Russian and Uzbek or Kyrgyz, while a few of the oldest men and women, deported from Ajaria, know Georgian. Georgian schools were introduced in Ajaria in the 1920s in place of Muslim schools (*mektebs*). Then, from the 1920s until 1938 the written language for Hemshinli was Azeri Turkish, during the short period of *natsional'nykh* (ethnic) Azerbaijani schools. Today, none of these old survivors knows either contemporary standard Turkish with Latin characters or old Ottoman with its Arabic characters. Nominally, the language of religion for the Hemshinli is Arabic. In fact, however, only a few can read Arabic inscriptions. Now, the main written language of the Hemshinli in the Krasnodar krai is Russian. It is of interest that in correspondence I have seen between Turkish Hemshinli from near Hopa (previously a part of Batum okrug) and their relatives in Russia there are two small texts on the back of family photographs written in Russian letters but in the Hemshin language.

Hamshentsi Armenians are as multilingual as Hemshinli. Aside from their own dialect, they also spoke Turkish in the first decades after their immigration. Literate persons used Standard Western Armenian as well. Armenian schools operated during the existence of the Armenian raion in Krasnodar, and they still function in Abkhazia. At present, after a hiatus of more than thirty years, Armenian teaching programs have begun again in the Krasnodar krai in some Sunday schools, elective school courses, and so forth. There are many literate people among the Hamshen Armenians who can read newspapers and books in Standard Eastern and Western Armenian. A national literary language is a bridge for them to pan-Armenian culture. They have also become increasingly fluent in both spoken and written Russian. Consequently, their native language is a more complicated multifunctional phenomenon. Hamshentsis and Hemshinli have no folklore relating to their native language except for a few fairytales, proverbs, and *mani* (rhymed quatrains of impromptu character, performed with the stringed instrument known as the *kamancha*).

To conclude, three major factors account for differences between Hemshinli and Hamshentsis in the use of Armenian, Russian, and Turkish. First, the degree of native language usage by mothers vis-à-vis the official language is a key element. Second, aspects of their culture, folklore genres, and so on are frequently verbalized in different languages, as Hemshinli and Hamshentsis differ in preference of one or another language for these purposes. Third, fluency in other languages differs between and within the two communities, often depending on the age group.

Religion and Identity

It is known that the French Revolution and its impact gave rise to nationalism, which promoted the concepts of the oneness of origin and language and of citizenship in place of religious or dynastic associations. Pontus and other regions in the east were affected by this process a hundred years later than Western Europe. At the time of Hamshentsi migrations to Russia, religion remained the main marker of identity. Religion still divides the Hamshentsis and Hemshinli. All Hemshinli are Sunni Muslims. In every house there is a prayer rug or piece of sheepskin, which is used for quintuple prayer (*namaz*), albeit mostly by elders. Only a few know Arabic, but many have a Quran in Russian translation. Most men are circumcised, and all men under middle age wear a little cap (*kudi*). Women and girls wear headscarves or kerchiefs. Hemshinli try to stick to Islamic dietary guidelines, but they drink vodka or other alcohol (mostly young men) in situations that are not ritually related.

Hemshinli as well as most other Muslims in the Krasnodar krai have no special edifice to serve as a mosque. They gather for communal prayer in individual homes. They do have a cemetery on the road from Kubanskaia stanitsa to Pshekhskaia stanitsa, however, thanks to the efforts of Gaspar Gasparyan, who persuaded the authorities to allocate a cemetery for Hemshinli and Meskhetian Turks. A local Hemshin spiritual leader, Hasan Salih-oghli of Vperiod, frequently performs the duties of a *mullah*, and in case of need the Hemshinli can also call upon the mullahs of the Meskhetian Turks.

One must speak guardedly about existing remnants of Christianity in Hemshin culture or about their crypto-Christianity. By contrast, in the early nineteenth century Minas Bzhshkian reported that during his travels in the Pontus that the Muslim Hemshinli traditionally cele-brated holidays that corresponded to the Armenian Christian Feast of the Ascension (*Vardavar*) and the Feast of the Assumption.[48] In 1890, Vital Cuinet noted that the Hemshinli still baptized their children, al-though this was now primarily for superstitious reasons.[49] The acade-mician V.A. Gordlevskii wrote that the former Christians of Rize pre-served elements of crypto-Christianity perhaps much longer.[50] How-ever, data that I gathered among the Hemshinli in the Krasnodar krai some 150 to 200 years later than these sources have not revealed any clear evidence of lingering Christian vestiges.

It is known nonetheless that relations between Christians and Mus-lims in the Pontus had certain unusual forms. Hamshen Armenians, for example, might choose their Turkish neighbors as godfathers, so-called *genkär*, *genkahar* (Standard Western Armenian: *gnkahayr*; Standard Eastern Armenian: *kavor*). In circumcision rituals, Turks could invite an Armenian to be the *kävrä* or godfather. At Christmastime, groups of masked Hamshen Armenian youngsters would make the rounds sing-ing carols first in their own village and then in neighboring Turkish vil-lages where there, too, people applauded and gave various gifts after a traditional performance of a staged kidnapping of a young beloved girl (*guluzar*) from the elder (*bab*) by a black man (*arab*). Such practices of purely ritual origin were also known in other areas where Christians and Muslims lived intermixed.

The Hemshinli freely use Armenian words such as *khach* (cross) and *asvadz* (God) instead of *allah*. But the first of these terms is also used in Turkish (Turkish *hach*; Armenian: *khach*). Nor is the second word necessarily proof of a Christian remnant because conversely the Christian Hamshen Armenians use the term *allah* to describe God in the text of their incantations: *guja guja gujgurija/alahdan arev kuzim/ hatumlardan kaymak isteru* . . . (guja guja gujgurija/I want the sun

---

[48] Bzhshkian, *Patmutiun Pontosi*, p. 97.

[49] Vital Cuinet, *Turquie d'Asie,* vol. 1 (Paris: Ernest Leroux, 1992), pp. 119-20; Bryer and Winfield, *Byzantine Monuments,* vol. 1, p. 337.

[50] Gordlevskii, *Izbrannye sochineniia,* vol. 3, p. 329.

from god/I want cream from the ladies). It seems to be similar to cases of taboo regarding direct use of the name of God.[51]

All Hamshen Armenians are Christians and formally belong to the Armenian Apostolic Church. From the period of the Stalin terror up to the beginning of the 1990s, Armenian churches disappeared in the Hamshen-populated areas. Those who were insistent on baptizing their children began to use Orthodox priests. Now, when the Armenian Church has again become active, there is a revival in the villages of the former Armenian raion of Russia, although the spiritual component is superficial. Few people attend church services, read the Bible, or know the prayers. The Christian faith for them is mainly a symbol of identity, just as it is for most Russians. Protestant organizations have stepped in to take advantage of this vacuum. For example, in Abkhazia which was devastated by the Abkhaz-Georgian war, most converts to Jehovah's Witnesses are Hamshen Armenians.

In general, present-day Hemshinli seem to be more Muslim than Hamshentsis are Christian. The fact that during the 1940s to 1980s the Hemshinli lived in Central Asia, surrounded by Muslim Uzbeks and Kazakhs, is probably a relevant factor. Islamization of culture can be determined as the process of cleansing it from neutral or apparently non-Islamic features, and this process is going on among the Hemshinli in the Krasnodar krai. In their fieldwork of 1997-98, for example, Anton Popov and other students of mine witnessed a Hemshin wedding. When the bride was entering the bridegroom's house somebody proposed to draw an X mark on a doorpost with a knife, a common rite in the eastern Pontus as well as in many areas of Georgia and the Caucasus. But the idea created a ruckus, "because the Cross is a Christian, not a Muslim symbol."

The mass conversion of the ancestors of the Hemshinli eliminated their Armenian environment but not their language. All Hemshinli I have spoken with realize they constitute a separate community and express it in their self-definition as *Homshetsik* (people from Hamshen). However, most of them do not perceive the Turkish *Hemşili* as a phonetic derivative of *Homshetsi*. They know that it goes back to the geographic place-name *Hemshin*, but with the exception of some well-read persons they know nothing about the term *Homshetsi* and explain it by

---

[51] Igor Kuznetsov, "Zaklinaniia ot zasukhi amshenskikh armian" [Anti-Drought Incantations among the Hamshen Armenians] *Sovetskaia etnografiia* [Soviet Ethnography] 1 (1991): 86-90.

using different folk etymologies. The Hamshen Armenians, on the other hand, do not use the name either in its Armenian or Turkish form. Usually they prefer to identify themselves with their historic geographic-administrative groups as well as generically as Armenian. Thus, Hamshentsis who live in the Apsheron and Tuapse raions usually call themselves *Janiktsik* (people from Janik) and *hayi* (*hay,* singular for "Armenian"). Since the 1960s intellectuals familiar with nationalistic and historical literature have begun to use the name *Hamshe(n)tsik* (*Hamshentsi,* a positional falling out of *n* is the characteristic feature for Western subdialects, such as Janik and Ordu). Examples of their activities in Erevan are literary gatherings and the publication of *Dzayn Hamshenakan.* Since the 1990s, both Hamshen non-governmental organizations (NGO) and folkloric groups have been created. In this period, three organizations with the name Hamshen sprang up in the Apsheron and Tuapse raions, as well as one in the city of Tuapse and one in the Novo-Mikhailovskii settlement. The artificiality of such new appellations is obvious. There are many people who have only the faintest idea about their origin. For example, one informant who is associated with the Hamshen Center in Apsheron explained to me that Armenians who live there are called Hamshentsis because they supposedly came from an area called Amsh and so on.

As for the Muslim Hemshinli in the Krasnodar krai, most have a double identity. The characteristic feature of their ethnicity is that they associate themselves with Turks. Many of them consider themselves Turks as well as Hemshinli. At Hasan Salih-oghli's house, one young woman wondered why I could be interested in the Turkish language and Turkish customs. There is a real religious and cultural affinity between the Hemshin and Turkish communities, not only because of historical linkages but also because of the strong contrast between them and the native Russian and Cossack population of the Krasnodar krai.

Immigration policies became more stringent and discriminatory following the election of former President Boris Putin in Russia and of Governor Aleksandr Tkachev in the Krasnodar krai. Cossack leaders, officials, and politicians once more uncovered the Meskhetian Turks (*Turki Meskhetintsy*), who have lived in the krai since the early 1980s. Various "patriotic" committees were organized and the mass media was filled with provocative reports emphasizing the irreconcilable differences between "our" Slavic (Russian, Ukrainian, Cossack) and the alien (Turkish) cultures.

Now both Hemshinli and Meskhetian Turks are unable to obtain refugee status and are deprived of many civil rights and social services. The Hemshinli are regarded as a subdivision of the Turks (Turk-Hemshin) as are the Terekeme from Meskhet-Javakheti, Turkified Laz, and Batumli Turks and Poshas from Ajaria. In the fall of 1994, there were preparations to create a Hemshin committee, but the organizers decided that they had a better chance to solve their problems by joining with the Turks in a common organization called *Vatan* (Homeland). They have now reverted to the idea of forming a separate committee. Steven Swerdlow of Columbia University has written about the impact of the discrimination in the Krasnodar krai on the development of Hemshin identity.[52]

It is of interest that Turkish informants, when asked about the identity of the Hemshinli, frequently answered that they are Turks ("the same as we are") but have, like the Kurds, their own language aside from Turkish. Like the Kurds, they are viewed as a rather primitive, semi-pastoral people, as distinct from the cultured sedentary Turks. This Turkish ethnic stereotype is seen also among the Meskhetian Turks vis-à-vis the Terekeme, another completely Turkish-speaking group but one that leads a semi-nomadic life akin to the Kurds. Interestingly, many Russian sources at the time of the annexation of the Batum okrug to the Russian Empire also speak about the affinity of the Hemshinli and Kurds. Obviously, this reflects a widespread preexisting view. A Laz informant from the village of Liman in the il of Artvin insisted that the Hemshinli are very much like Kurds. Perhaps, this has some connection with the economically and culturally semi-nomadic way of life that increased after the Hemshin forefathers adopted Islam. Of course, the Hemshinli themselves deny any association with the Kurds. But an important fact is that they denote as a subdivision of their community the so-called Kurdo-Hemshinli, who are said to have preserved a transhumant lifestyle much longer than the others.

Before their migration from Kyrgyzstan and Kazakhstan to the Krasnodar area, most Hemshinli made no linguistic and historic connections with the Hamshen Armenians. However, in the beginning of 1980s, a group of Hemshin leaders headed by Toprak Tursun met Barunak Torlakyan and then visited Armenia with his assistance. Having

---

[52] Steve Swerdlow, "The Hemshins of Krasnodar Krai: A Case Study of Ethnic Discrimination and Transnational Identity," Paper delivered at the Association for the Study of Nationalities, Columbia University, April 12, 2002.

come to the Krasnodar krai, the Hemshinli learned that their language is similar to that of their new Hamshen Armenian neighbors. Previously, any such contact with Armenians in Central Asia would not have been thinkable because of the strong peculiarity of Homshetsma. Ethnic minority revival in Russia since the 1980s has led to self-reflection among the Hamshentsis, too, in the form of attention to local history, study of Standard Armenian, and folkloric movements. Their intellectual elite gradually discovered in the Hemshin the lost descendants of Hamam Amatuni who had been forcibly Islamicized by uninvited guests and overlords—the Turks.

Two decades have passed since the first contact between Hamshentsi and Hemshinli, but there are negligible positive results. In Kalinin, Hamshentsis and Hemshinli live on neighboring streets, but both communities exist entirely apart. There is no common business where they work together and not a single mixed marriage. Recently, a Hamshen Armenian in the spirit of traditional bride stealing (*umykanie*) kidnapped a Hemshin girl. The matter ended unhappily, however, because the Hemshin elders insisted that the girl be returned. Some Hamshentsi activists tried several times to organize something like a round-table with Hemshin representatives. The main idea was to enlighten Hemshinli about their Armenian ancestors and to persuade them that the gradual transition from Islam to Christianity in its Armenian variant would be advantageous for them. However, most Hamshen Armenians continue to view the Hemshinli with caution and even suspicion, viewing them as Turks and remaining aloof from any mutual contacts. For their part, the Hemshinli are very reluctant to enter into serious discussions with Hamshen Armenians.

In my interviews, one middle-aged informant conceded that once-upon-a-time the Hemshinli had been Armenian, "but now we are Turks." A young educated Hemshin girl tried to connect names of different Hemshin family groups with Hamshentsi groups: *Jermaktsik* (Karaibrahim-oghli family group), *Janiktsik, Ardeletsik, Ordutsik,* and so on. But these are singular cases. It is conceivable that recent events can change things. Governor Tkachev's racist statements, the administration's propaganda against refugees and ethnic immigrants, including both Hamshen Armenians from Abkhazia and Hemshinli, incite fascist-like extremist public moods. There has been the mass desecration of more than twenty Armenian tombstones in Slavianskoie cemetery in Krasnodar as well as anti-Armenian violence in Korenovsk, Anapa, and elsewhere.

These conditions tend to strengthen Hamshentsi regionalist solidarity rather than a pan-Armenian ideology, and this may extend to their Muslim counterparts who have preserved the common cultural and linguistic legacy of ancient Hamshen. It may be that such a position has started to find a positive response among Hemshin activists who wish to dissociate themselves from the detested Meskhetian Turks. It is noteworthy that after the desecration in the Armenian cemetery, Hasan Salih-oghli, accompanied by his supporters, came to Krasnodar to consult with the Hamshen Center. Both Hemshin and Hamshen leaders prepared a letter addressed to experts and anthropologists of Institute of Ethnology and Anthropology in Moscow to provide information and answers about who the Hemshinli really are. Perhaps the next step will be the registration of a Hemshin NGO, distinct from the Turkish *Vatan* organization, and possibly even the reversion of Hemshin surnames to reflect their Hamshen origins. The process is still evolving.

Abkhazia: Nineteenth-Century Hamshen Home

Kuban: Nineteenth-Century Hamshen Settlers in Alpine Pastures
(*Yayla*), Lagonaki Plateau

Krasnodar: Messozhai Settlement,
Grinding Stone from Pontus

Abkhazia: Avedis Hamalian, Agaraki Village,
Native of Chibukluk Village of Ordu

430

Krasnodar: Terzian Settlement, Ornamental Rooster Wedding
Yaghlugh of Pontic Armenians

Krasnodar: Messozhai Settlement, Preserving Pontic
Hamshen Dance

INDEX